A Shearwater Book

HOPE'S HORIZON

HOPE'S HORIZON

Three Visions for Healing the American Land

CHIP WARD

ISLAND PRESS | *Shearwater Books*

WASHINGTON COVELO LONDON

For Brian, Carly, and Tyler

A Shearwater Book
Published by Island Press

Library of Congress Cataloging-in-Publication data.

Ward, Chip.
Hope's horizon : restoring vision while reviving wounded lands /
Chip Ward.
p.   cm.
Includes bibliographical references (p.).
ISBN 1-55963-977-6 (alk. paper)
1. Nature conservation—United States. 2. Restoration ecology—
United States. I. Title.
QH76.W37 2004
333.72—dc22
2003024794

British Cataloguing-in-Publication data available.

Printed on recycled, acid-free paper

Design by Teresa Bonner

Manufactured in the United States of America
10 9 8 7 6 5 4 3 2 1

CONTENTS

Contents

ABOLITION

PROLOGUE

Diving into Soup for Fun and Profit: Hubris and Progress in a Pothole

There is a spiritual basis to attention, a humility in waiting for the emergence of a pattern from experience.

—MARY CATHERINE BATESON

In the desert west of town, deep holes of hot water are scattered along the alkaline crust of earth, springs of varying clarity and depth. They contain a salty broth of barely discernible plants and creatures, warm reminders of the heat that emanates from the earth's volcanic core and the subtle and soupy nature of life itself. Water is always surprising on the desert, but to suddenly come upon one of these sockets of water is spooky, like sifting through a sandbox and discovering a glass eyeball. They seem out of place in such a dry and barren setting. Their murky bottoms are indefinite and mysterious, like cave holes or horse eyes. They smell slightly sulphurous, like rain-soaked matchheads. The fear of accidentally slipping past a crumbling lip into who-knows-how-hot water to the bottom of who-knows-what can be palpable. I will never forget the first time I saw one. For months after, it haunted my dreams.

As familiarity overcomes fear and mystery, playfulness follows. First you stick a toe in, then a foot. Sooner or later someone dares someone else to jump in, and before long you have a combination hot tub and swimming hole. That's what happened just west of town in the largest hotpot out there, a cavity of water that would hardly qualify as a small pond by Eastern or Midwestern standards but was more than adequate for recreation according to the lower expectations of my Utah neighbors. Talk to old-timers and they remember riding their horses or driving out for a socializing soak in the old warm spring that was one of the few amusements available in the lean and hard years of settlement, dry farming, and Depression. Eventually some ambitious young men poured cement around the border, and the wild swimming hole took on a more formal and institutional demeanor.

When I moved to a small town about an hour west of Salt Lake City, where the ski-rich mountains of Utah give way to the vast and dry reaches of the Great Basin Desert, I often heard about the good ol' times around that natural desert pool. But I never got a clear account of how it turned into the scummy stinkhole I found when I went looking for it. Amber shards of broken beer bottles littered the path and an old car was tilting into green water, looking as if it had crawled across the hot dust only to slake its thirst in the poisonously deceptive brine of the first watering hole it found.

When I asked what had happened to turn the beloved gathering spot into such a sorry mess, I got vague answers—time and neglect had taken their toll, and then vandalism finished the job. Much of what goes wrong in this largely Mormon state is attributed to rude drunkenness, or at least the absence of righteous behavior. There's nothing wrong with our perspective or values, we are told, other than our failure to adhere to them.

Then, in the late 1980s, someone decided to rescue the old hotpots and return them to recreational use. A desert entrepreneur formed a business to dig out one cluster of hot springs and expand them into a grand pool. The usual cement was applied to the edges to add definition. A dredge stood by, ready to dig out silted bottoms, while a broad Plexiglas roof supported by metal beams was erected over the warm water. A dive shop and classroom were constructed next to a gravel parking lot, and before long, year-round scuba diving lessons were being offered—a unique and convenient venue for those planning to fly from Salt Lake City to Caribbean and Baja vacations, where certified diving skills could add to the fun. The business was fueled by enthusiastic newspaper features that described the developer as an innovative and clever man who had the vision to bring the sea into the desert.

The facility also attracted curious desert landlubbers like my own family who were looking for some fun in the sun. We kept it simple and rented only snorkels, fins, and goggles. Linda and I told each other this day-long diversion would be an educational experience for our kids, who were raised in a dry clime and had never had the opportunity to snorkel in Hawaii-warm water.

As we flapped in our froggy gear down the cement steps into the pool, holding on to the already corroding metal railing, an attendant tossed lettuce onto the water and, to our utter amazement, summoned up a writhing swarm of parrot fish and other colorful tropical creatures. We oohed and aahed on cue. The attendant told us they had just added a shark—a small one, he reassured us, using his index fingers to demonstrate a two-foot length. Various guppies and mollies had also been tossed in to provide Mini-Jaws with distracting edibles. No worries for you, he said. Then, as we glubbed and bubbled away from the dock, he reminded us to dive down and look for a statue they had anchored to the bottom.

Our visit was fun, but it also felt weird to splash around in a pocket-size Caribbean on those white alkali flats west of town. There was something intuitively uncomfortable about it. We talked about going back there to swim but never did. Many years later I returned while giving some out-of-town friends a tour of the local desert. I was surprised by the changes I saw and then, as the predictability of the pool's fate sunk in, surprised by my surprise.

There was more gravel spread across the parking lot, and outbuildings had been added to the periphery of the canopy-covered pool. Despite the facility's expansion, there was little activity. One look at the water and it was apparent why. The pool was much greener and darker than I remembered. Algae had bloomed with a vengeance.

As we wandered around the pool's periphery, I tripped over a white five-gallon bucket filled with colorful little tropical fish. An elderly man in coveralls looked up, smiled, and explained that he and his wife had been invited to scoop out from the pool all the mollies they could because there were way too many of them. They had started to spread into neighboring undeveloped hotpots, too. The scooping couple planned to keep some of the little fish to sell and give away. Others would be used for garden fertilizer or food for bigger hobby fish at home. I had tripped over the losers, weeded out because their skin was dull, although I thought there were at least some keepers in the gasping, bug-eyed pile. What happened to the shark, I asked; wasn't he doing his job? He got too big, they said, and had to be removed.

Then it hit me that I was looking at an ecosystem that was spiraling out of its original delicate and finely tuned shape and morphing into the molly-choked mess before me. Prey and predator had been clumsily dumped in with no appreciation or knowledge of the well-honed reciprocal dynamic that a food web requires—the kind of symbiotic tapestry that only evolution can weave. The indiscriminate addition of amusing fish had also contributed their accompanying microorganisms, each carrying new variables to skew the pool's complex eco-dynamics. Years of people diving in their wet suits and gear had no doubt introduced a whole range of new bacteria into the evolutionary game. Human urine contains antibiotics, estrogens, viruses, and trace chemicals. Who knows what was on that lettuce?

Here was a little jewel of a habitat that had evolved over eons, a fragile symphony of temperature, minerals, and microorganisms, and it was being reduced, slowly but surely, to a pea soup of trash fish and scum. The people running it must have known they had a frustrating problem on their hands, one that would have to be managed meticulously, but did they really grasp the slow and inevitable degradation they were causing?

As my friends and I drove away that autumn day, my mind's eye thrust forward in time and I saw sections of missing Plexiglas, rusted railings, broken bottles, and stout weeds in the parking lot, and an old tire floating on a wet velvet surface of startling green. Now I knew what had happened the first time—new players, old story—hey, they were just trying to make a buck and have some fun. We have long assumed that's what land is for—profit or recreation. For deserts, especially, the question "What is it good for?" is frequently a prelude to abuse.

It is easy to see nature's wounds and to project them into the future. It is harder to imagine resilience, a landscape restored and whole. Where, I asked myself, is hope's horizon?

I read my description of the hotpots and their fate to another friend in town. "You're wrong about the shark," he told me. "There are two of them. They left them in, and they're big now, maybe two hundred pounds each. They're nurse sharks, so they're not really dangerous. They feed them frozen fish to keep 'em fat and happy. It's cool—you can watch them do it. And the water is better in the winter, since the summer heat makes the algae bloom."

"So you can see underwater then?" I ask.

"Well, yeah, sort of," he replies. "It's a great place to learn how to use a compass—ya know, navigate by numbers." He senses my disappointment. "Hey, lighten up! It's not like it's the Dugway Proving Grounds, ya know, with anthrax spores lying around and old rockets filled with nerve gas buried in the dirt." Dugway is an area the size of Rhode Island occupying most of Utah's West Desert. It was used by the military to test chemical and biological weapons back in the '50s and '60s. Its contaminated grounds are still off-limits and closely guarded by barbed wire and soldiers in jeeps.

"You're right," I tell him, "it's not Dugway. Not even close."

My friend has a shed for his dirt bike and boat. To him, my deepest thoughts are just plain goofy. In fact, I cannot make a strong case for that particular hole of hot water. Granted, an algae-loaded dive pot is not on a scale with the destruction of salmon habitat across the Northwest or the elimination of big predators all over the country, first in the East and then across the West. But it is of a kind. Natural history out here has an echoing and fractal quality. The difference between trashing a small desert hot spring and poisoning an entire desert with toxic waste is a difference of scale, not consciousness, just as trashing a stream is on a different scale than killing a wild river but shows similar patterns of thinking and behaving. We seem to think that any aspect of nature is expendable until proven otherwise and that each place we crash and consume stands alone.

"You're perverse," my friend told me. "You insist on seeing everything upside down and backward. A guy tries to improve something that nobody wants or uses, and you see that as a dumb mistake. It's like you're some kind of cultural dyslexic who looks at progress but sees things as only getting worse. Then you write it all down to document your disorder. Does it help you to do this?"

"Yes, it does," I answered. "If I can't reconcile my worldview with yours, I can at least give you a good account of what I am seeing."

What I am seeing is overengineering. Like the Everglades. We covered that inland sea of grass with a grid of canals and ditches until aquifers collapsed, estuaries rotted, and rivers became toxic, then had to spend billions to restore the ecosystem's cleansing and replenishing ebbs and flows, the very rhythms we worked so hard to thwart. We tapped free-flowing water too hard in California and are now reverse-engineering the San Francisco Bay and its estuaries. When the over-plumbed Ogalala Aquifer, which stretches under the Great Plains, goes down sometime in this century, the nation's breadbasket may become, once more, a bucket of dust. Those grand circles of green we see out the airplane window as we fly over the Midwest, those checkerboard farmlands, will blur and fade. Our engineering tends to be brilliant but brief, not sustainable across ecological time frames or even across the span of more than a few human generations.

Why do we insist on overengineering our landscapes despite all the self-evident failures we have experienced? Why do we still think we can engineer a fix for any problems we have caused, even when those problems are the consequence of the last technological fix? We persevere even when those in charge of promoting the latest fix are the ones who were in charge when the problem was created in the first place, or were in charge of previous attempts at a fix that failed. A kind of pervasive hubris resides on the face of our collective denial.

Is there another way? I began to wonder. What if we dropped that attitude—the one that regards humans as above and beyond the cycles and limits of the natural world—and understood how life's myriad strands of species, habitats, and dynamic processes are woven together? If we focused on the health of the land and conserving the integrity of the ecological processes that shape its life and, ultimately, our own well-being, what would we be doing instead?

After more than a decade as an activist confronting polluters and the regulators and politicians who enable them to pass on the costs and consequences of the damage they do, I wanted to encounter people who are exploring positive, instructive, and alternative visions of how to live on the land. Looking only at nature's wounds and playing defense all the time can be emotionally and spiritually exhausting. And frightening—my own quest to understand the link between environmental quality and public health began the day I realized I could stand on my porch and point to four homes where kids were in wheelchairs and I asked myself if I had moved my own children into harm's way. I have tried to capture the hard lessons I have learned as an activist trying to hold polluters accountable in my first book, *Canaries on the Rim: Living Downwind in the West.* I understand that to solve a problem, you must first acknowledge and define it, but at some point we must move beyond criticism and defense to proactive leadership. We need inspiring visions to guide us.

There is good news. Increasingly, environmental politics is turning to thoughtful proposals aimed at healing whole ecosystems that have been stripped of their diversity and connectivity and at abandoning technologies that are incompatible with life itself. In a three-year odyssey that took me from my backyard in Utah south to Arizona's Sonoran Desert and east to the thick and fragrant forests of Vermont and New York, then to the marbled halls of Washington, D.C., I collected the stories that follow. Each is about the expression and practice of a new vision, one that replaces established notions about material progress within a hostile world of fixed objects with a fascination for creative emergence within a web of communities. In this new approach, respect for and trust in ecological processes replace hubris.

This is not, however, an account of philosophers. Each vision is applied. Each critique is active and catalytic. Each encourages the development of local ecological literacy to retranslate our shared and prevailing behaviors, habits, and assumptions into new earth-friendly behaviors, relationships, and understandings. Michael Soulé grew weary of studying extinction and decided to try to save evolution itself and rework the map of North America to look radically different from the one we have been using. Rich Ingebretsen wants to uncork one of the most colossal reservoirs ever built and watch the drowned canyons below it emerge and recover. Corbin Harney, an uneducated Shoshone elder, is taking on the nation's engineering elite in his struggle to keep nuclear waste off his ancestral ground. You may be smart, he tells them, but you are not wise.

The individuals and organizations I focus on represent a tiny fraction of the tens of thousands of nongovernmental organizations emerging around the globe that are working on some aspect of conserving or restoring ecological health and integrity. Across the world, wetlands and streams are being restored, habitat is being reseeded, greenbelts and open spaces are being expanded, native seeds are being collected and cultivated, floodplains are being abandoned, and land is being set aside. In Georgia it's longleaf pine forest that is being restored, and in California it's butterfly habitat. On the Great Plains, bison are reappearing. In thousands of backyard woodlots from Michigan to Alabama, unsung citizens are making mindful changes on their own, inviting wild creatures back onto the land. State and local agencies charged with managing the public commons are finding new missions, pushed hard by local conservation and environmental groups.

I could have picked any one of those groups or projects to highlight in this book and still told the same story. Although they do not share a common agenda or ideology among them and there is disagreement on an array of issues, common patterns emerge. The new wave of activists aims for the reconnection and restoration of damaged and fragmented habitat. They don't want the damage that we are doing to ecosystems managed or merely curbed; they want it stopped, for the health and well-being of both wild creatures and humans alike.

I have divided the book into three sections to emphasize these themes—reconnection, restoration, and abolition—although the reality of creating a new paradigm for living on the planet involves all of them and more. That new model will recognize the intrinsic value of other species and the importance of diversity as a prerequisite for and sign of health. It will encourage the development of sustainable and fair economies. It will honor and create community rather than command ever more commodities.

The diversity of perspectives that can be found in this latest wave of conservation and environmental politics is a creative and potent mix that has already begun to bloom on the ruins of the culture that, from the latest terrorist attacks to emerging pandemics, is climaxing and crashing all around us. This book aims to provide an easy and colorful introduction to the potential for recognizing our biological communion with the world and then translating that realization into behaviors that honor the living communities that sustain us.

The activists described here might be termed humble visionaries. Visionaries because they see through the underlying assumptions that for most of us are so transparent and self-reinforcing that we do not see them at all. Visionaries because they see in our common future the robust environments that most of us can only glimpse dimly in humanity's distant past. And although their visions are bold, the activists themselves are humble, because the outlook they are trying to share and practice says, very simply, that we don't know everything and that natural systems are astonishingly intricate, reciprocal, creative, and self-organizing as they emerge and evolve all around us. We can learn to dance with those systems but not drive them. Heed that, they say. Trust that. Heed them, I say.

RECONNECTION

We could say a food brings a form into existence. Huckleberries and salmon call for bears, the clouds of plankton of the North Pacific call for salmon. The sperm whale is sucked into existence by pulsing, fluctuating pastures of squid.

—GARY SNYDER

ONE

Keeping Track, Watching Hawks

There is nothing so intimate or immediate as being eaten. This possibility increases dramatically when you dwell among large predators without the advantage of rifles, scopes, whistles, high-beams, hard walls, or pistols. On the other hand, there is no way of death that leaves more time for reflection than starvation. Prehistoric people paid close attention to animal signs and tracks because their lives depended on it. They lived in a world where it was well understood that all living creatures feed on and, in turn, are food for others.

In food webs, the insect eats a mite and is eaten by the fish that is eaten by a human who gets eaten by a bear. The bear, of course, is eaten by a flea that is being consumed by bacteria. Ask our indigenous ancestors to identify a bird, fish, insect, or mammal, and it is likely they would have provided a name, imitated its call or movement, told something unique about its behavior, and then described how to prepare it for dinner. To live is to feed. From fish eggs to frog legs, from larvae to hog heads, almost nothing is out of bounds. To be human is to find life tasty.

To know signs and tracks of wild creatures, you must be a patient observer. Our ancestors would not have called the attentive observation they practiced "natural history" any more than they would have called cave paintings "art." The word "nature," like the word "art," implies a separation from the subject one is naming. Ask a fish to define water. Humanity's formative generations who lived close by the wild earth observed the varied behaviors, patterns, relationships, and cycles of the living world not from outside a context of connection and belonging, but from within its embrace. Food was found locally, personally. It was a gift, and the wise person respected and honored the giver.

It is different today, of course. The mammal du jour is on sale at Wally World. Our food is fast or frozen. We consume millions of mass-made "personal" pizzas. Even our water is shipped, bar-coded, and shelved. We put seascapes and alpine vistas on our screen savers, but nine out of ten of us don't know what phase the moon is in or why we might care. We track data, not deer.

Except for people like Sue Morse, who is still tracking wildlife the old way—though not to eat it, but to save it by saving the habitats that sustain it. Sue is a co-founder and leader of Keeping Track, a Vermont-based group working with individual landowners, land trusts, public land agencies, and conservation organizations across the country to gather data on specific habitats and creatures that people want to conserve and understand. In the process, Keeping Track also teaches people about the role and value of biodiversity in a compelling, firsthand way.

A desire for better civic planning spawned the organization in 1994. As a rural planning commissioner, Sue discovered that the information available to those making decisions about land use was woefully inadequate.[1] State and federal agencies were not producing maps that included animal populations and details of their movements. A map of the interstate migratory routes for geese and raptors, for example, might tell you they would pass through your backwoods, but not where they might stop to rest and feed. Even conservation organizations were not making a systematic effort to include animals in the descriptions of land that guided planners and civic leaders. From local zoning boards to state legislatures to the feds, decision makers were working in the dark. Sue decided to turn on a light, at least in her own corner of the land.

She was well suited to the task. As a kid exploring the Pennsylvania woodlands on her grandfather's farm, she had found wildlife fascinat-

4

ing. In college she studied forestry but switched to Shakespeare. Then she had a tracking epiphany that fused her love of wild animals with her penchant for interpreting lyrical passages. Out one snowy day, shortly after she moved to Vermont, she realized she could look at tracks and "see" the animals that made them. Their relationships and stories could be interpreted, just as a literary passage could be: "Here is where the bobcat crouched and waited. Here it advanced and crouched again. These are the tracks of the hare it was stalking, and the nibbled leaves where the hare stopped to eat. This is where the bobcat attacked, and here is where it dragged and ate the hare."

Sue was hooked. She, in turn, hooked my friend John Derick. John was interested in building a trail system around the pretty college town of Middlebury and wanted to know where the trails should go and what could be seen. He now conducts his own tracking sessions, offering insights and inspiration to local residents and college students who accompany him on weekend outings. They, in turn, get hooked on tracking and pass their knowledge and enthusiasm to others. Ironically, Sue and her colleagues at Keeping Track have found a way to help laypeople develop a broad and inspiring ecological perspective by simply getting them to focus on the ground immediately under their feet.

At first Keeping Track focused on projects in Vermont and New Hampshire. The idea was simple. In communities where information was needed and desired, Keeping Track taught citizen volunteers the skills they needed to go out on the land in question and record what they found. As it turned out, there were always lots of volunteers, including local conservationists, school groups, hunters, landowners, hikers, and curious retirees. They were provided with guidebooks for tracks and scat, some on-the-ground instruction and experience, and a few tools such as clipboards, specialized rulers, and cameras.

Groups were usually given a key local species to focus on—a species whose presence and vitality was linked to the well-being of other species in the area. In New England, the focus was often on bear, mink, fishers, otters, weasels, or bobcats. As Keeping Track's reputation grew and the organization expanded to places as far away as Arizona and California, the focus turned to cougars and coyotes, among other species. Deciding which creatures to focus on introduces ecosystem literacy into the mix; participants are invited to think about relationships they may not have considered. Why, for instance, does removing a bear, bobcat, coyote, or other large predator from a landscape's food web mean an increase in smaller predators like foxes, skunks, and house cats—which, in turn, leads to decimated songbird populations?

Once trained, the citizen scientists would divide into teams to look at specific transects—sections of ground sixty feet wide and two miles long that can be defined using handheld satellite links to global positioning systems. Although GPS devices are used for accuracy, designating transects is not a geometry problem: participants must again look at land as habitat and see relationships to identify which transects are worthy of attention. Transects are visited at least once each season, year after year, until the data that are collected resolve into clear patterns of animal life.

Beyond the satisfaction of collecting useful data, participants gain firsthand experience with creatures in their backyards that they may have never seen or even suspected were there. And almost all of Keeping Track's volunteers find that experience exciting and uplifting. If, as acclaimed sociobiologist Edward O. Wilson believes, love of our natural world—what he calls biophilia—is an evolutionarily programmed feeling in humans, then Keeping Track is like a matchmaker that leads citizens to the big wet 'n' wild kisses they've been dreaming of. But you don't have to eat granola to come to the love nest—the backgrounds of Keeping Track's participants are diverse, ranging all the way from farmers to hunters.

On this morning, Keeping Track included me as well. I had come to the green forests of Vermont all the way from the tan deserts of Utah. As an activist there working to keep the desert from becoming an enabler for some very toxic collective behaviors, like the abandonment of chemical wastes and spent nuclear fuel on the desert floor, I came with a burning question. "In Utah we are willing to trade environmental quality and integrity for jobs, profits, and revenues," I had said in a hundred interviews, "but we may also be trading public health." After I organized a community health survey in my town that indicated widespread cancer, birth defects, and chronic illnesses, this was my litany as an advocate for precautionary policies. "We know how to make the land pay—how it can be used to make wealth. What we don't know is how the land generates and sustains health. At what point do the wounds we inflict on a landscape get translated into human sickness and suffering? That is the fine print in the deals we are cutting, and we have not learned how to read it."

Sue Morse might not answer those questions for me, but I hoped her insights would be helpful. Also, I had always wanted to learn how to track skillfully. When I arrived in the American West as a young man, I could track a bulldozer if it had an oil leak, but that was about all. After living for some years in the wildlands of southern Utah, I had at least learned to distinguish between common coyote tracks and cougar prints, which to the untrained eye look similar. I once tracked a mountain lion up a snowy canyon until the tracks disappeared in the rocks, only to find fresh cougar tracks behind my own when I returned. The experience was humbling. A full-grown cougar, after all, can bring down a bull elk in two seconds, and there I was playing Daniel Boone and tempting fate.

Sue Morse and John Derick were now taking us over land near John's Vermont home. John and his neighbors, including the leader of the local Audubon chapter and the manager of a lakeside summer camp, were walking over a transect to record what they found. My companions were involved in land use planning through land trusts, conservation organizations, and local governments, and it was important for them to understand what was going on there before making recommendations about how the land should be protected to conserve habitat.

The citizen trackers were particularly interested in signs that black bears might have left behind, like the claw marks in beechnut bark that are left when a bear climbs a tree looking for the tasty nuts. The branches of those trees are sometimes tangled together in telltale patterns, the result of a perched bear pulling the surrounding branches down and stripping them of their food, snapping off branches and stuffing them in the crotch of some limbs. Sue can recognize the tracks that distinguish one animal from another—dog from coyote from wolf from cougar, for example. Before she can make such distinctions, however, she must know where to look for them—she has to know what their makers eat and when, where they nest and den, where they seek water, their needs, likes, and dislikes.

Sue understands the routes they choose. Who would think to follow a ridgeline looking for teeth marks on a birch tree to know whether a bear had dropped into the beech trees down below? Bears, she explained, are not very social, and humans are not the only creatures who set boundaries. A jaw-sized signature in softwood serves as a warning to be read by other bears that a stand of beech trees is occupied. The other bears can tell if the bite is fresh or old, and can gauge jaw size to get a handle on how big the potential competition might be.

Sue Morse reads habitats. Animals leave memos in the mud for her. There are bulletins in the bark. Tracks are her texts. Hair and scat are punctuation.

As we hiked along, Sue found subtle signs of animals everywhere— a bit of fur here, an odor there, a claw or antler scraped across tree bark, teeth marks, blood from killed prey, a stone turned over for the insects underneath, and barely discernible footprints. Tracking is not a simple matter of memorizing signature shapes. Tracks made in the shade differ from tracks made in sunlight. The condition of the snow can distort a track so that it appears different in powder, slush, or crust. Tracks reveal an animal's gait, which is a clue to its body shape. A fox, for instance, has a narrow body and can put its feet in a straight line, one in front of the other, while a broad-shouldered dog makes more parallel footprints. The pattern of tracks also tells whether a creature was running or just ambling. If running, there may be clues that indicate whether it was chasing something or fleeing.

I was as excited as a first-grader learning to sound out letters. Powerful trackers, I learned, must be attentive, receptive, and honest to find tracks in the first place, and then intuitive and knowledgeable because they have to interpret what they're seeing while trying to supply what is missing. And there is always something missing. Tracks themselves are a sign of absence: the animal was once there but isn't now. Often Sue came across subtle signs that were ambiguous, prompting her to proclaim the guiding rule of tracking: "When in doubt, follow it out." We would then try to backtrack in search of crisper signs, a distinctive gait, signature scat, favorite foods, likely habitats, and telltale odors.

Standing aside, watching my fellow trackers, I found their attentiveness familiar. I often saw my dad, an ardent fly fisherman, in a similar trance while he watched glassy currents in mountain streams and fed fishing line into the air in a fluid S above his nodding fly rod. The more you learn to listen, the more you hear the world whisper, "Pay attention." Absent-minded rock climbers can literally get carried away. Even birders lose themselves while looking through binoculars and listening for calls. (Do they lose themselves or find themselves, then wake up singing a different tune?) Birds are like verbs in a grammar. To find them you must fit habit to habitat until the language of a landscape emerges.

Hearing that language is deeply satisfying. It's not just awe and wonder; it's a reassuring feeling of belonging. I never had much luck "going inside" to find myself, unless that needy and noisy voice that begged to be distracted or anesthetized was the real me. My "self," it seems, is not some organism without an environment but a process that feeds on inclusion, a kind of reciprocal, sensual dance I do with the world I am in. There is terror out there, teeth in the dark, but also sweet joy and magic.

We came across tracks pressed into glassy mud along a stream. Their crisp edges told us they were fresh. Raccoons, deer, mice, and beetles had left their marks. As I studied the varied calligraphy of bird feet in wet clay, I wondered if I was looking at some kind of precursor of the pictographic symbols I had seen on ancient clay tablets displayed in museums. At some point, did our species realize we too could mark mud and later papyrus with our own symbolic tracks, which would indicate in the present the onetime existence of something no longer here? I expressed this thought to my companions and speculated that our proud print culture, which so distinguishes us from the animal world, might even itself be a gift from that world to us. They smiled, nodded, and went on as if my conjecture was not so much thought-provoking as mildly annoying, even embarrassing. One person's revelation is another's evidence of brain damage. I put my eyes to the ground and resolved to keep it simple.

Months later I read the works of Paul Shepard, a patron saint of the deep ecology movement, and realize that my speculation about the animal contribution to our cultural development was not so far off. Shepard makes a compelling case that our brains, eyes, ears, and limbs evolved to hunt and gather. They were called into being by a wild habitat and the activities necessary to survive and thrive in that habitat. We learned about the world by observing our fellow animals so we could find and follow them. We gained consciousness while immersed in relationships with animals whose flesh we ate, whose skins we wore, whose antlers and bones we used as raw materials for our tools. Their feathers and claws adorned us. We admired their keen sight, speed, and strength, and their nonhuman capacity to disappear into the earth or soar high above it. Their powers seemed magical compared to our own. They permeated our dreams and were the subjects of our folklore and mythology. We sought their allegiance and were grateful for their gifts. Our rituals, dances, and art were created to attract them, appease them, and thank them. Our music imitated theirs. And our current "madness," as Shepard calls the modern condition of humanity, is in large measure the consequence of the serial amputation, over time, of our formative relationships with them.

Indigenous peoples across the globe commonly accept that knowledge is inherent in all things and that wild animals in particular convey meaning and teach. Even today we are fascinated by them, although we are more likely to encounter them on television shows than in the flesh. Wild animals live lean. They are naturally elemental and integral in ways we are not. We admire how, undistracted by cell phones, divorce lawyers, beer commercials, and a million and one of the other artifices we suffer, they live life directly. Although incapable of Socratic dialogues, they also have no hidden agendas or commercial interests. Their eloquence is in their behavior. Today's domesticated animals, according to Shepard, are inbred feedlot "goofies" we manage chemically and kill remotely, or pets that we turn into our alter egos.

There was nothing goofy about the animals Sue was tracking through the Vermont woods that afternoon. Those animals were mysterious and revealing—mysterious because they were hidden and stealthy, and revealing because their intelligence was evident where instinct and intent intersect. Sue told us she had found a deer that had been killed by a bear on a wild patch of forest she is restoring around her home. When asked how she knew the deer's killer was a bear, she told us how she had cut away the deer's hide from around its neck and measured the teeth marks in the exposed flesh beneath to approximate the killer's jaw size. Also, she noted that only the entrails had been eaten. A bear will do that in the spring after many weeks of eating buds and bark, she said. A high-cellulose diet in the winter and early spring will result in constipation that calls for a big dose of fresh deer guts. Ingesting the rich bacterial life in the deer's fecal matter apparently has a liberating effect on bears, and they know it.

Although most of us are aware of and have contemplated the fundamental relationship between predator and prey in the wild, on cable television if not actually in the great outdoors, we miss the more subtle microbial exchanges at work—not only the way shit happens, but the way it gets around. You could say Sue knows her shit and she'd agree, because animals are also distinguished by their scat. I watched her pick through scat with a thin knife blade and tweezers for evidence of bones, seeds, quills, insect parts, and fur—clues to the animal's habits, appetites, physical condition, and even its physiology. Coyotes use their big teeth and strong jaws to break, gnaw, crunch, and swallow bones. The scat of wildcats, by contrast, tends to be bone-clean because a cat has a rough tongue to lick and strip meat from ribs and hips. Heavy crunching is not necessary.

Sue's focus on scat reminded me of a friend who had studied vole poop for the U.S. Forest Service. A vole is a forest rodent—a food source for owls and hawks. But in addition, vole droppings contain a particular microbe that is also found on the root systems of spruce trees. These microbes play a key role in helping the spruce break down and absorb nutrients from the surrounding soil.

The Forest Service was interested in how plant succession occurs in areas that were once beaver ponds, after the beavers have abandoned their dams and the land has drained. Sometimes spruce trees grow right back in such areas, preparing the way for a succession of other plants and trees that restore the forest over the silted-in former ponds. Sometimes the land remains treeless for a hundred years. Even when foresters deliberately plant spruce trees in such areas, they tend to die. The Forest Service wondered why.

Then a link was made between the local vole population and the rate at which the spruce trees grew back. The more voles there were in the area, the more likely the spruce trees would repopulate the drained beaver ponds and thrive. As it turned out, the voles were reintroducing into the soil, via their excretions, the microbes needed by the spruce trees. Soil that was under pond water for years lost those microbes. Once the water left the land, voles could spread the microbes around in their droppings.

Who would have guessed that the health and resilience of a forest might be linked to the digestive tract of a tiny rodent? And how many of us are aware of or concerned about the health of soil at all? Snails, for example, are major consumers of forest floor debris and recyclers of animal and plant waste. Their presence or absence is a key indicator of soil vitality, yet most of us never give them a second thought.

Context and relationship are everything, as any skillful tracker learns. Ecosystems are loaded with circuits of energy and information that are constantly exchanged. Individuals are wrapped in communities that are wrapped in other communities. Understanding life's creative weave of dynamic and complementary relationships is the challenge before us. The world is not, as we presumed throughout the twentieth century, a collection of discrete and fixed objects that can be divided into their component parts and then neatly manipulated, but a much messier process we do not have a clear bead on. Despite our masterful understanding of the predictable, measurable, and linear sequences in nature, much of life is too complex and chaotic to be known. Everything is always in play. Invention and destruction feed on one another. A small change in initial conditions can grow in surprising ways as its influence is passed along. There are underlying and recurring patterns, and order always emerges from chaos eventually, but we cannot say for sure how it all fits together.

Mosquitoes interrupt my consideration of such heady questions. In the wet woods of Vermont, the gossamer little bloodsuckers can cover exposed flesh like fur unless you continually twitch, flap, fan, and, slap. From a distance, our party of intrepid citizen trackers must have looked a bit like a group outing for patients struggling with motor skill disorders. Maybe I have slapped myself silly. I press on but bring my thoughts down a notch by asking how Keeping Track uses the information it gleans.

"So what do you do with all these reports and descriptions?" I ask Sue.

First, she says, the data must be checked for credibility. Keeping Track hires and recruits wildlife biologists to advise volunteers, answer questions that arise in the field, and render judgments on the photos of tracks and marks that are not readily identifiable. Over time, the data sheets generated become a portrait of wildlife movement across the landscape that helps landowners and community governments to make informed choices. If it becomes clear that bears feed on spring growth in a wetland that may be filled, for instance, then second thoughts are in order. If a particular stretch of riverbank is a preferred path for otters, then an easement or some measure of protection becomes compelling. Maybe that proposed snowmobile trail gets moved or abandoned.

Encouragingly, landowners do tend to change their plans or take precautions when they get a picture of how wildlife moves across and uses their property, especially if they see the signs for themselves. That does not mean they dedicate their land to wildlife conservation alone, but they may considerably modify their decisions about development, cutting timber, and laying down roadbeds, for example, to account for the birds and animals that share the land.

Sue Morse stands on one end of that continuum of consideration. On her own parcel near Jericho, Vermont, called Wolf Run, she has demonstrated how species can not only be protected but invited back in.

It is not just a matter of seeing the signs firsthand that makes land use planners and property owners feel a stake in the health of the land's natural inhabitants. Community-based tracking projects also provide an opportunity for civic dialogue on compelling topics that are not normally raised. Anyone who has ever attended a zoning board hearing, for example, knows they can be the civil equivalent of chloroform. They have as much to do with ecosystem stewardship as a street-corner drug deal has to do with spiritual well-being. Yet that is the usual forum for community dialogue about land use. Such rigid and technical parameters discourage dialogue.

A trip to the woods with an experienced tracker like Sue, on the other hand, almost always means that volunteers go from curious to gung ho, and local groups quickly take on a life of their own. People talk to each other about what they value and why, and whether the criteria for public decision-making reflect those values and their new understandings about the way the world works. Local land use dialogues are also invigorated. The purely economic assumptions that formerly governed land use decision-making are often challenged and modified.

Tracking encourages cultural shifts as well. As groups of citizens cross the land, they may share their own knowledge and perspectives with each other. This often means that people who value the land for different reasons have to sort out their differences. An avid birder, for example, may sit down to rest or eat lunch in the woods with a hunter, a farmer, a teacher, and a banker.

The result of that dialogue is often recognition not only that the criteria for land use are too narrow and limited, but that natural webs are as intricate and complex as they are vulnerable. Somehow we must find ways to translate these new understandings into our vocabularies and then into our behaviors, individually and collectively. Keeping Track offers one way to do that.

For hundreds of years, humankind has focused relentlessly on how the land can be made to produce wealth. Relatively speaking, the question of how healthy ecosystems sustain human health and well-being has been raised only recently. Although we acknowledge such icons of conservation as Henry David Thoreau, John Muir, and Aldo Leopold, in their own times those men swam against the tides of rampant industrialism and prevailing notions that nature should be tamed, controlled, and used. It is only in our time that the insights and ideals of Thoreau, Muir, Leopold, and others have found expression in law and policy, if imperfectly.

In the 1960s and early '70s, national legislation protecting wilderness, clean water, and clean air was passed. Environmental impact assessments were added to the planning process. The health of the land and its consequent impact on public health became criteria for public decision-making. A kind of environmental assessment industry developed to facilitate the process. And, of course, corporations and their government allies eventually learned to manipulate the process when they could—to drive through every loophole, exploit every ambiguity, or simply submit bogus environmental impact statements.

This early legislation was an attempt to add new criteria to the public process at a time when a river flowing through Cleveland had recently caught fire and the very symbol of America, the bald eagle, was heading for extinction. There was a clear bipartisan consensus that something had to be done. The Environmental Protection Agency was created during the administration of no less a Republican than Richard Nixon.

The protections of the 1960s and '70s turned out to be limited, though, by assumptions that lay at their heart. We assumed pollution could be managed—just as we managed forests, perhaps. We assumed that the damage could be limited and controlled. We did not grasp the cumulative impacts. The terms "global warming" and "ozone depletion" had not yet been created. Ask someone back then about hormone disrupters, and they probably would have pictured a group of rowdy adolescents on a bus, not chemicals like PCBs and dioxins, which can wreak havoc on chromosomes and immune systems. Meanwhile, aquifers were drained, topsoil was washed away, and rain forests burned.

While our group sits with Sue on a plush carpet of moss covering a granite escarpment above a misty ravine, we discuss the limitations of laws and policies designed to protect the integrity of natural systems. "Too little, too late" is the prevailing judgment. Everyone has examples of how wetlands and woodlots they roamed when they were kids have been replaced by housing developments.

Vermont has managed to contain sprawl better than most. It is not as plagued by malls, highways, and subdivisions as other places I have visited, like Atlanta, Phoenix, Las Vegas, and southern California. Still, large swatches of habitat have been broken up by highways, fences, housing developments, and the like, making it hard for animals to hunt, migrate, and mate. In such conditions, wildlife populations thin and become isolated from one another. Reduced populations that are cut off from one another also suffer from a lack of the genetic diversity that is key to maintaining viability. Our trackers express concern for such threatened Eastern species as the lynx, blueback trout, and spruce grouse.

Disturbed habitat is vulnerable to invasive species—plants, insects, birds, reptiles, or mammals that are introduced to a habitat from elsewhere and then take over, pushing aside other species because of some attribute that allows them to compete with the natives for their food or other critical resources. John tells us how zebra mussels that were introduced into the Great Lakes from the Caspian Sea made their way down the Mississippi, then puddle-jumped on boat bottoms into New York and New England, where they triggered a series of negative effects. They removed particulates from water, making lakes and rivers appear clearer but also reducing phytoplankton—the food of other "filter-feeders" and their predators. They altered whole aquatic ecosystems by replacing a wide range of other aquatic creatures. And they colonized submerged surfaces so quickly and thoroughly that municipal utilities must spend fortunes to continually clear them out of the pipes they clog.

Adding alien species is tricky. Sue recounts the story of how, in just fifty years, a fungus brought to America in 1904 wiped out the

American chestnut tree population, which had dominated Eastern forests until then. In Florida, the water hyacinth clogs lakes and canals. Kudzu covers the South. I tell the trackers about the cheat grass and tamarisks where I live in Utah and the ways they vacuum up scant water and nutrients so that other plants can't compete. A mature tamarisk can suck up two hundred gallons of precious water a day. Nationwide, invasive species cost Americans well over $100 billion a year.

This ecologically literate group takes for granted the value of biodiversity, often defined simply as the variability of an ecosystem—the range and number of species that share overlapping habitats and can interact with one another. We have discovered only recently how robustly diverse life really is. As scientists push their scopes and instruments into unseen places, we have found a multitude of microscopic beasties in every thimbleful of soil, gardens blooming in Antarctic sea ice, and bacteria that have evolved to fit volcanic vents on ocean floors. During the grand and slow spiral of creation that science calls evolution, life pushed into every nook and crack, tirelessly feeding on and adapting to whatever circumstances it encountered until it became seamless and all-inclusive. Life is so diverse because the earth that calls life into being is so variable.

Nature is self-organizing and resilient but, like any problem solver, needs options—lots and lots of players, from microbes to whales. The more potential options are available, the more likely new relationships can emerge to succeed or mend those that have been disrupted and broken, and the more resilient a stressed ecosystem is likely to be.

Aldo Leopold, the intellectual and spiritual grandfather of conservation biology, famously observed that the key to healing broken habitats was to save as many of the parts as possible. The processes that create and shape diversity—fires and floods, for example—are also important. An ecosystem that is shaped by occasional fires, then, must be big enough to replace species that are lost to fires when they occur, or its diversity is vulnerable and temporary, perched on the edge of inevitable decline.

An ecosystem is such an intricate weave of reciprocal relationships that even small changes are echoed throughout the web. I tell the group about a superintendent at a national park who was beset by an abundance of wasps one season. The wasps made their nests in the eaves of park housing and tended to dive-bomb the rangers and their families when they entered and left their homes. After a summer of painful welts and screaming children, the superintendent ordered the wasps eradicated. The next year saw few wasps but an infestation of caterpillars in the park's historic fruit orchards. Trees were damaged and the fruit harvest was poor. The wasps, the park naturalists realized, were the caterpillars' most effective predators. Spraying the caterpillars to get them in check compromised bird and fish populations.

That's how it goes—you spray wasps but kill fish and apples. And we rarely consider the impact of our spraying on the microorganisms in the soil and water, although they are the staff of life itself. In the park, wasps were eventually reintroduced in hopes of regaining the dynamic balance that was lost when they were thoughtlessly killed.

I could have picked another story, but I like using the wasps' tale as an example because it underlines an important point. Wasps are easy to malign and kill, but even an unpopular insect has an intrinsic ecological value, and it is in our own self-interest to respect that. The Xerces Society, another nonprofit that brings together citizen naturalists and professional scientists, works to conserve the habitat of invertebrates because they are critical to ecosystems. The soil that nourishes our food was churned, swallowed, and excreted by worms, ants, mites, and millipedes. The fruits and vegetables that rise from that soil are pollinated by bees, moths, butterflies, and even flies. Mosquitoes serve as pollinators in the Arctic. From starfish to dragonflies, from lobsters to snails, lowly invertebrates make life possible in kaleidoscopic and unacknowledged ways.

The planet has experienced an alarming "crash" of species. Not just the popular animals, like panda bears and elephants, but an ever-cascading number of species have been drastically diminished in the past fifty years. The alarming rate of disappearance was recognized during the early phase of environmental legislation, in the 1960s and '70s, and as a consequence the Endangered Species Act was passed. Its renewal was being debated at the time I went out with the trackers, and they were worried.

On past trips to Vermont, I remember having to hop gingerly around tiny frogs that were ubiquitous on mossy logging roads. No more. Worldwide, amphibians are disappearing. Because of their delicate skin, the frog and salamander may be the modern equivalent of the coal mine canary, warning us of the presence of insidious chemicals in our water and soil. We can excuse the disappearance of an orchid-pollinating moth here and a pupfish there, but the cumulative impact of the loss of species, it is becoming increasingly clear, is a denuded world that we are not adapted to and cannot long survive without hardship, turmoil, and risk. Hug that tree for dear life.

But our trip into the woods is also a cause for hope and celebration. Some of us are sitting on moss-covered stumps under a canopy of leaves. This forest is third growth. Like most of Vermont, the land was deforested during the first half of the nineteenth century to make way for crops and pastures. Timber also provided cash for farmers who needed capital to buy land, seeds, and tools, and for entrepreneurs who supplied the lumber for burgeoning Eastern cities. Photos from the time show mountains of cut logs stacked against a barren and overgrazed landscape of rocky topsoil, an ecological wasteland. The deer disappeared, and the ubiquitous beaver was practically extinct. The moose and otters, once plentiful, became rare. Vermont boomed and then, like all abused landscapes, went bust. Thin soils were exhausted. Land-hungry farmers moved on to more promising frontiers, assisted by the construction of railroads and the decimation of Indian populations in their paths.

Down to a mere quarter of its pre-Columbian forest a hundred years ago, today Vermont is 80 percent forest again. The rambling stone walls of old farms thread dark forest floors. Hiking near my parents' house in Salisbury, I once stumbled across a ghost orchard—skeletal rows of dead apple trees under a ceiling of pine boughs. Although these forests do not contain the rich variety and majesty of old growth, they are recovering. The beaver are back, and so are the deer. They share the land with increasing populations of moose, black bears, and bobcats. There have even been reports of catamounts, the Eastern version of that master predator, the cougar.

Recovery happened while nobody was looking. Given 150 years of benign neglect, the tattered ecosystem started to sew itself back together. The old growth wasn't deliberately replanted with a monoculture of trees for lumber, so diversity had ground to grow on. It didn't hurt that the Adirondack Mountains, perhaps the largest wild landscape left in the East, lay to the immediate west. Wildlife found corridors back in and slowly reestablished itself as the fragments healed together. No one would claim that Vermont is a primeval and untouched wilderness again, but the natural recovery that has come with a hundred years of reforestation has been dramatic. Vermont is not a heavily populated state, so it had that advantage, too. Even so, Vermont offers compelling evidence that habitat can come back from historic degradation.

More than 2,000 miles west of Vermont, on the Nevada border, hawks swim high on currents of invisible air, spiraling slowly under a blinding sun. Howard Gross and the staff of HawkWatch International are perched on a sun-baked cliff below, squinting skyward and counting raptors. The raptors, mostly hawks and falcons, are migrating across the Great Basin Desert. They are going around a wide swatch of alkaline desert in western Utah and following a thin necklace of water sources that attract the small birds, rodents, and lizards they eat.

An escarpment in the Goshute Mountains provides a perfect place to watch the migration and count the kinds of birds the HawkWatch crew have become adept at identifying. They train thick binoculars on the sky and, based on a faraway bird's small dark profile and its movement, call out the particular names—peregrine falcon, sharp-shinned hawk, golden eagle, osprey, and kestrel—before I can find the bird at all. "Where? There! Where? There!" Our dialogue is somewhere between a children's game and a comedy routine—Marco Polo meets "Who's on First?"

HawkWatch doesn't just count, it catches. On an adjoining ridge, staff have set up a camouflaged blind. They hide behind it and hold a thin nylon line attached to a little leather harness fitted to a bird's body. Pulling on the line makes the bird jump and flap, attracting the attention of hungry migrating raptors far above. HawkWatch has an aviary of prey birds, like pigeons and sparrows, that they keep and care for in the low shade of piñons and junipers just below the ridgeline.

Just as a fly fisherman knows what nymph the fish are biting, Hawk-Watch's sky fishermen know which bird to tie on their line to tease down which raptor. A raptor's vision is acute, of course, and allows it to see small objects at great distance. Although they see the seemingly wounded and hopping bird very far below them, they miss the fine line tied to the bird-bait. When the tempted raptors plunge and pounce, they become entangled in a fine mist net. HawkWatch staff scramble from their hiding places and grab the startled birds before they can recover and fly away.

The birds are hurried to a hut where they are measured, weighed, and assessed for gender, age, and health. Bands are clipped to ankles. Once the data are recorded, each bird is slipped into a tube for its protection and carried to the neighboring ridge, where the raptor-counting volunteers mingle with various guests. Although the trip from Salt Lake City to the Goshutes takes two hours of highway driving followed by another half hour over a gravel road and, finally, a hot and heart-pounding hike up a steep mountainside, visitors are constant. Hawk-Watch treats the annual raptor count as an educational opportunity, and the highlight is the release of captured birds.

As a bird arrives, a small crowd gathers. The bird is slipped from its carrying tube and held by the legs, Popsicle-style. The HawkWatch staffer identifies the kind of bird, points to distinguishing markings, and gives the bird's age, sex, and condition. Questions are asked and answered. Then someone is chosen to release the bird, which is laid belly down in the palm of the chosen one's hand. The bird does not realize at first that it can fly free. The idea is to hold the hand still and see how long it takes for the bird to sense its freedom and burst into the air. The intricate, beautiful play of patterns across feathers, the long sharp talons, the intensity of the eyes—seeing raptors this close is a compelling visceral experience.

Months later, at Grantsville Elementary, just beyond the raptor flyway, two HawkWatch staffers wrap up a slide show on raptors and give the students the moment they have been waiting for. Jen and Mike unlatch the handmade box in front of the room and carefully lift out a Swainson's hawk named Argentina. Hit by a car and then nursed back to health by a raptor rehabilitator, Argentina has only one eye and can no longer survive in the wild.

Hawks' eyes, the kids have learned, are a work and a wonder. If a hawk or eagle were as big as a human, Mike and Jen tell them, its eyes would be *this* big. They hold tennis balls up to their eyes, and the kids laugh and gasp. "If I was an owl," Jen says, "my eyes would be *this* big." She holds a softball in front of her face. And that's not all—raptor eyes can zoom in like a camera and are as powerful as binoculars.

The number of raptors and their health are measures of the health of the habitats they visit. The classic example of chemical disruption of hawk habitat was DDT, a broadly used and much touted insecticide in the 1950s. My wife remembers playing hide-and-seek in the clouds of DDT sprayed from trucks on the woods and yards of her childhood New Jersey neighborhood. When falcons, eagles, and other raptors ate prey such as rodents, fish, and insects that contained DDT, the shells of their eggs became soft and the chicks defective.

The children are shown photos of an egg with a soft shell. Environmental problems that start lower in the food chain, Mike explains, tend to show up in the raptors later on. The fact that populations of such raptor species as eagles and peregrine falcons have rebounded quickly once chemicals were regulated out of their food chains demonstrates that once warnings are taken seriously, the negative impacts of human activity on wildlife can be reversed.

What he does not tell the kids is that in Utah, hawks migrate across a West Desert that is much abused. The military has used this desert to test chemical and biological weapons and to practice bombing. The West Desert includes a massive hazardous waste landfill, two commercial toxic waste incinerators, two chemical weapons incinerators, and a radioactive waste landfill. Many of their parents work at these facilities and vote for politicians who advocate for them. The families are dependent on the revenues such facilities generate.

Although the conventional wisdom holds that these facilities are well located because they are far from people and isolated, the raptors don't know that. It's a long way between meals when you're migrating, and a mouse is a mouse. Grasshoppers don't wear little skull-and-crossbones symbols to warn the unwary birds. Because of the contaminated environment they cross, there is good reason to watch the birds carefully and worry about their well-being.

HawkWatch's director, Howard Gross, is well aware that the raptors he studies face danger. I first met Howard when we worked together to pressure the state of Utah to test a West Desert magnesium refinery, Magcorp, for dioxin pollution. Howard, who grew up in New Jersey, was drawn to the wild landscapes of the West and moved to Utah to do graduate work in ecology. He was fascinated by the millions of birds that use the wetlands along the Great Salt Lake to nest and breed on their migratory journeys.

Magcorp was owned by a billionaire named Ira Rennert, who was notorious for building a palatial private estate in the tony Hamptons of Long Island while refusing to clean up lead mines he owned in the Midwest. Magcorp's dioxins were going into the lake and then into its predominant life-form, brine shrimp. The brine shrimp were going into birds. And some of those birds were going into raptors. Sometimes the world is a lot like those Russian dolls, one inside the other, smaller and smaller. Howard understood this and helped organize an ardent group of birders and other interested citizens called Friends of the Great Salt Lake to heal the wetland habitat along the lake.

The children at Grantsville Elementary are not just seeing a beautiful, charismatic creature and not just learning about its place in the habitat they share; they are learning about the evolutionary nature of life, although the word "evolution" is never used. The word "adapted," however, comes up a lot. The raptors are adapted for hunting. Along with their big keen eyes, they have sharp hooked beaks that they use as tools, as we use a knife and fork. The talons are sharp and strong enough to crush the bones in a man's arm, let alone some small rodent. The kids ooh and aah when Mike tells them that.

Raptors are found in forests, mountains, deserts, lakes, and marshes all over the globe, and each kind of raptor is adapted to its particular environment. Northern harriers, for example, lay more eggs because they nest on the ground, so more of their eggs get stolen. Females are larger than males, so they can guard the nest and cover all the eggs. Female plumage is duller than the fancier males because of the need for camouflage from other predators. The kids listen as if they've never considered the nuances of nature, but what they are hearing seems to make sense to them. Maybe they will not shoot birds when they get older and acquire guns. Gun ownership is common in Utah, and guns and adolescence combine in ways that are deadly for birds. Maybe they will even become birders themselves.

In Utah, known for its rough cowboy image, there are now two birdwatchers for every hunter, a quarter million by one estimate.[2] The number of people collecting information about the land, and the variety of activities they are engaged in, is also growing all the time. Such citizen scientists are not quite scientists and maybe not naturalists either. But by counting birds, butterflies, frogs, turtles, fish, and more, they are slowly drawing a portrait of the land and its creatures, revealing its connectivity and indicating its health. The field data they collect are the raw materials for more rigorous research.

Citizens groups collecting field notes also establish directions and priorities for research, and write grants and raise money to make it happen. They become powerful advocates for increasing the research budgets and resources of government agencies that do science. They disseminate the scientific findings to others through seminars, conferences, and newsletters. They host guest speakers and hold debates. And they learn the practical skills of science while gaining insights about the ways that local ecosystems work.

Birds, bears, and myriad wild creatures animate the landscape, and in doing so reveal its nature and needs. The ways bees make honey, birds nest, bobcats kill, and fish spawn can reveal more about the health of the watershed that nourishes your blood than any measure we have contrived, but only if we are paying attention and look for the connections. And we will pay attention only when we grasp that the health of watersheds and other landscapes is central to our own viability.

Healthy landscapes are key to economic vitality. As former Wisconsin senator Gaylord Nelson put it, "The economy is a wholly owned subsidiary of the environment." In 1997, a group of scientists and economists tried to assign a dollar value to the work of nature.[3] Their conclusions are compellingly described in *Nature's Services: Societal Dependence on Natural Ecosystems,* edited by Gretchen Daily. If natural systems, they asked, did not regulate the atmosphere and climate, purify and retain water, form and enrich soils, cycle nutrients, detoxify and recirculate wastes, pollinate crops, and produce lumber, fodder, and biomass fuels, what would it cost to replace these services? They came up with an estimate of $33 trillion, almost twice the combined gross national products of all the countries in the world.

This exercise may seem offensive to those who would no more put a dollar value on Gaia than they would price their own mothers. Or it may seem silly, considering that the services measured are irreplaceable—after all, when was the last time you saw an ad for a cheap deal on a climate? However high the values assigned to natural functions, they are, in a sense, arbitrary and understated. But the calculation underscores, for those whose bottom line is the almighty buck, that economies are embedded in and are a manifestation of ecosystems. It reveals the arrogance and ignorance of the argument that environmental criteria, rules, and conservation investments are too costly and an unacceptable burden on economies.

The assignment of dollar values to ecosystem functions can make more sense when applied regionally or locally. Gretchen Daily and Katherine Ellison have described several attempts, from Costa Rica to the Catskills, to assign quantitative values to ecosystem services that have been previously regarded as free, so that their value may be fully taken into account when comparing the costs and benefits of various choices.[4] When coastal wetlands are regarded as assets because they purify water and incubate fish that will eventually be harvested, they are more likely to be preserved and protected than if they are taken for granted. It would be great if we could all just love shellfish for themselves and feel related to them, but chances are someone with power will ask, "What's in it for us?" We can now answer that question. A healthy landscape is a productive landscape.

The civic dialogue about how to ensure clean drinking water for New York City provides an excellent example of how conservation can make cents as well as sense. The residents of New York City enjoy relatively clean water from the watershed of the Catskill Mountains. As rain and snow move downhill from the mountains toward the city, soil and fine roots filter the water while microorganisms break down contaminants. Plants in streams absorb the nitrogen in the water from car emissions and fertilizers. Wetlands trap sediment and heavy metals. A multibillion-dollar filtration plant is a pale imitation of the natural system already in place.

As the Catskills forests were consumed by farms, homes, and resorts, and as the resulting sewage and agricultural runoff tainted the water, the city of New York considered its options. It could replace the watershed's natural capacity to do the job it evolved to do. After $6 to $8 billion in capital costs, the operating cost would run to $300 million annually. Or it could spend $1 billion to buy and preserve forested land and upgrade septic tanks. After the initial costs, maintenance would be minimal. Preservation would also enhance flood control in the bargain. Plus, New York's urban dwellers would get some peaceful, pretty recreational areas to visit and enjoy. Now there's a no-brainer. Conserving a watershed might not guarantee clean water forever or preclude all other filtration, but it is a smart place to start.

Daily and Ellison combine the assignment of specific value to ecosystem services with an emphasis on accounting for externalities. An externality is a cost of doing something that is not paid by those doing it. Drivers of gas-guzzlers contribute to global warming but don't assume the costs and consequences. But when crops cook, soil blows away, and sudden storms push inland as a result of climate change, we all pay whether we drive alone to work in a Hummer or ride a bike.

Corporate polluters have long caused environmental problems that we all suffer and pay for, but that they do not have to account for. Bulky and nonbiodegradable product packaging, for example, goes into landfills taxpayers must pay for. Pervasive lead in our environment from years of leaded gasoline causes cancer and learning disabilities that continue to cost society plenty years after lead in gas was eliminated. When the costs of doing business are honestly faced and the value of nature's services is fully acknowledged, the balance sheet looks a lot different.

A critic of the Forest Service and the Bureau of Land Management might caution that our history of governing landscapes according to economic criteria is one of consistent misunderstanding and failure. Thus we should be wary of assigning values to natural systems in order to set priorities and make plans. That critic might say there is another bottom line that is beyond any number crunching because we are embedded in the natural world, and life is the process of translating an environment into flesh and blood. We express an environment bodily. This is not New Age prattle but self-evident science.

The amniotic fluid that is, in the words of ecologist Sandra Steingraber, our "first environment" is a mother-made micro-sea composed of drinking water and the juice of fruits and vegetables eaten by the mother.[5] Drinking water comes from clouds that drift in from the ocean and are gathered by mountains, cold fronts, and currents and then drained by storms that fill creeks, rivers, and lakes or seep deep down into aquifers. The juice of fruits and vegetables is a translation of raindrops, dewdrops, frost, and well water. Breast milk is also seawater and rain.

The same is true for the liquid of our cells. We are, after all, fluid creatures. We sweat, cry, urinate, salivate, and bleed. The nutrients our bloodstreams carry come from soil that was once leaf, stone, root, bone, carcass, carapace, and flowers. It is processed by worms and bugs. Through each fish, fowl, animal, and plant that we eat pours the generous energy of the sun. We may behave as if we are disembodied egos manipulating and mastering a world of dead objects, but our continual biological communion with the world is an undeniable fact of life. It is life.

So we are what we eat, what we drink, and what we breathe. And what we eat is a habitat, what we drink is a watershed, and what we breathe is a climate. I had to live in the wilderness to learn these fundamental lessons, but there is a simple experiment anyone can do to get the point—stop eating for three weeks, stop taking in fluids for three days, or stop breathing for three minutes. You'll get the picture fast. To be alive is to process an environment into flesh, bone, and experience. Life's process is profoundly inclusive. It includes constipated bears, the microbes in deer guts and vole poop, the water-fed blood coursing through your veins, and the eagle riding a spiral of high thermal wind with the image of that vole burning in her eye.

It's a Trickster World—Just Ask Coyote

A few summers ago I stood in sagebrush near Capitol Reef National Park, Utah, and heard a very old song—coyotes crying on the edge of town. It was not the mournful cliché wail heard in Western movies but a robust call-and-response jam session. I was intrigued and drawn to the sound, but the dog I was with shivered and retreated.

Those of us who have heard Coyote's sundown music often report that it makes us stop to think, interrupts the inner babble we are hearing and invites our senses to take over, to listen mindfully. We hear something primal and mysterious hiding in the dusk. We strain to understand a language we do not know. As I tuned in to the coyote I was all ears, but later my thoughts turned to evolution, to the contrast between that wild creature calling across the sagebrush and the obedient pet at my side.

The human-canine affair probably stretches all the way back to Paleolithic times, when hunters learned to follow wild dogs to easy carrion and migrating herds of delicious ungulates. Then, as now, we used dogs to hunt and guard. Who knows, we may have even regarded them affectionately—at least using their body heat on cold "three-dog nights."

Our intimate canine relationships have gone on for so long that our whims and needs have been translated into their evolutionary design with extreme and amusing variation. From pit bulls to greyhounds, chihuahuas to Saint Bernards, and poodles to dachshunds, we have bred dogs into every conceivable shape and behavior. We have hairy and hairless dogs, dogs with pointy snouts and dogs with wrinkled pusses. My niece has a dog she carries in her purse, while my former boss has one that barely fits in her car. We have lap dogs, watchdogs, seeing-eye dogs, retrievers, bloodhound trackers, pointers, and heelers.

And, of course, mutts—millions of mutts in endless combination. My neighbor owns the offspring of a wiener dog and a German shepherd who overcame the considerable physical impediments to their union and produced what looks like a long full-grown police dog padding around on three-inch legs. He barks a lot. If I looked like that, I would bark a lot. But no matter which breed a person prefers, ask him or her to list the characteristics of a dog and you will hear the words "devoted . . . loyal . . . companion . . . pet." Dogs are man's best friend.

Except one. After all these years, there is still one ancient canine cousin that retains its self-determined form and refuses to roll over: Coyote. Forget our deep doggy affinity, Coyote is hated. We kill hundreds of thousands of coyotes each year. In Utah, if you see one, you shoot it, trap it, poison it, or gas it—then hang its sorry hide on a fence. Most puppies melt our hearts, but across their native ground in the American West, coyote pups are burned and melted in their dens.

Our scorn for Coyote is in sharp contrast to the Native American view. Indigenous myth is rife with stories of Coyote, the Trickster: curious, creative, contradictory, playful, and lusty. He may not be likable or trustworthy in these legends, but his resilience in the face of adversity is noted and admired. Killed again and again, he always comes back to life. Those who closely observed his ability to adapt to changing circumstances such as drought or fluctuations in game appreciated his survival skills, since they too faced such challenges. Is it any wonder that people who lived in a dynamic landscape of fault lines, flash floods, and fire zones would weave through their folklore such a mischievous and utterly unpredictable character? Long before chaos theory, there was Coyote.

Unlike so many other animals, Coyote can adapt to new circumstances quickly. He is so exceptional that he survived and flourished while his less flexible cousin, the wolf, and other big predators such as cougars and bears perished. Coyote is also independent. The Navajo translation of his name is "God's dog"—not God as in Yahweh, but God as in Creator/Creation. Coyote's doglike loyalty, in other words, is to his own God-given wild nature. There is obviously much to learn from such an animal.

Even today, beyond the totemic content of native myths, Coyote is still instructing us, even if we are not listening. Coyote's lessons do not have to be retrieved from some ancient past when we too slept under a veil of stars in night air embroidered by his tune, but are present in the here and now all over this land. Including Manhattan.

Recently a coyote was captured in Central Park. To get to the park's pigeons, ducks, squirrels, and dumpsters, that coyote had to cross a scary bridge or follow a very long tunnel. Either she hitched a ride with a truck, or she braved heavy traffic, bright lights, and the cacophonous ambience of an urban environment that could not be more different than her ancestral ground.

The lesson is found not in the New York coyote's stealthy behavior, but in the ubiquitous presence of coyotes in America today, a presence underlined by the Central Park incident. Coyotes are everywhere. In spite of our long, violent campaign to kill them, the population of coyotes in America has probably doubled in the past century, and their habitat has exploded. Coyote does well in suburban settings, where he trades prairie dogs for hot dogs and other discarded food. Cats are also yummy and so are those little yipping dogs that hang out in Winnebagos. Unlike cougars, which must have blood, coyotes have been reported eating farmers' melons. Whether it's Los Angeles or Los Animas, it's all the same to the Trickster, who knows how to walk the edge of any habitat and drop in for a meal.

Our attempt to control Coyote has failed miserably. That is why we scorn him. He won't come, he won't fetch, he won't sit, he won't beg, and he won't die. Kill him and two come to the funeral. He is an affront to any culture that, having conquered the wild frontier, now prides itself on mapping genomes and distant galaxies.

We ought to pay attention to Coyote. In an age when we are splicing genes from flounders into strawberries and designing plants that contain their own indiscriminate pesticides, we ought to remember that there are limits to our ability to manipulate, finesse, and control. Viruses and insects are also resilient, complex, and unpredictable. Immune systems are loaded with tricksters. Stressed ecosystems—robbed of their healing diversity, soaked with pollutants, radiated beyond their tolerance, and then loaded with new and utterly unpredictable human-made biotech actors—can crash, kicking off new and unexpected evolutionary responses.

When we tinker with evolution, we may walk away with a proud thoroughbred and a shiny winner's cup or populate the neighborhood with weird barking mutts—and worse. Small changes in initial conditions can cascade through a natural system with surprising consequences that grow as they go. As Coyote is here to say, sometimes Nature is our dog and sometimes She is God's dog. Creation has directions, turns, and consequences that are often beyond us.

Given our power to stop, manipulate, and pollute the ecological and evolutionary processes that include us, we would be wise to be heedful and prudent—and mindful. That coyote singing to me in the sage told me it's a trickster world out there. I grew up in a culture that believes tricksters can be tamed. But if I could be tamed, the coyote was saying to me in her song, I wouldn't be a trickster. When I awoke in the morning, I set off to find Michael Soulé. If anybody could unravel the mysteries and surprises of ecological and evolutionary processes and patterns for me, it was he.

On a hot summer morning in 2002, I met up with Michael Soulé in western Colorado. He had just retired from teaching at the University of California at Santa Cruz, where he had chaired the department of environmental studies and still held the title of professor emeritus. Soulé is widely regarded as the midwife of a new science called conservation biology, which is revolutionizing how we regard ecosystems and their needs, and what we must do to meet those needs. He played key roles as the synthesizer of its themes, its organizer, its spokesperson, and, most of all, its visionary light. He had recently moved to Paonia, Colorado, and agreed to meet me at his new home there.

Soulé's name is not exactly a household word, although it could be someday. Conservation biology aims to understand biodiversity, then advocate new policies that put the conservation of biodiversity at the top of our land use priorities. The visionary work of Soulé and his colleagues is turning common notions of conservation upside down. Instead of building dams, we are breaching them. Instead of a cartoon bear in pants and ranger hat holding a shovel and advising us to stop forest fires, we are starting them. And instead of posses of hunters cornering and killing wolves, teams of scientists are releasing them into habitat that has not seen them for generations.

The turnoff to Soulé's home is hidden in hardy high-desert brush that has survived one of the worst droughts in memory. Four miles out of the little town of Hotchkiss, he'd told me, there's a marker acknowledging the historical importance of early Spanish explorers; take a sharp left after that. I realize I've missed the sign and circle back; fortunately, it's easier to see going the other way. A gravel road with hairpin turns winds up the slope of a dry mesa, the transition zone from farm fields to raw mountain range. "Look for the blue roof," he'd said.

Soulé's home is perched on top of the mesa, overlooking a wide valley—which, as it turns out, may soon be riddled with drilling rigs looking for methane gas over coal beds. The locals have just discovered that they do not own the mining rights to the land they have lived on, in some cases for generations, so corporations can just move in on top of them and begin doing business. There have been some heated community meetings, and the rural populace, though inexperienced at grassroots politics, is beginning to mobilize. Soulé decided to retire here after having hunted elk in the area for many years. That was before President George W. Bush gave the energy industry the green light to rape the valley below.

The broad mountain ranges in the distance are barely discernible through a smoky haze. Vast forest fires have been spreading across the West this summer. In fact, I have just spent two days standing on my brother-in-law's roof in Norwood, Colorado, watching big tanker planes dropping red fire retardant on a nearby wildfire. He was packed and ready to go if the roulette wheel of disaster, spun by the mercurial winds, stopped its arrow on his door. Fortunately, monsoon rains arrived in the nick of time.

On the way over to the North Fork Valley to see Soulé, I listened to a local politician ranting on the radio about environmentalists, whose resistance to logging, he claimed, was to blame for the unprecedented conflagration. I try to ignore fools, but this guy's opportunistic blame-setting pissed me off. "How about a hundred years of fire suppression that thwarted the natural process of thinning trees and clearing out undergrowth?" I ranted back at the radio. "Fire was controlled to protect timber and the lumber companies' profits. Now the public lands are loaded with fuel that's dried out by drought, ripe for a spark from lightning or human misconduct. I wonder who pays for your campaigns!"

I'm glad I'm on a rural two-lane blacktop, where there are few witnesses to my outburst, and finish my spontaneous editorial a mile from Soulé's door. The smoke-filled air, the occasional helicopters, and the townsfolk I've seen, their ears cocked for radio reports, combine to create an ambience of impending catastrophe—a fitting backdrop for a visit to Soulé, whose life's work has centered on another catastrophe: the massive extinction of species, the collapse of ecosystems, and the interruption of the evolutionary journey.

He greets me in the driveway and leads me into a spacious combination living room and dining room. Photos of Africa adorn the walls, seeming somewhat out of sync with the home's Southwest location and architectural style. It turns out that Soulé lived for several years in Malawi, where he taught at a university and studied wild animals.

He is a wiry man—lean and fit for a guy in his mid-sixties, tan and angular. His head is buzzed almost bald, and he has not shaved for several days, so his face is covered with gray stubble from scalp to chin. I can see he is busy, so I waste no time. "Tell me your story. How did you get from science to politics?"

"I was an academic scientist, and I never used the term 'public policy,'" he says. "I was [*Population Bomb* author] Paul Ehrlich's first graduate student, and had spoken in public quite a bit about population problems. I was involved in advocacy as a graduate student during the Vietnam War. But the interest in advocacy for Creation, or biodiversity, came quite a bit later."

Soulé grew up in San Diego in the 1940s and '50s, when the city was small and surrounded by canyons filled with chaparral. Abalone and lobsters could be harvested from tide pools. He collected butterflies, bugs, and snakes in the hills and canyons near home. "I saw paradise paved over for the benefit of real estate developers and politicians. I came to biology with some bitterness and sadness, knowing what could happen to an area. But I never thought of being an activist or advocate for nature, although I knew what was happening to it.

"The incident that triggered the development of conservation biology happened when I was on sabbatical in Australia in 1973 and '74. I got a phone call from an Australian scientist, Sir Otto Frankel, who had been knighted for his work on applied wheat genetics. He had read work I had done on island populations of lizards and told me it was relevant to a book he was writing on genetic conservation, on why we should conserve genetic variation. He invited me to teach a seminar in Canberra, and I did. Then he ended up inviting me to co-author the book he was writing."

Soulé and Frankel's book, *Conservation and Evolution,* was a milestone in conservation biology when it was published in 1981. They tried to identify the size of a viable population, below which breeding pairs of creatures would be so susceptible to the loss of genetic variation and so vulnerable to inevitable natural disturbances that extinction was likely. Soulé concluded that evolution itself, at least the continued evolutionary speciation of large mammals, was in peril. Although evolution continues apace, particularly among viruses and bacteria, the rise of new species of larger animals requires space and time for novel adaptations to fill available niches.

The earth is experiencing an unprecedented and historic avalanche of extinction. There have been five other great phases of extinction in history, but none of those were human-made. Now human beings—in large numbers, with sophisticated technology and boundless appetites for more stuff—are having the impact of an asteroid crash on the planet's biosphere.

The losses are staggering, and, just as alarming, evolution has nowhere to go. Few wild animals have enough space, opportunity, and genetic variation to keep evolving. While existing species of plants and animals will continue with moderate changes in their lineages over time, they are unlikely to split off and form new species. Dandelions and silverfish will continue to evolve, but the great apes and the magnificent rain forest hardwoods won't be players.

"Death is one thing," Soulé has written, "but an end to birth is something else, and nature reserves are too small to gestate new species of vertebrates. There is no escaping the conclusion that in our lifetimes, this planet will see a suspension, if not an end, to many ecological and evolutionary processes which have been uninterrupted since the beginning of paleontological time."[1]

Granted, your average Kmart shopper is likely to care more about the discontinuation of a favorite product or the cancellation of a TV show than whether wolverines get to morph along over the next 10,000 years, but to Soulé it matters. Speciation is how biodiversity is created. So if, on the one hand, we are witnessing a cascade of extinction and a loss of biodiversity and, on the other hand, the creation of new biodiversity is blocked, the health of the planet is in dire straits. By destroying and expropriating so much habitat for themselves, humans are now mediating evolution. And they are poised to do even more of that with genetically engineered plants, animals, and fish, cloned cattle, and emerging nano-technologies. "There is no precedent for what is happening to the biological fabric of this planet. As long as humans have hegemony over the earth," Soulé states flatly, "there will be no potential for recovery."

Soulé and his colleagues are deeply aware that the creatures they study have taken shape over millions of years, their behaviors and physiology changing in response to a landscape that also emerged over time. They are moved by what they have learned and experienced. Life on earth, they understand, is an awesome and intricate dance that has been going on nonstop for over a billion years, and now they can hear the music fading away. "For centuries to come, our descendants will eulogize or damn us and our integrity based on the integrity of the green mantle they inherit," Soulé says. "Aldo Leopold said that the price of an ecological education is to live alone in a land of wounds, to be acutely aware of the ways we are wounding Creation. It can be terribly sad."

Soulé tells me that he had to lecture his students about how to cope with despair because he depressed them by talking so much about extinction. Coping with gloom comes with the profession. "It helps to have an ecological perspective. It's a long-term perspective, almost a geological perspective. Ecological change occurs on a scale of decades to centuries. When you're in your twenties, you think that a problem that can't be solved in a year or two is hopeless. An ecological perspective tells you that problems have their own momentum. Problems that are a hundred years in the making will probably take that long to solve. A grounding in evolutionary biology teaches you to think on a scale that most of us are ill-equipped to consider. You get used to it.

"Yes, we're going through a very bad time for life on the planet. But," he adds, "we protect what we can and pass it on to the next generation. The builders of the great cathedrals knew they wouldn't see completion in their lifetimes, but they committed themselves and had faith. What we're building these days is more like a vessel, like an ark. There will be a time in the future when the world is friendly toward nature again. Then the species and patches of ecosystem that we protected and healed will spread out, will reanimate and revegetate the planet. Conservationists see themselves as Noahs with faith that human beings are fundamentally good and will someday come to their senses."

Another way of coping with despair is active engagement. When he returned from Australia to teach at the University of California at San Diego, he told a graduate student named Bruce Wilcox about his developing interest in applying theoretical and empirical science to the problems of nature conservation. "It hadn't been done very much. The activists and conservationists from the World Wildlife Fund, The Nature Conservancy, and so on were way over here, and the science was way over there. There wasn't much interchange between the scientists and the conservationists. I felt the conservationists were way behind in applying the science to protecting nature. Science was getting lip service, but that was about all."

Soulé and Wilcox decided to hold the First International Conference on Conservation Biology in La Jolla in 1978. That led to the book *Conservation Biology: An Evolutionary-Ecological Perspective* and sparked incipient scientific energies as well. Academic scientists who studied ecology, genetics, and evolutionary biology had long regarded applied biological sciences with intellectual disdain—likening them to wildlife management and forestry. But they began to realize that such egotistical detachment could no longer be afforded—not in the face of extinction and collapse.

Soulé and his colleagues had witnessed the folly of policymakers who made decisions without the best and latest science in hand. Now those government agencies, as well as philanthropies and land trusts, began asking the conservation biologists for recommendations on the design and management of land. Their concerns were wide-ranging, from the ideal site and size of protected areas and the evaluation of endangered or invasive species to chemical pollution and the impact of housing developments.

Traditionally, land use decisions had often been made in haste, driven by political dynamics, in an arena of competing interests and stakeholders. That was bad enough, but without the hard science, policymakers were forced to rely on dated assumptions about nature and on the dominant values of the most powerful economic interests. Natural resource planners and policymakers needed tools. Conservation biologists could develop those tools. "What was needed was a bridge," Soulé says, so he stretched himself out and became one.

The scientists who gathered in La Jolla were seeking a compelling direction that could be broadly shared, one that might challenge the traditional assumptions and dominant commercial and recreational values that underlay what they were painfully witnessing: the continued shredding of habitats and their creatures. Clearly, wildlands support more life than engineered landscapes do. And so-called "self-willed" lands, where ecological processes are unimpeded and the ecological players have been honed by evolution, tend to be much healthier than the landscapes we have managed intensively and badly.

Conservation biologists have witnessed more than their share of officially sanctioned stupid pet tricks. The goals and rules that guided powerful agencies like the Bureau of Land Management and the Department of Energy had about as much credibility, in their eyes, as the views of a Soviet engineer after Chernobyl. Yet in every agency, no matter how wrong-headed the information that misguided it and how dubious its performance, there was always a constituency pushing for change and hungry for better information and a new, compelling context.

The new context would rest on a much longer time scale and a much broader field of vision. It would heed the new understanding of the evolutionary, emergent, and regenerative processes and cycles of nature, and it would take biological diversity as its prime measure of habitat health. No one expressed that organizing context better than Michael Soulé: "I felt that conservation biology was analogous to public health medicine. Medicine also combines pure science with applied science. And like medicine, this new field of science would have a mission and its own ethical foundation or precepts." Conservation biology would be a kind of earth medicine, practiced to heal a planet that was losing its biodiversity.

Soulé also compared conservation biology to cancer biology.[2] Both draw from the work of many disciplines, not all of them biological. Conservation biology's multidisciplinary approach includes specialties ranging from wildlife management and forestry to physiology and genetic research. Both are applied in situations where there is not enough time, or there are too many shifting variables, to arrive at certainty. "Conservation biology," he wrote, "differs from most other biological sciences in one important way: it is often a crisis discipline. Its relation to biology, particularly ecology, is analogous to that of surgery to physiology and war to political science. In crisis disciplines, one must act before knowing all the facts; crisis disciplines are thus a mixture of science and art, and their pursuit requires intuition as well as information."

Conservation biology is science with a value-oriented mission to preserve biological diversity and maintain, even restore, healthy ecological systems. Or, it might be more accurate to say, conservation biology is a science that admits its mission. Unlike rocket science, which does not articulate its purpose outside of the defense industry contracts and government grant narratives it writes to obtain funding, conservation biology is unabashed about saving species.

Whether hip-deep in mud while counting salamanders along the rim of a pond or back in the office plotting the collected data with a computer, conservation biologists insist on all the controls and rules common to other sciences. Their research is peer-reviewed, but they are willing to venture beyond the usual boundaries of academia to navigate between the worlds of science and advocacy. They have struggled for many years to find a balance between the hard and thorough science they are trained to do and the expedient world of policy, politics, law, and engrained cultural behaviors.

For each scientist, the right mix of research and advocacy will be different. Some join debates, and some are content to inform the debates of others. Some charge barricades, and others have retreated to or never left the labs and fields where their knowledge was gleaned. But it is no longer possible for them to avoid looking over the rims of their glasses toward the messy world at large. Action, even imperfect action, is compelling when whole ecosystems are going to hell in a handbasket while we argue over who gets to carry it out to the car.

If conservation biology's cardinal theme is the importance of diversity, as the citizen trackers in Vermont and the hawk watchers in Nevada were learning, another central theme is the integrity of the ecological processes, honed by evolution, that support diverse life. There is no better example than wolf reintroduction of how powerfully conservation biologists like Michael Soulé have developed that theme to influence the public's imagination and the policies and philosophy of land use management. The notion of releasing wolves with radio collars back into habitat they have been expelled from would have been unfathomable to our forefathers. Our attitudes toward wolves are changing in revolutionary ways that accord with wholly new perspectives on how healthy ecosystems are sustained.

Historically, an entire regime of laws and policies guiding the use of public lands across the American West, from southwestern deserts to northwestern forests, was built on the confident assumption that we could manage habitat well. Federal, state, local, and private land managers, policymakers, and planners alike shared this assumption: self-willed land was inefficient, unpredictable, and inconvenient. Man was put here to manage. Tricksters could and should be tamed.

During most of the twentieth century, conservation, as practiced by federal and state agencies, often meant dam building. If free-running water could be captured, it could be conserved for human use. First you build a dam with a power plant; then you stock the reservoir behind it with game fish, build a campsite with toilets and a boat ramp, and carve out a road or two; and voilà!—conservation. Wildlife was managed so it could be harvested, meadows so they could be grazed by cows, and forests so they could be cut and fashioned into products.

The prevailing attitude toward the animals with which we share the planet was simple enough: some we could tame, harness, own, hunt, or eat, and the rest were expendable—unless they threatened those we could tame, harness, own, hunt, or eat, in which case they were "varmints" and must be destroyed. The value of a species was determined not by its relationships with other plants and animals, but by its relationship with humans. We are the animal that counts. Unfortunately, many of our critical assumptions about how nature works turned out to be wrong—dead wrong.

Although the labors of Michael Soulé and his conservation biologist colleagues are mostly unseen and unacknowledged by the general public, the shift in our understanding of natural processes that they have generated is no less profound. A brief history of our relationship with the coyote's less adaptable cousin, the wolf, reveals how far we have come. The war on North American wolves began almost as soon as our Pilgrim forefathers scraped their boots on Plymouth Rock and unloaded the boat. A bounty on wolves was enacted a scant ten years after the founding of the Plymouth Bay Colony in Massachusetts, where the General Court imposed a five-shilling fine for the unnecessary discharge of a gun "except at an Indian or a wolf."[3]

The colonists had brought with them shiploads of domesticated cows, pigs, and sheep, which had had their speed, agility, and intelligence bred out of them, making them easy prey. In the New World colonies, lost cattle could translate into starvation during lean winters, so the wolves' eager consumption of the guileless beasts struck them as criminal. Throughout the history of American settlement, popular accounts of wolves commonly described them as cruel and treacherous outlaws, enemies of civilization itself—a kind of Osama bin Lobos of the old frontier.

As the settlers moved into the American West, where wolves were abundant, their disdain for the animals grew. The first political organizing in the Oregon Territory was the so-called wolf meetings of 1843, aimed at enacting a bounty on wolves and taxing settlers to pay for it.

Killing wolves became even more profitable around the mid-1800s, after the beaver populations, which were the target of the earliest phase of the fur trade, had been trapped out. The powerful fur trading companies sought new wild animal resources to buy and sell, and bison hides took the place of beaver pelts. While Plains Indians had practiced sustainable hunting and wasted little, Anglo hunters killed whole herds, cut the woolly hides off the big brown bodies, and left the meat to rot in the sun.

As wolves were drawn to the burgeoning slaughter, hunters found them almost as easy to pick off as the bison. The broad-chested gray or timber wolf was often six feet long and yielded a nice pelt. Collecting wolf pelts became a popular way for seasonally employed miners and cowboys to generate income over long winters. They would load up on poison in the fall and bait carrion with it over the winter. Whole wolf packs died at such bait stations so miners could live to dig another day. Between 5,000 and 10,000 wolf pelts per year were purchased by the American Fur Company in Fort Benton, Missouri, during the 1860s.[4]

Under the grinding wheel of commerce, the noble wolf was translated into chewing tobacco, whiskey, soap, tools, whores, and jerky. Unfortunately, the poisoned wolf carcasses also killed eagles, ravens, foxes, coyotes, cougars, badgers, wolverines, and bears. Sometimes wolf hunters would trap a wolf, wire his penis closed so he could not urinate, and later cut out the engorged bladder. The accumulated urine was used as scent to bait new traps.

Once the land was stripped of the great bison herds and the Indians who hunted them, settlers drove in sheep and cattle to occupy the habitats they had captured and cleared. The remaining wolves found the lambs and calves convenient to kill and tasty to boot. Besides, the settlers had wiped out most of the wildlife that was the wolves' natural prey.

As wolves became less a resource to be harvested and more a threat to the cattle economy's crop of lambs and calves, wolf extirpation became a federal policy, and wolf hunting became maniacal. Traps, snares, poison, and dog packs were employed. Bait with fishhooks was thrown into dens so that the pups that ate it could be yanked out and clubbed to death. Wolf dens were even dynamited. One town in Kansas paved a road through a swamp with wolf carcasses.[5] Even the newly created national parks were not exempt from the formally sanctioned imperative to kill them all, every last one. The last wolves in Yellowstone National Park were killed in the 1930s.

Wolves were not alone. Bears and cougars were also hunted for bounties. Coyotes were on the list too, and still are, but unlike their "my-what-big-teeth-you-have" cousins, they survived. Coyotes can feed on disturbance, the way weeds do on torn-up ground. Not so for wolves and cougars, which are more solitary and shy, their survival behaviors rooted in territories that are vast and unbroken. After being relentlessly hunted and trapped off their native ground, those habitats usurped and fragmented, the beasts became mere ghosts on the land. And according to Michael Soulé, that haunted land suffers their absence terribly.

Soulé and his conservation biologist colleagues were instrumental in challenging the old bottom-up model of food chains and their associated habitat relationships. In its place, they outlined a more dynamic and complex system in which "top carnivores" play essential roles. This is an important concept in conservation biology. The old model imagined food relationships as a kind of pyramid. At the bottom are soils and plant communities. Plants are eaten by herbivores, which are eaten by carnivores. Remove the plants and the plant eaters die, and then the carnivores starve in turn. Our assimilation of this oversimplified notion may explain why we associate vulnerability with being at the top of the food chain. If this model were an ice-cream sundae, the big carnivores such as wolves, cougars, and bears would be like the cherry on top. And, as we all know, if you don't like your cherry, you can give it to someone who does, just throw it away, or put it in a leftover container. A delicious dessert remains. Under this model, the big predators were sovereign but expendable, not linked to the health of the whole through relationships with the other components.

Conservation biologists have discovered it's a lot more complicated than that. The food "chain" is actually a complex food *web* filled with reciprocal feedback loops. In this web, the top predators, especially the big, charismatic carnivores, are highly interactive key players. Pluck their cherry off the top, and the whole sundae might just melt down.

A classic example of this process emerged during a human-made ecological disaster in Venezuela in the 1980s, when development of one of the world's largest hydroelectric impoundments behind a dam at Lago Guri caused the flooding of the long Caroni Valley. The reservoir grew until it was 125 kilometers long and 70 kilometers wide. Hundreds of mountaintops became islands in a vast inland sea.

The old habitat's top predator, the jaguar, is a powerful, sleek, and beautiful cat, not an amphibian capable of island-hopping hunts. The jaguar's prey, mostly howler monkeys and iguanas, were stranded on the artificial islands with no jaguar in sight—a situation that was good for them in the short run, but not so good for the whole habitat in the long run. As they became superabundant, a cascade of consequences was set in motion.

Duke University's John Terborgh, a colleague of Soulé and one of the most influential tropical ecologists working today, studied what happened next. Seeds and seedlings disappeared as the overpopulated herbivores enjoyed an uninterrupted feast. Of the sixty to seventy tree species that were originally present, only five managed to reproduce.[6] Eventually, as the unchecked populations of seed and seedling eaters exploded, the forest canopy began to thin and forest succession was arrested, further skewing the ecosystem's dynamics. Although the Caroni Valley case involves many unique variables, it illustrates how predation contributes to the kind of dynamic balance enjoyed by most mature habitats.

Yellowstone National Park, the old crown jewel in the nation's park system, provides a case study closer to home. The removal of the wolves that ate the elk in the park has led to an overabundance of elk. But it's not just their numbers that are up—their behavior has changed too. Without wolves to chase them around, the elk have become fat and lazy. Complacent elk, instead of visiting a wide array of feeding areas, hang out along streams and rivers, where the livin' is easy.

As a result, the wet, fertile riparian zones along streams and rivers have become overgrazed. Tall grass and shrub habitat for other small animals and birds has disappeared. The calliope hummingbird and willow flycatcher populations have declined as their habitat was chewed to the nubs. Another result of overgrazing has been erosion that deposited silt into the clear mountain waters in amounts unlike anything the native fish had experienced during their slow evolution—and more than they could abide.

While the fish were choking on silt, aspen and cottonwood seedlings were devoured by hungry herds of stream-crowding elk, so no new aspens or cottonwoods have grown up. Forest succession, the cycle that renews forest growth, has been arrested. A forest where only stately old aspens are present makes a nice photo, but it is not the picture of health.

There is evidence that the absence of aspen seedlings, the major food source for beavers, has limited their numbers, too. Beavers create wetland habitats for all sorts of other species, so their disappearance from the landscape has in turn affected populations of fish, reptiles, amphibians, birds, insects, and other mammals both large and small.

A similar situation developed along the Kaibab Plateau near Grand Canyon National Park in the early 1900s, when mountain lions were removed and the deer population exploded. Photos from that time show rows of dead mountain lions stacked in pyramids by the proud hunters who had treed and shot them. Once the big predators were out of the picture, it wasn't long before the overgrazed piñon and shrub habitat began to collapse and the deer ended up starving in droves. In upper Michigan, where unchecked moose populations spread, it was balsam seedlings that disappeared.

In the past several decades, the absence of predation combined with the impracticality of hunting in Eastern suburbs has resulted in the overpopulation of white-tailed deer. Ticks that feed on the overabundant deer and carry Lyme disease have also become ubiquitous. Since wolves have an aversion to noise, lights, and traffic, automobiles will have to thin the Eastern herd out as best they can, one bummer at a time.

Big carnivores are interactive in other ways. By eliminating old and weakened members of a prey herd, they tone the herd. Dispersing prey not only keeps them from eroding habitat in the few areas where they would otherwise gather, it also keeps contagious illness from spreading as quickly and easily as it does through large, closely packed herds. Carcasses left behind by top predators supply food to scavengers such as eagles, ravens, magpies, and wolverines.

Another important destabilizing consequence of removing top predators from an ecosystem involves smaller predators and is called mesopredator release. The concept is simple enough. If you take out the wolves, the big cats, and the bears and leave in the smaller predators like foxes, skunks, raccoons, opossums, and house cats, their populations increase and as a consequence their prey—ground-nesting birds like quail, pheasants, grouse, and ducks—suffer. Even songbird populations can diminish. Thirty years ago, the farmland that surrounds my home in northern Utah was occasionally visited by cougars; coyotes were common there, and so were birds. Today the open fields are broken by new housing developments and roads. I see fewer species of birds on my walks around the edge of town, but there is no shortage of skunks.

The effects of mesopredator release are both behavioral and demographic. In the absence of their own predators, mesocarnivores become emboldened and may increase the length and type of their feeding activities. So when the little predators are "released" from their own predators, they eat up their own prey. When they have wiped out all their prey, their population starves or, as is increasingly the case, they develop a taste for human garbage. Dumpster diving, after all, beats dying, which is why we are seeing more skunks and foxes in suburbs and even in cities. Their presence is a sign of a desperation wed to adaptation as animals flee depleted traditional habitats.

Coyotes, as might be expected, can go either way. The trickster can act like a top predator and eat smaller foxes and skunks, or he can be treated like a midsize mammal and be eaten by a wolf. So the reduction of coyotes in some habitats can lead to mesopredator release and adverse consequences rippling through an ecosystem.

The abundance of coyotes in a habitat is itself an example of how food webs can be disrupted. Coyote populations can explode when top carnivores like wolves, which eat coyotes and compete with them for limited food, are eradicated. Ironically, the best way to reduce coyote numbers across the West may be to reintroduce wolves to eat them, compete with them, and push them away. So far, where wolves have been reintroduced and have reestablished their role in the food web, coyote numbers have dropped significantly. Western ranchers should take note: Shy and solitary wolves that have a healthy territory to roam through are less likely to approach populated areas and kill cattle than the coyote trickster that so vexes the ranchers and provokes their ire.

Connectivity is another major theme of conservation biology. Soulé explains that predation is an ecological process that can require a big territory for its big predator. Certain other ecological processes, like migration, also require abundant wild land. Unfortunately, there are few, if any, pristine places left, and those that remain, we are now learning, are too small and cannot be self-sustaining as islands in a human-made sea. We know this, he says, from island biogeography, a science most people have never heard of.

The biologists and others Soulé has rallied to the ranks of conservation biology are a generation of scientists who have come of age professionally under the profound influence of a book that is little known in the popular world: *The Theory of Island Biogeography*, by Edward O. Wilson and Robert MacArthur. Islands have long been a favorite focus for biologists looking for situations where variables are more fixed and stable than in vast mainland habitats, where boundaries are porous and variables are fluid. Thus, island biogeography is the study of the dynamics of ecosystems as expressed on islands. The field captured the attention of biologists in the 1970s because of what island ecosystems reveal about biodiversity, extinction, and connectivity. Wilson and MacArthur's book had a galvanizing effect on the thinking of Soulé and his colleagues.

You could say it all began with a fish fin in the eye. When Edward O. Wilson was a child, he carelessly jerked a fish into his face and suffered a traumatic wound to his right eye. With sight in only one eye, it was hard for him to discern birds or even mammals at a distance. His left eye, however, had powerful vision that could see the hairs on an ant's leg without a microscope. The young man's bent for observing nature close up and low down led to his becoming the world's foremost expert on ants. He traveled the world, including lots of islands, gathering rich data on the pesky insects.

When he met a talented young ecologist named Robert MacArthur, who had a gift for reading patterns in nature and expressing them mathematically, the two quickly developed a complementary partnership. Both believed that an obscure, peripheral, mostly descriptive and somewhat romantic discipline called island biogeography could yield insights into how species thrive, become extinct, or split off into new species. Wilson had the data, and MacArthur could apply the math to that data to support their theories.

MacArthur died young from renal cancer, but Wilson went on to win two Pulitzer Prizes and become famous, first as the inventor of sociobiology and later as an eloquent proponent of biodiversity. But his scientific and cultural legacy may have been set long before he won popular attention. MacArthur and Wilson's now classic work on island biogeography was issued with no fanfare, but its insights changed the way we look at landscapes and the creatures that inhabit them.

For starters, they said, bigger is better—a concept called the area effect. Generally, the size of an island is directly related to the number of species it can support over time. If an island is too small and its variety of habitats too limited, it will shelter fewer species and fewer individual populations of those species. When a natural disturbance like a fire or a hurricane wipes out most members of a species or destroys their habitat, the survivors are less likely to be replenished by a nearby population of that species if the island carries few such populations. And the survivors probably can't move over to the next valley to find another habitat or food source, unless the island is large enough to include multiple similar habitats.

The health and long-term viability of species also result from the genetic variation available. Inbreeding, as is popularly recognized in countless jokes about rednecks marrying their cousins, weakens the next generation. In the case of wildlife, a lack of genetic variation can make a population more susceptible to disease. If there is variation in a population's immune systems, some members will resist a disease and survive even though others may succumb. If all the members have similar immune systems, however, a disease that can overwhelm one may overwhelm all. Again, larger areas tend to carry more populations, which translates into more genetic diversity.

Nearer is better, too. This concept is referred to as the distance effect. If a population on one island is wiped out by a natural disturbance but can be recolonized by a population that can migrate from a nearby island, then extinction is less likely. In addition, if species have the chance to migrate between islands and encounter other populations, there is more opportunity to add genetic variation, which can be critical to survival if conditions change. Thus islands near a mainland or other islands tend to have more viable populations than similarly sized but more isolated islands.

These understandings about islands and habitat are applicable to the system of wilderness areas, wildlife refuges, and national parks that we proudly assume will preserve the wild animals we love to watch in documentaries and animated movies. Refuges and national parks are themselves large islands of wildlands in a profoundly human-altered and engineered landscape. Where buffers and bridges between legislated wild areas are not in place, we can expect the lessons of island biogeography to apply. But on the mainland there are additional variables to consider.

Fragmented habitats also suffer what are called edge effects, at the places where wildlife habitat and human habitat intersect, such as where a forest meets a road, a clear-cut, a farm field, or a lawn. Human activity that threatens animals, such as hunting and poaching, tends to take place and have the most impact along the edges of a habitat. Edges can also be more vulnerable to fire, pollution, parasites, and predation from house cats and dogs. Invasive species are more likely to show up along the edges. Some animals and birds are shy and avoid getting too close to the edges, where noisy civilization resides. As the size of a habitat fragment decreases, the ratio of its edges to its interior habitat increases; the various edge effects thus become even more significant for smaller fragments.

The distance effect is harder to translate for isolated land-based habitats. Obviously, populations of animals separated by great distances, with no means to bridge them, will not get together to trade genetic material or, in the event of a decimating disturbance, be able to rescue one another by filling out gaps in the population with new members or mates. For islands, distances tend to be straightforward: either swimmable or flyable, or not. But barriers to population interaction can be more varied on land. They may include geologic barriers, such as rivers, and human-made barriers, such as highways and subdivisions. The isolation imposed on land-based habitats by such varied barriers is called insularity.

Insularity occurs commonly in nature. It is present to some degree in almost all natural habitats. A stream habitat surrounded by forest can be as isolated as an island surrounded by water. How about caves, reefs, tide pools, gallery forests, mountaintops, and swamps? Where different habitats meet and blend, the landscape may be a dappled weave of habitats dancing with one another. In the far north, for example, arctic taiga forest surrounds tundra, and tundra breaks up taiga. If both habitats are healthy, the boundary areas they share can be a dynamic mix, and insularity is not a problem at all. But when insularity is the consequence of a large and lonely sea or a six-lane speedway featuring diesel trucks with flat raccoons on their grills, it can stand in the way of the connectivity that is a prerequisite for vital habitat.

It is important to realize that conclusions from island biogeography cannot be applied uniformly or everywhere. Nature is remarkably variable. For some species, like amphibians, the quality of the habitat may be far more critical for survival than its size. Some species are more adept at migrating than others. Birds, obviously, can repopulate over larger territories than can, say, ground sloths. Some species require larger territories or more particular habitats than others.

But the overall lessons from island biogeography have important implications for how wildland reserves must be designed and managed in order to be ecologically sound. To be viable over time, isolated reserves must be bigger, must include buffer zones to mitigate edge effects, and must have corridors between reserves to mitigate insularity. And if healthy ecosystems must include top predators like wolves or grizzly bears, which require huge territories to survive, then wildland reserves must be very big indeed.

When what has been learned about top carnivores' key role in maintaining habitat integrity is combined with what has been learned about island biogeography, the challenge of conserving biodiversity becomes hugely apparent, or apparently huge. When the parks, wilderness areas, and wildlife refuges we have established over the course of our recent history are viewed as islands, we begin to see that their conservation value and function have limits. We thought we were saving the wild beasts so our grandchildren could experience them, and we may have accomplished that. But whether those beasts will be around for our grandchildren's grandchildren is looking doubtful, because those inland islands are just too small. For many of the earth's beloved creatures, we may be only postponing extinction.

After the first conference on conservation biology, Michael Soulé took a break from the academic world of contending egos and campus politics. He resigned his tenured position at UCSD and retreated to a Zen center in Los Angeles, the Institute of Transcultural Studies. His sojourn to the Zen center was meditative in ways he hadn't planned. While there he edited the landmark compilation of papers presented at the conference, *Conservation Biology,* and worked with Otto Frankel, the Australian who had stimulated his interests earlier, to finish their influential book, *Conservation and Evolution.* He also tried to write a book that would integrate his Buddhist beliefs with insights from his work in conservation biology, but realized he wasn't "mature enough" to pull it off. "I had to do some more digging into the shadows," he says.

Now that he has retired from academia and is living in a more contemplative setting, he hopes to get back to the questions he wrestled with then. He is working on a book explaining the Buddhist–conservation connection and meditating again after an eighteen-year hiatus. His meditation teacher is his ex-wife and the mother of his children. He appreciates the irony. "Buddhism has become as important to me as anything because I see it as a way of being more effective. I see my own compassion for people as well as animals as a key to being able to synthesize a vision of a better place for all life. After the science and the conservation politics, it is what I need to work on now in my life."

By the time he left the Zen center to teach at the University of Michigan, he was considered a pioneer in his field. Almost as soon as he arrived on campus, in 1986, a Second Conference on Conservation Biology was called. It launched the Society for Conservation Biology, which for a time was the fastest-growing biological society in America, eventually leveling off at about 5,000 members. The journal *Conservation Biology* was begun the next year. "We needed to get the science out to the people who were making decisions and policy," Soulé explains. "We needed to communicate better with each other, but we also needed to talk to the world of policymakers and planning professionals, so they could consider what we had learned."

Organizing people from so many fields and professions, from wildlife biologists to plant geneticists, into one body with a means to communicate proved to be a catalyst for thousands of his fellow scientists, but Soulé remained frustrated. Having befriended Arne Naess, the Norwegian scholar, philosopher, and activist who was stirring the environmental community with his insightful exploration of deep ecology, Soulé began to articulate conservation biology's underlying ethics. "Biotic diversity has intrinsic value, irrespective of its instrumental or utilitarian value," he says plainly.[7] Here is an assumption that rocks the boat. It marks the confluence where hard science meets deep ecology.

The term "deep ecology" originated with Arne Naess, who developed the formal arguments for and definitions of it in the 1970s and 1980s. In North America, Bill Devall and George Sessions summarized and interpreted Naess and made his essays available. Alarmed by an ever widening ecological crisis, Naess was convinced that our anthropocentric worldview—the belief, so thoroughly assimilated that it was universally accepted, that man is the crown of Creation and that the natural world is there for his benefit and dominion—would lead inevitably to ecological devastation.

Environmental degradation, the threat of nuclear war, and the persistence of grinding poverty across the planet are all facets of a crisis of perception, Naess argued. That crisis, he concluded, compelled a new

49

context and orientation acknowledging the intrinsic value and interdependence of all species. Deep ecology expresses an ecocentric or biocentric orientation in which humankind, humbled by a history of ecological catastrophe, takes its place within the larger web of Creation. "Not man apart," as the poet Robinson Jeffers put it, but humans as a single strand in an inclusive and interdependent web. The challenge deep ecology makes to our culture is to shift our attitude toward nature from assertion to integration, and to shift the consequences of our actions from reduction and fragmentation to wholeness.

The arguments that deep ecology makes about intrinsic value resonate through long and familiar roots. Paul Shepard traces those roots as far back as the Pleistocene consciousness of hunter-gatherers and the animistic belief systems of indigenous people, who believed that the whole world, from rocks to rivers, is alive and that each creature commands respect. Similar notions have been advocated throughout history in Taoism, Zen Buddhism, and the Christianity of Saint Francis of Assisi. William Blake, D. H. Lawrence, and Gandhi all expressed a belief in the intrinsic value of nonhuman life and a profound understanding of connectivity, both of which are deeply ecological principles. In America, Henry David Thoreau and John Muir voiced the same sentiments.

In North America, the sensibility of deep ecology has been widely expressed through literature, not a catechism. You can hear it in iconoclastic author Ed Abbey's brave cowboy rants about the diminished lands he loved. You can hear it in poet Gary Snyder's ruminations on the kinship of creatures sharing Turtle Island, his name for North America, and on the need to heal the rift between mind and body, spirit and matter, culture and nature by reinhabiting the bioregions that sustain us. We hear its all-encompassing reverence for life in the "wild mercy" of a Terry Tempest Williams essay, in the grace of a Mary Oliver poem, and even in best-selling novels by Barbara Kingsolver. When it illuminates the quiet essays of Wendell Berry, it is most likely to be called wisdom. Although characterized by critics as misanthropic because it does not place humans before all other life-forms, the belief that every living creature has intrinsic value is widely shared and dearly held.

Soulé is quick to delineate the differences between conservation biologists' belief in the intrinsic value of species and animal-rights activists' concern for the welfare of individual animals. "We are talking

about populations of creatures," he says. "They are concerned with domestic and farm animals—chickens and pigs, dogs and cats—but wild
animals concern them only at the edges, like when people were beating
seal pups over their heads for fur. They don't care as much, generally,
about the protection of populations, the prevention of extinction, the
continuity of lineages, the complexity and diversity of life. . . . They
focus on the suffering of individual animals and how that relates to vio-
lence generally. There is a lot of overlap, but the 'intrinsic value' arguments are not the same."

He admires the compassion expressed by the activists and, it must
be said, envies the millions of dollars in donations they get to pursue
their work. He is even willing to give up meat and hunting to express
solidarity with them. But he and other wildlife biologists and ecologists
have witnessed more than their share of the suffering that is the common currency of natural food webs. While doing research in the field,
they see frogs gulp flies, fish snap up frogs, lizards snatch dragonflies,
snakes gag down lizards, and hawks tear apart snakes. They have
watched large carnivores pounce on elk calves and kill them in front of
their mothers. They have seen how licensed hunting can be a useful tool
for thinning populations that would otherwise slowly starve to death.
They are trained to take specimens for studying. Killing and the suffering that goes with it are a part of their background.

In our refined human cultures, the ideal death is a sleepy "natural"
death from old age, preferably with harp music in the background. In
the wild, the music of death is likely to begin with a scream and end with
a dinner gong—Spike Jones meets Hannibal Lecter. Whether or not we
discern it, those warm and fuzzy cubs we like to see on the promotional
literature for conservation groups have bloodstains on their menus. The
purpose of conservation biologists, then, is not to eliminate individual
suffering but to increase shared viability.

Poets may have made deep ecology sound sweet, but most people,
especially those whose power and wealth were generated by the pursuit
of conventional human-centered values, find its tenets hard to swallow.
Conservation biology is giving it body, in much the same way that the
science associated with the Gaia theory validated, stimulated, and encouraged holistic thinkers twenty years earlier. Conservation biology
translates the insights about life's intrinsic value, which are so key to

deep ecology, without losing the music that poets hear. When pines whisper and sea foam hisses, conservation biology names the tune, describes and documents the notes and chords.

"Arne Naess would come out to Santa Cruz and visit me," Soulé tells me while pouring a last cup of coffee. "We would camp down in Baja. While he was on campus, we would hold seminars together, and one afternoon we chose to discuss conservation in North America. We concluded that we knew what the problems were—we had a good handle on the causes of extinction and environmental crisis. The main problem was habitat loss and fragmentation. We also knew what the solutions were—we had the right prescription—but nobody wanted to admit it or apply it because it seemed too grand, too ambitious, too outrageous, too hopeless. And the solution is that we just reconnect all the fragments that are left and expand the system and thereby create an actual network with continuity, with linkages, across the whole continent. Because it's isolation or insularization of the remnant habitats that is causing extinction. We should reverse that."

After that seminar, Soulé wrote to Dave Foreman.

If Soulé was the catalyst for the science of conservation biology, Foreman was the catalyst for a kind of bold politics that Soulé hoped could translate the understandings of conservation biology and its sister, deep ecology, into political action. Foreman was legendary. He had been a formidable lobbyist for the Wilderness Society in Washington, D.C., until becoming disenchanted with the Beltway orientation of the big national environmental groups who, he believed, made too many compromises while ignoring their grassroots activists.

In 1980, Foreman and some friends founded Earth First! to express their vision of a reinvigorated grassroots movement for conservation that would aim to preserve and restore vast tracts of wildlands from one end of the continent to the other. Their slogan would be "No compromise in defense of Mother Earth." "Earth First!" Foreman yelled, pumping his thick fist in the air, and the new group had a name.

More fluid than formal, Earth First! was a loose, ragged organization that over time escaped Foreman's direction. As each year passed, its annual rendezvous looked less like a meeting of conservation activists and more like a ganja-fried gathering of Rastafarians. Foreman had trouble relating to the organization's emerging culture, especially after it was overtaken by activists who focused on a broad social justice agenda that strayed far from his original vision of saving wilderness. On the other hand, many in Earth First! had come to regard him as a retrograde sexist whose unwillingness to deal with the plight of communities in the path of his wilderness vision was short-sighted, if not callous. About ten years down the road, Foreman no longer fit into the organization he had envisioned and built.

Not fitting in was the least of his problems, though: Foreman had gotten busted. Earth First! took its inspiration in part from Ed Abbey's irreverent novel *The Monkey Wrench Gang,* and Foreman had written a manual on monkeywrenching, the term used to describe activities such as the deliberate pursuit of intimate and damaging encounters with large yellow logging machinery by moonlight. According to the law, dressing up as a bear, chaining oneself to a gate, and lying down in front of a bulldozer were one thing; sabotaging trucks was another.

In 1989 a handful of Foreman's Earth First! associates were arrested for plotting to cut power lines in Arizona that were connected to nuclear power plants in California. Foreman, the charismatic leader of the suspected monkeywrenchers, was thrown in jail for good measure. Prosecutors threw the book at them, and over the course of the long legal battle, it became clear that Earth First! had been bugged, wiretapped, infiltrated, set up, and betrayed by police moles and informers.

After two long years of legal maneuvering and three stressful months of trial, Dave Foreman was financially and emotionally drained. He promised to stop preaching the gospel of the monkeywrench for five years in return for legal closure. He promptly "split the sheets," as he called his divorce from Earth First!, and retreated once again.

In 1992 he started over, founding the Cenozoic Society. With John Davis, the former editor of the *Earth First! Journal,* he launched a new journal, *Wild Earth,* to forge links between conservation biologists and wilderness advocates. The journal also aimed to be a semischolarly forum for debate within the conservation movement about strategy, science, philosophy, and politics. In his latest incarnation, Foreman was trading tree spikes for wildlife linkages.

For Dave Foreman, the political pendulum had swung wildly, and Michael Soulé was waiting on the other side. Soulé's letter got right to the point: "I think it is about time that a few of us get together and discuss what America should look like in 2150. Such a plan would be map-based and would indicate all the major locations of wilderness area and the connections between them. We would assume such phenomena as the reversion of much of the Midwest to bison range and long grass prairie, the completion of the greater Yellowstone area, the interconnection of much of the old-growth forest in the Northwest and California, and a wilderness corridor from the Florida Everglades to Maine. Naturally this would require the abandonment of certain areas of the country by humans." He now regrets that last sentence and says he realizes that building a continental conservation plan will be an inclusive and democratic process involving much negotiation, trade-offs, and consensus building. The letter suggested a meeting in Santa Cruz and concluded with an incongruous line: "Anyway, you might want to think about it."

The letter didn't arrive. It was returned to Soulé, who had sent it to the wrong address in Tucson and had to mail it again. The second time he scribbled a new invitation to meet and then this note at the end: "We must plan the future."

THREE

Putting the Wolf at the Door

Vermont is green. Its name is derived from the French words for "green" and "mountain." No wonder—during the summer, Vermont's gracefully undulating old mountains are a universe of green hues. The ubiquitous cornfields and pastures between the mountains are also green, as are the tree-lined streets around the town squares that are referred to as greens. Sometimes even the politics are green.

Richmond is a small town, as are almost all towns in Vermont. It is a half-hour down the interstate from Burlington, Vermont's one big town. Just around the corner from Richmond's only stoplight is a row of classic brick storefronts circa 1920 to 1950. The Wildlands Project occupies the second floor of one of those old buildings, but the stairway to its office is hard to find. I walked too far and then backtracked until I saw a doorway tucked between a florist shop and an antiques dealer, fitting neighbors for an organization devoted to defending the biosphere and evolution.

The Wildlands Project's sign is also obscure and small. "That's by design," Leanne Klyza Linck, the project's current director, tells me as we walk across the street to a combination bakery and restaurant that seems to be the caffeinated beehive for the village's considerable population of activists, advocates, and volunteers. The Vermont Land Trust's local office and Keeping Track are also housed here. "We get threats, that kind of thing," she says casually, in a tone that tells me she'd rather not give details.

"I know what you mean," I reply, and I do. Activists learn to watch their backs habitually, the way desert hikers are mindful of rattlesnakes and scorpions without letting their potential presence spoil the journey.

Once we've had our coffee, Leanne leads me back across the street and up an old musty stairway. At the top, surprisingly, are bright white walls, clean hardwood floors, and clear glass partitions. The office is neat, spare, and filled with natural light. The Wildlands Project has just moved from Tucson to join the staff of its sister publication, *Wild Earth,* in Richmond. I have come to meet anyone and everyone I can.

I had been to the first home of the Wildlands Project, in Tucson, incongruously hidden at the back of a strip-mall row of offices better suited to real estate agencies and accounting firms than to a conservation group determined to "rewild" North America. The Tucson location had kept the fledgling organization near its leader and mentor, Dave Foreman, but the Vermont move put the project closer to *Wild Earth*'s staff, promising synergy and the savings from running one office instead of two. Leanne's big challenge as director had been to oversee the consolidation of the staff and the Wildlands Project's coordination with its many sister organizations across the continent.

The Wildlands Project may have lived in Tucson and resettled in Vermont, but it was born in California at the San Francisco home of Doug Tomkins. Tomkins started the North Face, but sold it before it became a well-known brand of outdoor clothing and equipment. No matter; next he and his first wife started Esprit, another popular outdoor line, which made millions.

An avid skier and mountaineer, Doug Tomkins found that his fortune gave him the means to visit the earth's wild places and to think about the challenges of preserving them. The philosophy of deep ecology made sense to him, so he started the Foundation for Deep Ecology. His home was the perfect location for the gathering of activists, philanthropists, and scholars who met in November 1991 to answer

Michael Soulé's invitation to "plan what America should look like in 2150."

When Foreman got Soulé's letter, he shouted to anyone who would listen, "Hey! Someone agrees with us!" Foreman had met Soulé once, briefly, and they had a common friend in Barbara Dugelby, a former student of Soulé's who had introduced them to each other. Now, six months after Soulé had written to Foreman, they were arranging the marriage of conservation biology to grassroots activism. Those at the wedding were a mixture of scientists and advocates, including scientist Reed Noss, scientist-activist George Wuerthner, and activists Rosalind McClellan, Mitch Friedman, Jamie Sayen, John Davis, and David Johns, an attorney who became the Wildlands Project's first director.

"I think we all sensed we were making history," Soulé told me. The meeting at Tomkins's home marked a new and powerful confluence of streams in the American conservation movement, one with the potential to radically shift the movement's course, broaden its reach, and deepen its currents. Years later, in an essay for *Wild Earth* entitled "The River Wild," Dave Foreman used the metaphor of a river's watershed to describe the course of that movement. In Foreman's vision, American conservation is the "River Wild," and the "headwater streams that flow together to make the River Wild are wildlife protection, stewardship, beauty, and forest protection."[1]

The headwater stream of wildlife protection can be traced all the way back to the sportsmanship codes endorsed by hunters in the early 1800s. Already then, game was disappearing. Hunters banded together in such organizations as the Boone and Crockett Club to curb the rapacious behaviors of game hogs, lest they hasten the elimination of wild game through wanton overkilling.

The headwater stream of stewardship also reaches back to the 1800s. It can be seen in the writings of people like Vermont's George Perkins Marsh and, of course, Henry David Thoreau—people who recognized and respected the integral natural relationships unfolding around them, even if they understood them incompletely. Humans, they said, were a disturbing agent, especially when unmindful of their place within the embrace of the land.

In the mid-1800s, the headwaters stream of beauty appeared and braided itself into the other strands of influence. This stream is a familiar one, expressing our shared love of great scenic beauty, and it inspired the creation of national parks and monuments to preserve special places. The final headwater, that of forest protection, wrote Foreman, "cascades briefly before a sharp ridge splits the stream. One side pours off into Resourcism River with Gifford Pinchot and the other falls into the River Wild with John Muir."

Pinchot was the father of the U.S. Forest Service, Muir the father of the Sierra Club. Pinchot is often called a conservationist, but his was conservation for purpose and profit. Muir, on the other hand, believed Pinchot was deluded, that he and his allies would tear apart the very heart and soul of the American land, its wild nature. That they would do so in the name of conservation, he found especially galling. Wilderness should be preserved as is, he argued. This fundamental divide continues today and can be heard in debates about forest-fire policy, road building, and more.

"Down-river," Foreman wrote, "the streams of wilderness, ecosystem representation, carnivore protection, and connectivity flow in," bleeding their tints and sediments to the larger current they join. When the streams of predator protection, island biogeography, and connectivity are added to the River Wild, Foreman continued, they will "churn the other currents together into a deep, wide, powerful river." The founding of the Wildlands Project in San Francisco in 1991 channeled those new streams into the River Wild.

Foreman's metaphor is apt. Our history of landscape conservation opens a window on our worldview—the assumptions and insights that shape our perceptions of the world and our place within it. That shared perspective, in turn, determines our behaviors, individually and collectively. Although we might not readily associate laws, policies, and publicly funded plans with the heart and mind of a culture, they are the practical expression of who we think we are, what we think is important, what we care about, and what moves us. The history of conservation in America reveals a growing awareness, a kind of awakening to where we are and how we fit in.

Exhausted by the Civil War and reaching the end of the frontier, Americans looked up and noticed places like Yellowstone, Yosemite Valley, and the old forests of great sequoias. They recognized and appreciated the sweep and grandeur of the American landscape and sought to conserve its most impressive expressions in national parks. Because scenic beauty was the main criteria for defining park boundaries, and because the lessons of ecology and wildlife biology were not yet available, our earliest national parks often preserve more ice and rocks than critical lowland habitat, especially if that habitat included profitable timber or pastures for cattle. The inevitable political conflicts that are a part of setting aside such lowland habitats were a further impediment to preservation beyond the shoulders of big mountains, as they still are today. We preserved wildlands as a scenic resource, with little regard for the ecological integrity of those lands. Given the state of our scientific understanding a century ago, it is hardly surprising that our criteria for preservation were limited. Nevertheless, the land protected by national park status over the years remains the core of our wildlands today.

As the Indians were beaten into submission and the frontier closed, the nation boomed westward. Just as Americans were realizing that our nation's most beautiful scenery was a limited and threatened resource, Gifford Pinchot and his academic and political allies realized that timber, ore, and game were also limited. Land scalpers were threatening to buy up and cash in on the great Western commons; in response, Pinchot was determined to impose a national policy that would conserve natural resources for the whole nation, then manage them efficiently. He was sure he could secure the greatest good for the greatest number through engineering and scientific management, and set out to develop the government agencies that could do the job.

While Pinchot and his colleagues made the case for rational and equitable use of common forest and mineral resources, John Muir and his followers argued that wildlands are not just an economic storehouse but an essential spiritual resource that should be preserved. After all, they argued, our unique American character was formed in the wilderness, and American culture grew from its encounter with a wild landscape. Early advocates of a national policy to protect and preserve wilderness, like Aldo Leopold and Bob Marshall in the 1930s and 1940s, railed against national park tourism and "Ford dust" in the backcountry, where one could still experience solitude while hiking or canoeing.

Leopold eventually broadened his perspective to include the need to protect whole ecosystems, or at least as many of the parts as could be salvaged. The shift from a reductionist worldview, which sees nature as a collection of parts to be manipulated for the material benefit of humans, to a holistic perspective, which regards humans as embedded in a larger self-creating and evolutionary whole, is profound. At one extreme, the world is viewed through the prism of the marketplace and measured with an economic bottom line. The other extreme is harder to translate into concrete goals and results.

That was the challenge of those who met at Doug Tomkins's San Francisco digs. How do you measure and convey ecosystem health? How do you get others to understand that beyond making products, enjoying scenery, or even being spiritually enriched, conservation and restoration of ecological integrity are key to our very health and survival? How do you shift a powerful and growing movement for conservation into a new paradigm? How do you make the ideal real?

The creation of the Wildlands Project, though no more dramatic than a living room conversation, is as good a marker as any for the moment when both the hard-won wisdom of Michael Soulé and the passionate vision of Dave Foreman, emblematic of the thinking of so many others, turned from thought to action. We've all had that experience—the moment when someone takes the fine idea that a group is sharing and says, "Let's make it happen!" It may slight others to attribute that kind of historical moment to the creation of the Wildlands Project alone, but for me it was a good place to start. I had traveled across the country to encounter those who were close to the turning point, and to get their stories.

While a roomful of conservation revolutionaries unleashed the waters of renewal in San Francisco, Leanne Klyza Linck was making her way up the organizational ladder within the Sierra Club. She worked on important legislative projects—the reauthorization of the Clean Air Act, Arctic and other wilderness bills, pollution issues, global warming. It was interesting, challenging, and necessary work, but a time came when she realized she knew more about the demographics of congressional districts and the habits of Congress members than the ecology of the habitats at stake and the lives of the creatures within them.

Even wilderness bills tended to focus on popular scenic values and the recreational constituents who could be organized for support of a particular piece of land, rather than the health of the ecosystem it belonged to. In the eco-illiterate process of preserving and protecting habitats, the voice of scientific reason was shortchanged by special interests and delayed by the reluctance of scientists to participate in political processes that seemed so at odds with their trusted methodologies, such as peer review and hard evidence.

"It was all too removed from nature," Leanne tells me, and yet her love of nature was why she was doing the work. "I saw *Born Free,* a movie about a family of lions, at my brother's birthday party. I was five years old, and that was it. Ever since I saw that film I have been committed to protecting wildlife and nature, and there was never a doubt that that was what I'd do with my life. I didn't have posters of movie stars on my bedroom walls, I had a poster of a rhinoceros."

Although she understood the vital role played by national environmental organizations, her disillusionment with them mirrored the earlier chagrin of Dave Foreman. "People in Washington aimed to do what they thought was achievable rather than what was right for nature," she lamented. "You compromise when you are stuck and have no place to go. You don't compromise from the start!"

She took time off to raise her baby boy and then worked for the Northern Forest Alliance, a coalition of about forty conservation groups, before going to the Wildlands Project. "I didn't see it as radical. Take the best science available and use it to identify what lands need to be protected in order to conserve biodiversity. Then do what's right. Think big and be bold. Have you seen the mission statement?" She hands me a brochure.

The declaration was mostly hammered out at the San Francisco meeting: "The mission of the Wildlands Project is to protect and restore the ecological richness and native biodiversity of North America through the establishment of a connected system of reserves." That direct opening statement is followed by two pages of specifics, highlighted by a vision statement that Foreman had been carrying in his head for years: "We are ambitious. We live for the day when grizzlies in Chihuahua have an unbroken connection to grizzlies in Alaska; when wolf populations are restored from Mexico to the Yukon to Maine; when vast forests and flowing prairies again thrive and support their full range of native plants and animals; when humans dwell on the land with respect, humility, and affection."

The Wildlands Project was set up to be decentralized—the antithesis of the big Washington, D.C.-based organizations. The project was intended to work in cooperation with independent grassroots organizations around the country. Local and regional conservation groups would do the legwork of identifying key species, understanding their needs, and designing land conservation plans because their members knew the land best. They were in place and had a closer handle on the immediate area's political conditions. They knew the stakeholders and understood the local culture. They were participants. The Wildlands Project would offer context and criteria, supply scientific expertise, and play a coordinating role.

Because the field of conservation biology was already well established by the time the Wildlands Project was launched, the context and criteria the project would employ were well developed. The overall, motivating context would be the alarming well-documented wave of species extinction and the need to conserve biodiversity, now understood as a measure of ecological integrity and resilience. In a special issue of *Wild Earth* dedicated to the launch of the project, Reed Noss outlined the criteria that would shape its strategy.

- First, protect all native ecosystem types. Traditionally, the American conservation movement had focused on ecosystems such as the Everglades, which had gained a popular following. But according to the gospel of conservation biology, all ecosystems have value and deserve protection. Each is a finely tuned and evolved natural system that is part of the greater whole in ways we do not fully understand.
- Second, maintain viable populations of all species. A viable population is one that can survive over the long run despite the inevitable disturbances.
- Third, maintain ecological and evolutionary processes. Hydrological processes, nutrient cycles, and biotic interactions must be understood and accounted for. Even disturbance regimes such as wildfires and floods, which shape habitat and the succession of species on it, must be accommodated. At the top of the list of important biotic interactions to be considered was predation, the red tooth-and-claw act that large carnivores have perfected over time.

- Fourth, design and manage the system to be responsive to both short- and long-term environmental change, and to maintain the evolutionary potential of not just particular species but their various lineages, since genetic diversity within a single species can also be critical to its survival and health in the long run.

These four goals for large-scale conservation planning soon became widespread, as they were adopted by serious practitioners from The Nature Conservancy to the World Wildlife Fund.

The emphasis on predators was especially timely. Wolf introduction programs were gathering support all across the West and even in the Northeast. In 1995, just four years after the founding of both the Wildlands Project and *Wild Earth,* gray wolves were reintroduced into the Greater Yellowstone Ecosystem. Whereas other pro-wolf groups relied solely on the romantic charisma of the wolf to garner support, the Wildlands Project stressed ecosystem integrity and the science that underlined the wolf's role as a keystone species.

Keystone species are those whose interactions with other species are so important that their removal results in the collapse of all sorts of interspecies relationships. Not only do mountain lions, wolves, and bears have a deep-seated appeal to humans that is easy to tap, but they can also be critically important to maintaining the order of whole ecosystems, as John Terborgh's studies in the Caroni Valley of Venezuela showed.

I have heard critics charge the "radical environmentalists" with using predator reintroduction like a Trojan horse. Because big territories are required for the survival of predators like wolves and bears, predators are not so much umbrellas for myriad other animals and birds in the food web, as wildlife biologists claim, but provide a cover for a radical land use agenda. Add that to the conservationists' insistence that forest fire is a natural disturbance that must be accommodated, and it is easy to see why my ranching and logging friends think environmentalists are burning down the woods and reserving what's left for the wolves. It's all in the eye of the lien holder.

Leanne understands the critique, but says it's not true: "The science is there. If you want healthy ecosystems, you can't ignore the predators, and big predators need big areas." The Wildlands Project does not apologize for thinking big, nor does it hide its agenda. Some scientists associated with the project have estimated that if society fully embraced the goal of "rewilding" North America over the next century, as much as half the land in the continental United States could be dedicated to conservation.

To achieve its bold goals for biodiversity protection, the Wildlands Project has developed a model design for a system of connected nature reserves. At the heart of the model are core areas consisting of already designated wilderness areas, national parks, and wildlife refuges, plus roadless areas in national forests and other chunks of unbroken wildlands not yet protected. These core areas would be surrounded by compatible-use lands that would function as transition areas between wildlands and humanized landscapes. The core areas and their buffers would be connected by wildlife linkages, originally called corridors until that term was rejected as simplistic and misleading. The linkages would be designed to make human-made barriers like highways and railways more permeable via overpasses and tunnels.

Core areas would be strictly managed to protect and even restore native species and natural processes. The buffering and transitional compatible-use lands would allow a looser mix of human activities and ecological considerations. Ideally, the mix of uses in the compatible-use lands would be determined by networks of people protecting networks of species in their own backyards. Wildlife linkages would provide secure routes for species to move between core areas in order to preserve terrestrial migratory species, to allow genetic exchange, and to allow species dispersal and repopulation in times of stress and crisis, particularly in response to global warming.

The assumptions underlying the core-area/compatible-use/linkage model were clearly stated at the outset in a special issue of *Wild Earth*. The influence of island biogeography was evident.

1. Species well distributed across their native range are less susceptible to extinction than species confined to small portions of their range.
2. Large blocks of habitat, containing large populations of a target species, are superior to small blocks of habitat containing small populations.

3. Blocks of habitat close together are better than blocks far apart.
4. Habitats that form contiguous blocks are better than fragmented habitat. Interconnected blocks of habitat are better than isolated blocks. . . .
5. Blocks of habitat that are roadless are better than roaded and accessible habitat blocks.[2]

Early on, as the guiding ideas were refined and recorded, Reed Noss came up with a humdinger he borrowed from fellow scientist Frank Egler: "Ecosystems are not only more complex than we think, they are more complex than we can think." If recognizing intrinsic value in all creatures great and small represents a break with prevailing cultural beliefs, the notion that we will never be able to fully fathom the secrets of Nature—to learn her laws, break her codes, and manipulate her body—is an outright slap in our cultural face.

Ever since the great Francis Bacon, father of Western civilization's beloved empiricism, advised us to "strap Mother Nature to the rack and make her reveal her secrets," we have been confident that the laws of nature can be known and that we can and should employ the knowledge we gain about them. Noss and his followers seem to be saying that we can employ what we learn about nature, but there are risks in doing so, because we cannot ever fully know nor measure, predict, and control the outcomes with certainty. The absence of certainty cannot preclude progress, but it should make us think twice, given our history of failed promises and obvious destruction, and it should make us look hard for alternatives that are more forgiving of our negative impacts on the world that sustains us.

Precaution, then, is a theme dear to conservation biologists, especially those who have witnessed the dire impacts on wildlife of air, water, and soil pollution by chemicals. In fact, much of what we now know about the alarming ability of endocrine-disrupting chemicals to wreak havoc on fetuses we learned after observing the devastating impacts of such chemicals on fish, birds, and reptiles. When male seagulls exhibited female mating behaviors and alligators were born with tiny dysfunctional penises, it was clear something nasty was in the water.

The endocrinologists I worked with on dioxin campaigns urged precaution to avoid contamination and enunciated a Precautionary Principle:

If you have scientific uncertainty and the likelihood of harm, you take preventive or precautionary action. You look for alternatives to risk rather than believing you can measure and manage risk. Conservation biologists urge precaution to avoid extinction.

The specific qualities and characteristics of core areas, buffers, and linkages were described and discussed at length in the pages of *Wild Earth*. Conservation biologists like Soulé, Noss, and Brian Miller were translating years of painstaking science and observation into an agenda that could be understood and enacted by grassroots activists, that could challenge or guide public land managers, and that could provide a specific context for everyone from forestry professors to land trust administrators. The Wildlands Project was to be a catalyst and advisor.

"It worked better in some places than others," Leanne explains. Each organization had its own local variables. An alliance of conservation organizations that focused on linking wildlands from Yellowstone to the Rocky Mountains and grasslands of Canada, and then all the way up to the Yukon, has grown into a powerful coalition that is far better funded and staffed than the Wildlands Project itself. On the other hand, some groups burned out early. Leadership was important; so were the potential for building coalitions and the ability of coalitions to cooperate.

"The message of the Wildlands Project was catalytic because there were all these people, scientists and activists, out there working on Band-Aid solutions to complex problems, and they knew it wasn't going to be enough," Leanne says. "We gave them a context that was powerful. The value of wilderness is that it is self-willed land where natural processes, not human agency, direct the ebb and flow of life. How can we extend that and restore even those processes that are seen as threatening, like wildfires, free-flowing rivers that periodically flood, and predation?

"Well, first there are a lot of questions, hard questions. Aldo Leopold said that when you make conservation easy, you may also make it trivial. We don't offer quick fixes here. But we do offer the best science we can find—and a vision. The relationships are also difficult and complex. Trying to keep track of all the local groups, all the coalitions, is like herding cats." The conceptual pieces, she said, fell into place faster than most of the staff would have predicted.

The Wildlands Project and *Wild Earth* helped to redefine the lexicon of conservation. Talk of core areas, compatible-use areas, and linkages dominates the new call of the wild. These ideas are now collectively referred to as "rewilding." I tell Leanne how I took my son to a freshman orientation program in the forestry department at Northern Arizona University in Flagstaff and was amazed to find displays on biodiversity, exhibits against grazing, and literature on ecosystem management. I asked a professor if the health of watersheds would someday trump timber sales on the "hooks n' bullets" agenda of land use agency staff. "Oh yes," he replied, "but it is happening slowly, too slowly, and we want to make it happen sooner rather than later. We want to be a part of that."

In 1993, the Y2Y (Yellowstone to Yukon) coalition was conceived and launched at a meeting in Alberta by Harvey Locke, a Canadian conservationist who was a Wildlands Project founder and board member. The project was becoming truly continental. In 1997, British Columbia put 11 million acres of the northern Rocky Mountains under protection, adhering to many of the concepts put forward by the Wildlands Project, and conservation projects were launched with the project and Mexican conservation groups.

Meanwhile, there were "vision mapping" sessions, conferences, workshops, consultations, and publications. People across the continent were organizing to develop regional maps according to the conservation biology principles outlined by the Wildlands Project and *Wild Earth*. By the spring of 2000, some thirty-one regional conservation planning efforts were under way. They reached across the continent, from Florida to Maine and from Central America to the Yukon. Each planning effort was locally led, and most included a coalition of partner organizations.

With thirty-one plans being created from the ground up, the Wildlands Project was feeling the frustration of making the case for continental conservation while herding so many hometown cats. "We reached a place where we knew we were changing minds, but we needed to show results. We decided to concentrate on the Sky Islands region in Arizona and New Mexico. If we could get out one big plan, we'd have a model that could inspire others, and we'd have something we could point to," Leanne explains.

In fact, the Wildlands Project's planning process and mapmaking were going on right next door to me in Utah. Having encountered its roots in the modest second-floor offices above the florist and the antiques dealer in Vermont, I flew home to get a closer look at one of its many branches. But first I visited the Sky Islands.

How to Fill Sky Islands with Parrots and Jaguars

For someone with an active imagination like mine, the Sonoran Desert Museum was a mixed blessing. On the one hand, the butterfly garden featured soft pastel blossoms that attracted a lightly flitting halo of delicate winged creatures in red, gold, yellow, blue, and white. Under a gorgeous Arizona sun, these exquisitely patterned and fragile pollinators could have been angels in heaven or the painters of some earthly Eden. On the other hand, there was a box of scorpions.

A docent played with the scorpions in the shade of an overhang, just outside a hallway of rattlesnakes in glass cages. The variety of rattlesnakes living in the Sonoran Desert is surprising. Deserts are hot and hard to survive in, but life persists through a wide range of adaptations to their peculiar conditions. The biological diversity of the Sonoran Desert is, in fact, significantly greater than that of any northern forest, "perhaps by an order of magnitude," a point the docent was there to make with his several species of flip-tailed stingers. The largest scorpion, which looked like a small lobster or a fat crayfish, actually packed the least poisonous wallop, he told me. The smaller species, apparently, were more potent. "If one of these little guys gets you, you'll be uncomfortable indeed. Yeah, real trouble. But I don't worry much about scorpions," he concluded. "It's the killer bees I find scary."

Later, after two hours of hard hiking off the parkway and up a ravine, I came across a swarm of busily sipping bees working on a glistening seep in the face of a rock wall. I had to climb that short wall to continue my uncharted adventure in Saguaro National Park. I was drenched with sweat and beginning to curse the Sonoran for being so stingy, stabby, pokey, and bitey. I had collected a diverse array of cactus needles in my ankles, knees, and hands; my limbs had become a kind of flesh catalogue for the ways succulents maintain their physical integrity in an arid biosphere. A plethora of scurrying lizards had made me jumpy—the damn things are solar powered, and in the full sun they moved like they were loaded with methamphetamines. The bees were the last straw.

What if I were attacked by "killer bees" while alone and so far from a trail? *I could die out here!* I thought. *Maybe I should turn back and go for a refreshing swim at the hotel.* But what if I quit and went back to the hotel in Tucson, only to find the pool filled with real estate moguls and their trophy wives comparing notes on golf games and nannies? It was a dilemma, for sure, but in the end the scorching September sun pressed my will away and I turned back.

Before returning to my hotel, however, I took one more stroll through the museum. Around a stucco corner, I came upon an old woman with a slim cane talking to parrots in a wired enclosure. The parrots were almost neon green, with thick purple bills and bright red faces. They tipped their heads and listened warily. The white-haired woman didn't seem embarrassed by my discovery of her avian conversation. "These parrots are beautiful, aren't they? They used to live in these parts, ya know, and when I was a child I saw them once. I was with my daddy on horseback. I never forgot."

"Maybe they'll come back," I offer.

"Oh, wouldn't that be wonderful! And jaguars, too!"

"Have you seen a jaguar in the wild?"

"No, but I've always wanted to."

"Me too," I said. "Me too."

In fact, jaguars have been sighted recently. One tripped a wire to a hidden camera set up by a remote water hole.

If the Wildlands Project and its partners in the Sky Island Alliance succeed, sightings of jaguars and parrots will not be so rare in the Southwest. The Sky Island Alliance can trace the legacy of its mission back to conservation biology's patron saint, Aldo Leopold, who was so inspired by the area's unique and rich diversity that he worked hard to preserve the Gila Wilderness during the late 1930s. Legislation passed in 1964, 1980, 1984, and 1990 protected core areas across the West, including the Gila Wilderness. Large tracts of wild habitat surrounding those core areas remained and could potentially be included in a conservation plan, but there would be challenges. Traditional practices like timber cutting, grazing, and mining competed for land, and as always, developers were poised to work the edges of public land, putting up subdivisions and condominiums where the market led them.

In the early 1990s, the Forest Service was working out a plan for the Coronado National Forest in southeastern Arizona and proposed designating it as a national recreation area. The status would offer the sensitive habitats less protection than a designation of wilderness, national park, or national monument, but would provide more opportunities to conserve the landscape than had been available before. The Sky Island Alliance was formed in 1992 in response to that proposal.

Conservationists were determined to be included in the Forest Service's planning process and to influence the final plan with criteria that emphasized the integrity of whole ecosystems and the ecological health of the diverse habitats they included. The Sky Island Alliance map, however, would not be limited to the public lands being considered. By expanding the land use context, the alliance hoped to make a more compelling case for every piece of the map it was making.

By 1994 it had a preliminary preserve design in hand that used many of the criteria and concepts advocated by the Wildlands Project. At the end of 1995, the Sky Island Alliance and the Wildlands Project pulled together a three-day workshop to kick off a much broader and inclusive design project, one that would even take in areas of Mexico and require cooperation across borders.

The Sky Islands themselves are mountains that rise up like islands in the dry sea of the Chihuahuan Desert. They form the heart of the Wildlands Project proposal, which weaves 17.3 million acres into a conservation system, the Sky Islands Wildlands Network, stretching from the Mogollon Rim in east-central Arizona and west-central New Mexico south to the Sierra Madre Occidental range in Mexico. The area includes an archipelago of forty mountain ranges rising from a sea of desert and grasslands in southeast Arizona, southwest New Mexico, and northern Mexico. Tucson sits on its western border, El Paso on its eastern rim.

It is a region where the Rocky Mountains and the Sierra Madre kiss: temperate, tropical, and subtropical climates converge and mix. Add that creative blend of climates to variations in elevation and geology, and you have a formula for superabundant biodiversity. From the hardpan floor of desert basins to the coniferous crests of the tallest peaks, there are five different life zones, each with its own mix of plants, animals, and birds. There are an estimated 2,300 to 2,800 species of flowering plants, at least 104 mammal species, and abundant populations of ants, bees, bats, lichens, snails, reptiles, and birds. Over half of the bird species in North America can be found in the region's Chiricahua Mountains alone. The border area holds the richest bee fauna in the world.[1]

The outline for the proposed conservation system, the Sky Islands Wildlands Network Conservation Plan, was released in 2000 and was the first of the big regional plans that the Wildlands Project had been coaxing along to be finished and presented. A model of both design and cooperation, it was, as Leanne Klyza Linck had told me in Vermont, "the answer to the comment and question 'Yeah, your ideas are great, but what have you guys got to show for all the work on design principles and methods?'" With the design and maps ready, a new implementation phase was at hand, even as the Wildlands Project was packing up its former headquarters in Tucson and leaving for Vermont.

Kim Vacariu and a skeleton crew were still in Tucson. I caught them on their way out the door. In this city, it turns out, those who would boldly surrender human agency to the natural ebb and flow of wildlands worked in a strip mall. I found them in a plain suite of half-abandoned rooms. There was no receptionist, so I wandered through the empty rooms, calling as I went. Kim greeted me warmly and apologized for the scattered office environment. The Tucson suite would be traded for smaller digs that would house the Sky Islands Alliance staff. A few boxes, stray office furniture, loose phone lines, and a couple of still-occupied desks were all that remained.

Kim is a handsome man, bearded and soft gray all over, but youthful, too—the kind of man you suspect may be either older or younger than he looks, but you are not sure which. He is not a scientist, but he knows the science well enough to frame a message that laypeople can understand. We go over the basics first. He pulls out a copy of *Continental Conservation: Scientific Foundations of Regional Reserve Networks,* by Michael Soulé and John Terborgh, and a special issue of *Wild Earth.* The cover is a close-up illustration of a wolf's intense black, orange, and yellow eye staring out from flowing patterns of fur that could be kelp beds in a tide, a tallgrass prairie in the wind, or whitewater cascading over shelves of stone. It is an arresting image.

I understand the need for biodiversity and the concept of connecting core wild areas and their buffers with wildlife linkages, I tell him, so we move on to the concept of focal species—species whose requirements for survival are key to a nature reserve's design. There are a variety of ways a species can be focal.

- An *umbrella species* is one that roams far and wide enough that protecting its habitat will ensure that the smaller habitats in the area, which are needed by many other species, are also included and protected.
- The members of a *keystone species* play a role that is so central to the ecosystem's ecological processes that they hold those processes together. A beaver, for example, plays a keystone role in a wetland, creating and maintaining a habitat around its dam that other species enjoy.
- *Flagship species* are charismatic and can win popular support for a plan. Eagles are a good example; they have a symbolic meaning that makes their survival powerfully compelling. Ironically, wolves are becoming charismatic in this sense, after a long history of being intensely demonized.
- Species that are *habitat-quality indicators* can also be focal. These species are especially sensitive to environmental degradation and can provide an early warning if an ecosystem is under stress. Amphibians, for example, that show drastic population declines across the continent may indicate the presence of chemicals that are powerful even in trace amounts.

- Even *prey species* can be focal if their presence and health are key to the survival and health of other focal species.

"The Sky Islands planning group was mostly conservation biologists and others who had training in the science and could read the literature," Kim tells me. "It was a collaborative process that involved a lot of peer review. Just talking about which species were important and why, how they related to one another, helped everyone to understand the issues, the challenges, what was at stake." Kim explains that maps start to take shape from this process, but fieldwork is critically important to make sure that the maps accurately reflect biological patterns in the landscape. Traditional maps designed to expedite mining, road building, and recreation emphasize geological features and access routes through them. The maps created to guide the design work by conservationists and their volunteers in the field, however, show water sources, vegetation, habitats, and other aspects of the biosphere as well, overlaid on the hard features.

All this science is well and good, I say, but how do you hope to implement such a big, inclusive plan? Even in the Southwest, where there is a lot of public land, there is also land held by private landowners and by the state. Don't these stakeholders feel threatened?

"The response to the release of the Sky Islands plan was surprising. We were braced for a negative reaction, but it didn't happen. Federal agencies, Arizona's Pima County, the state agencies, and even ranchers and others who owned land on the design map seemed to read it and take it seriously. It was an impressive piece of work—high-quality and credible. It revealed the landscape in new ways that compelled attention. The goals of the designers were worthy, and the methods seemed reasonable.

"On the Mexican side, they are not far along in their history of trying to protect their environment, so they have adopted our criteria for conservation as their own. This has been a formative experience for them, but even on our side of the border, the plan has become the blueprint everyone was looking for."

Translating that blueprint into an architecture of land use and management, however, will not be easy and could take many years. Kim is working to educate the public, especially landowners, about what the plan calls for and how each stakeholder can contribute. "It's as if everyone has a piece of the puzzle, but they don't know that. The goal is to get everyone to fit the piece he is holding into the puzzle," says Kim, who conveys an optimism that would be hard to sustain back in Utah.

This is not your father's conservation movement, relying on coffee-table books, letter writers, and lobbyists. The Wildlands Project and its network of people defending networks of nature reserves is not content to influence those at the policymaking table or even to sit at that table themselves. They are, instead, building their own table.

Ever thorough and programmatic, Michael Soulé and David Johns, the Wildlands Project's former director, have published an exhaustive connect-the-dots list outlining a model process for wilderness design. It starts with holding an initial workshop with identified key players; works its way through funding and community relations strategies, the gathering and analysis of data, and their review and publication; and culminates in a press conference to launch the campaign to implement the plan. This is how you put wheels underneath a paradigm shift.

I am interested in the groundwork. In our culture we preach cooperation but practice competition. Impasse, mistrust, and business-as-usual are pervasive. How do we overcome that? I ask Kim this question, as I do everyone I interview, and he adds his voice to a growing chorus that sounds like Democracy 101: better communication, openness, sound information, and an inclusive problem-solving process with lots of checks and balances.

Or maybe this is the same process that nature requires, to allow for lots of feedback, reciprocity, and diverse possibility. The principles that make for health in ecosystems, my informants seemed to be saying, also operate within a culture. You open up the decision-making process, they told me, and put citizens and stakeholders at the table early. It helps, of course, when the federal government sets a tone and creates a political environment that respects and encourages conservation.

My conversations with Kim took place before the Bush administration began rolling over every conservation gain of the Clinton era, encouraging the most reticent to resist instead of talk. Before President Bill Clinton, the federal agencies that managed our public lands and waters in the West were closed to the public. The doors were battered open during the 1990s, and secrecy and exclusion were on the run.

Agencies started to do outreach and search for consensus. Collaboration was encouraged—it was taught in workshops and written into job performance plans. Like everyone else, land use agencies were learning to appreciate complexity and uncertainty.

Despite the setbacks under the Bush administration, the old paradigms are collapsing from the weight of errors too serious and obvious to deny. Young blood with new ideas is moving in. How many will hang on under a presidential regime that is hostile to their goals is an open question. Thus it is more important than ever that citizen activists and advocates create counterpressures so that the reformers can survive.

When citizen activists pressure agencies to live up to their own findings and plans, to face the implications of the science and honestly implement policies, they give those within agencies who want to get it right the political cover they need to do so. Anyone in the Bureau of Land Management with a deep appreciation of the principles of conservation biology is likely to fit into the prevailing resource-leasing regime there about as well as a nun in a whorehouse. But some seeds have been sown. Lonely Forest Service employees are beginning to connect with one another and develop a voice within that agency. Reformers could also turn the BLM around, although it is farther behind on the road to conservation consciousness.

No matter how much ecological science and ardent fieldwork go into creating maps and plans like the ones outlining the Sky Islands landscape design, those plans must be negotiated and implemented in a political environment. In the West, that environment has seen some progress but also much gridlock. As the ecological principles are developed by conservation biologists and then assimilated by the public, the political environment is shifting.

Changes in political goals, rules, priorities, and criteria can be pushed by the legal teams and lobbyists of conservation groups old and new, but they must also be pulled by the expectations of citizens who vote the decision makers into power and then monitor their performance. When activists learn to overcome stereotypes, communicate shared values, and build sustainable relationships across old boundaries, they encourage the democratization of a decision-making process that was once the sole province of bureaucrats whose principal mission was resource extraction and allocation.

Impasse is tiring and frustrating. Wherever collaboration overcomes impasse, it will win attention. Learning the grassroots skills of communicating the vision and building consensus, then, is an essential complement to doing the work of conservation biology. In *Making Collaboration Work,* Julia Wondolleck and Steven Yaffee show how bridge building is becoming an explicit art, if not a science. They draw from hundreds of recent collaborative efforts to identify barriers and pitfalls as well as the methods and themes that characterize successful efforts. As practical guidelines for positive interaction become available, conservation visionaries can add them to their toolboxes for building landscape designs that realize those visions.[2]

Good grassroots methods alone won't get there. In the West, federal, state, tribal, and local governments must also sort themselves out and reshape their relationships because the federally dominated West has become a "procedural republic" of 260 million acres where process trumps results. The feds and Congress act as referee and ringmaster in a circus of competing studies, suits, hearings, press releases, bills, and countersuits. Government agencies contribute to impasse and inaction when they fail to share information and regulatory turf. They must learn to cooperate with each other, since adversarial interagency relationships are dysfunctional and block progress. Everyone complains—developers gnash their teeth over endangered species lawsuits, while conservationists wring their hands over dead salmon under dams still standing.

Distributing decision-making power away from the traditional centers of impasse may create possibilities for innovative resolutions. However, those resolutions will have to allay the anxieties of the national constituencies for public lands, who fear that decentralizing decision-making in the West will turn power over to the clear-cutters and dam builders who have competed so hard for advantage in the past. That fear seems very real in Utah and Nevada, but maybe less so in California, the Northwest, and Colorado. There, new constituencies for sustainable management are forming around watersheds and forests. Decentralization will also need to contend with the passionate belief that Western public lands belong to *all* Americans and not just the locals who would make land use decisions according to local needs.

Seen in the context of the contentious political stalemate generated by traditional competing interests, such as big timber corporations versus Washington-based conservation groups, the effort of the Wild-lands Project and its many sister organizations to define and describe natural boundaries and ecological processes is hopeful. The concerns for ecosystem and habitat health they have identified are inclusive. Over the long run, no one profits when a watershed is degraded, when an invasive species tips a balance, when a forest is blighted, or when soil blows away. If the political arena defined by traditional fixed political jurisdictions, titled and deeded lands, and legal zones does not facilitate progress in resolving conflicts, then perhaps changing the terms of the dialogue will be helpful.

If the Wildlands Project succeeds in places like the Sky Islands, all the stakeholders, from the most ardent conservationists to the most set-in-their-ways land users, may have to think across their borders and see how the individual piece of the puzzle they hold fits into a broader picture. Old assumptions will have to be retranslated onto new territory. From the practice of conservation biology, new perspectives emerge on all sides. Each succeeding generation will grow new insights from those achieved by the one before it. This is how Soulé's ark, the green cathedral of the twenty-first century, will be built. Though that green cathedral is human-made and will be seen from space, it will make more sense and be more sustainable than the current patchworks of cement and smoke that now march across satellite images. Ultimately, we cannot erase and go back, but we do make choices as we go forward—build an ark or build a dump truck.

The Sky Island plan is a "cultural landmark," according to Tom Butler, editor of *Wild Earth*. After a history of saying, "No, don't dam that or log this," the conservation community has finally said "Yes." It is easy to understand why conservationists have been obsessed with defense—the lands they cherish are under attack. Although the primary intent of the plans the Wildlands Project is helping to create is to preserve biodiversity and rewild wounded habitat, they can also be read—as Tom wrote in his introduction to the Sky Islands plan—as "cease-fire agreements on the way to a comprehensive peace treaty between human beings and Nature in the Americas."

FIVE

Making the Map Meaningful

The office of the Wild Utah Project is on the fourth floor of the old McIntyre building on Salt Lake's main street, just above a bustling light-rail trolley stop. It is directly across the hall from Families Against Incinerator Risk, a grassroots organization I helped build. Jim Catlin and Allison Jones are the core of the Wild Utah Project. My friend Carrie Richardson, a youthful and energetic FAIR volunteer turned board member, works with them.

Carrie is pregnant, and I have not seen her for months. She is gloriously round and shining. "Wow," I say.

"Yeah, I know," she replies. "I can't see my feet."

"You and half of America," I come back. "Hey, at least you have the prospect of seeing yours again."

She laughs, and I go into the office. Jim and Allison are in the field. Clues to their work are everywhere—mostly maps, books, and papers. The office is more academic than activist in demeanor. In contrast to the Luddite portrait of "radical environmentalism" painted by its critics, technology is key to this kind of conservation advocacy. Ironically, wild nature is defended by users of a global positioning system that sends satellite signals to handheld computers that are carried into the field. Data are collated, cross-referenced, and crunched by other computers back at the office. That information is carefully organized into reports and maps that are then e-mailed, put on disks, and mounted on web sites. Ancient insights about the wisdom of honoring the web of life are now supported by the most sophisticated high-tech instruments and tools available. Jim and Allison can both read the language of a watershed and translate that ecological insight into a spatial and digital domain that can be downloaded. First you climb a mountain, then you install software.

Later I join them for lunch at a stylish café around the corner and then follow them back to their offices. The Wild Utah Project—the Utah affiliate of the Wildlands Project—is working on one piece of the map and one part of a more inclusive plan for the conservation and restoration of the spine of the continent. The entire plan will eventually reach from the Canadian Yukon, down through the Canadian Rockies, farther south through the Rocky Mountain region of the American West, through the Sonoran Desert, and then conclude in the Chihuahua Desert of northern Mexico. The piece of the puzzle that Jim and Allison are working on is almost complete, and they are anticipating the implementation phase.

Implementation will require political fieldwork that is as rigorous and challenging as the scientific fieldwork that has preceded it. Advocates of the plan hope that what they have learned so far about building and maintaining coalitions will serve them well when negotiating the inevitable differences. Having a regional plan in hand is no guarantee that the project will be able to invite dialogue, engage decision makers, and influence priorities and policies.

In fact, the evidence is mixed. In the Sky Islands region of New Mexico and Arizona, for which the Wildlands Project has released a conservation blueprint, extensive discussion has been generated and, as a result, a broad range of coalitions and organizations, from local conservation groups to county planning boards, has endorsed the plan's criteria and methods. In Utah, it's a different story. There, a civic dialogue to reach consensus and communicate the lessons of conservation biology that have been absorbed by communities across the nation has been obliterated by political street-fighting over the raw data gathered in the wilderness. Politically, Utah is a hostile neighborhood to work in. It is a one-party state with few checks and balances. Good ol' boys rule.

Jim and Allison represent two generations of activists. Middle-aged Jim, the graybeard of the team, came to his calling via the Peace Corps. After service and travel in Africa, he was convinced that the straight pursuit of the engineering profession he had trained for would not satisfy his need for meaning. "I knew I wanted to do something different with my life," he says, "and I couldn't fit into an engineering cubicle." Back in Utah, he volunteered to look at transportation and land use issues for the local chapter of the Sierra Club. The experience was so compelling that he never let go, eventually abandoning his engineering day job to earn a Ph.D. in land use planning at the University of California at Berkeley before returning to Utah to become a full-time planner, organizer, and advocate. In 2002 he was elected to the Sierra Club's national board of directors.

Twenty-five years after Jim's formative experiences in Africa, Allison experienced her conversion to conservation in a less exotic setting. "It was in the girls' bathroom of my school. I was fourteen. I asked to borrow some makeup from my friend, and she told me she was not wearing makeup anymore, not until its corporate makers stopped using animals to test its products. 'You mean for safety?' I said, and she said no and told me about all the torturous things done to animals.

"I was shocked. I'd never heard about all that. I started an animal-rights group at my school, and we eventually eliminated dissection from the curriculum. When I went to the University of California at Santa Cruz, I started an animal-rights group there." She became a student of Michael Soulé's and studied conservation biology. Then she heard Dave Foreman speak, and the vision of the Wildlands Project clicked with all she had learned. "Of course this is the way you do it," she says, "and I wanted to be a part of that." After graduate school she took a starter job with an environmental consulting firm, then jumped to Wild Utah as soon as the opportunity arose.

As the conservation biologist of an organization still finding its feet and its funding, she had to find other paying projects to make ends meet. In her work for both the Wild Utah Project and clients on the side, she won a reputation for pulling together studies in record time, enlisting the support and participation of dozens of scientists along the way. Clearly, she can organize as well as do the science. She is the kind of scientist-advocate that extractive-industry corporations fear most: young, bright, articulate, likeable, and deeply committed.

Allison Jones exemplifies a generation of environmental activist-advocates who are entering the struggle way ahead of where their predecessors started. Well educated for the tasks at hand and well aware of the challenges ahead, they have benefited from the lessons their elders had to learn the hard way.

Jim Catlin still bristles when he tells how he was lied to. Unlike the younger generation, Jim and his peers learned the tough way that the political system governing the use of the American landscape can be biased, exclusive, and even rigged. In the beginning of his career as a conservation advocate, he asked the forest engineer and recreation manager for the Wasatch National Forest about "transportation plans" he'd heard about for the majestic Wasatch Mountains that tower over Salt Lake City. The plans would include the building of new roads through the mountain forests and the upkeep or abandonment of old roads. "There are no plans," he was told, "and no decisions have been made or are pending." He returned to the local Sierra Club offices to report his conversation, only to be presented with an inch-thick document, complete with detailed plans and maps, signed by the manager and engineer he had just interviewed. "They lied, they flat-out lied to me," he says indignantly.

"It was a big eye-opener. I have since learned that my experience was not exceptional. Resource managers routinely deny that information exists, or they twist their presentation of the information they are willing to share to convey misleading conclusions. Until recently, land use decisions were supposed to be made internally by professional staff, and the public's only role was to comment—do you like the plan or not?" In the years to come Jim would have to file Freedom of Information Act requests to get some documents, and in one case he would file a grievance against a Bureau of Land Management staffer who refused to let him copy documents.

In the West, where so much land is publicly owned, the way this land is managed can influence everything from tourism and housing development to transportation, revenue generation, and even water and air quality. Public land use decisions are often pivotal in shaping local and even regional economies. They express deeply held attitudes and values, set priorities, and affect the quality of life as it is variously, and sometimes contentiously, defined. When information is not openly available and public input is discouraged, management is not exactly democratic or smart. Checks and balances are missing in action, and bureaucrats take their orders from politicians who are influenced by those with the money to buy access.

"I can show you forest plans that are monuments of obfuscation," Jim says. "They're artificial structures of information because the conclusions of their studies and the promises of their policy pronouncements, even when they seem sound, are meaningless. There are always a couple of paragraphs buried at the end that contain exceptions so broad that they cover everything. The exceptions can be made at the discretion of the managers. When you confront the managers about logging or off-road vehicle use that shouldn't be happening according to their own findings, they just cite the exception and say it's allowed. You have to pursue each issue and stay on them. It's getting better in some places, but in Utah it has always been a struggle."

Jim filed an appeal of that Wasatch transportation plan and ended up walking portions of the proposed routes with the rangers who had written the plan. They had never visited the land in question. "We went to a place where a motorcycle trail was supposed to be bulldozed through the forest. It was completely inappropriate, and they knew it when they saw it, but they had never been there before that day. That helped. Eventually that project disappeared." The critical importance of applying on-the-ground experience to land use planning became apparent to Jim. If rangers wouldn't or couldn't do it, citizen activists would. "And that's the way you bring change to intractable agencies—by collecting clear evidence that is indisputable."

He stops himself and qualifies that statement. In fact, even when the understandings about habitat that have been developed by conservation biologists are acknowledged, and even when the evidence is right under their noses, federal land use managers can still have trouble with "clear evidence that is indisputable." The Departments of Agriculture

and the Interior, for example, agreed during the father-Bush administration that wetlands and riparian areas should be restored and re-
paired. They developed criteria for assessing the health of such habitat
and translated those criteria into a checklist that agency staff could use
to rapidly assess whether a pond or stream area is functioning ecologically or is at risk. But the final result of the assessment did not have to
be consistent with its parts. The checklist was designed so that those
using it could easily ignore the evidence they had gathered and draw
conclusions not supported by that evidence, especially if the evidence
would compel politically difficult actions, like removing grazing cows
from a watershed or closing a road that goes through a brook. Jim and
Allison are designing assessment tools for land use managers that make
it much harder to evade ecologically sound conclusions. In a land of
naked emperors, the royal tailors are blind; Jim and Allison are hoping
to restore their vision. They want such tools to be easy enough to understand that a rancher, a ranger, or a weekend wilderness pilgrim could
use them.

But sound assessment tools alone will not save wildlands. The scientific criteria must also be understood and applied in ways that are inclusive and empowering. Years earlier, while working for the Utah
Wilderness Coalition—an umbrella organization that includes the Wild
Utah Project as well as the Southern Utah Wilderness Alliance—Jim
had seen how the power of credible evidence developed by citizen
trekkers could be used effectively. He helped organize hundreds of them
to map Utah in order to identify BLM lands that qualified for officially
designated "wilderness area" protection.

The long struggle to designate wilderness acreage in Utah is, essentially,
a battle over what conservation biologists call core areas, places where
ecological processes remain, for the most part, whole. Core areas are,
logically enough, mostly roadless since roads fragment habitat, are
pathways for invasive species, and invite a level of access and use that
compromises ecological integrity. The establishment of core areas also
defines where buffer zones and linkages will be. All the players—conservationists, the oil and gas industry, ranchers, timber companies, off-
road vehicle riders and their vendors, and weekend hikers—know that
the way core areas are designated and configured will affect their in-

terests in the buffer zones between wildlands and the engineered landscape. Everyone is jockeying for position.

While most Americans, like the trackers I walked with in Vermont,
are trying to enhance buffers around the scant core areas that remain
and to create linkages between them, in Utah we are still arguing over
the shape and integrity of the core areas. The term "core area" is rarely
heard, however. Instead, we argue over "wilderness" as defined by the
Wilderness Act of 1964 and detailed in numerous policies, rules, guidelines, and findings developed over the ensuing decades.

Officially designated wilderness areas are also supposed to be nearly
or completely roadless. The Utah Wilderness Coalition's proposals for
wilderness designation were much criticized in the 1980s by agencies,
elected officials, and the media, who said the areas the coalition had
identified on maps didn't qualify because they were crisscrossed by dirt
and gravel roads. So the coalition decided to redo its proposal and take
a second look. It also needed a defense against RS2477.

That odd alphanumeric acronym for Revised Statute 2477 has become a shorthand reference to the struggle to determine whether an
area is "roadless." The statute's origins go back to 1866 when, in the
midst of a congressional debate over whether to sell off federal mineral
reserves to pay Civil War debts, the Senate amended a ditch and canal
bill to include the Lode Mining Act. A provision of that bill allowed
roads to be built and maintained across public lands so miners could
access their claims. That provision was revised in 1873 and then re-
pealed a hundred years later, in 1976, with passage of the Federal Land
Policy Management Act. The new law included a clause that protected
rights-of-way and allowed them to be maintained.

Some state and local politicians were hostile to wilderness designation because it would limit their options for developing everything from
vacation condos to new gas wells on or near the designated land. They
sought to put as many roads on the map as possible, in order to dis-
qualify those lands from designation. So road maintenance was often
translated by local county commissioners as widening, straightening,
and paving long-abandoned wagon roads, cow paths, and jeep trails that
existed before the repeal. But nobody had a handle on how many real
roads there were, where they were, or even what they looked like. So
in 1988 President Ronald Reagan's Interior secretary, Donald Hodel,

stepped in and defined those rights-of-way so broadly that they included pack animal trails, dogsled tracks, and any place where rocks have been moved or vegetation cut back.

The Clinton administration would later apply the brakes, but in the meanwhile rural commissioners were delighted. By claiming that any faint tire tracks in a dry wash constituted a road, they could identify roads almost anywhere. And they did. If a jeep had backfired or a horse had so much as farted in the backcountry, rural politicians in the West and Alaska claimed a right-of-way, often following up with bulldozers and graders to seal the deal before conservation lawyers could stop them. If roads crisscrossed a sensitive area, they argued, then wilderness designation and protection were out of the question. Maps of proposed wilderness areas soon resembled bowls of spaghetti.

Memory, imagination, and wishful thinking sometimes create a road in the minds of Western politicians, who have traditionally been wedded to resource extraction industries and grazing. They resent federal control over public lands, but they like the heavy subsidies, free services, and cheap fees they enjoy from the same evil feds whom they demonize for intruding on their economic freedoms.

Conservationists, on the other hand, want roadless areas to remain so because roads cut up habitat and enable soil erosion that undermines surface stability and loads streams and rivers with dirt. Roads create pathways for invasive species, and even the most rudimentary roads invite off-road vehicle abuse. The nation's public lands are now varicose with a road network several times greater in miles than the nation's interstate highway system.[1]

Conservationists understand that RS 2477 is a Trojan horse for mining, grazing, logging, and off-road vehicle interests. People who actually visit remote backcountry have also learned that the rights-of-way claimed on the maps of those friendly to the resource extraction businesses bear little relationship to reality. I once spent an afternoon looking for a road near an abandoned uranium mine that county officers said was an existing thoroughfare. Eventually we found the remnants of that road, covered by thigh-high brush, in between missing sections that had disappeared in floods and avalanches or had blown away or grown over completely. The claim was simply ludicrous.

"The best evidence is a photo," Jim says. "If you can show a picture of a cliff face that the county claims is a right-of-way and that appears on their map as a straight line between other roads, that's very powerful. So our strategy, which originated with my colleague Will McCarvill, was a very simple one. We broke those millions of acres to be surveyed down into territories that represent what one person can walk over in one day in one weekend. What one person can do is visit one supposed vehicle route, take photos and notes, mark a map, and bring it back. We repeated that process using five hundred volunteer field checkers over three years. They spent 70,000 hours doing this and took between 50,000 and 60,000 photos. I was project manager. We had some volunteers who practically abandoned their day jobs to do this work."

That survey method, he tells me, has become standard for the environmental community in the West when working on issues involving wilderness, off-road vehicles, and other impacts on habitat. "Activists refer to the method as 'ground-truthing,' and it has given us great authority, credibility, and leverage, especially after the media were taken out to the land in question and given the chance to compare what county officials said was there to what we showed them. Agencies now come to us and ask for the photos and evidence we can provide to guide land use planning. The quality and reliability of our work is assumed, and opponents have a hard time dealing with our information."

"You also developed a cadre of five hundred citizen volunteers who feel ownership and can offer firsthand testimony," I observe.

"Yes," Jim agrees enthusiastically, "and in fact we selectively brought in people from all over the country and teamed them up with local fieldworkers. That broadened our base and deepened the commitment." The out-of-staters then lobbied for Utah wilderness with their own Congress members, many of whom found that supporting wilderness in Utah was popular among their constituents. "You need it all," Jim concludes, "the fieldworkers, the credible information they develop, and the science that gives it meaning. You need both the broad political base and advocates in Washington, D.C."

Many rural Utahns resent that bills designating wilderness in their backyards are sponsored by Congress members from California, New York, and other states far away. But a formal designation of wilderness can be made only by Congress, and the lands in question belong to all of the American people. Like it or not, the commissioners of Kane County, Utah, can no more dictate the management plan for the Grand Staircase–Escalante National Monument, which is in their backyard, than New York City's council members can decide to paint the Statue of Liberty. Also, decisions about use of Utah's public lands may have a wide-ranging impact on vast federally owned tracts across the entire western United States, since they can set precedents for decisions elsewhere.

The citizen-powered inventory that Jim described is a dramatic development in a land use tug-of-war that has been waged in patriarchal Utah with an almost theological fervor. The state's one-party political culture is dominated by white Mormon Republican men, who command lockstep loyalty from a majority of Utahns. That hegemony is hard to challenge, because one-party rule in Utah promotes vigorous civic dialogue about as well as it did in the former Soviet Union. In the absence of diversity, political debate in the Utah legislature is the intellectual equivalent of marrying your cousin. Although Mormon naturalist Terry Tempest Williams has eloquently described the spirituality of the state's wild places and the need to show "wild mercy" for future life that lives by the same grace we do, the prevailing cultural attitude is as tender as a bulldozer clearing the path for an oil rig. After twenty years, the Utah Wilderness Coalition and its member groups are still trying to get Congress to pass a piece of legislation called America's Redrock Wilderness Act, which would protect that unique area of the state. The coalition has, however, kept bovine locusts, road builders, oil and gas drillers, thumper trucks, and an army of all-terrain vehicle riders out of the heart of millions of acres of desert land that meet the criteria for wilderness designation. It is hard to imagine what might have happened had the coalition not been there and resisted so effectively.

During the Clinton administration, the coalition won a historic victory when a vast swath of southern Utah canyon lands, 1.9 million acres in all, was designated as the Grand Staircase–Escalante National Monument. Although the lands in the monument are not as thoroughly protected as officially designated wilderness would be, and although the monument lands are but a fraction of the more than 9 million acres that the coalition has identified for wilderness designation, the victory was significant. It changed the terms of the struggle over land use to favor

conservationists. Utah governor Mike Leavitt and his rural political allies were furious.

In the spring of 2003, the Bush administration helped Governor
Leavitt strike back hard. The governor's lawyers had filed a lawsuit in
1996 aimed at keeping the Bureau of Land Management from conducting a reinventory of its Utah lands to identify potential wilderness
areas. The Utah pols feared that a new inventory, guided by maps
brought back from the field by Utah Wilderness Coalition volunteers,
would find a lot more wilderness than the first survey had. Although a
federal court in Denver threw out seven of the state's eight claims in
1998, the drastically diminished lawsuit continued to tick quietly like a
time bomb, poised to explode in the future. After the Supreme Court
selected the second George Bush as president, Utah quietly amended
the lawsuit in the spring of 2003 to challenge the BLM's right to designate or even study new wilderness. The state argued that Congress had
given the BLM fifteen years to identify and recommend land for wilderness designation in 1976, so any consideration given after 1991 was
moot. In effect, if Utah won the lawsuit, public discourse about wilderness protection would be forever frozen in time at 1991; even land that
was clearly wilderness could not be treated as such if its characteristics were not discovered and described prior to that year.

Utah's lawsuit also sought to strip all interim protections for land
under BLM consideration for wilderness designation when decisions
about roads, oil and gas drilling, and mining on that land were made.
If Utah got its way, the BLM would be effectively out of the wilderness
game altogether. The consequences would sweep the West. Millions of
acres of Western land that had been identified as potential wilderness
areas "too late" would be vulnerable to the kinds of extractive and recreational uses that would, in turn, compromise the very characteristics required for any future protection as wilderness. In the terms of conservation biology, potential core areas, buffers, and linkages would be
swept away.

Governor Leavitt's suit might have seemed ludicrous a few years before, but no one was laughing in 2003 when Interior Secretary Gale
Norton settled with Utah out of court. The lawyers for conservation
groups never even got to make their case before a judge. Under President Bush's regime, the federal watchdogs over our public lands simply

surrendered to the extractive industries and their local allies. Norton told the BLM to scrap its *Wilderness Inventory Handbook,* a critical tool for comprehensive land-use planning that articulated the criteria guiding such planning. The era of de facto wilderness protection, Utah's county commissioners gleefully proclaimed, was coming to an end. No more pesky citizens scoping out the landscape on weekends, reading the rule books, and showing up at hearings. Even the myopic rangers of the BLM would have to see it differently now, they crowed. Federal watchdogs would become lapdogs with one trick: roll over. Southern Utah Wilderness Alliance attorney Heidi McIntosh agreed. "It's going to force the BLM to pretend there is no wilderness out there. It will force them to act as though what they see with their own eyes doesn't exist."

To make matters worse, the second half of the one-two punch was thrown a few days later. Once again, Utah was the thread the Bush administration pulled to unravel decades of environmental law and policy that guide the entire nation. While the nation's attention was captured by American troops rolling across Iraq, Interior and Utah announced another settlement. After two years of closed-door negotiations, they signed a memorandum of understanding to establish a process by which road rights-of-way on federal land would be decided.

Under this precedent-setting agreement, the loophole known as RS 2477 once again became a freeway. County governments were put into the driver's seat while the public, excluded by the agreement from involvement in the decision-making process, was blindfolded and thrown into the trunk. Standards for what constitutes a road were so loosened that even cow paths could be claimed as roads and paved by local governments desperate for mining, oil, and gas revenues.

As wilderness protections were rolled back, prospects dimmed for the vision of the nation's dwindling roadless areas one day serving as core areas in a network of reconnected habitats. It seemed that the "geography of hope," as Wallace Stegner once described the West's remaining wildlands, would be divided into property for extraction and contraction.

Not so fast, says Heidi McIntosh, who describes the settlement as "illegal and unconstitutional." Conservation organizations will litigate vigorously. In Utah, anyway, common ground will be covered by the arenas of contention. Ironically, in August 2003 President Bush nominated

Michael Leavitt, the architect of the backroom deals on wilderness designation and road status, to be the next director of the Environmental Protection Agency, citing his record as a negotiator, problem solver, and consensus builder.

No outside observer examining the makeup of the Utah Wilderness Coalition would identify the Wild Utah Project, the local affiliate of the Wildlands Project, as its lead organization. Of the coalition's member groups, the two most prominent are the Utah chapter of the Sierra Club and the Southern Utah Wilderness Alliance. While the state's Sierra Club has adopted diverse objectives, including legal challenges to chemical weapons incineration near Tooele and a protracted battle to keep the Great Salt Lake's wetlands from being paved over, the Southern Utah Wilderness Alliance has a single goal—the preservation of Utah's unique redrock wilderness in a comprehensive Redrock Wilderness Act.

With more smart attorneys than Jim Catlin has staff, SUWA has a reputation across the West for its political and legal savvy, its powerful contributors, and its long reach. Its talented and dynamic staff are respected, even feared, by potential opponents, and newer grassroots organizations across the West regard SUWA as a model. SUWA hires Wild Utah Project staffers as consultants to inform the arguments it makes in court and in Congress. SUWA gets the glory, and SUWA deserves it.

The influence of the Wildlands Project on the struggle to define wilderness in Utah, then, is far from apparent. Each region of the continent has its own particular concerns and its own local and regional organizations addressing them. Each regional group, such as SUWA, has its own inspiring stories to tell, its own charismatic leaders, its own devoted and determined members. Each group would exist without the Wildlands Project; most of the groups' individual members are likely unaware of any connection with the project and its ambitious goals, or even of the project's existence. Nor could most members of these groups articulate a deep ecology perspective or articulate the principles of conservation biology.

Nevertheless, the members of the Utah Wilderness Coalition find synergy with the Wildlands Project through its local affiliate, Wild Utah. And the campaign to protect redrock wilderness fits into the

Wildlands Project's continental plan, whether or not it does so consciously and deliberately. The relationship between the Wildlands Project and organizations like SUWA, which are engaged in nuts-and-bolts legal and political struggles over the definition, designation, and defense of wilderness, is indirect. You can't find the organizations linked in an organizational chart, and the exchange of influence is hard to track and measure. The organizational relationships are more organic than linear.

The Utah Wilderness Coalition does not have to subscribe to the Wildlands Project's goals to work toward them, and this is true more broadly of conservation efforts across the nation. Local and regional groups are often engaged in fundamental struggles to protect and preserve their core areas or to sort out the boundaries of buffers and linkages, simply because these projects make sense from a local and regional perspective. Many use the concepts of conservation biology without doing so deliberately.

The Wildlands Project cannot even take credit for the powerful context that conservation biology has created for these scores of groups that are working to restore habitat vitality, biodiversity, and the integrity of ecological processes. The beauty of the project's plan for wilderness design may be that it draws from and builds on conservation proposals that are already active. It creates a compelling case for preservation and reconnection that can be empowering for those who see it, but one doesn't have to see it to make the plan meaningful.

Of course, the Wildlands Project's background role can put it at a disadvantage when submitting grant applications, as Leanne Klyza Linck pointed out to me in Vermont: The guy who hits the home run gets the applause, not the one who coached and inspired him. Organizations like SUWA, which focus on obviously urgent struggles with tangible outcomes, have an easier time engaging funders. It is more difficult for those who operate beyond familiar time lines and scales of tangibility, as do the Wildlands Project and *Wild Earth*. Context, concepts, direction, principles, and visionary inspiration are hard to measure. But in the final analysis, the marriage of conservation biology and activism has created a new map for making land use decisions, and when you're lost, the power of a good map is hard to deny.

ReWilding Earth

Almost every summer of my childhood, my family camped along the blue lakes of the Adirondack Mountains. The most vivid memories of my youth stem from the few weeks of each year I lived in that wet and craggy place, about two hundred miles north of New York City. The heartwarming interior montage includes casting lures from a pale green canvas boat toward black sunken logs along the forested shorelines. The trick was to cast near the logs and tease out the muscular bass that hid beneath them. I would watch the water at the end of my line intently, anticipating the startling silver splash of a smallmouth hitting those lures. I also remember catching plump frogs, climbing trees, and carrying home to New Jersey a thick and sodden pine aroma that permeated everything, including our clothes and hair. I have vivid memories of stepping in bear dung and daring my sister to be the first to jump into icy water above clear, round stones as smooth as glass.

The woods were unabashedly magical—loaded with ferns and fairies, roots and trolls, berries and bears. As my father and I returned from fishing each night, we would motor slowly through a channel between lakes. He steered from the stern with the motor gurgling low, while I leaned over the bow with a flashlight to scan the water for the house-sized boulders that loomed just below the surface. It was eerie.

Late one night, a bear came into our camp and crashed through our makeshift kitchen. Our dogs growled and barked and strained at their tethers. My mother held us tight and told us to be still. In the morning I examined the aftermath of the bear's rampage and was impressed by her power. She had left behind a talisman, an unopened can of tomato soup she had dented and raked, leaving claw marks across its torn label. We told stories at night by the light of a lantern, and I made up songs to sing to my sister, who thought I was hilarious.

Long beyond those idyllic summer days, I find myself once again on the edge of those blue mountains of boyhood, pondering how your typical Adirondack bear might get to Lake Champlain, about twenty miles to the east of the mountains, and take a dip in the cold waters of the lake's western shore. Tom Butler, the handsome young editor of *Wild Earth,* is my guide. If Michael Soulé and Dave Foreman were the Wildlands Project's visionaries, Tom Butler is the keeper of the flame.

The original vision of the Wildlands Project, delivered in bright kernels of ecological wisdom on the journal's pages, has become crowded with particulars as it is applied to a world shaped by the modern way of seeing and being. The hard-won scientific revelation that resides at the core of conservation biology—that all species are woven into a fabric of life that is fraying and fading—has to be translated and applied.

Tom's own visionary gifts are eloquently expressed in *Wild Earth,* where the latest science, fine art, and lyrical natural history essays highlight and complement each other. The journal has become a credible conduit for conveying the science of conservation biology to a lay audience, although the line between what engaged participants can follow and what is too technical, academic, and professional can sometimes be hard to discern. While the journal delivers practical knowledge, it is also inspiring and revealing. The art alone, mostly detailed drawings of plants, creatures, and landscapes, makes it an attractive and inviting literary experience.

"You hear it both ways," Tom says. "Some say it's too scientific—that the technical terms and concepts are too difficult and refined. And some say we could do more science. We try hard not to underestimate what the lay reader can understand. Activists in the field are smart and learn fast. Most of them have really been at that for years—it's amazing what birders and backpackers learn on their own. They read a lot, go to slide shows, see documentaries, and talk. There are lots of people who welcome the kind of scientific context they get in *Wild Earth*." He smiles, "No one complains about the beautiful artwork, of course."

The abundant illustrations of birds, fish, and animals in their habitats are key to communicating the Wildlands Project vision. Like the biodiversity it aims to conserve and restore, that vision is as diverse as the ecosystems that spread, overlap, and blend across North America. If the Wildlands Project succeeds in its bold endeavor, you might have a real chance of seeing a jaguar in the wild in Mexico. In California, you would remember the first time you saw a giant condor, its shadow impossibly broad. In Maine, you would look forward to your next glimpse of a lynx. On the Great Plains, buffalo would be common. In the West, of course, the wolf would be at your door, but you would not fret or fear. It is hard to convey in words how a thriving forest moderates climate or how the wounds to a crowded landscape are healing so that the ebb and flow of life is returning. Better to show a songbird hiding in tree limbs.

Perhaps, I suggest, the real vision of the Wildlands Project can be perceived just beyond the physical illustrations themselves, in the attitudes of respect, humility, and affection that the artists express regardless of their specific subjects. The work of making torn fragments of nature whole also requires a sustained commitment to creating vibrant human communities that are embedded in healthy ecosystems. When I study the finely wrought lines and careful attention to detail in the drawing of a toad, owl, prairie dog, or salmon, I am also seeing how ecological wisdom can emerge when one is patient and attentive. "Your artists," I say, "are modeling the behavior that can make it all happen."

I think it troubles Tom that Soulé and Foreman, as much as he admires them, get so much more attention than other contributors to the Wildlands Project's work. But if Soulé and Foreman were the sole visionaries, Tom's job would be much easier. There are so many scientists contributing fresh concepts about how healthy landscapes work and how their functions can be restored, Tom tells me, and there are so many activists and advocates with important insights to share. Sometimes the voices compete and contradict as the peer review process unfolds, and he has to listen carefully to sort out the arguments. He has to follow a score of regional projects that use Wildlands Project principles and winnow out the lessons to be learned. He also has to hear the poetry through the din.

Fortunately, he tells me, there is no shortage of people whose lives are inspiring, and he offers his predecessor at *Wild Earth* as an example. While we huddle under overcast skies and wait for the ferry that will carry us across Lake Champlain from Charlotte, Vermont, he recounts how John Davis, his best friend from his teenage years, would travel to work. Davis lived on the New York side of the lake and would ride his bike from there to the ferry and from the Vermont shore inland to Richmond. This made for several miles of hard peddling on both sides of Lake Champlain, to and from the ferry.

Davis was determined to practice what he preached, live off the grid, and avoid dependence on a gas-guzzling, pollution-pumping automobile. Many environmentally conscious people refuse to own cars, but Davis took it one step further. In the warm months, instead of using the ferry when he got to the dock, Davis would peddle to the shore, load his bike into a rowboat, and row miles across the open lake to reach the other side, then unload his awkward cargo and ride on.

Davis joined Earth First! when he was fresh out of Saint Olaf College in Minnesota. He showed up at Dave Foreman's Tucson home, rang the doorbell, and offered his services for free. Though taken aback, Foreman and his partner, Nancy Morton, took the skinny kid into their home, discovered his talents, and eventually made him the editor of *Earth First! Journal.* After Foreman got busted and abandoned Earth First! to find a new path for his continental conservation ambitions, Davis went with him and became the first editor of *Wild Earth.* Tom worked on the journal with his friend and eventually succeeded him as editor. Davis then left for California to work for Doug Tomkins and the Foundation for Deep Ecology.

Having pored over the early issues of *Wild Earth,* I ask Tom about the journal's evolution. It was clear in the early articles that the Wildlands Project would challenge underlying assumptions which are so thoroughly accepted by our culture that they are rarely stated—like "Economic growth is good," "Evolution peaked and concluded with us," and "Nature is here for us to use as we choose, and we can 'own' it."

There were missteps along the way. In an early issue, Davis wrote, "Do *Wild Earth* and the Wildlands Project advocate the end of industrial civilization? Most assuredly. Everything civilized must go (excepting hot showers and bottled beverages, which will have grandfather clauses running through 2070—at which time most of us will be biodegrading, with nary a thought of hot water or a cold brew)." His remarks were meant to be humorous. Further into the essay he added, "no one need advocate dismantling industrial civilization in order to join . . . some inconsistency is inevitable among those who try to speak for Nature." The shape of civilization's technology, Davis wrote, "will mostly be answered by future generations."

Right-wing cattle ranchers and property rights activists didn't get the joke and ignored the rest. They took Davis's comments out of their context and eagerly distributed them, seeking to discredit the Wildlands Project as a bunch of misanthropic, radical extremists hell-bent on kicking people off the land for the sake of animals. An important lesson was learned: when others hostile to your cause may be listening in, choose your words carefully so they won't come back to vex you.

Learning how to cope with the rules guiding public decision-making, the legal constraints, the conflicting viewpoints, and the contending interests went hand in hand with learning how to make an effective case. In the journal, philosophical pronouncements were tempered to reflect an emerging appreciation of the consensus-building process.

All the people I'd met so far on my quest—Sue Morse, John Derick, Howard Gross, Michael Soulé, Leanne Klyza Linck, Kim Vacariu, Jim Catlin, Allison Jones, and Tom Butler—were mindful of being inclusive in pursuit of their goals. Soulé in particular likes to emphasize that the Wildlands Project's broad time scale allows people to live out their lives ranching, logging, and otherwise making a living on the land while making provisions for greener uses to be phased in over generations. The more experience the conservation activists gained in negotiating for the land's protection, the more creative they became. The better they made their case, the more cooperation they invited.

As Tom and I huff our way up a steep ravine to a ridgeline where we can gain a better view, we stop to wipe the sweat away, catch our breath, and talk. We can see Lake Champlain below. The water is calm and looks like a slab of wet slate.

Tom's skills as an editor are self-evident in *Wild Earth,* so now I try to get a sense of Tom the political thinker. I am interested in how land use planning in the West differs from that in the East. Most of the West's land is federally managed—as much as 50 to 70 percent in many states. In the East there is little federal land, and so much ground has already been thoroughly modified and developed. Instead of a mere handful of federal agencies, in the East scores of land trusts, private landholders, and local governments may all have to sit at the table and sort out decisions together. I have noticed, I tell him, that there seems to be a greater awareness in the East of the irreplaceable nature of watersheds and the few remaining wild landscapes. It is as if Easterners have learned the hard way that degraded environments are expensive to manage, let alone fix, and that they also tend to be unhealthy. I see a willingness to work toward greener environments unlike anything I am accustomed to in the West.

Yes and no, Tom replies. He acknowledges that the land trust movement is one of the most hopeful recent developments in conservation. The movement has been booming for a couple of decades now, with the number of land trusts doubling during the 1990s. The trusts are variable in size: some are endowed with hundreds of millions of dollars from big foundations and corporations, while others are small, home-grown family affairs. Land trust targets also vary. They include wildlife habitat, ranchland, farms, historic sites, scenic views, and even urban parks, but they are generally a response to sprawl. On the one hand, the multiplication of land trust organizations shows the willingness of large numbers of people to set aside land for wildlife and to protect watersheds, although the desire for open vistas and outdoor recreation are also key motivators, he reminds me. On the other hand, the growth of the land trust movement is also a measure of the pace of the sprawl that gives them impetus.

The recent growth of land trusts also means that most are very young. Many are in the formative stages, in fact, and the Wildlands Project would like to help them set priorities for their work that include sound conservation criteria. The criteria that shape the trusts' purchase and protection of lands are critically important to the struggle to reconnect, restore, and rewild whole ecosystems. Land trusts, in contrast to traditional conservation groups, do not focus on management practices for public land, but purchase property directly or negotiate conservation easements to keep private property as open land. The easements—voluntary but permanent restrictions on development—are an important tool. They can allow or prohibit specific economic uses such as logging and livestock grazing, often in return for some tax advantage.

Because of their straightforward approach and voluntary nature, land trusts are inclusive. They can be supported by politicians who are otherwise wary of being associated with "enviros." They can attract ranchers and businessmen who are sensitive about property rights. They can even attract developers, who know that well-placed open land purchased by a land trust can increase the value of adjacent property. Conservationists generally support them, and in many cases have initiated them, but they are also wary. They worry that easements and other land trust instruments may be less permanent than supposed.

The Wildlands Project has addressed land trust conferences and sponsored workshops for trust staffers, and it is knocking on every door it can find to make its case for conserving land that has ecological value or that can be puzzled into a regional plan. Even where public lands are the conservation focus, land trusts can play an important role in creating compatible-use lands around core areas and linkages between the cores—if they understand that it is important to do so.

As hard as the Wildlands Project and other like-minded conservationists have tried to influence the principles of the land trust community, many in the movement have not yet embraced the insights of conservation biology—the critical need for big, wild, and interconnected habitats where all its members can flourish. Tom notes that all land conservation is now practiced against the backdrop of a global extinction crisis unprecedented in 65 million years. "That's the challenge we face—ending a mass extinction. Conservationists, and land trusts particularly, can face it directly or not. But I think our descendants would want us to leave them a world of beauty and complexity, with grizzly bears and California condors. We will fail them if we save a few bikepath greenways, stop a few strip malls, and use scarce conservation dollars to prop up marginal and destructive activities like industrial forestry and public lands grazing."

The latest trend for land trusts is to gain easements on and purchase "working landscapes." In other words, the lands still get grazed or logged. Although cows may be preferable to condos, and the added benefit of preserving local cultures based on subsistence ranching and selective logging is appealing, no cows and no cutting can be better for habitat health than some cows and some cutting.

Tom worries that land trusts are making compromises on future land use that are unnecessary. He is particularly distressed by how many land conservation plans apparently emphasize scenery over ecological value, and by how willing some land trusts are to allow logging on the land they hold—in some cases even insisting that the land be logged. "They may not be allowing for future uses that better achieve biodiversity conservation *and* are more profitable than logging—like putting land into carbon sinks," he argues, telling me about the experimental agreements in which landholders are paid to leave climate-moderating forests intact. Forested land that is being logged now might be more lucrative in a future economy where ecological services are acknowledged and rewarded. The value of wetlands and aquifers might also be treated differently.

Working with the burgeoning land trust movement is key to the Wildlands Project agenda because the purchases and easements that land trusts make will be essential in the development of the regional conservation plans that the project and its myriad allies are working on. Getting familiar with the movement is a challenge. There are the big players, such as The Nature Conservancy, Conservation International, and individuals like Ted Turner, who spend billions of dollars to put millions of acres out of development's reach; and then there are hundreds of little groups that freckle the path of development.

Fortunately, the movement includes many individuals who want to get the maximum ecological bang for their bucks and are receptive to the lessons conservation biology can teach about biodiversity and linkages. In the summer of 2002, the popular television program *Nightline* featured the efforts of Conservation International to purchase linkages between core areas. The reporter took pains to explain the concept of core areas linked by "corridors," admitting that the notion had sounded strange to him at first. He also interviewed Edward O. Wilson, who attributed the criteria guiding Conservation International's recent acquisitions to Michael Soulé.

One landowner who understands the power of land trusts is Jamie Phillips. Tom and I visit him on the New York side of Lake Champlain at his farmhouse. Jamie, a retired New York City fashion photographer, is buying up Champlain Valley land, as he says, "by opportunity and epiphany." His Eddy Foundation, generously supported by his parents as well as his own funds, is becoming a major landholder along the west shore of Lake Champlain.

Jamie guides us through his house to an enclosed wooden porch that looks out on the stately, pagoda-like pines that rim the clearing of his farm. After introducing us to an old brown dog snoozing on the floor, Jamie takes us to a map of the local region that he has fastened to a wall. Although he at first impressed me as a graying hippie who is now an avowed Buddhist trying to "embody dharma," now he reminds me of an army general or, perhaps, a football coach as he points at the map and discusses strategy. He is trying to piece together a passage for bears and other wildlife that might go from the Adirondack Mountains, on the west of the lake, over Boquet Mountain and then east to a stretch of Lake Champlain shoreline that is still undeveloped, the Split Rock Wild Forest. This is about a third of the way up the lake's narrow length.

"This really started when John Davis sat on a ledge over by Split Rock and asked, 'If I was a bear, how would I get from the mountains through the Champlain Valley and down to the lake?' He outlined where a wildlife linkage would go, and it made sense. Trying to put all the pieces together—dealing with landowners, easements, the market, and so on—gets very complicated. It is easy to become cynical. I am relying on positive energy," he explains. "So I often say, 'Just buy it!' and then figure out how to make it happen."

He and other local conservationists are buying in earnest because land is still cheap on the New York side of the lake. Lots of people driving up the price of property over in Vermont would love to live in the rustic Champlain Valley, but they can't commute across the lake in winter after the ferry closes down. For the past few winters, however, the lake did not freeze, so the ferry ran all year long. Global warming may be changing the local weather enough so that the lake is no longer an icy barrier to winter travel. If that climatic trend continues, the kind of large purchases Jamie is making will be curtailed by high prices as the wannabe buyers from Vermont spill into the New York market.

Jamie is on his way to visit farmland he owns along the Boquet River. He is working with a handful of local farmers on an experiment that, although not an official part of the Wildlands Project agenda, is related to it. The problem: small local farms are not profitable enough to compete with agribusiness corporations. But when farmers give up, their fields can get subdivided and their woodlots carved into vacation homes, further fragmenting habitat, increasing edge effects, and impeding migration. So Jamie is trying to figure out how to return small farms to sustainability—that is, profitability. He has arranged for a local bakery to buy a tasty strain of wheat that will be grown organically on small local farms. The higher price of the wheat and the niche market for it will, he hopes, play a key role in keeping the farms alive. For its part, the bakery is gambling that there are enough food-conscious buyers willing to pay more for a unique, hardy-tasting, and healthy loaf of bread. Jamie thinks lots of people are literally willing to put their money where their mouth is, so he's optimistic.

The relationship between how land is abused and how we eat is a growing concern among conservationists like Jamie. Factory farms pollute groundwater and rivers, and they produce animal waste on a scale that cannot be absorbed by the land they occupy. Food that is locally grown on a smaller scale is generally easier on the land and is often tastier and more nutritious as well. "Think globally, eat locally," I offer. He laughs and agrees.

I get a better view of what John Davis's imaginary bear is up against when Tom and I climb to the top of the next mountain ridge. The view to the west shows that the Adirondack Mountains are surprisingly unmarred. More than a hundred years ago, New Yorkers did something wise and ahead of their time: they decided to protect the watershed for downstate New York by making the Adirondacks "forever wild," a description and status conferred by no less than the New York state constitution.

Although the interpretation of that phrase is open to debate a hundred years later, the way New York treated its Adirondack watershed is a model of how to protect land. The Adirondacks are the biggest wilderness-quality habitat on the East Coast today. The land to the east, however, is broken. There is a troublesome freeway between our mountain perch and the high peaks—but still, it doesn't look impossible. Wildlife linkages could happen. I have seen models of broad landscaped bridges that can be built over highways so wild animals can cross over.

And this is New York, as populated and fragmented a state as any in the nation. If rewilding makes it here, it can make it almost anywhere.

As we sit on a stone ledge with a sweeping view of farmed valleys and the shimmering lake below, I challenge Tom about the radical nature of the Wildlands Project's goals. "Most people I know think you guys are extremists," I tell him. In fact, when property rights advocates and corporate Republican types want to discredit the environmental movement, they often point to the Wildlands Project as an example of how the enviros are off the cultural map.

The Wildlands Project's goals, Tom replies, seem extreme only to those who are in denial about the catastrophic human impacts now unfolding all around us. It is our own overpopulation and overconsumption of the world that is extreme. We can argue about the number of species lost and the rate, but the massive wave of extinction we are experiencing is undeniable. Overpopulation and its impacts are especially obvious. Burgeoning human populations are eating habitats down to the nubs. Nations and corporations compete to consume and control what remains. It was bad enough when a nation abused its own land and then moved on to conquer and rape ecosystems abroad, but now the competition has been refueled by unregulated global corporations and takes place in an environment of contracting possibilities for recovery. Add to that the possibility of biological and nuclear terrorism as the competition between the world's haves and have-nots intensifies, and the future is almost too vulnerable to consider. What happens when suicidal bombers become ecocidal bombers?

Anyone who is scientifically literate and ecologically mindful can see the fragmentation and degradation of habitat all around, and global warming will only accelerate the changes that habitats must adjust to. On the conservationists' handy list of apocalyptic problems, overpopulation is at the top. For conservationists at the beginning of the new millennium, the root of all evil is overpopulation—or the "population bomb," the term coined in the landmark book by Paul Ehrlich, who would become Michael Soulé's mentor and a co-founder with him of the field of conservation biology. Changes that happened in geological time at an ecological pace are now occurring at warp speed. Nature is experiencing evolution on acid. Gaia and Shiva are dancing before our glazed eyes.

If human populations are using up habitat, what about the Endangered Species Act? The act is a legal tool for offering protection to species in the path of development, based on their vulnerability. A company can't put in tracts of ranchettes, for example, on land that a rare desert tortoise is already using for its habitat. Developers hate the act, claiming it is overused by zealous anti-growth conservation groups. Look hard enough at any piece of ground, they say, and you can probably find some species that is using it. The Endangered Species Act, they say, was supposed to be used sparingly, not as an assault weapon to mow down property rights.

My conversations about the Endangered Species Act with conservation activists, on the other hand, reveal ambivalence. There seems to be a consensus that the act is a necessary tool in the effort to defend biodiversity and eventually rewild wounded lands. But how exactly to apply it is hotly debated. On one side of the divide are the many conservation and environmental advocates who worry that overusing the law may provoke a backlash from developers, landowners, taxpayers, and corporations. On the other side are conservation biologists who offer compelling scientific testimony in the struggle to apply the law and passionately defend it. A prominent representative of this camp is the Center for Biodiversity, headquartered in Tucson and best known for its sweeping application of the act's provisions without hesitation or apology.

The Center for Biodiversity's literature boasts about the vast tracts and many smaller parcels of land it has removed from development. The list of no-holds-barred legal challenges it has mounted on behalf of varied species is long and continually growing. Its web site and newsletter describe interventions for everything from tiger salamanders to leopard frogs, from fairy shrimp to killer whales, from cuckoos to cutthroat trout, and from gumplants to fruit bats. The center's activists and attorneys seem determined to ensure that every pupfish gets its day in court. Imagine its lawyers as wildlife defense attorneys frantically filing for the reprieve of species on death row. Don't even think of lecturing them on overusing the appeals process.

The mainstream national conservation and environmental organizations had made the integrity and power of the Endangered Species Act a high priority and were eager to discuss the specifics with me, but the radical conservationists I encountered were focused on a bigger picture. To them, the act, though important, was like the emergency room of biodiversity. Yes, we need a place where the critically wounded can get treatment and relief, but building a world where species are safe and can thrive is the larger goal. As my grandmother might say, an ounce of rewilding prevention is worth a pound of Endangered Species Act cure. Tom, while praising the efforts of the center to protect imperiled creatures, turned my questions about the act away from legal and legislative issues toward why the law was needed in the first place. He was interested in talking about why, in the long run, such stopgap measures could not stem the avalanche of extinction that prompted them.

We sit in the sun and talk for hours. It becomes apparent why *Wild Earth* is inspiring. Tom's vision includes dark and dangerous horizons. He seems to have grave doubts about whether we will face up to our crisis in time to get through it. Like most environmental activists, he wrestles with despair. It is a challenge to live in a world of wounds with eyes that see them clearly and to deal daily with a culture so at odds with your own vision of what is and should be. It is not going to be enough to change the goals we collectively and individually pursue, the rules and laws that guide us in our pursuits, the plans and policies we make. We are going to have to change consciousness and its culture.

A couple wanders up the trail in the middle of our discussion. The woman totters unsteadily across the rocks where we are sitting and takes in the view. These two are not your typical hikers. Their shoes are ill-suited for the task they have chosen, and they carry no rucksack or water bottles. They are wearing clothes more appropriate for a museum or tour bus excursion. The man is out of shape, red-faced, and sweating. He has apparently been doing more supersizing than exercising lately. I try to determine whether his complexion is the result of sunburn or a stressed heart, and silently review my last CPR class.

"It's wonderful, isn't it?" the woman asks, ignoring her partner's labored breathing. We agree. He eventually recovers and they walk around smiling at the view, take some photos, and then leave. "Look," I say to Tom as they disappear down the trail, "even people whom you might not suspect harbor love for wild landscapes. They worked hard to get up here."

"Yes, but an appreciation for scenery alone will never get us from where we are today to where we must go. That's the old conservation movement," he says. "Many ecosystems and creatures that need to be preserved and restored have little or no aesthetic appeal. Becoming ecologically literate is just one step, albeit a critical one, toward building a future that accommodates and is infused by wildness."

At the delta of my journey down the River Wild, Tom Butler gets the last word. After telling me how his three-year-old daughter, Grace Gavia, chose to add loons to the family's blessings at the dinner table—"Gavia" is a species appellation for the birds—he sums up the sweeping divide between the totemic consciousness emerging in his beloved toddler and the acquisitive consciousness of the prevailing empire of belief she was born into. "Science can help us achieve our conservation goals but at the end of the day, it's an ethical choice. You see the world either as a community or as a collection of commodities. Community or commodity—that's the difference."

SEVEN

I Used to Stomp on Grasshoppers,
but Oysters Made Me Stop

I used to stomp on grasshoppers. Any chance I got. If one crossed my path on a country road or a sidewalk, I would heel-hunt it into the ground. *Bam-splat!* Another one bites the dust. My dislike of grasshoppers was active, violent, and righteous. I was a god, walking this earth and dispensing life-or-death judgments on the lowly creatures that crawled and jumped beneath my feet.

The animosity and contempt I felt toward grasshoppers was the result of personal experience. Since moving to Utah's West Desert more than two decades ago, I have experienced two grasshopper infestations. An infestation, or plague as it is commonly called, must be experienced to be appreciated. I have seen groves of trees in summer stripped down to their winter profiles by a million tiny relentless jaws. I have seen gray, weathered fenceposts gnawed down to raw blond wood when swarms of hoppers ran out of vegetation to chew on. I have driven roads cobbled with their carcasses. I once drove over a flood of grasshoppers making their way from a field they had reduced to stubble to fresh food on the other side of the road. As I drove over them, they leaped by the thousands, hitting the bottom of the truck and making the rattling cacophony of an upside-down hailstorm.

What I have experienced, though, was nothing compared to the plagues of the past, like the swarm of locusts that crossed the Great Plains into Colorado in 1875. That year, Rocky Mountain locusts became a kind of superorganism of metabolic wildfire more than 100 miles wide and 1,800 miles long that eclipsed the sun and gleaned a whole landscape down to bristles and dust. Settlers reported that the insects even ate the wool off living sheep.[1]

Though not historic in scale, my experiences were nonetheless powerful. I can vividly recall tiptoeing, arms crossed protectively around my body, through a field of long, slender stems that were bent and trembling with the weight of grasshoppers lined up head to tail along their lengths. Halfway across, I was overcome by nausea. The grasshoppers were voracious. Prolific. Creepy. Once you have lived through their plague, you do not hold much affection for these insects or appreciate their return. One less grasshopper, in my book, was a welcome development. And so I stomped on them.

Oysters made me stop. I can explain. Some years ago I came across a remarkable account of oyster behavior in an essay, "High Tide in Tucson," by Barbara Kingsolver.[2] A scientist named F. A. Brown collected some oyster specimens along the Connecticut shoreline for research he was doing on the cycles of intertidal oysters. He took his little prisoners to a basement lab in landlocked Illinois. For the first couple of weeks in their new time zone, the oysters kept their Atlantic coast schedule. As the tide was rolling into Connecticut, they would open up in unison to feed on the briny plankton they expected to arrive. As the tide in Connecticut rolled out, they would shut tight and wait for the next tide. This, after all, was the pattern of their prespecimen lives, and one that was kept for eons by their clammy ancestors.

Then, over the next two weeks, an unexpected shift occurred. By the end of that time the oysters were still following a tidal pattern, but not on a schedule charted by man or woman. What was going on? Brown and his students crunched some numbers and made a startling discovery. The oysters were in perfect sync with what the Atlantic tides' schedule would have been had they pushed on beyond Connecticut, across the length of New York state, over the Midwest and eventually rolled into the oysters' Chicago basement lab.

Think about it. First, it's remarkable that these ancient and brainless slips of simple salty flesh, with no eyes, ears, or voices, could do anything in unison that was not the result of some heavy-duty simultaneous outside stimulation, like hooking a car battery to their aquarium and throwing the switch. To Brown and his colleagues, who were familiar with the myriad ways that plants, animals, and insects communicate and coordinate through hormones and other chemicals, the oysters' ability to act in unison was not surprising. But it was amazing that they somehow managed to anticipate a distant and subtle planetary rhythm without benefit of cues from the sun, moon, or stars, let alone the powerful moving ocean waters that had sustained their slow beat until they were captured and shipped away. How did they do it? What atmospheric, geologic, or biologic music do they dance to that we humans, with all our high-tech calculating capacity, cannot fathom?

Kingsolver's essay made me rethink my relationship with grasshoppers (and just about everything else). Grasshoppers, it seems to me, are potentially far more sophisticated than oysters. What do they know that I don't? Maybe the ebb and flow of their population is a response to some subtle planetary shift that I, in my blind and righteous sophistication, am not able to discern.

I began to take a second look. One of the first things I learned is that my original opinion of grasshoppers is not universally shared. Certainly not by the conservation biologists I encountered on my journey, who taught me about the intrinsic value of all species, the mysteries and wonders of ecological processes we do not fully comprehend, and the value and role of natural "disturbances" like fire and flood. My "kill the pest" attitude was similar to the approach we have followed when wiping out predators. It was not the least biocentric. So I stepped back and tried to see grasshoppers from the different perspective I had been learning.

How would those grasshoppers look to a bird? Mighty good. Our plague is their feast and fortune. Skunks, too, see it differently. Although I have some serious questions about the value and purpose of skunks in the grand scheme of life—again because I have had several negative experiences with that species, including getting sprayed twice—I am quite fond of birds. They animate the landscape, embroider the sky, and fill my mornings with song. I envy their ability to swoop and soar. In the winter, I find myself searching the horizon for twirling ribbons of starlings, awed by their collective tubular dance, the choreography of undulating columns of black birds. I look in shrubs for the tiny seedeaters that remain behind while others have migrated far and wide. I watch them huddle, hop, and peck. I miss their singing cousins and long for their return in the spring.

Birds, of course, are valuable not just for the aesthetic pleasures they bring. They are important as pollinators, and pollinators make life on earth possible. Also, by carrying undigested seeds in their droppings, they are important as seed distributors. Birds, you could say, are teamsters of biodiversity—each poop a Peterbilt.

As any HawkWatch member with a pair of binoculars can tell you, birds are also significant indicators of the health of the environment. Just as canaries in coal mines warned miners of the presence of dangerous fumes, birds give us an early warning of other environmental dangers. In the year following the Chernobyl disaster, for example, a precipitous decline in songbird populations in North America and Europe offered powerful evidence of how far radiation from Chernobyl had reached and the potent effect it had. The absence of birdsong that year was not just a sensual deprivation, it was a powerful message that we are all downwind and downstream from one another.

Birds don't just work and warn; they also reveal. As any bird-watcher knows, to do it right you must slow down, be still, and look and listen intently. You must understand habitat and learn the principles of wind and weather, climate, and seasons. You must tune in to behaviors that are rooted in cycles of mating, nesting, growth, and migration. In other words, to find and know birds, you must learn the primal, nonhuman language of life. Ask bird-watchers why they do it and they will likely describe the peaceful and reflective aspects of birding: how it can be a tonic for the mind and spirit in an age of stress and striving. They can tell you about moving lessons they have learned from birds—lessons about life and about how to simply be. I find it ironic that today's popular culture is so obsessed with angels with wings who look like us, while we ignore the winged creatures who surround us, already here and available to guide us to peace and understanding. But these angels eat grasshoppers. If I am so fond of birds, I reasoned, then maybe I should be more tolerant of their food.

Being attentive is key. The more I learn about the intricacies of food webs and nutrient cycles, the more I appreciate how every plant, animal, and insect, even the lowly bacteria, can play an essential role in some life process we humans do not fully understand or appreciate. An entomologist I know is fond of reminding his less bug-oriented friends that we are utterly dependent on life processes that bacteria and bugs contribute to in important ways. Beetles, he loves to point out, could exist very well without humans, but humans, who are dependent on soil that beetles help build and process, could not exist without beetles. Although life's individual threads may seem insignificant, pull any one of them and you cannot be sure what will unravel and how the consequences will be magnified as they travel along the tapestry of being.

I always knew that stomping on grasshoppers was petty and foolish behavior. Now, in the light of my attempt to understand conservation biology, I have to admit it is also arrogant. Who am I to judge the value and purpose of grasshoppers? What do I know about the natural cycles that underlie their rise and fall? The way a landscape consumes itself, shits itself out, reseeds, and starts over is often a matter of disturbance and even catastrophe. The specific conditions and chemical signals that push grasshoppers, crickets, and locusts into all-consuming migration are not well understood. The thinking that prevails today is that drought causes populations to crowd together for scant food. Proximity triggers chemical signals that lead to hyped-up breeding, and increased breeding leads to faster consumption of available food, thus compelling migration in search of new food. At some point, physiological changes appear. Wings lengthen for extended flight. Although I cannot see the tipping point where microchanges become mega, I should at least be able to recognize an ecological process when I see it, even if it is not appealing.

Fires and floods are two other ecological processes that have gotten a bad reputation because their opening acts are so clearly destructive. The changes and exchanges in nutrients they kick off are more subtle, slower, and harder to perceive. Perhaps rampaging hoppers also have hidden functions.

I do not have a firm handle on the mystery of how life on earth unfolds and keeps its dynamic balance while perched on the edge of chaos. I can't be sure exactly how I fit into the larger patterns that sustain me or the role that grasshoppers and oysters play in that pattern that connects one to all. As Reed Noss argues, life on earth expresses an intelligence and underlying order that is too complex for us to fully grasp, try as we may. Maybe a little humility is in order.

We are of this world—"dust to dust," as they say. Before we acquired the cultural habit of capturing our moldering flesh behind teakwood and oak six feet under, our bodily fate was to be fodder for the juice and sinew of a world that lived on after our demise. Just as we now refuse to blend in the end, we also deny the utter rootedness of our lives in a wide world that loops through us and feeds back to us in an intricate weave too complex to fathom.

Fact one: we are embedded in this world. Although we are, and should be, recognized for our unique human abilities, from writing symphonies to traveling to the moon, it is also fair to say that we are what we eat, what we drink, and what we breathe. Again, if you stop eating for three weeks, stop taking in fluids for three days, or stop breathing for three minutes, your body will make the case for you that the process of life is the constant transformation of environment into physical being.

The food we eat is synthesis of water, sunlight, and soil. Soil is the rich mix of plant debris, bits of sand and stone, and the decomposing flesh of every living thing you can name as it is consumed and transformed by communities of worms, insects, and microbes. A microbial world we barely know hums through us. An acre of soil includes ten tons of microbial and invertebrate life, the weight equivalent of ten Clydesdale draft horses, galloping not overland but underground.

We are also fluid creatures. Our blood tosses the salt of seas. Tears, amniotic fluid, sweat, piss, and our vulnerable wet flesh from head to toe contain whatever is carried in the currents, storms, and tides that sweep the globe and in the streams and rivers that drain the rain and snow. The same breeze that lifts the wings of birds also fills your lungs. Our continual biological communion with the planet is undeniable and profound.

Once the direct pathways between the biosphere and our own blood and bones become clear, the health of the land should become a self-evident concern of self-interest. If biodiversity is a key to planetary health, as conservation biologists attest, then biodiversity should become a measure of the success and well-being of humans that is as significant and important as the gross national product. Life's buzzing, blooming, and howling variability—from caribou to cactus, from marigolds to loons, from mussels to moss—makes life viable. To the extent that we damage that robust diversity, we are engaged in self-destructive and unsustainable behaviors because we are connected to what we are destroying. If we chop it up, it dies and eventually so do we, or we limp along in a diminished and dysfunctional world. Paradoxically, it is in our self-interest to be selfless and generous, for the health of the world is ultimately our own.

We know how to make the land pay—how the land can make wealth. We do not know how the land makes health. That requires a different language than the one we are adept at using. That new language of health, the one that conservation biologists are trying to invent, will be a challenge to acquire because it differs radically from the language of wealth. Wealth says more, health says enough. Wealth says accumulate, health says flow. Wealth says compete and win, while health says reciprocate, integrate, and reconcile. Wealth says manage and measure, health says jam and dance. Wealth assigns value, health assumes it. Wealth adds, subtracts, and divides. Health makes whole.

Yes, wealth is needed and can certainly be good and welcome. I enjoy my comforts. I am glad I do not hunger. I like being entertained. People across the globe have indisputable material needs that are not being met. But common sense and wisdom tell us that health is the ultimate bottom line. Rich soils, benign weather, breathing forests, filtering wetlands, clean freshwater, and abundant seas are hard to quantify and measure for the very reason that they are so important and valuable. "Incalculable" is the word to describe their worth.

After sacrificing environmental health for profits, power, jobs, and revenue that benefits a relative handful of the world's people for hundreds of years, it is time to restore the balance. Time to end the imbalance of power that strives to lock in the obscenely unequal distribution of wealth which allows a small elite to grow ever richer while a massive population struggles and suffers for a fraction of the rewards from their own labor and lands. Across the globe, the landless poor slash and burn, strip the land of trees for fuel, deplete soils, and poach wild game until they are forced to flee into crowded urban slums, where they sell their labor for slave wages and succumb to tainted water and food. Ecological destruction and social injustice are twin engines of global corporate capitalism as it is currently configured.

Time also to restore the balance of our minds. We cannot find the courage and creativity to address the central imbalance while holding on to the attitudes, assumptions, and beliefs that are so closely related to the very problems compelling our attention. This is not a matter of adopting a new ideology, although we will certainly be challenging a prevailing worldview if we challenge the criteria that underlie our current policies and choices. It is more a matter of learning by doing differently. Today we provide kids with lots of opportunities to compute, compete, keep score, accumulate, manipulate, and fix. We do not normally give them chances to contemplate, compost, and plant. Every legislator I know wants a computer in every classroom. I have yet to meet one who thinks each classroom should have its own garden. Being able to balance the books is a required skill. Bird watching and bulb planting are optional.

Sue Morse, John Derick, Howard Gross, Michael Soulé, Leanne Klyza Linck, Kim Vacariu, Jim Catlin, Allison Jones, Tom Butler, and many others I have encountered over the past few years are gaining and sharing understandings about how the natural world connects, communicates, and creates. Cutting off feedback loops when we don't know the role they play or the impacts of losing them, reducing the pool of possibilities and weakening a living system's resilience, and introducing alien variables are all reckless and risky practices.

The work of understanding the health of whole ecosystems and reweaving the broken strands is the way we learn to survive our own mistakes. It will point toward ways of living more lightly on the land. It may open new ways to converse with nature and create new languages, maps, and lenses. That work is the seedbed of a new culture focused on diverse, restored, and robust nature that will, like the ecosystems it seeks to heal, emerge and self-organize from the seeds we sow.

The dilemma for those of us trying to carve a new paradigm for our times is that philosophy does not precede perception. Like a well-honed nose and a universe of rich aromas, belief and perception call each other into being. How do you describe harmony and wholeness, their value and necessity, when the world around you is cacophonous, splintered, and dissonant? Healing and "rewilding" wounded lands, then, is not only the way we ensure our own physical vitality and sanity, it is the way we can learn the hard work of reconnection. Reconnect the land. Reconnect our bodies to the land. Reconnect body and spirit.

We will need places to learn how to do that work, and there are probably no pristine places left. Early Amerindians wiped out mastodons, and their descendants used fire as a tool to shape grasslands and forests to their needs. They irrigated, built villages, cut woods, and otherwise left their indelible marks, though certainly on a scale that pales next to our own impact. As island biogeographers show us, even the wildest places we have agreed to protect are islands withering from isolation and disconnection with the larger landscapes that once included them.

But large tracts of land with integrity and diverse life, the surest sign of health and the potential for resilience, do remain. Even in the crowded East, fragments of wildlands are often close to one another, begging for attention and reconnection into whole systems. Saving wilderness and near-wilderness provides us with places to start, learn, and practice how to help the earth's own healing powers take hold.

Health is the natural state of living systems that are allowed to function with integrity over time. That is what I have learned. It is right to honor Nature and wise to heed her. To stay healthy, we must be humble.

I used to stomp on grasshoppers. Oysters made me stop.

RESTORATION

What is a thunderstorm, to a bird?

—JOHN HAY

ONE

Flash Flood: Driven by Unquenchable Thirst
into the Path of Danger

We were driven by thirst across a landscape that could not quench it. The hike into the remote canyons of the San Rafael Swell over heat-reflecting ledges of bare stone was long and hard. We started while the morning sun was still pushing its bright yellow fingers into canyon recesses. By noon, the temperature hit 100 degrees Fahrenheit on the desert floor. Precious shade was intermittent, so we made the most of what shade there was, hugging the slim shadows that pooled along the cliff walls and aiming ourselves under the green and glassy hands of the occasional cottonwood tree along the route. By the time we reached the little oasis at the mouth of Chimney Canyon and its rare spring, we were eager to fill our depleted water bottles.

The San Rafael is a vast uplift in south-central Utah. If you want to know why we war over water in the West, the San Rafael is a good place to start—as dry as a bone, as they say. But awesome, too. Wilderness advocates argue that "the Swell" is the geological twin of Utah's Capitol Reef National Park and its uplifted universe of sandstone nooks and crannies, the Waterpocket Fold. As such, they argue, it deserves full wilderness protection, if not national park status.

Those who place a greater priority on resource extraction and off-road vehicle recreation than scenic beauty and habitat integrity have held off the conservationists for decades. In the 1960s, when Capitol Reef and Arches got national park status, the Swell was originally part of the package, but it was pulled out because it was thought to hold reserves of uranium useful for making nuclear fuel and weapons of mass destruction. Now the threats to the Swell come from all-terrain vehicle, jeep, and dirt bike riders, who want to turn the place into a theme park for off-road vehicles.

My hiking companion, Bill Hauze, and I were out to exercise our legs, find some solitude, and explore the maze of redrock canyons, untouched by cows or gearheads, that lay right behind the small oasis we were fast approaching. "Let's pump water so we can guzzle some right away," I suggested as we reached the first cottonwood tree. "Iodine is too slow." In even the most remote canyons of the Southwest, naturally occurring water must be filtered through a pump or treated with iodine tablets to avoid a case of giardia, a dysentery-like affliction caused by a ubiquitous bacteria that is the legacy of the correspondingly ubiquitous presence of its host and carrier, cow crap, on Southwest public lands.

I was eager to show Bill the hidden splendors of the canyons that I had first visited with another hiking buddy, Steve Allen, who is legendary for his knowledge of Utah's redrock wilderness and his standing-room-only slide-show fund-raisers for the Southern Utah Wilderness Alliance. The Chimney Rock complex of canyons is a gallery of stone art brimming with life, its diverse plants, birds, insects, and reptiles animating a sensuous realm of flesh tones and smooth shapes. The name is not unique—the West is covered with "chimney rocks"—and naming a canyon after its typical, though beautiful, sandstone spires while ignoring its uniquely stained and exquisitely sculptured walls misses the mark. It's like calling a goddess Dick.

As we kicked through the scattered debris of an abandoned prospector's camp that also shared the little oasis, my suppressed thirst moved up my throat and curled like a hairy beast in my parched mouth, where it waited impatiently behind lips as dry as lizard skin. Moments later, I knew something was wrong—the cattails that should have been plump and dark brown were faded and wispy. Where the ground should have turned spongy and wet, we found nothing but powdery soil and dry rushes. Adrenaline flooded into my limbs.

"Damn!" I said to Bill. "This is not good." The understatement was a thin veil over my heart-pumping panic. The dry spring was not just disappointing, it was life-threatening. An agonizing death involving thirst-induced fever, shock, and delirium is not a top-ten way to leave this life—not that any way is great, but falling off a cliff is certainly more thrilling and sudden. The view is better, too.

We could not go on without water. In fact, the risk from dehydration was real. We were a full day's hike away from the truck, which we had left at the trailhead at Tomsich Butte. We had no cell phones to call for help, and we were way out of range anyway. It would be a long night without water and a torturous walk out the next day. But we had no choice. Unlike my desert-savvy friend Steve Allen, I had not found and marked on topo maps every water-bearing pothole hidden in the deep folds and thin crevices of the sandstone landscape.

I remembered to breathe deeply and think. There were other springs tucked up in the canyon behind the gnarled cottonwood tree that leaned over the dusty ex-oasis where we stood. During a previous trip to the Chimney Rock canyons, we had reached them by climbing through a narrow break in a canyon wall that was just a few yards away.

We dropped our packs, gathered empty water bottles in our shirts, and started climbing. In a few minutes we reached two shaded pools by a mossy seep, deep enough to dip the bottles under the surface without disturbing the easily aroused bottoms, plenty deep for pumping. We spread wet bandanas on our baked foreheads and let our fears evaporate. It felt good to be free of the backpacks we had left on the floor of the dry wash below.

In the desert, the water we might take for granted almost anywhere else can become a sweet and sensual joy—even when it is amber-tinged and warm. On backpacking trips I have been thankful for green water and returned to civilization with a newfound appreciation for the tinkling music ice makes against a glass and the way it startles the tongue. "How can something so simple and elemental be so delightful, so exquisite?" Bill didn't answer, but smiled and sighed. He finished filling his bottles and headed for an overhang laced with pink columbines and pastel wisps of green grass. I followed, then rested with him. We napped briefly in the silence, awakened only by the high-pitched whistle of hummingbirds and the soft thrum of a dragonfly. The clap of thunder, however, brought us to our feet.

Just over the canyon edge, the sky went from deep blue to an ominous dark, bruised color in an instant. Summer is flood season in canyon country. Ocean mist is sucked up off the coast of Mexico and pushed inland. It rises with the afternoon desert heat and banks up against island mountain ranges and escarpments, where it billows into brilliant white thunderheads that eventually darken and collapse. We looked up to see a jagged bolt of electricity crackle as it arced across the cliff tops. Moments later, booming thunder shook the canyon walls so hard that rocks broke loose and clattered down. Then fat drops of rain splattered all around us like little water balloons. The rain polka-dotted the pale surfaces of stone, puffed the dust, and nodded the broad leaves of the cottonwoods. Ropes of rain followed, then sheets.

There is precious little soil to absorb the rain in "standing-up country," the high deserts of the Colorado Plateau that are known throughout the world for their rocky buttes, bluffs, and towers. There are few plants to shield the ground from driving rain, and only sporadic webs of roots to hold scant soil in place. The face of slickrock has been carved into channels, basins, and rills that gather rain and spill it to the canyon floor. Ribbons of running water are braided into reddish cascades that run over cliff walls onto desert floors until the canyons become galleries of waterfalls that are as varied as the sleek dips and lips that the water pours over. On the bottom, dry washes become torrents that churn colors of chocolate and blood, sand and ash.

The silence and stillness of deep-cut rock masks the potential for periodic catastrophe. It can take a river in the incrementally shaped landscapes of the East several days to reach a flood stage that can be merely twice the river's normal flow. In the dry canyons of the more dynamic West, a stream or river can reach a hundred times its volume in a matter of hours. And it is not just the river bottoms and floodplains that fill with runoff. In the West, a storm can break out of view and send a wall of water down a canyon drainage several miles away with no more warning than the faint rumble of distant thunder.

Just as backcountry skiers have to learn the language of avalanches and sailors must be attuned to squalls, Southwest hikers must listen for floods. In places like Muddy Creek in the San Rafael, or Buckskin Gulch on the Utah–Arizona border, I have seen thick logs and shrubby debris jammed between canyon walls thirty feet above the merely wet ground. These serve as powerful warnings that slot canyons can fill up fast where there is no way to run. Even wider canyons can be impossible to exit during floods.

Like the one we were in. All that spilling water had to go somewhere, and the crevice we had climbed through was where it was headed. As that simple realization sank in, we looked at each other's faces and read each other's thoughts: we could be stranded up this canyon overnight with no packs and no gear. We broke away from the storm's thrall and bounded down the banks from our overhang shelter. The anxiety we had dismissed only an hour earlier returned with a vengeance.

We bolted across a growing torrent of muddy water just moments before it became too swift to enter. Too late. We reached the notch in the canyon wall just in time to see it fill up with latte-colored froth. Worse, we could see our packs below and realized they could easily be swept away by the water that was now swelling in the wash below us. Damn! Why hadn't we left them on higher ground, away from the bottom of the wash? The prospect of no food was not much pleasanter to face than dehydration had been. The desert seemed to be toying with us. It was big and we were small. We desperately scoped the ledge we were on for another way down. One route we tried didn't go down, but luckily the next one we tried did, and we snatched up our packs in the nick of time.

Once we had our packs on, we started climbing as high along the canyon wall as we could, eventually dropping under a long alcove, where we spent an uneasy night listening to one flood after another pulse through the narrow canyon below. As the rumbling chorus of floodwaters grew louder and closer in the pitch-black night, Bill and I wondered if we were high enough to escape the reach of the muddy monster we could hear below us. We plotted how we could climb up higher and cling to thin ledges if we had to. In the forest, you might be treed by a bear. Here in the dry desert of the San Rafael Swell we were treed, ironically enough, by water.

The thought of being swept up and away in the dark was strong enough that we ignored the risk of sleeping in rodent dung possibly saturated with deadly hantavirus and pushed ourselves farther up into the crevices of our stone-cove shelter. Getting a lung-clenching case of hantavirus seemed an acceptable risk compared to the more immediate danger of being soaked, rolled, dashed, and drowned in the dead of night.

There is something about a cave that invites a story. As we waited for the parade of storms to pass us and subside, we told each other about our "first" floods. I will never forget mine. It happened on a summer day in Capitol Reef, along the lush banks of Pleasant Creek just below the Sleeping Rainbow Ranch, where we were living. We watched a storm break over the face of Boulder Mountain, several miles away, and suspected a flood was coming, although the sun-drenched stillness offered no hint or clue. We watched and waited for so long that we decided nothing was coming our way after all.

Just as we turned back toward the ranch house, we heard an utterly unique and ominous *shush* of gravel and the knocking percussion of stones rolling and clapping against one another underwater. The weird sound grew louder, followed by the oddest sight I'd ever seen. The advancing tongue of the flood was like a rolling wall of grass, sticks, tumbleweeds, and leaves. It looked dry and seemed to be migrating slowly. Its speed, however, was deceptive.

Once the debris pile it was pushing with its nose had passed, the flood revealed a full-throttle power that was humbling. Anything swept up in that rushing current would be as helpless as a rag in a hurricane. The roar of boulders bouncing along beneath the swollen water was so loud that we had to shout at each other to be heard. When the banks of the creek started to cave in and wash away, we walked a safe distance from the boiling stew of earth and rain. A couple of hours later the waters ebbed, and by the next morning Pleasant Creek was reduced to fresh puddles threaded by a thin, meandering banner of chalky water. Weeks later, a carpet of fresh grass embroidered by wildflowers pushed up through the drying mud. Bees and butterflies danced to a chorus of birdsong across the flood's green wake. Frogs plopped into fresh water that was covered with tasty bugs skating on gossamer legs. Potholes teemed and swarmed. Buds poked up along the edges of stranded and stagnant pools. The flood's hammer blow was followed by a delicate caress, and in a million nooks and crannies life was nurtured and renewed.

Our stories over, we rolled up like burritos in our blue ponchos, slept fitfully, and were occasionally awakened by strobes of distant lightning as a procession of thunderstorms spent themselves over the desert swell. By morning they were gone, and we awoke to a quiet world washed clean and brimming with bright light. The desert air had been scoured clean. The overwhelming rumble of the night was reduced to a subtle music of trickling and dripping. We climbed down from our uneven perch to sparkling washes with swollen pools rimmed with silken mud and smooth quicksand. The air soon filled with chirping birds, the thrum of busy insects, and the celebrating chant of frogs. By midmorning there was no hint that the canyon could be anything but still and benign.

Life evolves according to the circumstances. One size does not fit all. Although the grammar and syntax of life may be common, ecosystems speak the vernacular of whatever landscape generates them. Just as we have learned that forest ecosystems can accommodate, incorporate, and express fire, we now know that in canyon country, floods are an expression of canyon geology. Canyon plants, animals, and insects have evolved around that unavoidable fact of life.

Just as wildfires clear debris, release nutrients into the soil, and reset the successional clock for renewed growth in forests and prairies, floods build beaches and make niches for canyon life, especially in the spring, when runoff is high. Wildfires and floods are natural disturbances that play key functions in their ecosystems despite their unpredictable timing. Just as a forest fire can break seeds in its wake, thus renewing growth, flash floods in canyon landscapes pulse moisture and nutrients into dry reaches where life has evolved to bloom, breed, and recede quickly.

Canyon country is scattered with hidden pockets of water called potholes, which can hold anywhere from a couple of quarts to thousands of gallons of precious water. Because floods replenish the water and nutrients in potholes, they bloom with sudden activity after it rains. Floods fire the starting gun in a procreative race that evolution has fine-tuned to fit the circumstances. Two days after a big flood, the typical desert floor becomes the scene of a bug and toad orgy.

Desert mammals rely on potholes for drinking water. Floodwaters also reload precious seeps and springs, create quicksand reservoirs, and are pumped up into the fleshy architecture of succulent plants. Floods carve the land into niches, and a persistent, creative life force loads those niches with microbial critters, insects, birds, plants, fish, and animals that fit together to become communities, tuned into and dependent upon one another.

As our biosphere unfolds, it makes loops, links, and cycles even in the challenging heat of a desert, where evolution's touch has been fine and particular. Like fearsome wildfires, slickrock floods are so dramatic, deadly, and unforgiving that we may miss the necessary and beneficial role they play in the dynamic of the ecosystems they shape. Stop that pulsing flow with a dam, and you stint the desert's life-giving artery. Or you could say that flash floods are the rug a dam pulls out from under the desert's evolutionary players.

Floyd Dominy didn't see it that way. He led the federal Bureau of Reclamation during its era of prodigious dam building across the West. Some, including Floyd himself, would say that in the 1950s and 1960s he *was* the Bureau of Reclamation. To the emperor of the federal government's flood control empire, floods were not an awesome natural wonder but a nasty and annoying characteristic of Western landscapes that inhibited their efficient development. If agriculture and civilization itself were to succeed, according to Dominy's proud vision, Western waters must be tamed and harnessed. Rainfall alone would never make the desert bloom. Rivers are rare in the West, and Dominy's bureau was determined to mine them all for the fluid gold they carried. The unruly wet chaos had to be made predictable so it could be harnessed and used.

On the top of Dominy's list of water demons was the Colorado River, the liquid heart of the West. "The unregulated Colorado River," Dominy proclaimed, "is a son of a bitch . . . either in flood or a trickle."[1] To be useful, the river must be manageable. To be manageable, it must be predictable. To be predictable, it must be dammed.

And so it was.

TWO

Flashback: From Suicidal Fool
to Prophetic-Hydro Hero, John Wesley Powell's
Strange Trip Downriver

Katie Lee stood naked under a bright column of light on the warm lip of a sandstone spire, her back to the camera, arms raised in praise, circled by stone. All around her the amazing world was curved and seeded with grace. It was 1962 and Glen Canyon was still a sandstone Eden, carved and nourished by the warm red flow of the Colorado River as it meandered through the last remote corner of the continental American landscape to be explored and mapped. Katie often interrupted her fledgling Hollywood singing and acting career to hitch rides with river guides through the sinuous and tranquil Glen Canyon wilderness that lay across the Utah–Arizona border. In return for entertaining guests with her guitar and smart conversation, she rode for free. The photo taken by a friend would become a popular poster almost forty years later. "The light there acted upon you," she claims.

I first met Katie in 2001 at a fund-raising dinner for the Southern Utah Wilderness Alliance, where she sang and then read from her book, *All My Rivers Are Gone*. Still lean and lively, Katie remains attentive to and proud of her appearance at eighty years of age. She can still command rapt attention from an audience when she sings and plays her guitar on stage. Her songs tell stories about her beloved Colorado River and its paradise lost, Glen Canyon. The portrait she draws of the canyon is unabashedly intimate.

Katie conveys her opinions with humor and flair. It is not hard to imagine the younger woman she was in those river-running days. "That Katie is a pistol," they would say back then, and she still is. She's also one of the few humans left on the planet with a vivid memory of Glen Canyon before it was drowned behind the massive dam that bore its name. I wanted to bottle her and take her home.

She told us how trips through side canyons like Little Labyrinth, Fluted Canyon, Cascade, Twilight, and Wishbone touched her deeply, inspired her songwriting, and shaped a lifelong understanding of nature and beauty. Photos taken by Tad Nichols, one of her fellow wilderness pilgrims, reveal why. Glen Canyon was unlike any other American landscape: a unique, graceful riparian realm where cottonwoods and myriad smaller flora and fauna were fed by rivers, streams, springs, and seeps flowing through majestic stratas of redrock that arched up under cobalt blue skies. The walls careened and swooped. Each one offered a gallery of sculpted and stained surfaces, burnished by the wind.

The Colorado Plateau's canyons are a galaxy of red earthtones, but some walls shine white and some glimmer deep blue, reflecting the desert sky. Patterns underlay other patterns, so that the vertical lines of stains from orange and chocolate mud that drip and run down cliff walls from above braid with older stripes of dark desert varnish. Those vertical ribbons spread across circular patterns polished into rock surfaces and across horizontal stone ribs, scattered holes, and chaotic cracks. Each wall is a kaleidoscope of angles, edges, shadows, patinas, and pentimentos—a mysterious riot of intersecting lines and patterns that is as challenging to read as the palm of your hand.

Those who had the good fortune to experience Glen Canyon commonly describe it as enchanting, a quality that resonates in lyrical place names like Rainbow Bridge, Cathedral in the Desert, Hidden Passage, Music Temple, Firelight Island, Tapestry Wall, Quaking Bog Amphitheatre, and Wild Horse Bar. And then there were the canyons, like Slickhorn, Fizzle, Dove, Dangling Rope, and Nobody's Bizness. Compare the perception that generated those names with the perspective that generated more common place-names that make plain the hot, un-forgiving nature of the Southwest. My place in Torrey, for example, is between Hell's Backbone and the Dirty Devil River.

The hidden wonderland that Katie and her friends celebrated in photos and songs was not always regarded as benign and beautiful. As habitat, canyon country was usually perceived as tough and sparse, an arid place that allowed humans no margin for error. It took a long time for ancient peoples to learn how to live in the deep gorges carved by muddy rivers, like the Colorado and San Juan, that meander and spill across southern Utah and northern Arizona. For a long time they vis-ited the canyons only to gather pine nuts and herbs or to hunt bighorn sheep, deer, and rabbits. Eventually they replaced their temporary camps with more substantial pit houses. Those crude shelters dug among gnarly piñons and junipers can still be seen on top of the broad mesas that cage the rivers below. Sifted and churned by the wind for a thousand years, lithic scatters—flakes of shiny red chert left over from chipping out arrowheads and primitive stone-cutting tools—are also plentiful.

About eight hundred years ago the Anasazi, or "ancient others" as the Navajo named them, ventured lower to grow corn and gourds where enough river silt had piled up for gardens to be seeded and tended. Their sheltering architecture evolved to so mimic the angular stone walls towering around them that they blended to near-invisibility within the canyon landscape. They learned to craft the kind of tools, pots, and baskets that more sedentary people use to store grain and seeds or to mix foods and carry water. They filled redrock alcoves with granaries resembling the mud nests of wasps and swallows. Over time, they be-came so adept at using this narrow habitat that they flourished, cover-ing the land with hundreds of vertical sandstone villas and carving on varnished walls thousands of haunting images, including bighorn sheep, snakes, solar signs, and angular spirit-beings with weird halos and spooky demeanors.

Archaeological discoveries of seashells, precious gemstones, and par-rot feathers reveal how far and wide the Anasazi traded, reaching south into what is now Mexico. Despite the powerful Aztec example to their south, the Anasazi resisted the maize-growing/city-state model. While their Aztec cousins built armies and pyramids, the Anasazi continued to hunt, gather, and garden, suggesting that they felt secure and comfortable in their ways. They left no written record other than the strange symbols found in petroglyphs and pictographs, but there is little evidence that they engaged in war, sacrifice, or grand civil ambitions throughout most of their thousand-year history, although things may have soured considerably toward the end.

As has happened so often to various populations throughout time, the Anasazi adapted, learned, prospered, and flourished until they reached the limits of the land's capacity to absorb their collective impact. Years of drought pushed them across some invisible threshold, and their society collapsed. In the last era before their fall, however, they briefly leaped to a much higher level of cultural organization, displaying astronomical acumen, cosmological sophistication, and architectural expertise far beyond those of other indigenous hunting and gathering cultures.

In northern New Mexico's Chaco Canyon, two hundred miles southeast of Glen Canyon, there are clusters of spectacular stone rooms and ceremonial kivas. They stood at the hub of a network of roads that drew thousands of pilgrims to ceremonies that remain mysteries to us today. The discovery that the spiral carvings on nearby canyon walls are pierced by daggers of sunlight during solstice and equinox events led to the realization that the windows and walls at Chaco are also aligned to record astronomical events with breathtaking accuracy. These discoveries add an aspect of cosmological finesse to the considerable organizing skills required to build Chaco. Several generations of ancient Chaco residents were organized to bring down thousands of thick timbers from faraway forests to support ceilings above blocks of stone, which also had to be cut and carried.

Why and how such impressive hives of kivas bloomed in Chaco Canyon is the subject of much academic speculation. Chaco's exacting focus on distant, abstract points of light, rather than on the earthbound spirits commonly worshiped by hunter-gatherers, adds to the mystery. What propelled that shift? Unlike the Eastern and European environs, where change is continuous but incremental, the West stays the same and then changes suddenly. It is racked by earthquakes, avalanches, fires, and floods. Did the chaos of the canyons—the relentless regime of flood and drought—drive the Anasazi's eyes skyward toward the order they discovered above them? Was Chaco an ambitious attempt to harness that order, an attempt that collapsed into an Anasazi diaspora? What lessons does the collapse of the first civilization to settle the Southwest hold for us today?

The recorded history of the American West that shapes our assumptions about how that environment behaves may be too brief to give us accurate expectations. There are significant signs that the region's recent weather history may have been uncharacteristically benign. Tree ring data and river deposit cores indicate that prehistoric times saw droughts on a scale we have never known in our relatively short sojourn across Western landscapes. The Anasazi experiment culminated in one of those epic droughts that may be more characteristic of Western weather cycles than those of the last two hundred years.

Theories about the collapse of the Anasazi's experiment and their disappearance abound, fueled by evidence of warfare, cannibalism, and messianic religious activity at the end. In that final, dramatic period, the Anasazi constructed eye-catching, impossibly precarious cliff dwellings along the high, slim ledges of canyon walls—the first gated communities in the Southwest, sans golf courses and swimming pools. One look at that aerie architecture and the breathtaking routes and one has to ask, "Who were these people, and why did they do that?" More specifically, I often wondered, "How do you raise kids on cliffs?" Teaching a child to walk is dangerous enough in a home filled with stairs, armchairs, and tables with sharp edges. Imagine doing it on the thin ledges of a sandstone precipice.

The Anasazi intrigue me because their emergence in unlikely canyons was as amazing as their disappearance is mysterious. I have visited their broken castles and looted granaries, scuffled in their corncobs, charcoal, and potsherds, and studied the walls they carved and stained. I have wondered where they went and why and how. The answers I find in my public library vary, but each is humbling. There is a morphological fact of life: things must fit. Somehow the Anasazi's adept dance with a fickle habitat slipped. Down they came and away they went, leaving a mixed bag of hints and clues in their ghostly wake.

The most intriguing signs of that lost and hidden history are the hundreds of petroglyphs of Kokopelli, a shamanic flute-playing figure known for his hunchback, club feet, six toes, and, in many crude depictions, big erection. Minus that troubling member, Kokopelli has gone on to become a prolific subject of Southwest jewelers as well as a logo for real estate developers and mountain-bike stores with espresso bars. Was ol' Koko an actual charismatic leader who was congenitally challenged, or the symbol of a kind of Pied Piper spirit? Was he a visionary with a compelling message? We will never know. There is no written record—no Anasazi version of the Magna Carta or *People* magazine. Many of us who have wandered far in the redrock canyons that hold his ghostly image have heard his haunting music, though.

How the Anasazi's last crises played out and where they fled may be a drama remembered and guarded only by Hopis, Zunis, and other Pueblo peoples, who claim their own origins in the migration of Anasazi refugees. (Some say the Anasazi fathered the Shoshone.) Oral cultures don't fax, file, or publish. Their most important stories are passed along within a context of ceremonies and initiations that, despite the best efforts of anthropologists, are still not completely open to the descendants of Europeans, who are commonly regarded by Native Americans as spiritually clumsy, careless, clueless, and indiscreet.

One look at the Pueblo architecture on the mesa tops occupied by those tribes today, however, and the physical continuity with the Anasazi ruins is striking. Behind Pueblo walls today, the sacred powers are still practiced in kivas pierced by *sipapus,* those spiritual umbilicals connecting the people to the earthly underworld from whence they first emerged. No matter what happened to the Anasazi as they passed from culmination to collapse, and no matter what cultural connections remain, the Anasazi story seems instructive in a dim, foreshadowing way: misunderstanding the limits and dynamics of your watershed isn't a formula for a happy ending.

After the Anasazi, most Indians avoided the canyons altogether. Navajos wandered in now and then, and Paiutes occasionally hunted, gathered, and camped. Utes eventually pushed out the Paiutes and exploited the margins of that world. The ruins, thought to be the dwelling places of potentially malevolent Anasazi spirits, were off-limits. Later, many of those perfectly preserved villages were looted by cowboys hunting for pots to sell. The walls were often torn apart in a search for hidden caches of fabled gold. But Glen Canyon was still loaded with untouched ruins, an archaeological treasure trove.

Abandoned by the Anasazi, canyon country was next a barrier to Anglos looking for easy routes from Santa Fe to California. When early explorers like Friars Francisco Atanasio Domínguez and Silvestre Vélez de Escalante struggled across that dry reef searching for a way to descend to the Colorado River and cross it, they ended up eating their horses and surviving on grilled cactus before they got out. The diaries and letters of Southwest explorers leave no doubt about the hardship they endured while learning the awesome topography of an uninhabited landscape that was about the size of France and still unmapped for most of the nineteenth century. The deep sandstone gorges, the convoluted saw-cut slot canyons, and the domes, needles, fins, and spires that inspired Katie Lee left explorers frustrated in the extreme. Here was a land that could not be plowed, grazed, or even crossed. "Profitless," "abominable," and "appalling" were typical characterizations found in their journals and letters home. It was not until 1869 that John Wesley Powell finally navigated that portion of the Colorado River, which crossed the last blank areas on the map of the continental United States.

The planet was a few billion people lighter then. Although the ravenous consumption of habitat that marked westward migration was in full swing, at least in the eyes of the bison and the Indians, white settlers didn't grasp the full extent of the damage they were doing. Biodiversity was not in their vocabulary. No, they saw the world as rich and believed we were put here to tame the wild land and enjoy her fruits as God granted.

The post–Civil War migrations westward were regarded as adventures in almighty Progress. Descriptions of the exploration and settlement of the American West usually take the form of dramatic narratives of adventure, perseverance, toil, hardship, and glory. Spreading farms, roads, canals, ports, and forts westward across the continent was our manifest destiny.

Western migration was also a convenient means of draining the unmet yearnings of the unwashed landless, who believed redemption from a rude life was just over the Western horizon. The explorers were followed by soldiers, surveyors, and settlers. Many years later, the soil blew away—but that's another story, one that adds misunderstanding and waste to the themes of Western history.

John Wesley Powell was a surveyor, but one who read the land with a naturalist's eye as well as a lens. He rode into the West on the back of manifest destiny, working as its soldier and civil servant, and ended as the era's visionary—although he would not be recognized as such until many years after his death. His observations would be used to feed competing agendas.

Dam builders, for instance, emphasized Powell's argument that it would have to be government's mission in the West to develop and distribute scant water for the people. Floyd Dominy, a kind of visionary in his own right, was so inspired by Powell that he named his proudest engineering project after him: Lake Powell.

Dam opponents, on the other hand, understood that although Powell never used the word "ecological" in his writings or speeches, his vision of Western settlement on the arid lands he surveyed was uniquely holistic and conscious of ecological processes and limits. Monster dams, they argue, are counter to Powell's democratic and humble vision.

Who was the man whose ideas inspire such conflicting visions? Powell's father was an itinerant preacher who followed the breaking wave of westward migration through Ohio, Illinois, and Wisconsin when those areas were still wilderness frontiers. Powell grew up exploring the old forests and their wild rivers while grabbing his education where he could. After serving as a major for the Union army in the Civil War and losing his right arm to a steel ball at the battle of Shiloh, Powell taught college geology. Whenever he could break away from the classroom, he did.

His experiences while exploring around the American West led him to suspect that the square-peg paradigm of wet agriculture that had developed in the eastern United States would not fit into the West's dry round hole, but he needed a closer look. In 1869 he got his chance. He secured funding for a dangerous and epic "geographic expedition" from Green River, Wyoming, through the unexplored length of the Colorado River, to the confluence of the Virgin River near the present-day town of St. George, Utah. The journey would cover about four hundred miles and include the Grand Canyon and Glen Canyon.

Just as many pre-Columbian Europeans believed that the Atlantic horizon dropped off into the belly of a monster, many pre-Powell Americans thought that the Colorado River dropped off the rim of their known world into the belly of a threatening wilderness untouched by compass or conquistador. Powell's journey down that serpentine ribbon of brown silk and froth was a last chance for exploration in the heroic tradition, which was rapidly fading.

Powell's epic quest took place at a hinge point in history. Already, robber barons were aiming newly forged rails from Eastern steel mills at prairie expanses, and plans were being hatched to move the recalcitrant heathens out of the way of the settlers, who were gathering on the lip of the frontier with their wagons, farm implements, and cattle. The same year Powell embarked on his journey down "the Great Unknown," the transcontinental railroad was linked at Promontory Point, a few hundred miles north in Utah's Great Basin Desert. The event was a collective rite of passage for the country, which had just shed half a million lives to resolve its future as a united nation. The ring of steel hammers on a golden spike at Promontory was the frontier's death knell. It was time to fill in the last details on the map so that land, water, and other resources could be divided, managed, and used. Lewis and Clark had been succeeded by telegraphs and trains. Powell's trip would be the last great continental adventure.

Before embarking on his journey, Powell did his best to scope out what lay downstream along the Colorado from the scant records and stories of those who had tried and failed before him. Most Americans considered his proposed trip to be nothing short of suicidal. Nevertheless, he gathered his war-crazed brother and eight other surly vets and wannabe mountain men to go along. Boats arrived at Green River by rail from Chicago. Scientific instruments, food, and other supplies for ten months were packed into four wooden dories.

The expedition encountered some whitewater rapids during the early leg of the trip, but they were minor compared to those downstream, where the river cuts through the Colorado Plateau. As thrill-seeking rafters will attest, the Colorado River is a combination of placid meanders interrupted by surprising hydraulic avalanches. Even the most carefully guided modern adventures include bangs and scrapes. Life-flight helicopters are a regular feature above Colorado River gorges today, called in by cell phones and guided by satellite-coordinated guidance systems. Powell's band of geologic argonauts could only cock their ears for the ominous roar of approaching waterfalls, whitewater, and whirlpools. Where flash floods had caromed huge boulders into the river's path, restricting and twisting the water's flow, the resulting rapids could be unparalleled. Some waves were the size of three-story houses.

Powell's boats were poorly designed for the quick maneuvers required to navigate whitewater, and the men had no experience or instruction in the tricks of a river-runner trade that had not yet been invented. To avoid the most robust whitewater, the men hauled their clumsy wooden boats and heavy supplies across steep ledges and jumbled slopes of loose and broken rock, but they still had to brave many unavoidable rapids in their brittle dories. Early on, the raging waters claimed one boat and the precious supplies it held, leaving them no margin for further error during the remainder of their trip.

In between sweaty, heart-pounding episodes, Powell marveled at a landscape that was so new it had no names, no history, not even a vocabulary to describe it. To indicate things to each other, they had to point. The land of pillars, arches, and caverns was unlike any other they had seen. Massive zebra-striped walls towered over vast arched chasms. Sand-strewn winds had polished the cracked, varnished stone surfaces to sculpt beautiful abstract patterns in the cliff faces, so that long stretches of canyon were like giant art galleries. Where seeps of surface water poured through fractured walls, they were rimmed with opalescent moss and hanging gardens of columbines, monkeyflowers, and maidenhair ferns set against rust walls and blue skies. Countless side canyons led to shaded glens of cottonwood trees, embroidered by tall delicate grasses, strange shrubs, and lush succulents they could not identify.

Powell, the only scientist among the group, saw it all as a seamless whole of geology and evolution, woven intricately over time and ever-morphing under the physical forces and laws of nature. His vision was not shared by all, though. One member of the party surveyed the same scene and wrote in his journal, "Country mostly worthless."[1]

Powell's expedition took longer than he planned—too many slow portages around the Colorado's muddy maelstroms. The men had counted on enhancing their food supply with game they hunted in the canyon, but edible wildlife proved spare and elusive. It is hard to enjoy the scenery when you're down to rancid bacon and matted flour, hard to relax when you are dreading the next foaming terror around the next blind bend. In addition to their daily dose of fear, backbreaking labor, and slow starvation, there was the heat that can burn the skin, cook the brain, and dry out vital organs.

By the time Powell's expedition reached the last set of threatening rapids, three members of his crew had decided they'd had enough of the major, his cranky brother, the rotten rations, and the foaming waves of chaos. Instead they would climb out of the "prison" canyon and hike to a nearby settlement. When they reached the canyon rim, though, they were promptly killed—supposedly by Shivwits Indians, but possibly by Mormon settlers, who suspected they were federal agents looking for polygamists to persecute.

Powell and the remaining crew survived the last set of rapids and emerged at the confluence of the Colorado and the Virgin River, where they surprised a small group of Mormons that had been sent to look for signs of the overdue party. The Mormons had been scanning the water for debris and corpses flushed downstream, as they assumed that the trekkers had perished. They were hoping to find and salvage some of the party's maps and notes to provide clues to the unknown regions upriver.

Instead they greeted the major and his thin and battered crew as the explorers escaped the confines of the Grand Canyon at last. News of Powell's death-defying journey soon spread across the land. They had done the impossible, and the last unknown canyon had been revealed. Powell went down the canyon as a suicidal fool and returned as a hero. He would soon add "prophet" to his title—although, like most prophets, he was widely ignored in his own time.

Powell emerged from his bold journey and subsequent expeditions with a firm conviction that not only was there too little water to transform the arid West into farmland and civilization, but what water there was could not be moved so that it could be used. Bright and curious, Powell was an astute and careful observer. He believed in science, and the facts told him that the arid West did not contain enough water to irrigate all of its dry land. He argued that it would be prudent to create political boundaries based on watersheds instead of arbitrary measurements.

His detractors, among them the most respected scientists of the day, argued that "rain followed the plough," meaning that the moisture turned up from tilling, along with the smoke of locomotives and the noise from bustling human activity, could hasten cloud formation and attract rain. These same folks were fond of firing cannons in the air to encourage precipitation. Powell's attempt to discuss the limitations of available water in a civic environment of wild speculation, corruption, and bogus science went unheeded.

The engine for much of the speculation and corruption was a set of land policies that Powell also critiqued as wrong-headed. Homesteaders were given either more land than they could farm, in the case of well-irrigated land, or way too little, in the case of waterless land that could only be grazed seasonally or dry farmed. Deals were cut and rules bent to make up the difference as speculators jockeyed for advantage in a game they had to cheat at to win. Estimates of how much land should be distributed to individuals were based on assumptions about farming that may have been true in the wet landscape and climate of eastern America, but didn't hold up in the West. Most of the land could not be farmed at all, Powell argued. If used for grazing instead, the allotments must be vast to support cattle, more reminiscent of the estates of feudal Mexican land barons than the democratic homesteads of the Midwest.

Compounding the irrational system of land distribution, water was apportioned as it would have been in the wet East, encouraging inefficient hoarding upstream. To make the most of what water resources were accessible, Powell argued, water and land had to be used in common, with the federal government taking the lead in building dams where they would do the most good. He envisioned populist commonwealths organized to govern local watersheds, the limitations and possibilities of each discerned locally. Democracy married to an intimate local knowledge of water resources, he reasoned, would assure wise stewardship of the arid West's scant water. The government would help with the dams and ditches.

Although Powell's beliefs were well reasoned and would eventually be seen as self-evident, his call for communal, equitable use of natural resources guided by a thorough examination of the facts was not well received in an era of get-rich-quick social Darwinism. Policy was crafted back East, where most were completely ignorant of the West's limited soil and water conditions. The need for precaution informed by local experience and knowledge over time was not understood. Getting to know a watershed happens slowly because important seasonal and cyclical patterns unfold at an ecological and geological pace. A race to capture a burgeoning market, on the other hand, happens in an ecological instant.

Those with enough capital and power to develop the resources did not want to be checked and slowed by messy democratic practices. As is the case today, money bought enough access and influence to drive plans and policies. No one, neither poor settlers nor rich railroad barons, wanted a reality check. That would have to wait for a later era of soil depletion, overgrazing, dust bowl Depression, and desperate migration away from the very lands that had once seemed so promising. By then, the development of water would be as much about cash flow as about any rhythm of its own. Water became captured by an infrastructure with a powerful constituency that could not let it flow on its own.

Long after his death, Powell's ideas about the need to develop and use the waters of the arid West cooperatively and efficiently were revisited. His words were often used to rationalize an era of monster projects and water welfare that probably would have struck the thoughtful explorer as just as rash and ill-considered as the policies of his day. Powell envisioned democratic water governance, organized around individual watersheds, that could tap local knowledge and be responsive to local circumstances and limits. He would not have recognized as part of his vision the interstate compacts, massive multistate infrastructure for water storage and delivery, and powerful federal bureaucracies and giant construction corporations that now characterize Western water development. Nevertheless, the Colorado River, the liquid heart of the West, was dammed in his name.

The construction of dams and reservoirs along the Colorado took place over three decades, from the completion of the Hoover Dam in 1936 to the completion of the Glen Canyon Dam in 1963. Those dams could be thought of as monumental parentheses enclosing America's era of big-dam building, which plugged every major river in America several times over. Hoover Dam and the Grand Coulee Dam on the mighty Columbia River, finished in 1941, also launched an engineering regime that aimed taxpayer-funded technology at wild water. The Glen

Canyon Dam was one of the last grand dams. By then, damming had become a big business that would eventually be exported with a vengeance to rivers in developing nations across the globe.

We went from one extreme to the other. First we put more farmers on the land than the available water could support, if the farmers used the water-intensive practices they carried with them from the East and Europe. Then we developed so much of the land's water that it could be wasted without consequence, at least for a while. Although our responses to Western aridity have varied widely over time and seem contradictory, they may simply indicate that our misunderstandings are complete. We still think we can implement strategies to compensate for, or even overcome, the one central and defining characteristic of American deserts—their dryness. Dry climates make for dry biospheres. Dry biospheres do not readily accommodate subdivisions of Kentucky bluegrass lawns, golf courses, coal slurries, cows and their alfalfa, and countless canals and big pipelines. We drowned Eden to make that happen.

By 1963, water was deepening behind the tall walls of the big dam on the Colorado that was begun in 1959. The wild and muddy river was stopped in its tracks. It ran cold and clear where it emerged below the dam. The side canyons of Glen Canyon began to fill. In 1966, after so many life-affirming adventures in its arms, Katie Lee took one last trip to embrace Glen Canyon as the waters of the Colorado gathered behind the newest dam and covered her beloved canyons. "I won't watch you die," she thought.[2] She turned her back, walked away, and didn't return for more than thirty years.

"Glen Canyon saved my life," Katie Lee told me, "and then it broke my heart." She never stopped mourning her loss. Then she met Rich Ingebretsen.

THREE

Dammed If You Do, Damned If You Don't:
Dominy vs. Brower

To Katie Lee and the river runners, Floyd Dominy was evil incarnate. Dominy wanted to cage and control the wild beauty they loved. He was a powerful, clever, and relentless foe. But Katie and her river-hugging compatriots were out of step with the rest of the country. To most Americans who had heard of him, Floyd Dominy was a hero—cantankerous, perhaps, but much admired.

The loud, animated, cigar-chomping champ who personified the dam-building era and called himself the messiah of water development grew up on the arid plains of Hastings, Nebraska, in the early 1900s. He was raised in an environment where the capricious weather, in the form of droughts, blizzards, hailstorms, and tornadoes, is impressively threatening.

Floyd Dominy detested the anarchy of nature and went to college to learn how to engineer it into submission. Though he was mechanically gifted, he grew bored with engineering and ended up an economics major at the University of Wyoming, where he became the hard-charging captain of the hockey team. After college he tried his hand at teaching but, as he later told journalist Ken Verdoia in an interview for Utah television, "I didn't have the patience to be a good teacher."[1]

His true calling was just around the corner. As the Great Depression settled across the country, a severe drought sucked the western plains dry. Massive dust storms roiled across this vast surface, lifting away precious topsoil and setting off the Okie migration depicted in John Steinbeck's *The Grapes of Wrath*. Dominy was hired to work as an agricultural agent in Campbell County, Wyoming, where cattle with black tongues and protruding ribs were wandering through the dust of burnt-out range-land, across abandoned homesteads and the graves of buffalo hunters.

Farmers were desperate, and Dominy was touched by their struggle against overwhelming odds. He rolled up his sleeves, cocked his white Stetson, and got going. In four years, from 1933 to 1937, he oversaw the construction of hundreds of dams—mostly creek stoppers and wash in-ternments designed to slow intermittent storm-water runoff for thirsty cows, but a Herculean task nonetheless. And it worked—he freckled the dry land with ponds where cattle could sip and low.

Power and prestige followed success. From Soda Wells to Wildcat and Recluse, he was, in his own words, "king of the goddamned coun-try" at the tender age of twenty-four.[2] No one got in his way, and he had no tolerance for "pettifogging minutiae" like regulations and inspec-tions. His Wyoming performance made him more than a local hero—his reputation as a dam-building whiz reached all the way to Washing-ton, D.C.

When the dams were completed, Dominy took his family to see the Rose Bowl Parade in Pasadena, stopping to see the Hoover Dam along the way. "I was highly impressed," he told Verdoia, "that anybody could build such a magnificent structure and make it work. I never dreamed I would someday be in charge of operating that dam." But that honor lay in the future. He was next asked by the Roosevelt administration to build farms in the South Pacific to feed soldiers during World War II. He tackled those projects with his usual self-assured drive and suc-ceeded again and again.

After the war, he took his can-do zeal to the Bureau of Reclamation so he could plan and build dams, his highest calling. Brash, bright, and both funny and intimidating, Dominy rose rapidly through the ranks from dirt sampler to assistant commissioner. He could dazzle and charm an audience one moment and terrorize his employees the next. He was a master organizer who was cunning, clever, and mean.[3] In 1959 he knocked his predecessor aside and became director, then built a bureaucratic empire. Like Powell, Dominy could be called a visionary. But his vision—of a West where every river was tapped and plumbed—was heroic, not humble. His projects were technologically daring and politically compelling because they provided contracts, profits, and power.

During the 1950s, Congressmen Wayne Aspinall of Colorado and Carl Hayden of Arizona were his allies, and for good reasons. First, Colorado and Arizona were thirsty and competing for the West's limited water resources. The control of where dams went and who got the water were intimately linked. Both politicians were senior members of Congress who had risen to powerful positions, Aspinall as chair of the House Interior Committee and Hayden as chair of the Senate Appropriations Committee. With their support, Dominy could defy the presidency itself if he had to. Presidents come and go, Dominy realized, but plutocrats live on. And the language of Western plutocrats was water, in which Dominy was fluent.

Although most Westerners have never heard of the Colorado River Compact, it may be the real mortar that holds the Glen Canyon Dam in place. The compact is an agreement among the seven states that comprise the Colorado River Basin—California, Colorado, Nevada, Arizona, New Mexico, Wyoming, and Utah—about how to divide the river's water. The catalyst for the compact was California's explosive growth in the early 1900s. The neighboring basin states were alarmed at how Los Angeles and its rich allies were conquering, colonizing, and controlling every watershed they could reach with aqueducts and canals as they outgrew locally available water resources.

The laws governing water rights were based on a simple premise that did not encourage wise and prudent use: water belonged to whoever swallowed it first. Clearly, California had an insatiable thirst and the money and expertise to slake it, while the other states were sparsely populated, poor, and underdeveloped. However, the combined congressional delegations of the basin's poor-cousin states of Utah, Arizona, Nevada, and Wyoming did give them a kind of political equity and the means to challenge California's ecological imperialism. Like it or not, California had to deal with its country-mouse neighbors.

In 1922, then Secretary of Commerce Herbert Hoover brought the basin states together, and they hammered out a compact. In the long tradition of dividing ecosystems and watersheds to conform to political jurisdictions and needs, the Colorado River Basin was artificially divided in two. The lion's share of the water for the river and its tributaries originated in the snowpack of the majestic mountain ridges of Colorado, Utah, and Wyoming, with smaller contributions made by the uplands of New Mexico and Arizona.

Under the compact, the mountainous "upper basin" states—Utah, Colorado, Wyoming, and New Mexico—would be entitled to only about half of the estimated water, despite their enormous contribution. They would have to divide their portion among themselves. Almost all of the remaining water would go to the "lower basin" states, primarily California, since they were the only states growing so fast that their local watersheds were already getting tapped out. To sweeten the deal for the eight-hundred-pound gorilla in the group, California was also promised any water committed to but unused by its underdeveloped partners.

The small share remaining would go to poor Mexico, waiting by the spigot at the end of the line. Eventually, the dams built under the compact deprived Mexico of even the rich silt that once fed the wetlands and farms of its Colorado River Delta, turning that lush oasis of biodiversity into barren hardpan. But this would take decades to happen, and then longer to acknowledge. After canoeing through the delta in 1922, Aldo Leopold described it as a "milk and honey wilderness" of "a hundred green lagoons" that may have been the most biologically diverse ecosystem on the planet.[4] Today, forty years after the last dam generated by the Colorado River Compact was completed, the delta has suffered a biological holocaust and all of the delta's Mexican farmers are gone, many having fled north across the border.

The Cocopa tribe, which called the delta home and built its culture in mindful relationship with its ecosystem, is fading away, just as the species that evolved there and sustained the tribe have faded away before them. What good is knowledge of a local ecosystem if it has been destroyed? The shredding of Cocopa culture in the deleted delta was an early example of the loss of cultural diversity that so often accompanies the loss of biodiversity: big dams not only wipe out habitat but displace the indigenous people who live within it.

Once the Colorado Compact deal was done, each state delegation had to go home and sell it to its legislature and governor. This proved to be difficult but largely doable. Arizona, however, resisted. The other states decided to go ahead without her. At one point emotions ran so high that Arizona sent an armed militia, laughingly dubbed "the Arizona navy," to the river. Eventually the state realized it could not hold out alone and signed on the dotted line.

Once nature's watery spoils were divided, the mechanics of appropriation had to be designed. The federal agency that would do this was the Bureau of Reclamation, created by the Reclamation Act of 1902. The Reclamation Act was the congressional response to decades of drought on Western lands, the failure of speculative local irrigation companies to cope with Western aridity, and the failure of privately built dams, like the one that collapsed above Johnstown, Pennsylvania, in 1889, killing 2,000 people.

Settlers were fleeing the dusty West, parched cows were dropping dead in droves, and out-of-work cowboys like Butch Cassidy were robbing trains. The federal government came to the rescue in what some argue was the first national experiment with welfare. The bureau would apply the best irrigation methods known, borrowing heavily from the expertise of the Mormon settlers, who had built a green city on a dry plain in the Salt Lake Valley. The need for electricity to fuel development in the rural West added considerably to the incentives for building dams, since they were a "twofer"—dams could help bring irrigation water to parched soil as well as light cities and power factories.

Humans are probably hard-wired to hack and hammer; even the Anasazi tried a rude dam or two. Civilizations are certainly organized to measure, legislate, budget, and build. The Colorado had an unpredictable flow that would be challenging to measure and meter. Government geologists had dreamed of taming the chaotic river for years and had scoped out a few possible sites for a giant dam that could do the job. The site had to be narrow, steep, and solid, according to the parameters the fieldworkers carried as they poked around, looking for just the place to chain the beast. Tall dams were also better for making hydroelectric power on a large scale.

The Glen Canyon Dam site was an early contender but was eventually judged too far away from roads and potential water and electricity users. Instead, Boulder Canyon was selected for the epic construction project, which created the Lake Mead reservoir as well as "Boulder Dam"—soon renamed Hoover Dam, after the man who had brokered the Colorado Compact and served as president during the dam's construction. The project was the largest public works project of the Depression era, a colossal engineering feat celebrated in a Woody Guthrie folk song and often compared to the building of the pyramids. Nobody had thought a dam so big was physically possible.

Hoover Dam's boosters credited it with mythic accomplishments. Who could argue with a public works project that gave gainful employment to thousands of hungry laborers, brought life-giving waters to millions in the parched American interior, and produced electricity to boot? Several monster-sized construction companies, including Morrison Knudsen, Kaiser, and Bechtel, were also created in the process. The Bureau of Reclamation, given broad powers and lucrative contracts to disperse, became a bureaucratic empire that would go on to build hundreds of dams, lay thousands of miles of pipeline, and scoop out canals galore. It was aided and abetted by scores of local water districts, almost always governed by political appointees who were unaudited and unaccountable, and who learned well how to grow fat on water-project contracts.

After the completion of Hoover Dam and the Lake Mead reservoir on the Colorado River where it spilled from the Grand Canyon into Nevada, it was the upper basin's turn. The compact had given the upper basin states some security, but when California's boom resumed after World War II and the city of Phoenix quadrupled in size as well, the upper basin states expressed understandable concern that folks in California and Arizona were getting into the habit of using water that was supposed to eventually go to them.

Their fears were compounded by the realization that there was not as much river water available as originally assumed when the compact was negotiated. They had divided up water they wouldn't have. Under the terms of the compact, the upper basin states had to guarantee delivery of 75 million acre-feet of water to the lower basin states in any rolling ten-year period. Unfortunately, the erratic seasonal pulse of the Colorado River is an echo of its longer pattern of cycles: there are wet years and dry.

Floyd Dominy and his Bureau of Reclamation, however, had a plan to thwart nature. In order to allow for drought years and still have enough water to meet upper basin needs while sending a guaranteed volume to the partners downstream, they argued, the upper basin needed storage capacity. Dominy convinced the lower basin states that they also had a stake in building more dams. After all, it is good business to help those who owe you to stay solvent.

In the early 1950s, the Bureau of Reclamation fine-tuned a plan called the Colorado River Storage Project, which expressed the vast scale of its power, influence, and hubris. Four dams and reservoirs would be raised—one at Bridge Canyon on the Colorado just downriver from Grand Canyon National Monument; one above Lees Ferry in Glen Canyon; one on the Green River at Flaming Gorge, by the Utah–Wyoming border; and another on the Green River, in Dinosaur National Monument's Echo Park. The dam in Echo Park would straddle Whirlpool Canyon, named by Powell on his famous trip.

The entire Colorado River drainage would be plumbed and regulated. Fortunes would be built, of course, and careers made. There would be winners and losers. That's the way it is when you make progress, harness nature, build and expand. Few doubted. Civilization and wealth, we told ourselves, were impossible in the American West without water development and electricity.

We somehow did not understand that there are limits to how far you can engineer your way around aridity. Water development has stimulated growth that we now understand may not be sustainable. Western droughts, especially in an era of global climate change, may be more persistent and intense than we anticipated. As Western watersheds have been plumbed and mined, whole ecosystems have been shredded, from the salmon-rich river systems of the Northwest to the Colorado River Delta in Mexico. A day of reckoning seems to be close at hand. But in the heady days of dam building, those who did express doubt and challenge the prevailing view were pushed aside by those chasing contracts with big bucks.

At the time, there was no National Environmental Policy Act to require a scientific assessment of the environmental impacts of building dams. "We would not be allowed to build Glen Canyon Dam today," says dam critic Rich Ingebretsen, a point that ardent dam proponents also make to support their case that current environmental policies are too onerous. The public consensus then did not question the necessity and benefits of damming rivers. As Dominy told Verdoia, "There were no naysayers in those days. Everyone thought that managing water was desirable and it was in the public interest. And we didn't have lint pickers behind every bush."

By the mid-1950s, the lint pickers were just over the horizon. Although there was no environmental movement per se, David Brower, who would go on to become the legendary "archdruid" of that movement as director of the burgeoning Sierra Club, went ballistic. In its earliest days, when it was still a genteel hiking club, the Sierra Club had been badly scarred by the loss of a battle over the drowning by dam of an idyllic alpine valley in Yosemite National Park. In 1917 the Hetch Hetchy Dam was constructed, over the strenuous objections of the club's avid campers, to slake San Francisco's thirst.

Brower had camped below Hetch Hetchy as a boy. He had heard the story of the club's battle to save Yosemite's twin and how the loss had broken John Muir's heart. Muir, the world-famous naturalist and a spiritual grandfather of the modern conservation movement, died a year after the U.S. Senate passed a bill separating Hetch Hetchy from Yosemite, thus damning it to be dammed. After the Hetch Hetchy controversy the feds had promised that they would never flood another national park or monument, but here they were again, endangering both Grand Canyon and Dinosaur National Monument. Brower felt betrayed. He had seen Echo Park and loved it.

The political battle over Echo Park was a preview of how modern conservation struggles would be waged. Brower and his allies discovered the power of publicizing the issue in the national media, generating thousands of letters to Congress to support the club's diligent lobbying efforts.

As a famous alpine rock climber and Sierra peak bagger in his youth, Brower was oriented toward mountain terrain. He had not seen Glen Canyon and was generally unfamiliar with and unappreciative of desert wilderness. During negotiations over the Colorado River Storage Project, Dominy protested that the loss of stored water behind the proposed Echo Park dam would have to be compensated for elsewhere if the project was to meet its water storage goals. Why not build the proposed

Glen Canyon Dam thirty-five feet higher, Brower suggested. In the fall of 1955 as the debate developed, Harold Bradley, president of the Sierra Club's board, did raft down the "unknown" Glen Canyon. He was moved and impressed by what he saw there but concluded, "I feel content to see Glen Canyon go under."[5]

After a protracted battle, a compromise was reached. Dams would go up in Flaming Gorge and Glen Canyon, but the Grand Canyon and Dinosaur national monuments would be spared. Later, as the massive dam in Glen Canyon was being built, David Brower floated down through the area's pristine canyons and experienced firsthand what had been, more or less, traded away in the bargain. Heartsick at what would be lost, he launched a last-ditch effort to spare Glen Canyon—despite the fact that the dam was on its way up and the feds seemed unlikely to abandon their investment.

Brower commissioned a book from Sierra Club board member and photographer Eliot Porter—*The Place That No One Knew,* a visually eloquent attempt to communicate to America what was at stake. It would become a model for the many coffee-table tomes honoring wild places that the Sierra Club and other conservation groups would use in later years to publicize their causes. The battle over Echo Park and Dinosaur National Monument also taught Brower how to tap Americans' love of their scenic treasures and generate public support for conservation. The reserved alpine mountain climber became a master of the sound bite. Common sense, Brower proclaimed, tells us to "walk around our gardens and not trample over them."[6]

The struggle between Brower's Sierra Club and Dominy's Bureau of Reclamation was a quest for hearts and minds. Competing visions were compellingly drawn. A famous full-page Sierra Club ad in the *New York Times* asked if it made sense to flood the Sistine Chapel to get a better look at the paintings on the ceiling.[7] This was a response to Dominy's argument that more people would get to see the marvelous canyon walls up close if they could float in on boats rather than run rapids or hike. The ad infuriated Dominy, who regarded it as misleading since it implied that the whole canyon would be filled. In the *San Francisco Chronicle,* Brower charged that "the Bureau of Reclamation is determined to make the Colorado River a place for Paul Bunyan on water skis and have a good time just going from dam to dam."[8] Dominy, in turn, speculated that 3 million people a year would eventually visit the lake, a seemingly Bunyanesque prediction that actually turned out to be correct.

The Bureau of Reclamation made its own attempt at winning the propaganda war by publishing *Jewel of the Colorado*. Its introduction neatly summed up Dominy & Co.'s worldview, the traditional one that shaped Western civilization: "There is a natural order in our Universe. God created both man and nature. And man serves God. But nature serves man. To have a deep blue lake where no lake was before seems to bring man closer to God." Besides, fumed Dominy later to Verdoia, he was just drowning a "few rattlesnakes and prairie dogs."[9]

In the end, Glen Canyon was sacrificed to block dams in Dinosaur National Monument and the Grand Canyon. Brower's complicity in the loss of Glen Canyon would haunt him for the rest of his days. In the battles over dams along the muddy Colorado, however, the Sierra Club became a powerful, modern environmental organization, an effective campaigner for the wilderness and environmental legislation of the 1960s and 1970s that has profoundly altered public consciousness and collective behaviors. In the process it was labeled a lobbying organization and lost its tax-exempt status, a blow that also propelled it beyond its former hesitance to engage directly in the political arena. Thus the modern conservation movement was born in the desert.

Brower's loss was Floyd Dominy's gain. Dominy had wanted more dams than he got, and he fumed at his opposition for thwarting his bureau's more grandiose plans for turning the Grand Canyon into a reservoir, but the massive dam at Glen Canyon, finally authorized in 1956, would be his baby. A dubious second act, according to its critics, the dam was proudly received by the Western political and economic establishment as one more heroic and progressive achievement—the right and necessary thing to do. But not easy.

First, there was the isolation. Not only was there no road into the site that could accommodate heavy equipment, but there was also no staging area. The little settlement of Page, Arizona, was selected for that honor and grew by several thousand house trailers overnight. Everything from groceries to church services was delivered out of big tin sheds. Food shortages were common, as the delivery routes into town were not well established or reliable. People who visited cities on weekend trips carried long lists of supplies needed by friends and neighbors. Workers were paid extra for their hardships.

Building Glen Canyon Dam was dangerous work. Workers dangled over steep cliffs on thin lines. At the end of their shifts, they jumped into nets spread below them, then crawled up the sides of the nets and out. Seventeen workers died in various construction accidents, and 365 were injured.[10] In all, the dam used 10 million tons of cement,[11] delivered continually in shifts day and night. The intense summer heat, which reached 104 degrees in the shade, required the construction of the nation's largest ice plant so that ice could be mixed into the concrete as it was poured to keep it from baking prematurely. Construction was halted for six months in 1959 when the construction company, worried that they had underbid the project and would lose money, decided that the town of Page had progressed to the point that hardship pay was no longer necessary. Workers disagreed and went on strike. By the time a settlement was reached, many workers had pulled up stakes and abandoned Page altogether, and a new workforce had to be recruited.

Despite hardship and setbacks, the massive engineering project was completed. Lady Bird Johnson cut the ribbon on the dam in 1966. To the surprise of the assembled crowd, Dominy revealed that Brower was in attendance and that the two were about to embark on a trip by boat down the lake, arranged by author John McPhee, who wanted to observe and record their encounter. The two had been adversaries for so long, debating each other at various hearings, that they had developed a grudging respect for and interest in each other.

The trip was an intense encounter, though. Brower and Dominy alternately made nice and tore each other up. Brower couldn't accept that the new "lake," as admittedly beautiful as he found it to be, was an improvement over the peaceful Glen Canyon it covered. Dominy fumed that he was a "bigger environmentalist" than Brower because "I've changed the environment, yes, but I've changed it for the benefit of man!" It was all moot anyway, Dominy concluded as he calmed down, because there would be no more big dams. Not needed, he told Brower; atomic power would now be harnessed to meet the nation's energy needs. With most of the West's water already impounded for development and dams no longer needed to generate power, the American era of big-dam building was over.[12]

Katie Lee wrote protest songs lamenting the drowning of her beloved canyons and then retreated to California and New York City to sing in coffeehouses. She still performs "The Wreck-the-Nation Bureau Song," her take on Dominy and the Bureau of Reclamation. "They didn't reclaim anything," she tells her audiences. "They revise, redo, retard, repress, replace, and reduce, but they don't reclaim."

On the liner notes of her CD, *Glen Canyon River Journeys,* Katie Lee articulated the humble side of the competing visions represented by Floyd Dominy, the arch-engineer, and David Brower, the archdruid. Glen Canyon, she wrote, "taught me about intimacy and the value of observation. Together, they resurrected my spirit with their beauty and taught me that time is not my enemy. The Glen gave me roots as tenacious as the willows along its banks."

As the waters behind the dam spread upstream, filling whole canyons, a Cub Scout named Rich Ingebretsen took a ski boat across the new Lake Powell and peered into the water beneath him. He was looking for the canyons he had visited a couple of years earlier on a hike to Rainbow Bridge. He remembered the music of the birds that filled the green shadows. His eyes strained, to no avail. The dark waters were unyielding.

FOUR

Faux Flood: Diverting Disaster by Inviting Chaos

Three generations of my uncle's family visited us from Louisiana over Christmas in 1982. Accustomed to a climate that encourages crayfish, magnolias, water moccasins, and mint juleps, they hoped to see snow— maybe slide down it on a sled or even try skis. Catch it on the tip of a tongue.

It began snowing the day they arrived in Salt Lake City, and it never stopped. Big fat feathery flakes filled the air, drifted about, and floated down for days on end. A record depth of snow accumulated, burying cars and shrubbery until they resembled a herd of giant marshmallows nosing through a landscape of half moons. I had to enlist a neighbor to drive my cousins' rental car from the airport to my home for them, as they had as much experience driving on Utah snowpack as I had wrestling with bayou alligators. In fact, they couldn't navigate the blizzard well enough to get to the motel a few miles away, so we put them up at our house.

The roads to the ski resorts were closed by avalanches, but my cousins didn't care. They were experiencing a "forty-year storm" and were content to walk around in the quiet splendor of falling snow, admiring the flocked trees and taking photos of the chaotic pile of boots sloped against our back-door wall, a talus slope of unfamiliar footwear. "Wait 'til they see this in Baton Rouge. . . . " To my swampland cousins, mittens were as exotic and intriguing as a ceiling fan over a veranda would be to an Eskimo, and catching Utah powder in the act was akin to seeing a pride of lions basking on the sun-drenched Serengeti plain.

For a week in December, Rocky Mountain clichés paraded before them in a postcard version of Utah in winter. As is the case in all blizzards, the zen-like moments were occasionally interrupted by pratfalls, and I felt fortunate that they survived their visit with only a few bruises.

That storm was the grandest of the winter, but there were many others, with the snowy season continuing well into the spring. Then, in June, the way it often does in Utah, the weather went from a cold, wet spring to a hot, dry summer overnight, as if some mischievous sky gnome had thrown a switch. The bright heat beat down on that empire of snow and soon turned it into silver threads of water escaping high altitudes. Icy streams boiled over their banks, rivers flooded, and farmlands became reflecting pools. South of Stockton, Utah, a little seasonal pond became Rush Lake and drowned the Hogan Ranch so thoroughly that for twenty years afterward, where Mr. Hogan's cows had once grazed, cranes and pelicans perched on rusting strands of barbed wire sagging above grassy expanses of shallow water.

Most of the unusually deep mountain snowpack that year melted down in just two weeks. Roads were cut off by rising waters. Across the state, sandbagging brigades were organized by Mormon Church leaders to save property from raging waters. Sandbags along State Street in Salt Lake City channeled floodwaters through the city. One enterprising soul caught a trout in the middle of town. In that spring of 1983, the double-sized runoff from the enormous area drained by the Colorado made its way to the lowest groove in the landscape, the river itself.

The Glen Canyon Dam has a unique system to deal with runoff. Instead of allowing waters to spill directly over the lip of the dam, as many smaller dams are designed to do, or around the dam's shoulders, Glen Canyon Dam diverts rising waters into tunnels that have been dug through the sandstone at the base of the dam. Tunnels were originally built to divert the fast waters of the Colorado away from workers and equipment so construction could proceed on dry ground. When the dam was completed, the diversion tunnels themselves were plugged, but a system of tunnels with intakes that opened upstream from the dam, designed for weather-related diversions, was opened.

Normally, every gallon of water that is spilled back into the river is used to turn massive $200 million turbines that produce electricity. Moving water is money. In June 1983, however, the diversion tunnels had to be enlisted for the first time in a desperate effort to divert the swelling floodwaters entering the river and reservoir. At first, all went as planned. Then, on June 6, workers inside the dam complex heard ominous rumbling noises and felt tremors and vibrations. The concrete giant was moaning and groaning.

Once they looked downstream, their fear became palpable. The mouths of the diversion tunnels on the other side of the dam were regurgitating huge pieces of chewed-up concrete, shredded bits of steel rebar, and red bedrock. The rushing Colorado was digging itself a new path under the dam. If this kept happening, the undermined dam could collapse. Such a catastrophic failure could in turn overwhelm Hoover Dam downstream, setting loose 100 million acre-feet of water altogether—the equivalent of ten straight years of Colorado River flows. Imagine an inland tsunami.

If enough water escaped at once, a domino effect could collapse downstream dams at Davis, Parker, Headgate Rock, Palo Verde, Imperial, Laguna, and Moreles. California could be hit with a flood of biblical proportion that not only would tear out a century's worth of infrastructure, but would likely carve southern California's geology into a radically new pattern.

The prospect of losing the technological jewel of the Colorado suddenly seemed real. The catastrophic failure of the Teton Dam in Idaho several years before made it easier to consider as a serious possibility. The Teton had filled too fast, and rising waters pushed through the canyon walls that abutted the dam and then dissolved a third of the dam itself. A torrent of water twenty-stories high crashed through three small towns downstream. Most of the residents fled in time, but fourteen were killed, 4,000 homes and 350 businesses were damaged or destroyed, and the topsoil from thousands of acres of farmland was scoured away.

If history were to repeat itself here on a grander scale, the sediment-starved Colorado River Delta in Mexico might be replenished in the blink of a geological eye. Or maybe the river would escape its banks the way it had in 1905 and 1907, re-creating an inland Salton Sea. Or maybe it would find a whole new route to the sea. The Glen Canyon engineers, a bunch of dam boosters if ever there was one, were not about to find out. The pride of their profession was on the line. Their careers too, of course.

After shutting down the diversion system to make inspections, they discovered that the waters rushing down through the diversion system were eating out massive sections of stone where the downward tunnels from upstream diversion gates elbowed into the tunnels that went out and around the center of the dam. Shutting down the diversion system meant that the reservoir would rise faster behind the dam, threatening to eventually overflow the giant wall and wipe out the power plant that lay below the dam on its dry side. They had to find that delicate balance on the edge of chaos, letting out enough water one way or the other to keep the dam from being overwhelmed, but not so much that the river waters chewed their way through the diversion tunnels and then under or around the dam.

For most of the month of June, engineers and workers experimented, jury-rigged, guessed, argued, hoped, and, above all, prayed. Every day there was a crisis. At one point the height of the dam was extended with plywood barriers, just in case. By the end of the month the reservoir had peaked and stabilized, just seven feet from the top of the dam. An initial inspection of the diversion tunnels revealed massive cavitation. One cavity measured 36 feet deep and 150 feet long, and extended 10 feet wider than the tunnel itself.[1]

The damage done that spring—the enormous cavities washed out along the diversion tunnel elbows, the gouges in bedrock, the steel rebar and concrete spat out—is not well known and certainly not well publicized. The fact is, a massive icon of engineering prowess, often called one of the engineering wonders of the world, almost went down.

The floods of '83 were a humbling wake-up call. The possibility that the Colorado could dig a hole under the Glen Canyon Dam or that the dam itself could fail remained remote, but the enormous consequences if it did fail had been brought to public awareness. The permanence of the dam was no longer assumed within or outside of the Bureau of Reclamation, which operated it.

Had the dam retained its invincible reputation, Rich Ingebretsen might be quietly practicing medicine in Salt Lake City. Dave Wegner might have retired and relaxed. But that was not to be.

Dave Wegner had worked for the Department of Interior for twenty-one years, mostly for the Bureau of Reclamation, the agency that manages dams. He was a scientist by training, and his specialty became the habitat and ecosystem of the Grand Canyon, about fifty miles downstream of the Glen Canyon Dam. Over the years he and his colleagues had the chance to observe and record how the native species of the Grand Canyon were disappearing and being replaced.

Native species were adapted to an environment shaped by the warm water, rich in sediments and nutrients, carried by the muddy Colorado and its tributaries. But that muddy formative brew had been replaced by water that became cold and clean as it dropped its load of silt in still water and was chilled in the reservoir's depths. The water's change in content and temperature affected everything in its path. Silty water, for example, called forth native humpback chubs, while clear cold water allowed stocked trout to thrive. But the absence of floods was also important.

Wegner is a flash-flood junkie. "Floods shape and define the habitat," he explains. "We call them natural disturbances, but they are an ecological process that is key to making habitats downstream, building up beaches and sandbars that create niches for a variety of species, especially native fish. When the floods went away, so did beaches. Pools and backwaters along the river disappeared. With no floods to remove them, tamarisks and other vegetation took hold and crowded in. That ecosystem needs floods, and it hasn't been getting them since the dam went up."

Floods happen. They've been going on for millions of years. Ocean waters evaporate and rise into clouds. Clouds are pushed landward by wind currents until they pile up against inland mountain ranges that milk their moisture. Snowmelt and rainfall descend mountain slopes in rivulets that braid into streams that also weave together until they reach those low paths of least resistance where they crescendo into rivers. The rivers carry nutrients and soil, and deposit them on alluvial plains as they head toward birdfoot deltas. Along the way they flush marshes and other wetlands. They recharge aquifers and watersheds while providing wet habitat, food, sheltering banks, and transportation for myriad birds, reptiles, fish, animals, insects, and so much microscopic flora and fauna that we have identified only a fraction of them. When river waters eventually reach the sea, the cycle begins again.

Rivers are the arterial networks for a global hydrologic system that nourishes life's diversity and makes the planet inhabitable. They even pulse the way arteries do, rising and falling according to the time of day, the amount of sunlight on feeding snowfields, and the seasons. They become thin with drought and fat after storms. What we call a river is not a thing but a living process. Water animates evolution, food chains, and climate. Gaia is one wet woman. Since rivers carry her lifeblood, the introduction of 40,000 human-made aneurysms along such a key fluid medium must have consequences, and some of those are now apparent.

"Are all dams bad?" I ask.

"No, not at all," is his answer, "but rivers have needs and the land has needs, too, for water. We didn't consider those needs when we built so many dams, and we need to go back now and take a hard look." During our dam-building boom in the first half of the twentieth century we saw inconvenience and waste in wild water, in contrast with the advantages of dams, which provided electricity, recreation, and irrigation.

Now the downside is known. Dams obstruct fish migration and hold back the silt, gravel, debris, and nutrients that create healthy habitats downstream for plants, insects, fish, animals, and birds. They disrupt the interaction between a river and its banks, further skewing habitat. They alter the balance between surface and ground water. Ecological costs, like lost fisheries, have economic costs, too.

Ironically, a decade after spring floods almost took out Floyd Dominy's proud dam, a debate raged within the Bureau of Reclamation about the need to create floods through the Grand Canyon, the very thing that the Glen Canyon Dam was designed to suppress. Scientists from the National Academy of Sciences eventually supported Wegner and his colleagues, who were studying how new management practices could become more environmentally friendly. Instead of regulating the flow of water through the dam and down the Colorado according to the needs of the hydroelectric operators, they suggested, why not try to imitate nature's floods? Although 90 percent of the sediment load carried down the river was dropped in the reservoir behind the dam, some sediments accumulated, they reasoned, deep in the river's channels. A sudden and prolonged release of large volumes of water might churn that sand and silt to create more of the beaches that had been disappearing. The stands of invasive tamarisks that crowded the banks might be torn loose and eventually replaced by native willows.

In March 1996, under a growing chorus of criticism both from conservationists outside the government and from its own scientists such as Dave Wegner, the Glen Canyon operators agreed to make an experimental flood. Television crews were on hand to witness the event. For two weeks, high water was released down the river. When the spigots were turned off, sure enough, new beaches could be seen. Secretary of the Interior Bruce Babbitt stood before a bank of microphones and cameras to declare the $1.5 million, 100-billion-gallon experiment a success. River management could be adapted to fit the need of the river and its ecosystem.

Not so fast. Adaptive management's success was short-lived, if not illusory. "The man-made flood of '96 was missing some key elements," Wegner says. "There is a whole array of integrated effects you get from a natural flood that weren't in the artificial flood. Timing and temperature are important—how and when the waters rise and fall—because temperatures vary seasonally." A natural flood, he goes on to explain, is not just a gush of water that scours sand up from one end of the canyon and pushes it downstream. It is, rather, a subtle wet weave of sediments, nutrients, and temperature that crests and ebbs according to the ancient and elemental rhythm of rain sweeping across a whole landscape. In Wegner's view, what was set loose from the big dam was an ill-contrived, one-dimensional imitation primarily aimed at enhancing a recreational use. "Of course, what the public sees and wants are beaches to camp on when they run the river. Temporarily, we did get some beaches."

In 2002, when I interviewed Wegner, the bureau was planning to do another experimental flood. They would time the flood for the late fall, when the sediments from the flash floods of late summer and early fall, which enter the river below the dam, are still in the river channel. They hoped that those sediments will be churned up and form beaches that will last longer and be more viable habitat than those in the earlier experiment. After a century of learning how to build bigger and stronger dams, the Bureau of Reclamation is now trying to simulate the very geological and ecological processes that its dams short-circuited. The results, so far, are not promising.

Wegner is skeptical about whether the latest variation on the artificial flood experiment will work, unless the bureau's engineers can "add value" to the flood by including sediments and nutrients or changing the temperature of the floodwater. These are dubious possibilities. In fact, since the failure of the 1996 floods became apparent, other schemes to mitigate the dam's negative effects on the river habitat's living systems have been proposed. One option being explored is the construction of a two-hundred-mile-long slurry from one end of Lake Powell, where sediments accumulate, to the other side of the dam, where the sediment-starved river begins its journey through the Grand Canyon. The slurry project would be very expensive for taxpayers but lucrative for construction companies. "At least they can say they are doing something, and that may be why they are doing it," Wegner says. "But we know now that, yes, you can move sand around, but you cannot imitate a flash flood.

"The 1996 flood got a lot of publicity, and it was mostly described as a success," he continues. "But we followed up on it. By September, 85 percent of the beaches that had been created in March were gone. The flood was an exceedingly successful experiment in that we could learn from it, but it didn't do much for the canyon habitat. It failed to make a difference." Wegner was not shy about his scientific conclusions, but he is coy about what happened next. He admits that the bureau was not happy when the shortcomings of its experiment were underlined, but calls his decision to leave a mutual one. It was, he says, "time for me to move on." Of course, one man's "move on" is another's "get out of the way." Other scientists who concluded the artificial flood was a failure were also pushed aside. After the study of the flood's aftermath was complete, a fresh batch of scientists from other agencies was brought in, and Wegner was out the door.

It had been a long haul. Wegner's career had begun in the 1970s, about the same time that the National Environmental Policy Act was passed. Because it required assessment and documentation of environmental impacts as part of a public decision-making process, NEPA's potential power to alter development agendas was huge. At first, though, little changed. It took the courts many years to decide what the two-page law meant. Many destructive projects were still built after it was passed, because implementation of its provisions was uneven and often halfhearted. Also, to implement it, an entire management infrastructure had to be created and then refined.

But critics of the Glen Canyon Dam argue that if it and other big dams had been proposed after NEPA requirements became law, they most likely couldn't have been built. Both dam critics and NEPA critics like to point this out. Either way, the Bureau of Reclamation was not an agency that welcomed potentially career-stopping new rules and priorities.

Wegner looked around and chose to go to work for the Bureau of Reclamation. "I decided to work in agencies that were having the biggest effect on the environment, and the Bureau of Reclamation was the key agency for rivers in the West," he said. "So I made a conscious decision to work there, realizing that I would be working in a society of strict engineers who have a definitive way of doing business and that understanding the environment has not been their calling card."

His role, he felt, was to challenge questionable assumptions, suggest alternative perspectives, raise awareness, support compliance with environmental regulations, model more democratic behaviors, and push the gates of power open in a hundred little ways. "I saw the bureau make significant changes over time," he told me. "Those of us inside the organization who wanted change chipped away at the monolith of the bureau, and slowly we got them to accept the environment in their criteria and even as a priority.

"In the early '80s, when we started our environmental studies, Secretary of the Interior James Watt sat me down in his office and said, 'There is no way on God's green earth that we are ever going to change the operations of the Glen Canyon Dam, no way we'll do an environmental assessment of its operation.' He told me, 'Your job is to keep the environmentalists out of my office.' Well, we did do that environmental impact study on the dam, and in '96 we changed the operations for an environmental purpose. Now they're considering decommissioning dams across the land, so that's significant progress. There's room for a lot more change, sure. To their credit," he laughs, "they put up with me for twenty-five years."

Outside the gates and unconstrained by the politics and parameters of the Bureau of Reclamation, Wegner's vision was liberated. "It got me thinking in a deeper philosophical perspective. It was clear that just doing a flood by opening the gates of the dam periodically wasn't going to solve the problem of lost habitat and the extinction of native species. That was a Band-Aid approach. We needed to look from a much more expansive perspective and consider removing the dam. Whether you like that or not is immaterial to me as a scientist. We ought to be open enough to at least study that option, especially now that we are eliminating the artificial flood option. Otherwise, the adaptive management process that is supposed to understand how the river's health can be restored is just going to be a study of the river's death."

Agency studies showed that Lake Powell had reached a volume that was accompanied by a surface area so large that as much or more water was evaporating off the surface and seeping into soft sandstone walls as was running into the reservoir annually. The reservoir, once filled to the brim, became a massive evaporator rather than a collector of river water. An environmental impact study showed other problems. The dam contributed to the salination of soils in the basin, and aggradation of sediments was choking off tributaries, because when running water from those tributaries hit the slackwater of the reservoir, sediment loads dropped out of the moving water. Over time, those dropped-out sediments piled up, creating rapids-killing mini-deltas where the tributaries entered the reservoir-stalled river.

After years of scientifically studying the dam's actual impacts as opposed to its promised results, Wegner found his doubts as hard to contain as a spring flood. He also was no longer constrained in the scope of his study. Just as communities across the nation were opting for dam removal to restore the ecological functions of their watersheds, Wegner had also reached a turning point. Decommissioning was not off-limits now. "In the whole history of the Bureau of Reclamation, we have never looked at the dam and its impacts in the context of the entire Colorado River drainage system, and that is what needs to be done," he says. "We use water very inefficiently. We manage it in ways that encourage waste. No agency has ever looked at the entire picture of water and electricity use in the Colorado River Basin to see the effects of our management on everything from wildlife species in Wyoming to fisheries off the Colorado Delta. That's the context we need to see."

While inside the bureau, Wegner had argued for doing a study that included the option of draining the reservoir. Outside, he was free to hook up with others beyond the agency who were pushing for the one study that had not been done—a thorough look at the costs and benefits of keeping the reservoir versus draining it. In this study, questions about how to replace the electricity the dam produced would also be addressed, along with other practical considerations, but the health of the river ecosystem would be the bottom line.

Wegner was good to go. He fell directly into the arms of Rich Ingebretsen, who had been waiting for him to jump.

FIVE

Flash Forward: The Draining Debate
over Powell's Dead Body

Rich Ingebretsen had a wild idea. He was floating down the Colorado River in a raft when it came to him. He smiles and admits, "The idea was so radical you couldn't even say it." Rich Ingebretsen was going to drain Lake Powell. All two hundred miles of it. The river would run free. Glen Canyon would return.

Rich tells me, in a manner typically devoid of self-promotion, how he "founded" the Glen Canyon Institute while sitting alone with his thoughts in a sunlit raft. It was 1995. "Of course," he adds, "for the first couple of years I was the only member." His isolation didn't bother him. His confidence was complete. Anyone presented with the clear evidence of the case he was constructing would see that the dam was a disastrous mistake. It was just a matter of time.

Rich Ingebretsen has mastered the art of being in two places at once. Not just a professor of physics at the University of Utah but a practicing physician as well, he also finds time for what has become his passion and his torment—challenging fundamental assumptions about water management in the West. The ideas of this soft-spoken doctor strike terror into the hearts of jet-ski dealers and houseboat owners. While other doctors are honing their golf swings, Rich Ingebretsen is planning to drain Lake Powell.

Despite a schedule that would reduce most of us to nervous tics and persistent rashes, Rich seems calm, relaxed, and self-assured. A handsome, clean-cut man who looks younger than his years, Rich looks more like a Mormon bishop than a radical environmentalist. In fact, he is a faithful Latter-day Saint who is also a radical environmentalist, a walking oxymoron. Rich has a friendly, open, almost boyish demeanor that might be mistaken for innocence. In conversation, you don't get the feeling that Rich regards his visionary ideas about draining Powell as extreme at all.

The science, he is convinced and ought to know, is on his side. The implications are obvious for anyone who cares to take a look at the facts. As for the physical practicality and political possibility of actually breaching a world-famous dam, a proud icon of Western progress and a cornerstone of a complicated water compact, Rich is matter-of-fact. "I had thirteen goals when I started the Glen Canyon Institute, and we have accomplished twelve of them," he states plainly. "Draining the lake is the only one unmet. But we have a ten- to fifteen-year plan, and I think we are on schedule."

As far as Rich is concerned, draining the reservoir is simply inevitable. Yes, he admits, he is ahead of the curve on this, but everyone else will eventually catch up. People, after all, are basically good and want to do the right thing when they realize what it is. Sure, it looks as if he's up against overwhelming resistance, "but it's not where we are that matters, but where we are going. Trends are not just important in the stock market or your personal relationships, you know, and there is a huge trend toward restoring ecosystems all over the world."

We are sharing dinner in a restaurant that was recently imported from Chicago to Salt Lake City. There is a lot of meat on the menu, and old sepia photos of men with substantial girths and thick handlebar moustaches on the walls. He suggests we order halibut because it is rich in omega-3 oils that are good for the heart. He's the doctor, so I agree. I've just finished a long day at the nearby Salt Lake City Public Library, where I'm an administrator, and I'm so hungry I could eat upholstery with motor oil. But I'm happy to opt for the halibut and omega-3 oils instead.

Rich has had a lifelong love affair with the canyons that cradled the Colorado River in its sinuous sandstone arms and then trapped the water that gathered behind the big dam that was built when he was just a boy. His Cub Scout troop took a trip to Rainbow Bridge, a graceful and radiant sandstone arch in Glen Canyon. It was love at first sight. Little Rich encountered a Shangri-la of waterfalls, pools, birds, and animals. Sadly, it was a love doomed from the start. Riding across the "fledgling lake," Rich remembers his Scout leader explaining the process that would slowly drown those magical realms. The leader pointed, as leaders do, to the level the new reservoir would reach on distant canyon walls. The logic of water piling up behind massive cement walls until it flooded every side canyon was easy to grasp. Later, camped in a beautiful canyon alcove along the river, the group's leader gestured with a sweeping arm and said, "Next year this will all be underwater."

Rich intuitively understood the immensity of what would happen. The lush grottoes, arches, and ancient Anasazi ruins that Major Powell passed on his epic voyage were disappearing under the deepening waters of the reservoir named for the one-armed Columbus of the canyons. Eventually, after years of filling up, "Lake Powell" would stretch for two hundred miles over the canyon complex. One of the wonders of the natural world was drowning in a slow, deliberate flood of biblical proportion behind Glen Canyon Dam, itself a marvel in the worldview of engineers and land managers.

When he describes this childhood experience, his voice becomes thin, his eyes moist. Eight years later, as a young man, Rich learned to water-ski on the newly formed Lake Powell and he boated over that alcove he had camped in as a boy. Looking down into the unyielding veil of water now covering it, the sadness of that childhood experience returned. He felt cheated, but he accepted his loss, though reluctantly. The modern logic of trading water for wildness was not questioned in those days.

Eventually anger succeeded sorrow. Every rafting trip he made down the Colorado over the next several years convinced him that the impact to his beloved river would continue. The Colorado's name, which means "reddish brown" in Spanish, was inspired by its muddy character. Churning across soft redrock sandstone and fed by latte-colored flash floods, the Colorado carries one million cubic feet of sediment into the Powell reservoir every day. He calculated that it would take three dump trucks per minute, all day, twenty-four hours a day, nonstop, to match the sediment flow into the reservoir. If you took a year's worth of those dump trucks and lined them up bumper to bumper, the line of trucks would wrap around the planet three times.[1] Rafters joked that it was too thin to plow and too thick to drink.

Before the dam was constructed, that silt was carried south to the river's vast birdfoot delta in Mexico, where the silt was dropped and spread as the Colorado spilled into the ocean. Before the dam went up, the Colorado Delta was known for its biologically diverse and teeming wetlands, lush foliage, and rich soil. Silt-starved since the dam's completion, the delta is now a stony, dry, and diminished realm of ecological ruin. Meanwhile, unseen and underwater, the delta's former sediment supply is filling the reservoir floor and backing up along the Colorado River bed. "Each year I could see the difference," Rich says. "We were losing rapids as the silt was dropped in the slowing water and then built up. It was clear that the wildest whitewater river in America was choking on its own silt as it backed up. It made me mad."

This time around, Rich Ingebretsen was no helpless Cub Scout. He was a well-educated scientist who had mastered physics and medicine. He began to study the "lake" that had been formed and the dam's impact. What he learned at the time amazed him. The conventional wisdom on dams was all wet.

Damming big rivers and making vast reservoirs out of them was accepted practice in the American West for most of the past century. Dams were considered the practical icons of progress, unquestionably needed and unquestionably good. Sure, let Ed Abbey and his cantankerous ilk, with their stubbornly romantic attitude toward Western wildlands, mourn and complain—the American West must be tamed, and that meant dry land must be irrigated. Dams were how you did it. Development required electrical power, and dams provided that, too. "Dams solve a basic problem," says Rich. "They compensate for uneven seasonal flows. But just as importantly, they also solve the political problem of how you appropriate water and distribute it. I think they are a bad solution to those problems, but it has taken the public a while to catch on."

The public likes fast fun in wet places. Each year, thousands of boaters spill across Powell's startling blue surface to play, party, and enjoy the redrock splendor of the once lofty reaches of the Glen Canyon maze, which can now be touched at the water's edge. Better to appreciate the paradise before you, they say to those who deride "Lake Foul," than to pine for a paradise lost. Even Abbey understood that he was out of step. The colorful characters who populate *The Monkey Wrench Gang,* his now classic novel of the region, and dream about breaching the Glen Canyon Dam include a burnt-out veteran, a mad doctor, a sexy revolutionary, and a polygamist cowboy. They are a radical fringe, disdainful of the dominant culture's priorities, which honor economic growth, prosperity, comfort, and even lake surface recreation. They are round pegs in square holes. Aside from the ranting complaints of misfits, what could be wrong with a dam?

Everything, claims Rich. His Glen Canyon Institute has methodically catalogued the accumulating evidence of the negative consequences of throwing a massive dam across what had been America's last great uncharted river, the liquid heart of the Wild West. The case the institute is making contradicts cherished notions. How did he reconcile his radical civic ambitions with his religion and a church hierarchy not known for its ecological literacy or concern? Big smile. "You know, my mother is a devout Mormon, and she thinks my work on this is divine—I mean, inspired. My religion teaches me to rejoice in the Creator's work. It's okay to save His wonders from certain peril." I tell him my dad was an avowed atheist whose reverence for nature gave me my most important spiritual insights.

His "group of one" changed in 1995. Ignoring friends and colleagues who warned him that "people will say you are crazy," Rich decided to scope out who else was interested in studying the environmental impact of the dam and the feasibility of breaching it and restoring Glen Canyon. What better way of giving those who were interested an opportunity to express that interest than a debate between two legendary arch-enemies, Floyd Dominy and David Brower?

Dominy was the duke of the dam-building era. Brower had fathered the modern conservation movement. During the formative struggle to develop Western water policies and the infrastructure shaped by those policies, Dominy and Brower were team captains. Floyd Dominy's team was the federal Bureau of Reclamation, the powerful government agency that organized agricultural interests, developers, construction companies, and local politicians around massive water control projects. Brower headed the Sierra Club, the most powerful environmental organization in the nation, forged in struggles to preserve the wild rivers of the American West. Think of them as the managers in an epic Water World Series—the Water Buffaloes vs. the Tree Huggers.

Thirty years after their monumental struggle over the shape of the Colorado River system, the future of the Grand Canyon, and the fate of Glen Canyon, Rich called them from his cramped office in the physics building on the University of Utah campus. Now in their eighties, bleached and bent by time, their memories stewed in decades of reflection, the two adversaries agreed to meet, reminisce, and debate. They flew to Salt Lake separately, and each met Rich first.

Both arrived cranky—old men annoyed by late arrivals and misunderstandings about schedules. Brower struck Rich as a bit stiff and haughty. "He comes across as highly literate, very different from Dominy, who is all nuts and bolts." Dominy was a surprise, "a little old man who needed help getting up," Rich recalls. Never mind; he soon discovered the former BuRec chief to be as assertive as he expected. When Rich tried to flatter Dominy by acknowledging the power he had within the Bureau of Reclamation, Dominy corrected him. "I *was* the Bureau of Reclamation!"

In their first meeting with each other in thirty years, since the river trip John McPhee had arranged, they were gentle and solicitous. When Brower inquired about Dominy's wife, Floyd replied quietly, "I lost her nine years ago, Dave," and Brower's eyes brimmed with tears. The old animosity had mellowed, diluted by years of hard living and the lessons that long life brings to old men.

Their beliefs, however, remained strong. The two giants in their time spoke before a packed house of six hundred people on the University of Utah campus. Dominy proclaimed, "I'm proud that I'm known as the builder of Glen Canyon Dam and the creator of Lake Powell. I'm very proud of the fact that the ten most visited areas behind dams have more visitation than the ten most visited national parks." He also listed the number of megawatts, revenue dollars, and jobs generated by the famous dam he had built, in an unabashed tone that seemed to say only a fool would question whether dams are engines of prosperity and progress. The Wild West, as historian Donald Worster once observed, was tamed not by the six-gun but by the impounded waters of wild rivers. And Dominy was the dam sheriff.

After Dominy boasted, Brower confessed. He had dropped the ball that Dominy picked up and ran with, he explained, and had lived the rest of his life in regret. "I was deeply saddened by the dam because Glen Canyon was one of the most beautiful places I'd ever seen in my life or ever would see . . . possibly the most beautiful canyon on the planet."

But now he hoped the tragic mistake could be corrected. The dam was "overengineered" and had destroyed most of the Grand Canyon ecosystem downstream. Lake Mead alone could meet the water needs of the Colorado River Compact states. Only rich people with boats and trailers could play on Powell. Why not find a way to bypass the dam and at least drop Lake Powell two hundred feet so it was a third of its present size and long sections of the river would reappear? Yes, huge piles of sediment would build up over the years and clog Glen Canyon and its web of side canyons, but over time floods would wash them away. "Let the river recover," Brower implored. Trying to sound reasonable and accommodating, he suggested that we "leave the dam there, and when it is needed—after Lake Mead downstream has sedimented up—then fill Glen Canyon. That will give us at least two centuries to enjoy Glen Canyon."[2]

"Nonsense!" fumed Dominy. "Accept the fact. It is there, and it's going to stay." Dropping the level by two hundred feet would reduce Lake Powell's storage capacity to 6 million acre-feet, from its current 26 million acre-feet. There was no need to "tinker," advised the man who stanched the mighty Colorado and drowned Eden. Before the lake, he reminded Brower, only a few hundred people a year hiked into Glen Canyon, but millions now played on Lake Powell. Visitation trumped all that ecological and spiritual mumbo-jumbo, according to the commissioner. "I make no apology for my years in land development and as a dam builder."

The battle of ecology versus engineering ended in a disagreement over sediment. Brower claimed that sedimentation would fill in Lake Powell completely in less than three hundred years and that mud would clog the penstocks, making the dam useless for power generation, a lot sooner than that. Dominy was adamant that it would be more like a thousand years before the lake silted in. Three hundred years or a thousand, Brower's point was made: the proud technology of man would alter the landscape for only a blip in geologic time. Future generations would have to learn to live without a dam and reservoir anyway, so why deprive our grandchildren and their grandchildren of the splendors of Glen Canyon in the meantime? Asked by an audience member what a future generation would do once the reservoir silted up and the toxins concentrated in the sediments had become a problem, Dominy was glib. "I'll let the people who are around then worry about that," he chuckled. The audience did not share his humor. The auditorium was dead silent.

At the conclusion of the evening, as the audience members dispersed to their cars, many of them carried an intriguing new vision. What if the side canyons they loved to hike and climb, on either side of Lake Powell, didn't end at the water's edge but continued all the way down to a free-flowing Colorado River? What would they look like? A bathtub ring of deposited minerals would obscure the artful patterns of the canyon walls, but for how long? Years? Decades? And what would it be like to watch the pentimento of those true colors emerging as the mineral layers thinned and faded? If the millions of gallons of water that soaked into soft sandstone walls were free to seep back out, would the canyon fill with fresh flora and hanging gardens? As they imagined the possibilities, the dam that had for so long seemed mighty and inevitable came to look more like a big mistake that could be corrected.

After the evening's event, Rich took the two speakers to a bar to unwind. Brower drank martinis "straight up with no distraction," and Dominy sucked down bourbon. The debate continued informally. Suddenly, Dominy became angry. He yelled and pounded his fist on the table. "The whole place noticed," said Rich, "and everyone but Floyd was embarrassed. Then, just as suddenly, he was friendly again.

"Dave tolerated a lot. He forgave him his outburst," said Rich. Dominy could just as quickly show heartfelt goodwill. Despite having once called Brower a "sanctimonious bastard," Dominy respected him as a worthy opponent, and an opponent who had brought some fame to the engineering bureau chief. "Besides," he told Rich, "I like anybody—pimps or cab drivers—anybody."[3]

The next day Rich drove them to the airport. Brower departed first. Dominy turned to Rich, his expression troubled. "Dave doesn't look good, does he? I worry he won't be with us much longer." The two men never spoke again.

In the next few years, Rich would visit both Dominy and Brower in their homes. "Dave's home was always full of people. He had so many friends. His relationships were long and deep. He may have seemed a bit reserved at first, but underneath he was wise and caring." Dominy, on the other hand, lived alone in one room of his house, a structure that felt like a mausoleum, Rich says. It was cold and empty, and part of it was closed off. Dominy was estranged from his children and feuding with former colleagues at the bureau. He had two dogs but wouldn't let them into the house, even when it rained. "Floyd Dominy," Rich concluded, "didn't have a long-term relationship with anybody or anything."

One night at dinner, Dominy suddenly leaned forward and asked, "How serious is this effort to drain Lake Powell?" It was as if he had finally realized that it was not just a crazy notion.

"Very serious," Rich replied. Dominy thought for a minute. Here was Rich Ingebretsen, a squeaky-clean Mormon doctor, not some dope-smoking, monkeywrenching radical. If a man like Rich could entertain the notion of draining Lake Powell, what was the world coming to?

How would it be done, he asked. Rich said he had been told that the old bypass tunnels would have to be drilled out so water could pass out of the reservoir and around the dam.

"Can't do it," snapped Dominy. "There's three hundred feet of reinforced cement in those now!" He reached for a clean napkin and spread it out, whipped out a pen, and started to scratch furiously, his eyeglasses resting on the end of his nose. A diagram of the dam and the surrounding canyon walls emerged.

"I've been thinking about this a lot," Dominy explained. "This is how it could be done." New tunnels would be drilled out through untouched sandstone on either side of the dam. They would have to be low enough to draw out sediments. "Clean water is hungry water," he explained. Too much clear water would eat up Grand Canyon. He gave the napkin to Rich, who was awestruck. Floyd Dominy, the supreme master of American dams, had just handed him a blueprint for draining his most prized creation.

Dominy tucked his pen back in his pocket. "I'm very sorry about Glen Canyon," he said, "It was a shame it had to go under."

SIX

A Ridiculous Idea Whose Time Has Come

Representative Jim Hansen tends to twitch. He's a restless kind of guy, some would say impatient. Not a good listener. First of all, he's made up his mind, and he knows he's right. Enduring the comments of the "extreme environmentalists," as he refers to anyone greener than the Chamber of Commerce in his native Utah, gives him a full case of ants in the pants. His body language during my encounters with him at town meetings, hearings, and lobbying visits tells me that he enjoys listening to us about as much as finding a nest of hornets in his desk drawer.

On September 24, 1997, though, he couldn't wait to hear from Adam Werbach, the very young president of the Sierra Club. Hansen had hoped to have the great David Brower himself appear before a joint hearing of his Subcommittee on National Parks and Public Lands and the Subcommittee on Water and Power chaired by John Doolittle of California, but Brower couldn't attend because his wife was ill.

Werbach had been recruited to the post of club president at the tender age of twenty-two by a new board that included Brower and such radicals as Dave Foreman. They wanted to underscore the club's new focus on the grassroots and the young, a remarkable turnabout from the previous era, when the club had morphed into a Beltway political machine frequently accused of engaging in too little vision and too much compromise. Tearing down the kid would be a poor substitute for the drama and fun of exposing the folly of the grand eco-prophet himself, but Werbach would be easier to burn at the stake. He'd have to do.

The national Sierra Club had shown its true colors, and Hansen was eager to wave them in front of Congress and the media. Under the influence of Brower and Foreman and over the objections of the Utah chapter, the club's board had endorsed the draining of Lake Powell— had decided to advocate for the wild idea, if not the dubious means of achieving it, that had been popularly introduced in Ed Abbey's 1975 best-seller, *The Monkey Wrench Gang.*

Distilling his anger over the loss of Glen Canyon, Abbey had imagined "some unknown hero with a rucksack full of dynamite strapped onto his back" climbing into the bowels of the dam to blow it away.[1] Now the irreverent characters in Abbey's story were becoming the models for a scruffy, radical, eco-activist culture growing around the periphery of the West.

Although the club wasn't proposing to take the dam down with dynamite and was, in fact, unsure how the reservoir behind the massive dam could be drained, proposing that it be drained in any way at all, in Hansen's view, was a drastic breach of the covenants that had governed the West and enabled its development. It was one of those radical hippie ideas expressed by Rastafarian trust-funders in Boulder and Berkeley, the tree sitters and spikers of the Northwest forests, and the salmon worshipers and wolf lovers. To an ultraconservative Republican and staunch Mormon like Hansen, such people were clearly crazy and dangerous.

Another Utah Republican, Garfield County commissioner Louise Liston, expressed the cowboy consensus when she told me that "environ mentalists" (she pronounced the term in two parts, as if naming a psychological disorder) went into the wilderness mostly to get naked and get high. In Utah, she is well known for her remark "They come here with $20 and one set of clothes, and when they leave a week later they haven't changed either." I often remember that remark when emerging from a weeklong backpacking trip, covered in dust and reeking—and having encountered nary an ATM or an item on sale for days.

Although Brower couldn't attend, the octogenarian was completing a round trip of sorts. He had been ousted from the Sierra Club in 1969. His bold, ambitious struggles had made the club into a national political power, its membership rising from 7,000 in 1952 to 77,000 in 1969,[2] but they had also overextended its finances. Brower was impatient with those who could not glimpse his vision as it emerged, and he'd aggravated the board and his staff many times. When he turned against nuclear power in 1969 and came out against the construction of a nuclear plant at Diablo Canyon in California, the board balked.[3]

In those heady days before its deadly, long-lived waste had accumulated and become a concern to so many, most people considered atomic energy a desirable power source, cleaner than coal-fired power plants and not tied to dam building like hydropower. Many in the conservation community had mixed, even favorable attitudes about it, and Brower's jump off the atomic fence seemed to confirm a rashness they distrusted.

With author and anti-technology activist Jerry Mander, Brower launched a Sierra Club ad campaign called Spaceship Earth, which made some club stalwarts uneasy about the scope of their leader's goals that pushed way beyond the club's traditional concerns. Even old friends of Brower's like Ansel Adams, the famed photographer and a Sierra Club board member, and Wallace Stegner, the acclaimed writer, questioned his leadership publicly. After a brutal conflict, Brower was forced out of the club's leadership. Although Brower's board opponents have been characterized as short-sighted bean counters, there is evidence that Brower's use of Sierra Club funds was very questionable. The full story has not been told.

He immediately went on to found Friends of the Earth, the first environmental group to put ecology into a social, political, and international context. Fifteen years later, after he had driven that organization into a financial wall, the staff and board rebelled and Brower was overthrown once more. He then founded the Earth Island Institute, which became known for its pioneering eco-activism.

In the early 1990s, a quarter century after Brower's overthrow, the Sierra Club had become big, rich, respected—and, some would say, too prone to compromise and out of touch with its grassroots. The Sierra Club was under internal siege by a group of such radicals who called themselves the John Muirs, after the legendary naturalist and Sierra Club founder. Led by Chad Hanson—who was proposing a ban on all logging in national forests, an idea greeted with disdain by the board—the John Muirs thought the club had grown fat, comfortable, and timid. Its legal and lobbying strategies were designed to enforce and further the historic legislative and policy gains of the 1960s and early 1970s, but it was unable or unwilling to carve out a fresh and inspiring political agenda.

The age of the club's average member was creeping up into the mid-forties. The trademark tin cups that clubbers would take camping were going on fewer outings and being used to soak more dentures. Polls showed that 80 percent of Americans now regarded themselves as environmentalists, a remarkable measure of success, yet the degradation of the American landscape, and even the nurturing atmosphere that enveloped it, continued. It was time to reinvigorate the club with bold ideas and challenging campaigns.

Chad Hanson's logging ban was defeated in a 1994 vote, but it would succeed a couple of years later and become a major priority of the organization by 2000. Meanwhile, the John Muirs were gaining seats on the club's fifteen-member board of directors, and in 1995 Brower, endorsed by the Muir faction, was elected to the board by the club's general membership. That was the same year Rich Ingebretsen launched the Glen Canyon Institute with the Brower-Dominy debate at the University of Utah. In 1996 Dave Foreman was elected to the board, joining Brower. That year Dave Wegner's human-made floods were released through Glen Canyon Dam to see if the geological and ecological functions of naturally occurring floods could be replicated artificially.

Foreman was also on a round trip. After years of dressing up and walking the halls of Congress for the Wilderness Society, he had become disillusioned with the Beltway orientation of the large, established environmental organizations. He had broken ranks and ranted, raved, and rallied with Earth First! until the full weight of the law had put an end to that outdoor party.

But not before he and Ed Abbey revealed a "crack" on the face of the Glen Canyon Dam. In the early 1980s, as Foreman was gathering around him the disillusioned reformers and woolly outcasts who would form Earth First!, Ed Abbey was becoming their cantankerous, irreverent, and charismatic patron saint. Before creating his story of the merry band of monkeywrenchers, Abbey had written an instant classic, *Desert Solitaire*, and a series of hard-hitting essays that gave an early voice to an emerging perspective on the land. In "The Damnation of a Canyon," he proclaimed that "a fully industrialized, thoroughly urbanized, and elegantly computerized social system is not fit for human habitation. Great for machines, yes. But unfit for people."[4] In "Down the River," he wrote, " The love of wilderness is . . . an expression of loyalty to the earth, the earth which bore us and sustains us, the only home we shall ever know, the only paradise we ever need—if only we had the eyes to see."[5]

In 1981, in a picture-perfect act of political performance art, Foreman, Abbey, and their Earth First! friends stood atop the Glen Canyon Dam and unfurled a three-hundred-foot-long piece of polyurethane plastic designed to resemble a giant black crack. They pinned it to the face of the dam. Thus was a creation of Abbey's imagination transformed by Foreman into a giant visual aid that was transmitted across the nation via the wire services and news media. Rich Ingebretsen has no recollection of that event, but Brower certainly noticed. Glen Canyon was still on the political map.

By the time Brower returned to the Sierra board, fifteen years after that act of imaginary insurrection, he was ready to revisit the formative issue of his political life. Rich gave Brower his cue. The debate with Dominy stirred his blood. During a visit to Utah, a TV reporter asked Brower if any major environmental organization had endorsed the radical proposal that Brower and Dominy were debating. "Not yet" was the response. Rich quietly suggested to Brower that maybe the Sierra Club should look at it. "I've been meaning to take care of that," Brower told him.

Rich also gave Brower and the Sierra Club precious and catalytic data. At a dinner he organized at Salt Lake's aristocratic Alta Club, Rich sat down with river runners, scientists, and government bureaucrats to encourage a dialogue about the future of the dam and its reservoir. To his utter amazement, the Bureau of Reclamation scientists, whom he had expected to be defensive, stole the show. They came to the dinner with documents they discreetly handed over. Studies had been done, they said, and you'll be interested in the findings. The idea of decommissioning the dam was not so crazy, they told Rich and his guests, and deserved to be on the table.

Their research and models showed that massive amounts of water were being sucked into the soft sandstone that held Lake Powell in place. Evaporation from the reservoir's surface during the long, hot desert summer was enormous. Add up the figures, and the lake was losing as much water each year as was flowing into it. The Bureau of Reclamation's own data showed that more water would be available each year from the Colorado River if Lake Powell didn't exist. The lower the lake went, the more water would become available. This idea was counterintuitive, but the data were strong. The BuRec bureaucrats had handed Rich Ingebretsen a loaded gun pointed at the very heart of the myths that held the Glen Canyon Dam in place.

Rich was as surprised by the forthrightness of the bureau's staff as he was heartened by the picture their numbers presented. "Remember, outside of the city of Page, Arizona, we don't directly use any water from Lake Powell for irrigation or drinking," he explained. "The water is for insurance only, to guarantee the upper basin's flow to the lower basin states in time of drought. But what the bureau's own data showed was that in reality, Lake Powell is like having a giant evaporation pond upstream. It doesn't guarantee anything; it just wastes water."

This information added a powerful new dimension to the critique of the dam. Aside from the ways the reservoir's clean, cold water was altering the Grand Canyon ecosystem, and aside from the drowning of the canyon paradise beneath it, the Glen Canyon Dam and its reservoir didn't even accomplish its underlying objective. For the reservoir's large constituency of recreational users who rented houseboats or liked to jet-ski and water-ski, or who sold goods and services to those who rented houseboats or liked to jet-ski and water-ski, its failure to conserve water was beside the point. But to those who debated public policy, the failure of the dam to accomplish its formal, validating objectives was important.

Brower brought the proposal to drain Lake Powell before a meeting of the Sierra Club's national board of directors, where it quickly passed by a unanimous vote. Only after the vote did some board members question what they had done. "We might want to keep this to ourselves," suggested one board member, according to the report Rich got. No way. Brower immediately called everyone he knew in the media.

The leaders of the Sierra Club's Utah chapter were caught off guard. Lake Powell was in the chapter's backyard, but the Utahns had not been consulted. Defending a controversial proposal to drain the reservoir was not a priority of the state chapter. They were focused on a protracted struggle to designate wilderness areas in Utah, and soon they would be consumed by a struggle to stop a proposed highway from running over the rich wetlands described by Terry Tempest Williams in *Refuge,* her eloquent and lyrical ode to the Great Salt Lake and its migrating birds.

The Utah chapter saw the drain-the-lake proposal as an annoying, unnecessary, and credibility-damaging distraction from these other campaigns. Why tilt at windmills when there is real work to do? But a dissident faction in the river-running town of Moab favored draining the lake, objected to the objections of the state chapter (which was based in Salt Lake City), and formed a Glen Canyon Group. The controversial proposal was heatedly debated in many other chapters across the nation—from Los Angeles, where meetings disintegrated into fist-pounding yelling matches, to New York City, where factions filed lawsuits against one another.

The Sierra Club was suddenly becoming radical. In 1996 the national board signed off on both Chad Hanson's logging ban and Brower's drain-the-lake resolution. The lion's share of the club's Washington lobbying budget was redirected to grassroots campaigns, and a training camp for organizers and activists was initiated. In an obvious attempt to attract young people to the organization, Adam Werbach, barely out of college, was recruited to be the club's president. Clearly, the radicals were in the cockpit and the staid Club was veering off the map with a very old man and a boy-pilot at the stick.

Back in Washington, the anti-environment elite were flabbergasted and elated. The guardians of political culture who gave us Mutually Assured Destruction, Star Wars, trickle-down economics, and, eventually, Enron accounting regarded themselves as the guardians of reasonable discourse and maybe even the keepers of "reality" itself. Clearly, the radicals were in the cockpit and the staid Club was veering off the map with a very old man and a boy-pilot at the stick. And reality was long established—the perogatives of property, profit, and progress took top priority, had to be protected. Environmental regulation challenged those perogatives and there was too much of it. It was getting harder to make that case. But this! This time, they crowed, the nature worshipers were way over the line. Hot dog! Seeing his chance to paint the word "wacko" across the Sierra Club banner, Congressman Jim Hansen called a hearing.

The congressman from Utah's second district wasted no time. He was licking his proverbial chops, and David Brower and his looneytunes friends were on the menu. In his opening statement before the hearing, Hansen said, "Any discussion of this issue brings some disbelief from some observers."[6] Although known for mean-tempered confrontations with those who oppose the military use of Utah's West Desert or are critical of the traditional cattle, mining, and timber interests he supports, Hansen was on his best behavior. "This hearing is designed to put all the facts on the table and analyze the potential impacts of such a proposal," he proclaimed, "so that the public and the media understand the consequences." He then outlined a roster of witnesses loaded with every water and electric power bureaucrat he could muster.

Representative John Doolittle of California spoke first. Chair of the Subcommittee on Water and Power, Doolittle waxed eloquently about Lake Powell's "majestic reach." The lake was a "beautiful gem" and "one of life's truly refreshing treasures," he said. Furthermore, its grandeur "would not exist and could not be enjoyed if we had not had the foresight and courage to create this wonder." God himself might have shown more modesty in describing His accomplishments. Those "who wish to rewrite history," Doolittle advised, must realize that "there is a time when all of us must let go."

Chairman Hansen displayed all the dignity and patience he could summon, leaving the name-calling to others on the committee, especially Utah representative Chris Cannon. Cannon's political base was the staunchly conservative, patriarchal community known as Happy Valley, home of Brigham Young University, the pride of the Mormon Church. The niceties over, Cannon took the mike, sputtering with outrage and feigned disbelief. To forgo "protection from ravenous floods" was "a ridiculous idea," he fumed. The dam was a fact and, like it or not, it was "too late to change that now simply because some have grown sentimental for Glen Canyon. What existed then could never be restored. To suggest otherwise is silly. I daresay this is the silliest proposal discussed in the 105th Congress." So much for hearing the other side's case.

"I have seen environmental proposals in my district that can only be described as dumb, some monumentally dumb," Cannon said, in reference to the Clinton administration's decision to create the Grand Staircase–Escalante National Monument in Cannon's backyard without his approval, "but now, Mr. Chairman, we have dumb and dumber." Then, in a parody of late-night TV talk-show host David Letterman's top-ten lists, he named the ten environmental ideas "that might be even dumber than draining Lake Powell." These included removing the Statue of Liberty from its island, returning Mount Rushmore to its primitive state, repacking tunnels into Manhattan, and, the topper of them all, "designating a 1.7-million-acre national monument in southern Utah without any hearings."

Cannon's diatribe was so sarcastic that Hansen warned the others to show some respect. No matter. Representative John Shadegg of Arizona took up the cudgel but wielded it with a righteous swing. "Time," he intoned, "moves in only one direction," and that was "how God intended it." In case the environmental extremists didn't understand whose side God was on, Shadegg told them that "man's creations honor his God" and attributed the raising of this "spurious issue" to "ego, sentimentality, guilt, and a desire for profit." Representative Joel Hefley of Colorado called the proposal a "nutty idea" that put the Sierra Club, logically enough, on "the nutty fringe," while Senator Ben Nighthorse Campbell of Colorado made a guest appearance to call the Sierra Club proposal "a certified nut idea . . . a joke." Idaho's Helen Chenoweth warned that proposals to bring down dams on the Columbia and Snake Rivers would be next. A number of Congress members not on the joint subcommittee dropped by to contribute their views of the proposal. Extreme, absurd, and silly, they said.

Bureaucrat after bureaucrat followed, putting those "facts on the table" that Representative Hansen had promised. They took the mike to count up the millions of visits, the megawatts of power, the acre-feet of water supplied, and the tons of coal that would have to be burned to compensate for the loss of the dam's electrical generating power. Revenue losses, they said, would be crippling. The recreationists alone generated millions of dollars in sales, spending money on everything from $100,000 boats to motel rooms and meals, fuel, and even the handmade turquoise necklaces spread atop blankets and sold by Navajos beside the highways leading to the reservoir. The grave revenue implications for local medical services and schools, should the lake be drained, were underlined in red. The devastating potential impact of draining on the town of Page was described in detail.

The bureaucrats took pains to explain the complicated system devised for delivering water to the lower basin states and maintaining an "insurance policy" upstream for the upper basin states. Do away with Lake Powell, they warned, and you will not be able to compensate downstream—Lake Mead cannot take the difference or, as the Honorable Mr. Doolittle put it, "You can't have it all in Lake Mead and we're all just fat, dumb, and happy." At every opportunity, committee members asked leading questions and repeated the answers they wanted to underscore.

Finally Adam Werbach got his chance to speak, with Dave Wegner at his side. The Club had recruited Wegner for the occasion to explain the science of their case, science that Rich Ingebretsen and he were beginning to compile for an anticipated study by the new Glen Canyon Institute. "I represent the Sierra Club's 600,000 members across America in supporting the restoration of one of the most special places on earth, Glen Canyon, for our families and our future," Werbach said. He recalled the words of the right wing's own icon, Arizona senator Barry Goldwater, who had expressed regret for his vote in favor of the dam's construction. Werbach explained how the change from silty warm water to cold clear water had altered the ecosystem of the Grand Canyon and how the absence of seasonal floods had reordered the landscape downstream. Recent studies, he said, also showed that one million acre-feet of water a year was being lost from evaporation and seepage, enough to meet the needs of the city of Los Angeles.

Lake Mead alone contained more than enough water to meet the region's needs, he argued, and water conservation could make even more water available. Most of the "overstored" Colorado River water, Werbach said, went to plants, not people. It supported crops like cotton that

consume huge amounts of water and cannot be grown on a desert without price supports, tax breaks, and subsidized water. The obligation
of the upper basin states to send water down to the lower basin, as established by the Colorado River Compact, could be met without the
reservoir, he said, citing an Environmental Defense Fund study that had
used the Bureau of Reclamation's own models. The electrical power
the dam produced was not essential and not worth what was being lost
in the bargain. "Regardless of where you stand on this issue," Werbach
told the joint subcommittee, "it clearly makes sense to examine the
facts." Just agree to a review, he implored the members. "The Sierra
Club supports evaluating the trade-offs and opportunities of draining
Lake Powell through an environmental assessment."

In the question-and-answer session that followed, Werbach tried to
have Wegner, the scientist, field the technical questions. The Congress
members would have none of it. They wanted an unobstructed target,
and the Sierra Club's boy director looked like he had bull's-eyes painted
all over him. But Werbach held his own. He deflected the technical debate by emphasizing that the club had voted to advocate draining the
lake as a way to kick-start a dialogue, "to begin a conversation with society to see where we come out." A scientific assessment would be key
to guiding that civic dialogue. The subcommittee members, however,
made it clear they saw no reason to study a proposal that, in their minds,
had no merit. When asked if the Sierra Club would go ahead with its
own study, Werbach said the club would help the Glen Canyon Institute with their study.

Finally, after watching Werbach endure a withering barrage of remarks and questions, it was Wegner's turn. He introduced himself. "I
am a scientist by training. I am not a politician. I am not a businessman.
I am not a bureaucrat. All I am is a simple scientist trying to get at
the facts. Those facts, gathered over the last fourteen years, are that the
Grand Canyon and Colorado are in serious need of restoration." The
endangered fish and bird populations, he advised, couldn't be sustained
otherwise.

He diplomatically praised the subcommittee members for their
tough questions and offered to make those questions the framework for
the citizens' assessment he was proposing to "document the science."
He then conveyed a brief history of the Glen Canyon Institute,

emphasizing that "we are a volunteer organization. None of us get paid. We are private citizens. We are scientists. Today we are here seeking wisdom; we are here in this place of power and trappings to look at how we can move forward with this whole proposal." He ended his introduction poetically and passionately. "We are people who believe in fish," he said. "We are people who speak for birds."

Hansen and his esteemed colleagues must have enyoyed the confirmation that they were dealing with a fish-hugging birdbrain, but they were more concerned about whether public money would be required for the scientific inquiry extolled by Wegner. The Glen Canyon Institute was not asking for a dime, Wegner replied, but they did support the Sierra Club's request for a publicly funded study.

Representative Shadegg then acknowledged Wegner's reputation. "In all the world," he said, "you are one of the most renowned experts on the Grand Canyon." Having bowed briefly in Wegner's direction, Shadegg quickly called on Robert Elliott to refute Wegner's testimony that the Grand Canyon's species were endangered by the way the river is operated. Elliott was the president of Arizona Raft Adventures and a spokesperson for America Outdoors, an association comprising six hundred small businesses that outfitted backcountry trips over public lands. He had earlier testified that restoring the river would add so much silt to it that his rafting customers would not be able to get clean at night. It would mean the water would be so warm that their perishable vegetables could not be refreshed in cold water overnight, he said. Elliott then assured the joint subcommittee that the ecosystem of the Grand Canyon was actually more robust than ever, citing his recent two-hour conversation with a biologist in Flagstaff. "It is also my observations from just antidotally [sic]," he said.

That was good enough for Shadegg. When it came to deciding public land and water policy in the West, a good ol' boy apparently trumped a pointy-headed tree-hugger any day. If Wegner was looking for wisdom in Congress, he was more likely to find molars in a snake or wit in a sea bass.

Hansen wound up the hearing with a suggestion to Adam Werbach that the Sierra Club find a target for their anti-dam inclinations that didn't have "so much multiple use"—Hetch Hetchy in Yosemite, for example. "I might go along with that," Hansen teased, but warned Werbach that if he wanted to bring down the Hetch Hetchy Dam, he would have to face the large California congressional delegation. Hansen had had some experience with them, he told Werbach, because they were so vocal when their military bases were targeted for closure. (As a final note before adjourning the hearing Hansen noted, for the witless, that his suggestion about Hetch Hetchy had been purely "tongue in cheek.")

The Glen Canyon Institute's "Citizens' Environmental Assessment" was concluded in 2000. The institute had filled their advisory board and board of trustees with talented, articulate people like Dave Brower and Katie Lee. They raised money and won grants, hired the first staff member, and eventually opened an office in a cottage in Flagstaff, Arizona. Scientists and researchers were recruited to do the study. A small staff tracked the study, publicized the work being done, and created literature and a web site to describe its findings. Thousands of new members were recruited to provide political and financial support.

The institute's growth pleased Rich. "We definitely tapped into a kind of resentment out there," he said. "People were tired of putting up with the dam, the reservoir, and the ongoing degradation they caused. And a lot of people never fully accepted the loss of Glen Canyon. What we were saying was exciting—we don't have to settle for the way it is—and the 'Citizens' Environmental Assessment' was making our case."

The assessment compiles information from eight separate studies commissioned by the institute.[7] It begins by noting that it refers to "Lake Powell" as "Powell reservoir" throughout, because a lake is a natural body of water, whereas a reservoir is a human-made body of water. Powell reservoir, it explains, was built before most of the nation's environmental legislation was enacted. Had laws like the Endangered Species Act, the Clean Water Act, or the Archaeological and Historic Preservation Act been in force at the time, the dam could not have been built. The degradation the dam has caused the Grand Canyon ecosystem was not anticipated then, it says, but we have learned much since. The government's faux floods, or "periodic flow management measures," designed to restore ecological integrity, have fallen short of their goals.

But what about the dam's stated purpose—its raison d'être—the storage of water to ensure adequate supplies to lower basin states? Even there, the assessment says, the dam is a failure. "Powell reservoir loses 570,000 acre-feet of water per year due to evaporation, compared to

102,000 acre-feet evaporated along this section of the Colorado River prior to dam construction. This difference is enough water to supply Salt Lake City each year," the assessment reports. The amount of water evaporated "is worth $150 million at Salt Lake City water prices." If only 10 percent of the amount that evaporates off Powell's surface flowed across the border to Mexico, "a substantial portion of the Colorado River Delta could be restored."

The amount of water evaporated since 1963, when the dam began to fill, is almost equal to the current amount held within the reservoir, the assessment notes. The total amount of water lost to seepage during the reservoir's short history is 10,000,000 acre-feet. Add it up and more than two years' worth of river flow has been evaporated or seeped away. Evaporation increases salinity, too, causing water users more than $25 million annually in damage to household appliances, auto cooling systems, reduced crop yields, decreased cleaning efficiency, and desalinization measures.

Without the reservoir intact, the delivery of water to lower basin states will continue with only minimal additional fluctuations, which could be easily compensated for by water conservation measures, the assessment states. Upper basin states won't notice any difference in water supply, except for Page and the nearby Navajo Generating Station, which can have water piped in directly from the river instead of from the reservoir. If the unneeded but impounded waters of Powell can be passed along through the series of dams below it to the Colorado River Delta, the delta can be wet and rich with diverse life once more, and the fisheries at the mouth of the river will be reinvigorated.

The statistics established by the assessment concerning the accumulation of sediments are also damning. Each year, the unfettered Colorado River carries 60 to 80 million tons of sediment toward the Grand Canyon. Eighty-five percent of those sediments are trapped behind the dam, "thereby depriving the canyon of much of the sediments and nutrients necessary to maintain beaches and natural aquatic habitats," not to mention causing the virtual disappearance of the lush wetlands around the Colorado River Delta.

Again, the experimental floods of 1996 brought only minimal and temporary benefits to Grand Canyon habitats. While the Grand Canyon is starved for silt, "the process of aggradation deposits sediments upstream above the level of the reservoir" and is choking off the tributaries, such as the San Juan River and Cataract Canyon. Depending on the rate of silt flow and fill, the reservoir will "totally fill with sediment in two hundred to eight hundred years," but power plant intakes will clog up much sooner. Without the reservoir, the built-up silt would be carried away quickly, dissipating the naturally occurring selenium and mercury that are building up and concentrating to dangerous levels.

Some species that have been introduced into the Grand Canyon ecosystem since the dam was built, like trout and many birds, have thrived in the new conditions, the assessment acknowledges. But hundreds of species that were native, including humpback chubs, razorback and flannel mouth suckers, frogs, and reptiles that took millions of years to evolve in place, have been endangered by the sudden shift in habitat conditions. Add to that the change in flow patterns and the accumulation of raw sewage generated by boaters, and you get a portrait of an ecosystem under duress. And, of course, should the kind of catastrophic spillway failure occur that almost happened in 1983, when the Colorado began forging a new path under the dam, there is no way to guess what might be torn apart downstream.

Yes, the assessment concludes, people love the reservoir for "flatwater recreation," but they put approximately "one million gallons of hydrocarbon pollution" into it each year, including 20,000 gallons of spilled raw gas and oil. Those dirty-bird tourists could engage in more sustainable activities like hiking and rafting if the reservoir was gone, so the economic changes would be less a matter of degree than of kind. Depending on how fast the reservoir was drawn down and how this was accomplished, there would be time for readjustment. Energy conservation could compensate for the electrical power lost.

The first step in solving a problem is to acknowledge and define it. The "Citizens' Environmental Assessment" was not meant to fully describe how the dam would be bypassed and how the reservoir would be drawn down, but to outline the problem. It describes consequences that engineers did not consider and that the dam's defenders would prefer to ignore. It was not intended, it notes, to be the last word on all these impacts of the reservoir, but "to demonstrate sufficient support to justify a full Environmental Impact Statement" that "includes the decommissioning of the dam and draining of the reservoir" as an option.

It was hard to imagine that an Environmental Impact Statement would ever be done as long as Jim Hansen served on the House Interior Committee and had a chokehold on the Interior Department's budgets. But Hansen retired from Congress in 2002, and the idea of taking a long, hard look at the need for Glen Canyon Dam and its Powell reservoir had grown more acceptable as time passed. Although the Bush administration was sure to keep the dam busters in check for the time being, Hansen worried out loud that the day would eventually come when a study would be funded.

Meanwhile, Rich Ingebretsen was ever optimistic. On a rainy April day in 2002, we huddled in his dark office and talked about the prospects ahead. "Our generation could revisit decisions that were made in a less enlightened time and use man's genius and vision instead of his inertia," he said, leaning forward in his swivel chair and smiling quietly, his voice almost a whisper, somewhere between a secret and a prayer. "There's a drought on. We can't afford to allow all that evaporation. The lake is dropping quickly and is going lower than it has been since they were filling it up." By the following year, boat ramps would be stranded high and dry, and the ferry at Hite would have to be moved to avoid emerging sandbars. Maybe the lake would drain itself.

"Soon, canyons that were drowned for decades will reappear," Rich said. "We'll see Cathedral in the Desert emerge. Yes, there will be muddy, bleached, and stained walls, but it will wash away sooner than people expect. Water will pour from the seeps where it has been hiding. It will be wonderful to watch the canyons restore themselves, clean themselves out, and bloom so that life can return there and our grandchildren can enjoy them. People will understand what we lost, what we could have back. And we won't let them refill the lake. We're getting ready to challenge them in court. Money and support are coming in from all over." His eyes go glassy for a moment as he stares out the window into the torrents of swirling spring rain, the pink blossoms bouncing in the wind. The smile quickens. He can almost see Glen Canyon.

SEVEN

Fire in the Water: Salmon as Gift or Commodity

Helen Chenoweth was disingenuous. The Republican congresswoman from Idaho had warned her colleagues on Jim Hansen's Subcommittee on National Parks and Public Lands that if the threat to Lake Powell was tolerated, proposals to breach the dams along the Snake and Columbia Rivers would be next. In fact, as she knew well, the Snake River dams had already been targeted. Vigorous campaigns for their removal were under way by the time of the congressional hearings on the proposal to bypass the Glen Canyon Dam. But Chenoweth, who would soon lose her seat in Congress, was giving voice to the dam-domino nightmare scenario so feared by dam-friendly politicians, in which the first big dam to go down leads to attempts to breach other dams, which in turn would be increasingly harder to defend.

And indeed, the drain-the-lake proposal did strike a chord with those already struggling to bring down lesser dams in order to restore salmon habitat in the Northwest. It resonated with a growing environmental movement weary of conducting "stop the damage" campaigns. It lifted their vision of what might be possible to another level, a level that included restoration as a worthy and realistic goal. It heartened those who understood intuitively the wisdom and necessity of moving beyond defending the integrity of wilderness habitats and whole ecosystems under assault and of raising the stakes to include widespread restoration. It complemented the arguments of critics of the Forest Service, the Bureau of Land Management, and other agencies that view their utilitarian mission as "professionally" managing public lands for "multiple uses," including clear-cutting timber, mining, grazing, dam building, and recreation, sometimes all on the same acre.

To move a dialogue to the question of whether a mistake should be corrected is to win the debate over whether what happened was a mistake at all. To successfully characterize a keystone project of the governing mind-set as a mistake is also to underline the flaws in that mind-set, thus setting the stage for the creation of new perspectives and directions. Those making the case for incremental changes in the governing criteria for land use—the academics, the planners, the reformist politicians—often criticize visionaries like Rich Ingebretsen for being "extreme" and distance themselves from ideas and behaviors they regard as embarrassing. In the overall dynamic of the civic culture, however, those visionaries often push civic dialogue into new areas and create a context that is loaded with opportunities for the reformers to advance their more particular and modest agendas.

In Chenoweth's Idaho and across the Northwest, salmon were on the agenda. Although the bodacious drain-the-lake proposal jumped to the front and center of the national dialogue about the value and viability of dams, that dialogue had been going on for two decades, focusing on dams in Northwest watersheds that were endangering salmon. It is easy to see why. The struggles across the country over bringing down dams and restoring riparian ecosystems all boil down to one question: Should rivers be defined as sacred arteries of interwoven life, or as useful hydraulic engines of profit?

And if dams are icons of progress, salmon have become the sacramental totem of wild rivers. There is no finer example of how a wild species evolves to fit the geology, climate, and biosphere of a particular place than the hook-nosed native salmon. During the geologic history of the Pacific Northwest, mountains rose, lava flowed, coastlines shifted, and climate changed. Those transformations took place over hundreds of millions of years, and the ancestors of today's salmon kept pace and diversified to fit the shifting circumstances. Their physiological morphing happened over a million generations, and about 2 million years ago, modern salmon emerged.[1] In the last geologic phase before the present one, glaciers formed and covered the land and then ice melted, carving the intricate and complex drainages we know today, with their diverse patchwork of habitats. Modern strains of salmon emerged then, fine-tuned as ever to match the diverse geologic and biotic particulars of the drainages they inhabit.

Salmon's diversity is a key to their survival. As circumstances change, some strains are at a disadvantage and others are favored, but a variation of possibilities ensures that some will survive to carry on the evolutionary journey. Changes in the habitats that nurture salmon, of course, must be on a scale that allows biological change, with all its trials and errors, adaptations, mutations, and new habits, to unfold at its evolutionary pace. Clear-cuts, erosion, pollution, and damming happen in an evolutionary instant; they represent a human-made fast-forward way beyond the ancestral rhythm of habitat change that salmon have survived for thousands of years.

The wild salmon is the one and only wet species that travels between the fresh waters of the continent's high-altitude interior and the salt waters of the open sea. Its journey seldom fails to inspire awe. Emerging from a clutch of delicate, sunset-colored eggs, fingerling salmon have an unfathomably good memory for the currents, patterns of stone, and subtle chemical differences marking the place of their creation, which enables them to return there to mate and die. A year or two after they hatch, they heed a primal downstream call, leaving their rain-nourished, gravel-laced womb of sunlight, shadow, and snowmelt for deep seawater hundreds of miles away. They brave threats and distances worthy of a mythic hero.

Young salmon smolts face upstream and homeward as they go down to the sea from the mountains. Like Ginger Rogers in the arms of Fred Astaire, they do the whole dance to the ocean backward. They are so obsessively heedful of the sea's siren song that they don't bother to look for food along the way. They starve as they go, so delay can be deadly. The ability of salmon to imprint meticulously and then make a round-trip journey of thousands of miles, so that they return to the exact bend in the river where they hatched, is way beyond the comprehension of those of us like me who still have trouble locating our cars in the Wal-Mart parking lot. And that is only the opening act.

Once in the ocean, salmon must adjust quickly to the changes in water chemistry and temperature, then add silvery muscle and fat for the trip back home. Everything from the oxygen levels in their blood to the colors of their scales must change for them to thrive at sea. They range far and deep in seawater but eventually return to whatever coastal seep they emerged from, so they can join another epic struggle upstream and return to reproduce in their exact hatching place in ancestral waters. As little as 1 percent of the young salmon that leave the freshwater for the ocean will make it back home to breed.

The survivors carve shallow grooves into the marrow of riverbeds and lay eggs, in the case of females, or fertilize eggs, in the case of males. And then they die. After death, the salmon enters into its last circle dance. Nutrients from the salmon's decaying body nourish its riparian habitat, making it healthy for its progeny, who will in turn emerge, descend, recover, return, mate, die, decay, and feed. Salmon are held sacred by Northwest peoples because they are life-giving food to a wide array of creatures like bears and eagles, which are also powerful and highly regarded, and because they embody generosity, courage, wonder, mystery, steadfastness, hope, and renewal. The life story of a salmon is a performance of the signature movement of life itself—a grand and unifying circle. It all starts with a bright row of reddish orange eggs, their reflections flickering under the surface of clear and rippled water like primal fire.

Dams change everything. They present impenetrable barriers and deadly delays through the warm, predator-rich slackwaters that collect behind them, and they have treacherous spillways or flesh-shredding turbines—all hazards the salmon encounter over and over along their journey. About 99 percent of the salmon fingerlings that leave their high-altitude interior homes never make it back under the best of circumstances, and a gauntlet of engineered steel and cement is not the best of circumstances.[2] Today the wild salmon, an evolutionary masterpiece that is as genetically tuned, refined, and diverse as any species on earth, is disappearing and endangered.

But dams are not the only cause of the salmon's precipitous decline. As late as 1950, the region's extensive forests were largely intact.[3] In the fifty-odd years since then—pushed by the demands of a burgeoning populace, pulled by the opening of new global markets, and then driven, in the 1980s and 1990s, by lumber companies' need to make profits and pay off the debts they had incurred in a cutthroat financial environment—the Northwest forests were mowed down like so much wheat. Many of the remaining tracts of old-growth forest were removed.

Logging begins with the bulldozing of muddy dirt roads. Trees are torn out by the roots that also hold the forest floor in place. As trees are cut down, massive logs are dragged across soft, moist soil surfaces. The result of all this activity is rapid erosion and the subsequent silting of the gravel beds needed by salmon to spawn. Obviously, when fewer spawn, fewer survive. Logging is bad enough, but dams deliver the coup de grâce to the fragile strains of native salmon that remain.

The Grand Coulee Dam in Washington state alone doomed hundreds of ancient strains of salmon. Dams along the Columbia River destroyed 90 percent of the inland West's wild salmon in twenty-five years. They have since been retrofitted to accommodate fish migration, but success has been mixed at best. Although bypass tunnels and screens can keep salmon from getting sucked into powerful turbines, most fish become exhausted and die upstream in the slackwater behind the dams before they can get to those bypasses. Those going the other way may be offered fish ladders, which have been ineffective almost everywhere they have been tried. Fish elevators have also been disappointing. Today, dam operators are experimenting with loading fish entering slackwater into trucks or barges and then hauling them to the other side of the dam, a procedure the fish seem to find stressful and confusing.

When big dams were engineered, the dynamics of a living river were neither imagined nor considered. The state and federal agencies currently working to reverse the ill consequences of dam technology are earnest and concerned, but there is a limit to technological fixes in the face of a technology that is as incompatible with ecological process as it is massive, fixed, and rigid.

The mighty Columbia of legend, the artery of a thousand watershed habitats for the sacred salmon of Northwest tribes and settlers, has been tamed. The salmon are mostly gone, replaced by aluminum plants that feed on hydroelectric power. The aluminum went into airplanes, which in turn fueled a thriving Northwest Cold War economy, which in turn drew millions of new inhabitants who believed they needed the trapped water to drink and to wash their cars. Dams often create their own fierce constituency in that way—build it and they will come.

In the Northwest, dams often set the pattern for subsequent development and are widely perceived as indispensable, making the destruction of the dams along the Columbia and the restoration of salmon habitat hard to imagine. But the four dams that impede the Snake River, which is part of the wide Columbia–Snake drainage, are a different story. Although they are the type of run-of-the-river dams that provide no flood control, only a small fraction of the region's electricity, and only minor water storage, the Snake River dams are defended by many of Idaho's politicians as if they are of critical importance. Economic studies clearly show that the restoration of native salmon populations would benefit riverside communities, which could thrive beside robust salmon grounds, with thousands of jobs created.

When the U.S. Department of Commerce's National Marine Fisheries Service, the government agency charged with protecting salmon as a "commercial resource," proclaimed that the dams "pose no jeopardy" to the recovery of native salmon, Judge Malcolm Marsh called their science "arbitrary and capricious."[4] A subsequent study, the most thorough of its kind ever done, concluded that the fish could not survive for long with the dams in place. Salmon lovers rejoiced—their case was made. Their glee was premature, however. The Snake River dams may be excellent examples of the kind of ill-considered pork-barrel projects built during the Cold War era, but they have attracted a powerful constituency and are zealously defended by slackwater politicians, who spread fear and misinformation about the consequences of their removal. Congresswoman Chenoweth was a fine example of this pheonomenon. Never known for her critical-thinking skills, Chenoweth is famous in the West for exclaiming that salmon could not be endangered, since her grocery store shelves were stocked with cans of them.

Those cans were packed, of course, with hatchery-raised salmon, which bear about the same relationship to wild salmon as a Tyson's

chicken bears to a bald eagle. Raised in ocean pens in quantities characteristic of industrial agricultural operations that grow and process
hogs and chickens, hatchery salmon have only half to a third as much
of the healthy omega-3 oils as their leaner wild cousins. They are not
nearly as nutritious as wild salmon are. Wild salmon are in the pink, but
the flesh of hatchery salmon would be as pale as flounder if synthetic
dyes were not added to their food.[5] Hatchery salmon are grown mostly
in Norway, Canada, Chile, and Britain.

Chenoweth's ecological illiteracy was at the heart of her anti-
environmental agenda, and many of her Idaho constituents bought it
hook, line, and sinker. But not all of them: bumper stickers reading
"Can Helen, not salmon" began to appear. A couple of years after the
Hansen hearing, she quit after embarrassing details of an extramarital
affair were revealed.

Because of Idaho politicians' attachment to the dams, instead of the
prescribed dam removal dozens of elaborate technical schemes have
been proposed and several implemented to circumvent the river's natural functions. One of these is the "juvenile-salmon transport system,"
which causes salmon smolts to be trapped behind dams, where they
may starve to death or be hunted by birds, before being scooped or
sucked into tubes, trucks, and barges that bypass the dam and dump
them on the other side. It costs millions of dollars, and it doesn't work.
The trucks spread diseases, and many fish die.

Meanwhile, drastically dwindling populations of native chinook,
coho, steelhead, and sockeye salmon have been seeded with millions of
hatchery eggs to compensate for the absence of egg-laying survivors,
also to no avail whatsoever. Although a hundred Northwest hatcheries
make fish in long cement troughs and dump enough into rivers and
streams to keep the opening-day crowd mollified, hatchery fish spread
disease. In addition, they usually lack the skills needed to survive in the
wild, yet they eat up the wild salmon's food supply. Slurries have been
proposed, too—anything but a free river and a healthy ecosystem. And
the dams would be cheap to breach.

No matter. A few powerful businesses do benefit from the dam, and
they have sewn themselves into the political fabric of the region. While
the wild salmon populations continue to be torn apart, that political

fabric has, so far, held. Barge companies, for example, want to keep barging along. Northwest barge operators lobbied for dams and fight to keep them in place because the slackwater highways that the dams make are key to barge owner profits. Those profits also translate into revenues that politicians want. If the slackwater byways were restored to whitewater rapids, the freight and goods now shipped by barge traffic would simply shift to parallel highways and rail lines. Consumers wouldn't know the difference, but a handful of barge owners would.

The accumulated economic benefits from tearing out dams might be much greater than the economic activity currently generated by dams, and those economic benefits would certainly be more widely and inclusively disbursed, but the economy that is in place trumps the one that is only imagined. Dams make electrical power and make avenues for the subsidized transportation of cargo. They attract development, and people like to recreate on their reservoirs. But removing dams and restoring salmon in the Northwest would draw sport fishermen, rafters, and kayakers, who would in turn benefit hundreds of small businesses in small towns all along the freed rivers. But those who have not yet benefited from that change are not yet here to campaign for it.

As food for man, the wild salmon can be replaced by its hatchery-held cousins, who share the wild salmon's form but not its substance. If we are what we eat, however, we might pause before that popular entrée and think about this. Hatchery salmon are not the awe-inspiring blessings of Northwest watersheds woven by evolution into the fabric of time and land, but products of managed incest, bred in cement casements and then trucked and dumped. They marry their first cousins endlessly until the marvelous genetic features that evolved over eons are gone and they become, in the words of one Northwest critic, "homeless seagoing spam."[6] Worse, genetically altered salmon, humanly engineered to add weight at rates inconceivable in the wild, may be a kind of evolutionary pollution if their altered genes get mixed into wild native strains. No one understands the natural implications of manufactured fish, but commercial fish-growing operations find the profits from fatter fish irresistible.

The dams' destruction of wild salmon is particularly grievous to Native Americans in the Northwest, whose cultures evolved alongside the salmon. First the varied strains of salmon laced the Northwest water-

sheds. Then the prehistoric people who drifted around and across re-
ceding Ice Age glaciers discovered them. Accustomed to eating deer,
elk, duck, and seal, it took them a while to learn how to harvest marine
life, but they eventually adapted to the resources at hand. When the
salmon were running, they could fill their nets and spears so easily that
it was as if the salmon were offering themselves freely. But that was not
always the case. The Northwest is a tapestry of habitats, each with its
own circumstances and disturbances. While one watershed is experiencing an exceptionally rich run, another is having a lean one.

In *Salmon Without Rivers,* his excellent history of the Pacific salmon
crisis, Jim Lichatowich explains how the development of a widespread
gift economy made local cultures viable in good times and bad.[7] The
Native American notion of a gift was not a commodity or property to
be possessed, but an act understood as reciprocal in nature: My giving
you a gift is an expression of my power that conveys prestige upon me,
the giver. Your acceptance of my gift implies obligation. Someday I will
be in need, and you will have the power to return my gift to me.

The formal expression of this cycle of obligatory returns was called
a potlatch. A potlatch could take place at a celebration of a marriage, the
naming of a child, or other community events. Potlatches became the
engines of commerce. They also served to redistribute wealth: a community experiencing abundance during a good year in their watershed
would provide for a community experiencing scarcity in theirs, with a
guarantee that the gift would be returned when the circumstances were
reversed.

The gift economy expressed a worldview that emphasized the reciprocal nature of all relationships. Trees, salmon, ravens, rocks, and
shellfish were kindred spirits—equivalent beings capable of exchange,
obligation, respect, and understanding. If an animal gave its flesh or fur,
the eater or wearer was obliged to honor and acknowledge the gift, or
it would not be given again—respect and abundance were intertwined.
The gift economy of native Northwesterners was remarkably harmo-
nious with nature's own economy—more like music than math.

Though the gift of wild salmon may not be revered by all, there is no
denying that the native salmon's decline signals the distressed condition of our holistic commons. Many things kill and impede salmon, like
silted runoff from logging roads and pollution, but there is no cause of

their decline equal to dams. When, in the name of progress and development, we stow the flow, the sacred salmon dies.

The decline of native salmon is the consequence of our collective choices, as hashed out in the political and economic arenas of the Northwest, about the meaning, purpose, and use of commonly held natural resources like rivers. The questions "What is a river?" and "What is a river for?" are not just philosophical, because the answers have measurable consequences for natural communities of fish, birds, plants, and animals and also imply winners and losers in human communities. The Nez Perce see salmon as a gift from the Creator and the river as a generous living being. Barge operators see rivers as transportation vectors. Fly fishermen see sport and delicious food, while kayakers see fun.

Restoration proposals pit well-established constituencies against imagined ones. Those imagined constituencies may be present in a nascent way, but rarely do they have the power accumulated by well-established interests. Since the day the first white settlers took over native watersheds, water rights in the West have traditionally gone to those who used water first; political power has accrued first and foremost to those user groups that got into the political process early. The construction companies that built the dams, the utilities that grabbed the new hydroelectric power, the aluminum plants that used the cheap power from the utilities, and the barge operators who used the new slackwater grabbed the power to shape water policies and the management process itself. They got seats at the tables where the decisions about water were made, built lobbying groups, contributed campaign bucks to politicians, and forged political alliances. They also lay down assumptions about what is rational, right, and real. Now they are entrenched. The rights of the Indians have always been violated with impunity, on a scale comparable only to the denial of the rights of wildlife to healthy habitat. The sport fishermen, salmon-loving eco-activists, kayakers, birders, and others who question the wisdom of dams have been too late in getting to the door that is mostly now barred by those who want to keep power for themselves.

Organizing those groups so that they can challenge the current system is crucial, of course, but the metaphorical struggle is also important. The way to enlist supporters who can see beyond the tangible benefits in place from a given system is to raise awareness about the drawbacks and inequities of that system, its failures and liabilities. At the same time that the problems of the current system are described, a compelling vision of a different system must also be created. In the struggle over the viability and future of native salmon versus the future of Northwest dams, two premier symbols collide. One is the engineering icon of technological prowess that tames wild landscapes. The other is the living embodiment of the reach and resilience of evolutionary creation.

Ultimately, this is no slim intellectual struggle over metaphors, but a fundamental divide about the meaning of life, the place of humans within the cosmos, and the future course of civilization. Metaphors make maps, and maps guide plans, policies, laws, and budgets that not only mark the land but are also blueprints for how we see, who we become, and the webs we weave with one another. Under one vision we get healthy and sustainable watersheds plus the quality of life they offer. The other perspective turns rivers into barge conveyances and convenient electricity for aluminum factories while shredding food webs that support whole ecosystems, ecosystems that ultimately enclose our own health and well-being.

The emergence of the wild salmon at the heart of the struggle over restoring Northwest watersheds also signals a shift in the wider environmental movement in America. The Clean Water Act, a premier and characteristic result of that movement's earlier focus, limited the damage allowed by corporate polluters and made a huge difference in the quality of our collective water resources. But it also assumed that the ongoing damage allowed by the law could be managed, regulated, and controlled. Industry, after all, was not going away or even changing from its guiding paradigm. The era's assumptions about the rights of private property, the need to progress materially, and the wisdom of technological means were not challenged by the new law.

As a consequence of that legislation, rivers were cleaned up significantly. You never hear of one catching fire anymore, as a river running through Cleveland did thirty years ago, unless a barge hits a bridge and fuel is spilled. The Clean Water Act worked as far as it was intended to go. But enforcement of the act didn't often result in restored habitats, healed ecosystems, or new economies.

Restoration aims at a grander scale of change. It seeks not just to remove the chemical pollution from the tap, but to free the river itself.

Restoration trusts the integrity of the river's flow and flood, the way it loops and leans across the land, creating a marsh here and rapids there. Restoration acknowledges that water creates life and that to deprive land of water is to rob it of life. It aims to put living fire back into wild glacial streams and to heal the land that watersheds nourish.

EIGHT

Following the Money Through Fear and Loathing

"Rivers are metaphors for life itself," Zach Frankel tells me as we sit in the offices of the Utah Rivers Council. One wall is dominated by a plastic relief map of the state. When I look more closely, I see that a small piece is missing in the middle, the county we call Happy Valley, the home of Brigham Young University and the cultural heart of Mormondom. Zach tells me he found the big map in a dumpster. He carried it back to the office and mounted it on the wall. It serves not only as a useful reference tool but also as a symbol of the frugality that is at once a core characteristic of grassroots activism and the theme that Zach and his colleagues at the Utah Rivers Council teach. They think we waste water and then hoard it so we can waste more of it, at the expense of wildlife and the land. That, according to Zach, is a shame.

"Rivers are metaphors for life, but water, of course, is the lifeblood of the land," he says. "Every creature on the land needs clean and fresh water to live. Rivers support more plant and animal species than all other habitat types combined. Here in Utah, for example, about 80 percent of wildlife species are supported for a portion of their life by a river.

Streamside vegetation purifies runoff by removing nutrients and improves water quality for humans. Rivers provide migration corridors for fish, birds, and mammals. "

Although most of us might not put such a fine grain to it as Zach does, the importance of water is self-evident, especially in arid Western states. Somehow, he continues, that basic understanding has not led us to revere our watersheds and manage their use in a precautionary way, but instead has primed us for a reckless and self-defeating race to use up watersheds.

It is impossible to address water policy in the arid West without confronting denial, ignorance, fear, and wishful thinking—a messy mindset that both contributes to and is a consequence of bad policy. We surround ourselves with golf courses, Kentucky bluegrass lawns, and exotic species of water-sucking trees that mask our desert and high plains environments and make them look like wet Eastern landscapes, where the limitations on water use that we do not want to confront do not exist. But Westerners know in their bones that we are vulnerable to long droughts that could curb our waterlogged habits abruptly—the parched ghosts of the Anasazi haunt us. We know it is not wise to overdraw a thin and fickle watershed, and we are becoming aware that tapped-out ecosystems suffer.

This dawning awareness, now forced upon us by prolonged drought, is a harbinger of change, and Zach wants to shape that change. He believes that our ignorance and denial is enabled by water policies that mask the real costs of water and encourage waste. And there is a self-fulfilling prophecy at work, too. Our drive to tap, drain, plumb, and use more water is driven by a fear of massive water shortages, which we may, ironically, be hastening by the wasteful uses of water made possible by the very water development projects we think will save us.

We misunderstand the nature of our crisis, Zach tells me. Several years of drought have raised fears that there may not be enough water for our insatiable and profligate needs. There is indeed enough water to go around, he says, but only if we use it wisely and find the means to reward conservation of water and discourage its waste. Current water policies often do just the opposite. It is important to change those policies and the habits they enable, not only so the human community benefits, but also so the wildlife communities that share our watersheds have enough. In Zach's humble vision, a healthy landscape is well watered, providing habitat to all the members of watershed communities, from people to birds and animals. Golfers do not trump wetland species, citizens are informed, and their leaders practice rational policies that make sense.

Zach bristles when others dismiss his ideas as too radical. What could be more extreme than the destructive, irrational, and futile behaviors that now pass as the conventional wisdom on water use? Call him a citizen advocate; he hates the term "environmentalist," finding it divisive and misleading. "How many people walk the streets and call themselves Wobblies because they believe in the right to a forty-hour work week," he says, "or call themselves suffragettes because they think women should have the right to vote? We all believe that. And we all think the environment is important and should be protected. The term 'environmentalist' often conjures up someone who is extreme and unyielding, a social misfit. It's absurd, because these issues are all about mainstream politics and the principles we all share. So I start out as a member of the public who is concerned about how the government is spending my money and the results they are getting from that. But then I get labeled an environmentalist by someone who wants to shield their self-serving water project from view by diverting the attention to me. They want to undermine my credibility with the label."

When the Central Utah Project, a very expensive pipeline system, was targeted in the 1970s and 1980s by critics who pointed out that the CUP had not been audited for more than a decade, the annual report of the Upper Colorado River Commission, which supposedly monitored the progress and performance of the CUP, claimed that it was being "subjected to unmerciful, unreasonable, and unconscionable attacks by ecology and environmental extremists." You know, like the ones who think that auditing the financial records of water districts every twenty years or so might be a good idea. Emotional people like that. Wackos.

It seems to me that Zach has successfully escaped the wacko stereotype and is moving his ideas into the mainstream of Utah's political culture. The governor has adopted his once radical notion that big, publicly funded water projects should no longer get a hidden subsidy from state sales, income, and property taxes. The media quote him. He is acknowledged by all familiar with his work as an up-and-coming mover and shaker. But for several years, several years ago, Zach lived out of the trunk of his car and made do on only a few thousand dollars a year. A bright graduate of the University of Utah and then a grad student at the University of Washington, Zach Frankel was employable at the usual forty-hour-a-week pace, but he preferred kayaking, scuba diving, rock climbing, and skiing.

"I'd put a thousand dollars on my credit card over the summer so I wouldn't have to work, and then pay it off with a seasonal job the following winter," he explains, waxing poetic about the joy he experienced in wild places and the lessons to be learned from living simply. When you weed out most of the material possessions we strive to acquire and discover that a leaner perspective is possible, he said, Wal-Mart never looks the same again.

Even fresh water, precious life-giving water, had become a commodity, he realized. It was a resource to be marketed, and it was being marketed to death. This was particularly troubling to him. "I have this affinity with water—rivers, the ocean, even my love of skiing, really, because snow is water, too."

When Zach was a kid his parents took him on river trips, and he found himself drawn to living water in a powerful way. On one journey downriver when he was about five years old, he disappeared underwater. His parents, of course, panicked. "But I was fine," he recalls. "I remember sitting at the bottom of that pool and just looking at what was going on all around me on that river bottom. It was amazing. I felt calm." Not quite at home, however, and he was pulled to the surface for air.

Years later, he had more oxygen-friendly opportunities to observe river life while scuba diving through rivers in Washington and Idaho as he studied river ecology. Fish fascinated him—their sleek beauty, the way they moved together in schools like undulating ribbons, the myriad and subtle ways they complemented their fluid environments. He saw otters swimming under the water and birds diving into it.

Zach first did conservation work in the Northwest, but in the early 1990s he came home to Utah, where the Southern Utah Wilderness Alliance hired him to do an inventory of rivers as part of their effort to describe all the aspects of the state's wilderness. He went on to author a book on Utah's wild and scenic rivers, then decided that his research for the book, and the case it made, would be a good starting point for a nonprofit advocacy group focusing on Utah's rivers, their condition, and their future. He wanted to return to the Northwest but couldn't persuade others to start such a group without him. So he founded the Utah Rivers Council himself.

That was eight years ago. He shakes his head and smiles. The organization and its mission have had an unexpected eddying effect on the course of his life. "I thought I'd only be working on wild and scenic rivers," he says, "but instead we got involved in dam busting right away. We put a campaign together to stop a dam on Utah's Diamond Fork River, and then did the same for the Bear River." The Bear River campaign was especially important because the Bear is the largest water source for the Great Salt Lake, one of North America's largest wetland ecosystems. The Bear continually nourishes and recharges irreplaceable wetlands around the lake. A dam that impounded the river could lower the lake's level and dry up critical habitat for migrating and nesting birds. Getting people to conserve water rather than building more dams, on the other hand, would mean that there would be more water for wildlife.

The campaigns were unambiguously successful. They killed the dams they took on. And the process of making a case against particular unnecessary dams made Zach look at water development in general.

Zach had the context down. He knew rivers inside out, literally. He knew the science. He also clearly recognized the difference between seeing a river as both a primary metaphor for life and, truly, the life-source of the land itself and seeing a river as a mere resource, as a vehicle for profit and power. What he needed to learn was the process that turned living rivers into polluted, plumbed, rigid artifacts of their once vibrant beings. How did that happen?

The mechanisms were simple enough but hidden, he discovered. They were as familiar and old as corruption itself. Water had been turned over to politicians who were inaccessible, uninformed, and unaccountable. They had learned how to make the water infrastructure they presided over generate straight cash and contracts for themselves, their relatives, and their construction-business cronies. In an earlier era, Western communities got federal funds to do whatever water development projects they could think up. Lobbyists from agribusiness and growing Western cities like Las Vegas and Phoenix squeezed Congress hard for pork-barrel projects that were beyond the influence of the general public. Waste and corruption were tolerated because, throughout the West, water development was assumed to be necessary and good. It was the way we made the desert bloom.

That unquestioning era ended as conservation organizations began to underline the ecological destruction wrought by those projects, which increasingly were less about crops and more about golf greens, casino fountains, and industrial slurries. Congress took a closer look and found that tax dollars were being spent badly. Also, at a certain point most of the free-flowing rivers had already been dammed and diverted. By then, however, a culture of pork-barrel spending on water development had become well established.

"Water in the West is controlled and directed by water districts," Zach says. "They are the large wholesalers of water in Utah and across the West. What is a water district?" He answers his own question. "They are the same sort of utility provider as natural gas, electricity, cable television, and telephone service. They are a commodity deliverer that makes money from the sale of water instead of gas, electricity, cable, phones, and so on.

"But unlike phones and gas," he continues, "they are not private companies regulated by a public utility commission that is supposed to ensure that rates are fair to consumers and that expensive new projects are carefully weighed before going forward. Water districts aren't regulated at all! They are governmental agencies controlled by directors who more or less appoint each other and usually stay there as long as they please. Here in Utah they have taxation powers like a city council, but they are not elected into office. They aren't even responsive to elected leaders who, for the most part, won't take them on. They operate more like a private company, out of the public eye and out of reach."

The same lessons we found true two hundred years ago are true today, he explains. "Taxation without representation leads to really bad public policy. So here we have the Wasatch Front, with the highest per capita water use and rapid growth in the middle of a drought, and instead of implementing an aggressive water conservation campaign immediately, the water districts promise to cut water consumption over twenty, thirty, or forty years—*after* they spend billions on dubious water development projects. They want to spend the money. It's about the money."

Not surprisingly, such blank-check government has led to corruption. "Following the money in Utah water development," Zach laughs, "is easy—there's usually one stop. Take the Central Utah Project. It's been going on since 1956, but there have only been two audits, one in '89 and again in '99. The audits revealed that members of the board appointed by the governor were pocketing money. The chair of the board at one time received $90,000 in consulting contracts that were a violation of state law. And he couldn't even account for what he did. He produced invoices that described no work. Other board members were also drawing salaries from the CUP with no clear jobs. One member got $500,000 in construction and consulting contracts. Family members, of course, got sweetheart construction contracts. Staffers were buying themselves and their spouses ski tickets, dinners, personal airline tickets, cars, and memberships. A general manager got a bonus of $70,000, and not all the other board members even knew about it. So there is very little oversight going on." Not all districts are that corrupt, he concedes, but there is a clear pattern of shenanigans and misappropriated funds across the board, from local districts to the big federal projects and agencies.

To make it worse, those who freely spend public dollars on themselves then wrap it all up in what Zach calls a "patriotic sense." "There is this myth in the West that water development is a pure good: We need to tame nature by damming and diverting rivers for use. Flowing rivers are wasted water." Until quite recently, most Western water projects got a political pass that was not available to most publicly funded projects— except perhaps the defense industry during the Cold War era or anything called homeland security today. During the early pork-barrel era, when the West's water infrastructure was built, special interests ruled and citizens had little say. It wasn't until the passage of landmark national legislation like the Clean Water Act and the National Environmental Policy Act that citizens could get through the door and sit at the policy and planning table.

"I have not heard an adequate description for this kind of corruption," Zach observes. "We call corrupt politicians who govern water 'water buffaloes,' but that doesn't quite hit the mark."

"Water hogs?" I suggest.

"No, that could be anyone who wastes water. It's different," he says. Vampires, maybe?

After uncovering the madness and its methods, Zach Frankel had to figure out a different way. If unaccountable taxation feeds political corruption and results in gluttonous water usage, then cutting off the taxes that the water vampires feed on is a first step. The idea is simple and very mainstream: reconnect a relationship between supply and demand based on price. The Utah Rivers Council has been all over it, telling media, municipal governments, and legislators that as long as water is divorced from the laws of supply and demand, water will be artificially cheap but remain heavily subsidized by taxpayers. If you look at water rates alone—the amount of money the consumer is charged directly—Utah has the third-lowest water rates in the nation and the cheapest rates of all of the thirteen Western states. It also scores among the very highest states in per-capita usage. Arid Utah's direct water charges are half those of a resident of wet Seattle. How can that be?

The answer resides in the property taxes and sales taxes paid by the typical Utahn. Everyone belongs to at least one water district and pays a portion of his or her property taxes to support those districts. Some unlucky taxpayers belong to three water districts. Each district has an office and staff to support, its own equipment, and a list of pet projects it wants to undertake. Utah's water is not nearly as cheap as its directly paid water rates suggest. The real costs of its water, driven up by overlapping little bureaucracies with padded staffs, sweetheart deals, and overengineered projects, are hidden in residents' tax bills and divorced from usage. But only those with a penchant for the details of the revenue process are likely to know that.

The Utah Rivers Council is changing the terms of the debate, encouraging more open dialogue, and shifting the agenda for public discourse. The council is turning water into a taxpayer issue because there's a powerful case to be made on the economics of water alone that most people of all political persuasions can understand. To beat the Bear River and Diamond Fork dams, they talked to every city council member and every legislator they could corner. Look at the fiscal impacts and the complete costs, they told them, and then look at the less expensive alternatives that the water bureaucracies are refusing to consider. Water utilities responded angrily, claiming that eliminating their property-tax crutch would ruin their bond ratings and leave them fiscally emasculated. The council compared bond ratings for districts that did and didn't use property taxes and found little or no difference.

There are signs that the awareness of water development as a taxpayer concern is growing. For starters, sales and income taxes have also traditionally supported water development, but these practices too are now being questioned. In his 2003–2004 budget Utah governor Mike Leavitt, desperate to fund education for the state's burgeoning population of children during a recession, proposed to take the sales tax away from water projects and apply it elsewhere. The local media is starting to outline the implications of using property taxes and sales taxes for water development. Even the conservative Sutherland Institute has chimed in on the common sense of tying water use to price.

First of all, the argument goes, when rates do not reflect usage, key incentives to cut water use are missing at a time when the West is in an extended and severe drought. There are encouraging signs that we are ready to relate to our landscape differently. Cheered on by a "slow the flow" public relations campaign in 2002, Utahns cut their water use significantly and voluntarily, making evident the power of water conservation. Salt Lake City has identified its two main methods of meeting future water needs as conservation and recycling. Xeriscaping—low-water-use landscaping that relies on drought-tolerant native plants—has suddenly become fashionable. Having realized that outdoor watering accounts for about 70 percent of the city's water usage, Salt Lake City is practically mandating xeriscaping for public facilities.

The state has a long way to go, however, because even as it learns to use less water per person, it is adding more people all the time. Mormon Utah has the highest birthrate in the nation. It is unlikely that the state can cut water use much further without creating positive incentives that encourage water conservation and negative incentives that discourage waste. And all of those good citizens who get it, who understand the need to conserve and want to do so, need feedback—information that tells them how they are doing. People do not generally read meters, but we all look at our water bills.

I, for one, welcome the change. When I moved to town from Capitol Reef National Park, I missed the dry, wild landscapes I knew in the canyons, but I embraced the regime of landscaping domesticity I saw around me. I had kids, after all, who wanted to roll on a lawn. I grew up with a lawn. My infatuation did not last long. Unlike the lush lawns of the easy-growing East, my Western lawn must be soaked regularly to prevent baked soil and dried-out blades. In the Southwest, the difference between a rich green lawn and a fire hazard can be a mere week without water in July. Keeping a lawn going in the summer requires a frantic cycle of cutting the lawn before it requires a hay-baler and then quickly spraying water on it so it doesn't dry up under the hot summer sun, only to be rewarded by another bumper crop that has to be cut right away.

Hardy native plants like sagebrush and cactus are gaining appeal for me. There is actually a wide array of plants native to this region that have evolved to withstand our typical seasonal stresses. Landscaping with native plants reduces water consumption significantly. But we all have neighbors who have turned green lawns into a kind of suburban cult, with reservoir-enabled sprinklers as their fetish. Under the current system, if I stop watering my lawn and replace it with hardy shrubs while my neighbor acts like he is on a one-man campaign to grow muskrats and mosquitoes next to his patio, our monthly water bills will be only slightly different.

Stroll any suburban neighborhood on a hot day and you can catalogue the ways we waste water. First there are all those green lawns of Kentucky bluegrass, the preferred ground cover all over America regardless of whether you live in Kentucky or Las Vegas. Kentucky bluegrass is thirsty, sucking up twice as much water as more hardy species like buffalo grass and blue grama. Around the lawn we plant non-native trees and shrubs that may also suck up more water than the local rainfall provides. Then we give our landscaped lawns about twice as much water as they need, even for all those imported exotics we planted. Automatic sprinkler systems help us do that. They are convenient but usually timed to stay on too long, and they go on even when they are not needed. Or they go on during the afternoon, when evaporation pulls much of the water into the air instead of the lawn. And they tend to water streets and sidewalks as well as yards. "We still have rivers," Zach says. "They just flow down our gutters instead of covering trout."

The pattern Zach describes—artificially low rates that encourage overuse, subsidized by taxes collected by self-serving water developers—is not unique to Utah. Dozens of grassroots organizations across the West are also making the case for water reform in their own watersheds. Many Western communities have found success in using market-based water pricing. Through this and other programs, by 1997 Los Angeles reduced its water usage to 1970 levels, even more impressive given the 25 percent increase in population between then and now.[1] Most of the drought-stricken West is looking hard at water reform and conservation. As communities apply what they learn, success stories will be rolling in.

The hydro-sins of the suburbs are a mere drop in the bucket. Most of the water used in the West goes to agriculture. In the West, Zach tells me, about 85 percent of the water is used for agriculture, while only about 15 percent goes to urban uses, including all that inefficient outdoor watering. Of the 85 percent, some water goes to crops that are ridiculously water-intensive and not appropriate to grow in the desert, like cotton and rice, but most of it supports alfalfa for cattle, which soaks up a lot of water. Cows themselves, of course, are water-intensive beasts as well. In the East and Midwest they can graze the bottomlands and get by well enough without baled supplements. Not so in the West, where too often they trash precious riparian areas on public lands and still have to be watered and fed bales of alfalfa most of the year.

If all the cows in the West were to get mad and go away, the water that goes to cow food would be available for other uses. The Western cattle industry produces a very small portion of the nation's overall beef supply, around 3 percent, but it takes the lion's share of the West's water. If the price of water becomes realistic, water now used for agriculture may get redirected to city and suburban users, who now subsidize the water used for cows. More water might be left for the river itself. As former Colorado governor Dick Lamm once observed, "Water does not run downhill, but towards money."[2]

It goes back to the days of John Wesley Powell, Zach says. "Congress encouraged the settling of the West with a pioneer mentality that 'rain followed the plough.' That was wrong, of course. We also irrigated land that shouldn't have been irrigated because there wasn't an adequate water source. Dry-land farming was unrealistic. We were accustomed to the East and lots of rain. We misunderstood the environment." Ironically, cultivating crops that were not sustainable in the long run marked the beginning of our water development follies, and now withdrawing such irrigated farmland may be the key to averting the water shortages that appear to be looming in the West. Turning farmland into housing developments has dire consequences for habitats and their creatures as well, but private dwellings suck up less water than do farmlands.

"It's a lifestyle choice too," says Zach. "The younger generation doesn't want the struggle of ranching anymore. They don't want to do hobby farming when they can make more money developing the land and selling the water. One way or the other, there will be plenty of water to go around as agriculture gives up ground." He is not advocating sprawl as a means of countering bad water policy, but simply relaying an economic fact of life: when agricultural water is translated into urban water, there will be much more water to go around. The fear of running out of water is overstated.

What about hydroelectric power from dams? Isn't that an important benefit of large-scale water development? Won't that power be even more important if we experience energy shortages? Again, Zach says, energy conservation could trump power generation if we addressed the disincentives to change our wasteful habits and the absence of incentives to do better. The estimates of how much electricity could be conserved are far-ranging and often reflect how bold and innovative the estimator is willing to be, but everyone concedes that cheap, plentiful power has encouraged inefficient use, just as cheap water enables waste. If the capital costs of dams are figured in, hydroelectric power is not cheap. The era of energy profligacy may be over.

As for those alarming "shortages" of electrical power in 2000 and 2001, they turned out to be the result of deregulation wedded to greed and corruption, and now, Zach says, there is a glut. But there are limits to building our way out of shortages with more power plants that damage the environment and are resisted locally wherever they are proposed. If Utahns can learn to conserve even 5 percent of what we now use, or replace dam-generated power with alternatives like wind and solar, the power generated by the Glen Canyon Dam would be unnecessary.

Okay, I tell Zach, let me summarize. We start by misunderstanding our arid environment and developing water-intensive agriculture that is not sustainable in the long run. We get hooked on water development to feed that agriculture. Water development becomes an end in itself as politicians and their business allies feed at the water-project trough at the public's expense. By hiding the costs of our water in our tax bills and keeping water rates artificially low, they encourage waste and the very demand for more water that drives, in turn, more development. Conservation is ignored. The land suffers. How do we break the pattern?

His answers sound like Democracy 101. When there are no checks and balances, there are no brakes on spending and no incentives to do well or think differently. Zach rails at the hypocrisy of Western politicians, especially Republicans, who condemn wasteful government and taxation but tolerate the wasteful way water is managed. "Lowering taxes to curb government doesn't apply to the water districts and their fat projects, only to battered women's shelters and education. Water projects get an exemption from democracy and a double standard on performance," he claims.

"Socialism for the rich and free enterprise for the poor?" I offer.

"Exactly!"

"How do they get away with it?" I ask.

"Fear has a lot to do with it," he replies. "Water, especially in times of drought like these, isn't like telephone service or cable television. We're not afraid of running out of cable stations and cell phones like we are afraid of water shortages. Water providers play on that fear and constantly warn of shortages." The other utilities are judged on criteria like profitability and performance, but water development is hostage to a basic fear that trumps those standards.

Another insight, which Zach calls tertiary, focuses on the way we are divided from one another. He cites the best example he knows of the empowerment that can result when people drop labels and encounter one another beyond the limitations of stereotypes. During the struggle to stop the Bear River dam, the Utah Rivers Council asked people whose lives would be affected by the dam to write statements about themselves, their work, and their families and attach them to a banner, along with photos of themselves. They were farmers, ranchers, contractors, excavators, real estate agents, professors, schoolteachers, and the like. The banner was taken to a hearing and pinned to the wall. It stretched out of the room, down a hallway, and up the stairs.

The variety of people whose concerns were colorfully and personally expressed on that banner melted the contrived boundaries the participants had perceived. It was a moving eye-opener. The room was no longer full of "farmers" and "environmentalists," just people who had a lot in common, whose cares and needs were real, who could now address each other's concerns directly, unmediated by misleading assumptions. "Healthy dialogue is so important," he concludes, "and we have to work at making that happen. Discourse is so important. That discourse has to include an open look at the fiscal impacts and whether other options are available. There are other options besides more dams, pipelines, and diversions, but we don't talk about them."

As Zach Frankel passionately points out, usually missing from the debate about dams—their "necessity" versus the damage they do—is a full acknowledgment of how water conservation could make a difference. Water conservationist Amy Vickers added it up for me during a conference I attended in Atlanta. The conference was for librarians from all over the nation, but Amy was taking advantage of the gathering to share information and raise awareness. She travels widely, offering her services as a consultant, doing lectures, meeting with media, and otherwise preaching the gospel of water conservation.

Yes, she acknowledged to her audience, booming population growth everywhere is a major factor in sucking up water supplies, and, yes, drought compounds the problem. But in America, our notoriously thirsty lawns and our habit of landscaping with ornamental plants that use copious water are also huge factors. Ditch-flowing irrigation for crops is too common and incredibly wasteful. Nations that have mastered drip irrigation, like Israel, grow food with a small fraction of the irrigation water we use.

We could harvest gray water, rainwater, and storm-water runoff for irrigating urban landscapes. We could capture huge water savings by fixing leakage, installing composting toilets, retrofitting inefficient fixtures, and making appliances like washing machines and dishwashers more efficient. We could stop letting local governments cut deals that offer cheap water to businesses instead of incentives to cut waste. We could require water conservation plans as a prerequisite for building permits. We could stop allowing our precious water to be polluted so it can't be used, period.

This is not just a problem in Utah. Although some regions of the nation seem waterlogged and worry more about flooding than about conservation, much of the nation, from the arid Southwest and southern California to the Great Plains, experiences periodic severe droughts. Even in the wet Midwest, aquifers that are taken for granted are getting tapped out. Global climate change may mean disruption of expected and familiar rain patterns that, in turn, may disrupt water supplies, even in those regions where water has not been considered a problem. Conservation is a trick we all need to learn.

If we spent a fraction of the money on conservation that we have spent on building dams, Amy says, we could have avoided the water crisis we are beginning to acknowledge, rather than ruining countless riparian habitats in the process. Ultimately, however, we may need to make fundamental changes in our behaviors. Our eating habits, for example, are particularly water wasteful. "It takes 120 gallons of water to produce a pound of tofu, but a pound of beef requires 1,200 gallons of water. Raising beef in the arid West, where the lion's share of water goes to beef crops like alfalfa, is a particularly questionable use of scant water. And then there are all those golf courses in places like Phoenix and Las Vegas, where only the sand traps are natural."

As nonrenewable aquifers dry up, says Amy, we will have to confront our wasteful ways. Meanwhile, she will continue to cross the nation like a hydro–Paul Revere, spreading the warning that the day of reckoning is upon us, as water sources we took for granted are tapped out. The West may have enough water to go around after all if we learn to conserve and create incentives to do so, but in the case of other big aquifers like the Ogalala Aquifer that sits beneath the Great Plains, we may have turned the notion of "too little, too late" on its head. We have used too much too soon. Aquifers that took thousands of years to form have been tapped down in less than a hundred years, faster than they can be replenished. Her primary mission is to show municipal governments how to do better, to be water wise. She knows she is also up against ingrained habits. But dams, pipelines, and treatment plants are big and expensive while conservation, she argues, is cheap. That's a powerful and popular bottom line in her favor.

On the other side, of course, are those who build and maintain our water infrastructure, those whose business is water, who would like to capture that bottom line altogether. They want to move the raw material of their industry from public to private hands, from the commons to the corporation. Although the United States has not experienced the rapid and complete privatization of water distribution that is now emerging in the underdeveloped world, local governments are increasingly tempted to hand over troublesome water problems to private consultants. Hired experts can be very helpful if they are used to inform civic discourse about options and impacts, but water is too important to turn over to them alone. Water is, perhaps, *the* most important resource we hold in common, and its purpose, meaning, and use should be commonly determined.

The privatization of water sources is a detour Amy hopes we don't take on our way to water wisdom. It's bad enough that we are polluting, diverting, and depleting the wellspring of life at an alarming rate, but faced with a demand for freshwater that outstrips the natural supply, it would be woefully misguided to turn to the same profit-driven corporate system for solutions that polluted, diverted, and depleted our freshwater sources in the first place.

Even in the western United States, where water policy is a case study in the pitfalls of poor government, turning water development and distribution over to corporations wouldn't make our water practices more accountable, more inclusive, or smarter. Where Western water policy is failing, it is often driven by the business allies of water bureaucrats, out to make a buck by building big projects or tapping into subsidized hydroelectric power. When decisions about water development are manipulated by private businesses seeking to make money, the interests of taxpayers and the needs of ecosystems are often ignored.

Ironically, the solution to bad government is not necessarily no government but sometimes more government, or at least better government. In some cases, private companies may offer positive contributions. What are most important are that the public stays on top of all water development and allocation decisions, whether stewarded by government agencies or private corporations, and that they learn well and exercise their rights effectively.

Unfortunately, governments across the globe are abdicating their responsibility to supply their people with the clean freshwater they need to live. The World Bank and the International Monetary Fund urge Third World governments to hand over their aging, costly, and inadequate water infrastructures to private corporations like French-based conglomerates Suez and Vivendi International, Britain's RWE/Thames Water, and America's own Bechtel. Privatization promises to rebuild antiquated water infrastructures that need huge infusions of capital and then run the new infrastructures efficiently.

"Efficiently" also means "profitably." *Fortune* magazine has called water "one of the world's greatest business opportunities," saying that it "promises to be to the twenty-first century what oil was to the twentieth."[3] It looks different, of course, if you live in a poor village and find that the community water supply that you and your children need to live has become an unaffordable commodity. Water riots may also become a common feature of the twenty-first century.

In the public arena, wise choices are generated by decision-making processes that are open, inclusive, informed, and accountable. The history of water development in the western United States offers ample evidence of what happens when public officials and their corporate allies are given an exemption from democracy. It is a history of blank checks and baloney. Zach Frankel and his many counterparts in grassroots groups across the West have pierced the veil of myths, lies, and misunderstandings and are introducing long-overdue reform and democratic discourse.

Although the water policies and practices they are advocating are not fully formed, they are introducing a revolutionary perspective to the process. Beyond the necessary focus on nuts and bolts like rates and taxes, this is what I hear: water management will not be truly wise and sustainable until we adapt to natural complexity and respect natural diversity. Only then will we learn to restore and conserve our watershed. An appreciation and regard for rivers as arteries of life may seem like common sense, but in a culture that views water as a commodity to be divided from its natural community and controlled, that perspective is also visionary.

"You have learned to stop new dams, but what about the big ones that are already up? Is Rich Ingebretsen crazy for thinking the Glen Canyon Dam can be breached?" I ask Zach. "Will the big ones come down?"

"Yes, certainly, that's the whole point—we can do that, let the waters flow freely again, let the rivers come alive, let the lands that rivers nourish grow healthy again. My dad told me that his generation made an industry to build dams, and mine would have to create an industry for taking them down." And Zach agrees that since that era of big-dam building started in the American West, it is appropriate and right that the era of decommissioning the big ones also begins here in the West.

NINE

White Elephants in the Boneyard of Pride

If rivers are the ultimate metaphors of life, as Zach Frankel proclaims, and there is ample evidence from religion and literature to support that view, then dams can't help but be powerful symbols, too. They are the human-made technology that captures and controls the wild and free flow of life.

To critics like Zach Frankel and Rich Ingebretsen, then, dams are stints in the heart of life's most powerfully resonating process. On the other hand, their proponents regard them as the foundation of civilization itself. The powerful clash of such potent symbols may explain the disdain conservationists feel for dams large and small, a response that some criticize as disproportionate to the damage dams do compared to other environmental horrors. Accumulating evidence, though, reveals that the critics' dim view of dams is in fact farsighted.

Following the era of the big dam in America, and fueled by self-inflating bureaucracies, careers, contracts, corruption, and greed, a worldwide dam-building boom bypassed all knowledge, research, and precaution. In a movement led by the U.S. and the U.S.S.R, the two superpowers during the twentieth century, big dams became big business. As a result, most of the world's rivers are now plumbed.

Silenced Rivers: The Ecology and Politics of Large Dams by Patrick McCully, director of the International Rivers Network, is the most comprehensive and devastating critique to date of the impact of dams on habitat and people. Despite the absence of a single formal assessment of even one big dam project's impact on ecosystems or local cultures,[1] growing and compelling evidence shows that big dams damage watersheds, habitats, communities, and even the economies they are supposed to buoy. Refusal to assess goes hand in hand with a lack of accountability. Dam opponents must not only make their case on their own but then struggle to find out who controls the floodgates. Only lately have dam critics gained credibility. Until then, dam building was viewed as an expected, acceptable aspect of civilization—the more evolved the society, the bigger the dams it built.

It is an old story. We have been damming rivers for thousands of years, since our hunter-gatherer ancestors turned to farming and discovered the wonders of irrigation, but for most of human history dams were small weirs of brushwood and earth designed to simply divert water. These early dams were modest and impermanent, reflecting the small scale of the farmlands and settlements that used them. Eventually, expanding agrarian cultures built much larger stone and earthen dams to both divert and store water. These dams were equal to the growing scope of the organizing powers, engineering prowess, and cultivating needs of the people who made them. They did not really alleviate the scourge of floods, commemorated universally in myths and legends, but they empowered burgeoning agrarian economies and their expanding populations by bringing rivers onto the land and ensuring a water supply during dry times and seasonal shortages.

The Romans made a fine art of dam building. By the time Columbus stretched his sea legs in the New World, penned water was also being used to power water wheels. England was covered with water mills, and New England followed suit. By the beginning of the Industrial Revolution, half a million water mills were powering Europe's factories and mines.[2]

Although damming has a long history, it wasn't until the twentieth century that large dams, thirty feet and higher, became common. As the height of dams soared, of course, the acreage of impounded water grew proportionately. The United States, Europe, and the Soviet Union, as usual, paved the way for big freshwater engineering projects. In the United States, the earliest big dams, like Grand Coulee, Hoover, and Shasta, were touted as the proud evidence of capitalism's engineering and organizing prowess. Today in the United States alone, the area of reservoir-covered lands is equal to Vermont and New Hampshire.[3] Our Cold War rival, the former Soviet Union, was not to be outdone, however, building vast reservoirs such as Kakhovskaya, Bratsk, and Krasnoyarsk. These reservoirs are the second-, fourth-, and ninth-largest reservoirs in the world. All are larger than Lake Mead or Lake Powell. Eight of the twenty largest reservoirs in the world were built in the lands of the former Soviet Union.[4]

The Soviet Union provided an ideal culture for dam building. To build big dams and drown the land, you must be able to marshal the required resources and stifle voices that question the wisdom of such projects. The Soviets' centralized authority, command economy, unchecked bureaucracies, forced gulag labor, and utilitarian philosophy that exalted the heroic control of nature made it easy to sweep any resistance out of the way. "Water that reaches the sea is wasted water," Stalin famously proclaimed.

After the big powers had thoroughly plugged their own rivers, export of dam building followed. The Soviets sponsored dams like the Aswan in Egypt and others in Europe, while the United States spearheaded projects like the Owens Falls Dam in Uganda. Big dams are not generated at the grass roots but are pushed forward by those elites and their agencies who have the power to command, muster, and move others. It is no surprise that China, which had eight large dams at the time of its Maoist revolution in 1949, now has 19,000. Finally, the massive dam movement spread southward into the Third World, fueled by international funding from the World Bank and the International Monetary Fund. In the Third World, water development usually involved schemes to turn communal lands used for local food production toward large-scale cash-crop production, aggravating the conditions of hungry, landless peoples.

Today the world is thoroughly dammed. The International Commission on Large Dams, the top dam industry association, estimates that the world's rivers are now blocked by more than 40,000 dams higher than fifteen meters, 35,000 of those constructed since 1950.[5] The pace and scale picked up at the close of the twentieth century—of the twenty highest dams in the world, fourteen were built since 1970; of the twenty dams with largest reservoir capacity, half were built since 1970.[6] The size of dams has increased until the weight of the waters they hold can trigger earthquakes. The reservoirs behind the world's big dams cover a total of about 155,000 square miles, an area the size of California. The collected weight of stored water has a slight but measurable impact on the speed of the earth's rotation, the tilt of its axis, and the shape of its gravitational field.[7]

Across the globe and in just a few decades, many rivers have all but disappeared or are barely recognizable. Cut into staircases of reservoirs, bled by canals, and confined by troughs and levees, rivers' relationship to the wetlands and floodplains they once nourished has been broken. The ecosystems that thrived along their banks have been sacrificed too, as rivers have been engineered into managed plumbing systems. Freshwater ecosystems are the most denigrated ecosystems on earth. Pollution started the job, and it is being finished by dams, those icons of development, progress, and engineering know-how. While pollution compromises water's content, dams undermine its dynamic process.

Dam building was pushed hard by powerful bureaucracies in the United States, the Soviet Union, and Maoist China. But worldwide, it was also fueled by large corporations and their financial lenders and allies. As behemoth dam-building corporations finished plugging up the rivers in their own backyards, they moved on to projects far away from their homelands. So Bechtel, which became big and rich while building the Hoover Dam, moved north into Canada and worked on the James Bay Dam, then eventually took on projects in Laos and China. Morrison Knudsen, another American corporation enlarged and enriched by building Hoover, moved on to Brazil, Paraguay, and Bangladesh's Kaptai dam and reservoir, which displaced 100,000 people. Canada's Acres Group had plenty to do in its own water-laced nation, a veritable wet dream for dam builders, but it also sold its expertise in Africa, Vietnam, and China. Like markets, rivers get tapped out, and then new ones must be found and exploited. Dam building has become a big business that must continually find markets for what generates its power and profits. As the dam-building industry moved out from its

American and European base looking for new customers, it learned how to lobby, persuade, manipulate, and grease palms when necessary—and it was often necessary.

Like its American and European predecessors, the overseas dam-building boom was fueled by the industries that profited directly from building—construction corporations, water-supply utilities, and big agriculture—and by the availability of funding through powerful international investors and international aid. During the Cold War, the Soviet Union and the United States both pushed to complete mega-dam projects in the Third World, in countries they competitively courted. The Soviets worked with the Egyptians to build the massive Aswan Dam project, until they lost favor there; then American advice followed. John Savage, the chief designer of the Hoover Dam, helped China design the Three Gorges Dam until the Maoist revolution in 1949, when he was replaced by Soviet engineers, who were also eventually kicked out, to be replaced recently by American and European consultants.

As development projects, dams had great appeal because they were perceived as impressive visible symbols of the progress of capitalism or communism, respectively. They were sold to the locals as a source of national pride, but in fact they came with a big hook. Dam building provides its sponsors with a manageable means of both empowering and controlling local allies through the distribution of cheap loans and fat contracts that, in turn, make those allies dependent enough on the sponsors to be influenced by them. Throughout the Third World, the lucrative contracts associated with dam building have fueled kickback corruption and contributed significantly to those countries' crushing debt. The economic benefits, meanwhile, have mostly accrued to the construction firms that built the dams, the politicians and bureaucrats who distribute the spoils for a price, and the agribusinesses that can afford to farm on the large scale that irrigation makes possible.

This pattern was also well established in the United States during the early dam-building era. The beneficiaries of irrigation water piped out from the San Luis and Oroville Dams, for example, include the Southern Pacific Railroad, the Blackwell Land Company, the vast Tejon Ranch, and oil companies with enormous agricultural land holdings like Chevron and Getty.[8] Although the production of food increases, it is often food that is shipped away, not food for local consumption.

Hydropower benefits have also been overstated and, like the advantages of large-scale irrigation, accrue to local elites—the poor still sit in dark slums, while the rich get to upgrade their seats on jet vacations. Even promises of flood control have not been fulfilled.

The compelling need to move impoverished populations away from spreading reservoirs is also convenient for authoritarian governments and their wealthy clients, who often seek to turn communal lands and small landholdings into larger agribusiness holdings. It is hard to know how many across the world have been displaced by dams, since people disperse and disappear. The governments complicit in their removal are not eager to count them, and they are too stressed and distracted to count themselves. But the estimate of the number of peasants who will be displaced by China's now complete Three Gorges Dam approaches one and a half million.[9] Patrick McCully estimates the number of people displaced during the last fifty years of international dam building to be at least 30 million and perhaps as high as 100 million.[10] Compensation and resettlement plans, he says, have generally been a cruel joke.

Although dams are supposedly designed for the benefit and welfare of all, the recent spate of big-dam building has had a steep human cost, especially for myriad indigenous and peasant peoples. Cultural Survival, a Harvard-based nonprofit dedicated to empowering the "human rights, voices, and visions of indigenous peoples," has described how the world's cultural diversity is shredded by dam displacement. Having gathered unique place-based knowledge of their homelands over thousands of years, such cultures are rich with understandings about the behavior and constraints of their habitats, especially their watersheds. They often practice the distribution and use of watershed resources in a way that has been sustainable for centuries. Cultures like these, which evolve locally and are grounded in a home habitat, do not relocate well. Tight patterns of interaction and reciprocal relationships are torn apart when members are displaced and disperse. Customs are diluted and rituals cease when the community can no longer easily come together to practice them.

For individuals, the psychic and practical costs of moving are also devastating. Aside from the very real loss of their land and modest wealth, indigenous and peasant peoples lose their identity. Their knowledge of their native habitat often cannot be translated into any advantage in the marketplace for migrant labor that they enter as they move through refugee camps and into squalid urban slums. Indian writer Arundhati Roy has passionately described the plight of hundreds of thousands of indigenous tribal peoples whose communal lands are threatened by dams like Narayanpur, Narmada Sagar, and Sardar Sarovar in her country.[11] The majority of the nearly 200,000 people evicted to make way for Vietnam's Hoa Binh and Ta Bu dams were ethnic minorities.[12] The Waimiri-Atroari tribe in the Amazon has been reduced to the edge of extinction by Brazil's Balbina Dam. The list of displaced indigenous people is both long and logical, since indigenous people are likely to be powerless, poor, and unrepresented—in short, easy for political elites to roll over.

It is hard, of course, to build the kind of robust civil society we extol in a nation full of people who feel they have been robbed, who are landless and impoverished, who don't know who they are and feel they don't belong. Such individuals can easily become prostitutes and drunks, terrorists and brutal soldiers, drug dealers and slaves—the kind who make the cheap clothes and other products we crave. In an odd twist, the ecological damage that Third World countries invite when they partner with the dam-building industry is transformed into cultural degradation as they ingest the displaced into their festering cities. These cities, in turn, become the breeding grounds for terror and disease, which spread back to the rich nations that funded the destruction of landscapes in the first place.

Sometimes the displaced resist. In 1976, for example, Maya Achi Indians in the submergence zone of the Chixoy Dam in Guatemala balked when they realized they were being moved to cramped quarters on poor land. Their resistance was short-lived, however. Guatemalan police and paramilitary units eventually slaughtered 378 Indians in tiny villages along the Rio Negro. These included more than a hundred women, who were repeatedly raped before they were garroted, stabbed, or shot, and more than a hundred children, many bashed to death on rocks. Orphaned Maya Achi children were taken as slaves.[13] Although the Rio Negro massacres were particularly brutal, forced relocations have long been common in the former Soviet Union, China, and many Third World countries. They continue today.

I think John Wesley Powell would have understood that no one values water more than a peasant woman who has to walk a mile to fetch it, and no one values it less than an urban dweller who pays to get it to flow from a tap or buys it bar-coded in a plastic bottle at a gas station. He would have seen through the myth that to be used efficiently, effectively, and sustainably, water must be turned into a marketed commodity that can be piped all over. Powell thought the federal government would help farmers and ranchers overcome the limitations of local government. He believed in harnessing nature through science and technology. But at the heart of his vision is an agrarian watershed democracy with local knowledge of water as a check and balance for wise and equitable use. I doubt that he imagined cotton growing on the desert next to an eighteen-hole golf course. Or farming villages drowned so electricity can be supplied to mines and factories in India. Dams, yes, but on what scale and for what purpose?

Dam building's impacts on land use—by forcing displaced people into undeveloped forests and opening up opportunities for further exploitation—are not typically calculated by those promoting the projects, but they are enormous. When indigenous and peasant farmers are displaced, they often clear-cut adjoining mountainsides to make new farms. The result is deforestation and soil erosion. The roads that are developed to bring workers and materials to remote dam sites are often subsequently used by loggers and miners. Critics such as Patrick McCully are beginning to bring attention to these lesser-known effects of dams.

New reservoirs are particularly obnoxious for the displaced populations that try to resettle near them, especially in tropical landscapes. Although lush vegetation is supposed to be removed from the dam's floodpath, the challenge of doing a thorough job is usually overwhelming and expensive. The result of shoddy clearing is lots of rotting matter that releases methane and carbon dioxide into the atmosphere, contributing to global warming.

Not only do new reservoirs stink, but they can also make you sick. Naturally occurring mercury in soil gets transformed during the decaying process into methyl-mercury, a powerful neurotoxin that bioaccumulates in fish consumed by humans, especially natives. For example, 64 percent of the Cree who live around LeGrande 2 Reservoir in Quebec, a component of the James Bay project, have blood mercury levels far exceeding World Health Organization standards.[14]

In the tropics, malarial mosquitoes breed in fetid dam-induced swamps, which are also excellent vectors for parasitic flatworms that cause a wide range of illnesses. The spread of river blindness and dengue fever has also been associated with tropical reservoirs.[15] Water hyacinths often move in to colonize young tropical reservoirs and can spread quickly, like a biotic fire, until the new reservoirs are clogged and choked. Liberal applications of carcinogenic herbicides usually follow, and their dangerous residues get widely distributed, first through the veins of irrigation and then into the veins of animals and people.

A dam can make sweet water salty over time. Even fresh water includes some salt content. Because so much flat water is exposed to the rays of the sun, evaporation is a major problem—not only for the net loss of water, but because the salt from the evaporated water is left in the remaining water, resulting in higher salt concentrations. Irrigation makes the salt problem worse because irrigation water washes salts out of soil and, eventually, back into the reservoirs. Since salt is corrosive, it damages machinery and pipes downstream. Crops, of course, don't tolerate salt well, and people are not fond of drinking water laced with it. In retrospect, the term "comprehensive river-bottom development," which dam-building agencies and corporations often use to describe their projects, is like calling a frontal lobotomy "complete cognitive treatment."

Assessment would be problematic, even if we were willing to do it. Because so many dams have been constructed only recently, and ecological consequences may be decades in the making, we cannot yet know their full impact. And what can we use for comparison, now that free-flowing rivers have become so rare? Unfortunately, most of the world's rivers were not fully studied prior to being plugged, diked, dredged, ditched, diverted, and drowned. We had limited knowledge about river dynamics and river ecology before the dam-building boom was off and running. Adding to the confusion, most dam projects, especially in the Third World, were pushed along despite inadequate or no meteorological, hydrological, and geological studies. And the studies that were done were typically based on a few decades of past weather and flow records, which were assumed to represent what could be expected in future years. However, such data can be highly misleading, as weather patterns can shift and vary much more over the supposed life spans of the dams than they have in just the last thirty years, especially if global warming alters weather patterns. A tendency to overpredict water availability and underpredict flood potential has already become apparent.

Dam feasibility and impact studies are rarely, if ever, peer-reviewed and are usually hidden from public scrutiny. Environmental assessments sometimes follow planning, as in the case of India's Narayanpur project, and usually downplay harmful ecological impacts. For example, a 1994 feasibility study of a series of dams on Vietnam's Mekong River, conducted by the Canadian firm Acres International and the French dam agency Compagnie Nationale du Rhône, stated that environmental impacts were expected to be "not severe." The fisheries volume of the study, however, concluded that the proposed dams might cause a "wholesale decline in the fishery throughout the lower Mekong River."[16]

Even formal tallies of promises broken and kept are absent from the record. No wonder. All of the big dams hold these characteristics in common: they cost much more than projected to build and operate, they produce less power than promised, they silt faster than anticipated, and they do more damage to habitats and ecosystems than planners claimed they would. If the broken promises and failures of dams are not documented and acknowledged, unrealistic expectations can continue to justify new projects, and public dialogue about the costs and benefits of dam construction will likewise be skewed. If the process of building big dams excludes credible evaluation altogether, as has been the case across the Third World, then it is missing a cardinal component of modern planning. Add ignorance of river dynamics and ecology, scant understanding of the variables at hand, and an absence of assessment, and it is clear that dam building on the global scale we have just experienced is a massive experiment with little or no controls.

That experiment began in earnest in the American West, where opposition to it is now burgeoning. Americans made the case for damming rivers. We are now making the case for restoring them. The rate of dam decommissioning in the United States has now overtaken the rate of construction.[17] Not all dams have to go, of course, but the excesses of the dam-building era must be addressed. If the United States takes down a big dam or two, we could start a trend. If we learn new ways to recharge aquifers and wetlands with free-flowing freshwater, new ways to conserve and recycle, Americans could point the way to the future.

The story of big dams should offer cautionary evidence that an undemocratic, ignorant approach to projects with massive ecological consequences is reckless in the long run. Regardless of whose arguments eventually win favor and shape the public agenda, the big dams' days are numbered. Dams trap silt, and silt builds up. According to Patrick McCully, increased storm activity associated with global warming and sudden climate change will just make matters worse. Rivers move mountains and carve canyons. Rivers make deltas. Given time, and maybe sooner than we expect, dams will fill in and become waterfalls, or they will break.

As the drought years at the turn of the twenty-first century dropped the level of Lake Powell, huge mudflats and mountains of silt were revealed, showing how quickly sedimentation is filling up the reservoir, how the Glen Canyon Dam's days are numbered. Should the eventual demise of Glen Canyon, Hoover, and Grand Coulee happen catastrophically or without planning and control, flooding events not seen since prehistory could result. Ask anyone who knows a river well what will happen in time. One way or the other, Glen Canyon Dam is destined to become a massive artifact of our technological prowess, our shortsightedness, and our collective hubris—a white elephant in the boneyard of our pride.

ABOLITION

*There are a thousand hacking at the branches of evil to one who is
striking at the root.*

—HENRY DAVID THOREAU

*If we appear to seek the unattainable, as it has been said, then let it be
known that we do so to avoid the unimaginable.*

—PORT HURON STATEMENT,
STUDENTS FOR A DEMOCRATIC SOCIETY

First, They Killed John Wayne

It was too hot to breathe. The big man in the bronze hat sweated hard and choked on the dust kicked up by the charging horses of the dueling warriors. Their spears glinted in the desert sun as the horses crashed and rolled in the dirt, spilling riders who jumped up and swung their swords. In between takes, he retreated to his trailer, but a shower would have to wait until he got back to the hotel in St. George, several miles from the movie set.

John Wayne's real name was Marion: Marion Michael Morrison. "John Wayne" was his stage name, and it fit the characters he played on the big screen—solid, big-boned heroes who spoke plainly and brooked no nonsense. Wayne's characters were brave and moral, but not complicated. They articulated a world of black hats and white hats. The good guys wore white, were white, did right. In the post–World War II years, John Wayne was a sure thing, like science, medicine, progress, and the American Way. In the 1950s and 1960s, he was what we imagined ourselves to be at our best—one of us, but taller.

We called him the Duke. Obviously the name "Marion" wouldn't fit such an iron-fisted persona, so he took a stage name that was the verbal equivalent of those movie sets he labored on, like the facade of an Old West street propped up by two-by-fours. It didn't matter—he looked good, and we believed in him.

Perhaps the oddest role Wayne played was when he traded his cowboy hat for a bronze helmet and became Genghis Khan in the 1955 movie *The Conqueror*. That movie would be easily forgettable were it not for the strange fact that about 80 percent of the cast and crew eventually succumbed to cancer.[1] By the time of Wayne's demise in 1979, cancer was as common in America as the postwar flood of synthetic industrial chemicals that stained the average citizen's blood cells, as common as the trace amounts of radiation drifting through our food webs. Even so, an 80 percent fatal-cancer rate constituted a suspicious anomaly, and the leading suspect was a monster that glowed in the dark, a demon so scary even Hollywood could not have imagined it.

The movie was made near St. George, Utah—about a hundred miles downwind of the Nevada Test Site, where a hundred atomic bombs were blown up, one after the other, to gain the technological expertise needed to build a Cold War nuclear arsenal. They contaminated the ground downwind, including the sand on the set of *The Conqueror*. And as if riding, rolling, and waiting around in contaminated sand wasn't enough, producer Howard Hughes had sixty tons of the stuff hauled to the RKO soundstage in Los Angeles in order to match the set for close-ups. There is evidence that the brilliant aircraft designer turned producer knew the raw material for the fantasy he was making was dangerous but ignored the risk and hid it from others.[2] As an aircraft designer, defense-industry tycoon, handsome pilot, and Hollywood producer all rolled into one, Howard Hughes was himself another powerful icon of the era. When he was a dashing and brilliant young millionaire, Hughes dated glamorous movie starlets and was considered America's most desirable bachelor, but he ended up an emaciated and reclusive wreck who refused to groom and bathe. He spent his last decades hiding in a Las Vegas tower, where, addicted to drugs, he surrounded himself with people who would not deny his needs as he defined them, no matter how outrageous. Among those in the cast who died of cancer were actresses Susan Hayward and Agnes Moorehead, as well as director Dick Powell. A direct link between their cancers and the radioactive fallout and contaminated sand may never be made, but they were in good company, as time would show.

In the 1950s, '60s, and '70s, the government conducted more than nine hundred nuclear weapons tests at the Nevada Test Site near Las Vegas. Rural residents of Utah and Nevada, like the movie cast and crew of *The Conqueror,* got dosed by fallout from the atomic blasts, carried to them on the wind. But unlike the temporary visitors from Hollywood, the residents stayed on, living in the radioactive dust that rolled over them after each atomic test. The fallout coated the clothes they hung in the sun to dry and the backyard swing sets where their children played. It settled on gardens, orchards, fields of grain, pastures, reservoirs, and the troughs of water kept for animals. Pets and kids rolled in it. It drifted into sandboxes, corrals, chicken coops, and irrigation ditches. It rested on windows, tires, and shoes. It settled on the flowers that young men cut for courtship and that young women braided into their hair.

The newly created Atomic Energy Commission was the government agency responsible for the tests. Created in 1946, right after World War II, it was given sweeping powers; later, the Atomic Energy Act of 1954 gave it a mandate to promote atomic technology. Unfortunately, the AEC quickly became a totalitarian bureaucracy that ruled from afar, almost impossible for an ordinary citizen to influence. Congress tolerated its undemocratic behavior. Secrecy and fear were its mainstays. Misinformation became the rule. But in the largely Mormon villages of southern Utah in the early 1950s, the AEC's word was the last word.

The permeating radiation was invisible and silent. It didn't hiss, rattle, bite, or burn. It came with no black hat or war paint. The sleepy little cow towns trusted the official government assurances that they were safe. But in the early 1950s strange things began to happen almost at once. First, ranchers' sheep bore hideously deformed progeny. The stillborn and twisted lambs were followed within a few years by human cancers that eventually reached epidemic proportions. Kids died first, from what was called at the time "childhood leukemia." No one knew why, and federal officials and local doctors were not helpful. A woman who lost her hair and endured continual rashes was told she was suffering from hysteria. Although Utah's Mormons were patriotic to the core, Pentagon brass considered them a "low-use segment of the population,"[3] hicks in the sticks whose ineffective dissent would be suppressed by a church hierarchy eager to underscore its loyalty to a nation that regarded Mormons as cultural oddities.

Although to this day epidemiologists are still debating the causes of the diseases and deformities, in the minds of downwinders, the civilians who lived downwind from atomic fallout, the impacts were clear by the 1960s. They lived in a world where balding housewives miscarried jellyfish babies and took their kids to chemotherapy, while their cowboy husbands tended irradiated sheep that gave birth to two-headed lambs. Towns like St. George began to resemble a John Wayne Western on acid.

As the years marched on, thyroid cancer became common. The invisible damage done to the chromosomes of those who survived and then reproduced guaranteed that a concentric wave of suffering would spread through the next generation of downwinders, children born with disabilities or cancer ticking in their bones. Unfortunately for the downwinders' cause, human health is variable, synergistic, complex, and dynamic, so direct links are hard to make. The anecdotal evidence of high cancer rates among downwinders is strong, but epidemiological studies consider the rural communities' populations to be too small to draw statistically valid conclusions. Despite the lack of smoking-gun evidence, downwinders organized in the 1980s and won limited compensation for those immediately downwind of atomic testing in the 1950s.

Mary Dickson, a friend and fellow activist, is a downwinder. She grew up in the shadow that atomic testing cast over northern Utah, survived a bout of thyroid cancer as a too-young girl, and then learned that her type of cancer was common among Utahns who lived downwind from atomic testing. You didn't have to live in southern Utah, near the border with Nevada, to be injured by radiation.

In fact, Mary points out, most of America was downwind. The weather, dynamic and unpredictable, carried radioactive fallout far and wide. Nuclear scientists believed that radiation from tests would dissipate fairly evenly, but in 1953, radiation from a Nevada test was sucked up into the jet stream and dumped over Troy, New York, in unexpectedly high concentrations. In the Midwest, fallout contaminated grain and milk that was then consumed by children with growing bones all across the country. For boomer kids, the "breakfast of champions" became a game of radioactive roulette.

Where high tech met high desert, thousands of "atomic GIs" were also exposed to dangerous levels of radiation. At the Nevada Test Site, where weapons were tested and the military practiced the developing art of nuclear warfare, troops were imported as guinea pigs. They crouched in the test site trenches during detonation of the "devices," then marched toward ground zero over sand that had been fused by the bomb's heat into shards of glass. At the moment of detonation, the atomic light was so intense that the soldiers saw through closed eyelids the ghostly vision of their own X-rayed bones in their hands and wrists. Pilots were instructed to fly through the mushroom clouds that rose above the trenches where the soldiers crouched. Ships full of sailors and soldiers witnessed blasts over the open ocean in the Pacific and also sailed right into harm's way.

Commanders wanted to know how the nuclear experience would affect combat functionality—was atomic warfare catastrophically traumatic, or merely a distraction that a soldier could be conditioned to overcome? It turned out to be cancerous, but—fortunately for commanders—in a post-combat way. In Nevada and in the Pacific, a total of a quarter-million servicemen were exposed to above-ground atomic blasts. They scattered back to their workaday lives after the Army released them. They remained untracked even after their cancers became so common that they themselves saw the pattern despite their dispersal.

Our atomic history, the story of nuclear weapons and power, backlights the current struggle over what to do with spent nuclear fuel and accumulated radioactive wastes from weapons production and uranium processing. Since expert assurances drive decision-making and influence public opinion today as they did then, it is important to know if the record of such experts is credible. Sadly, the nuclear establishment has been as consistently wrong as it has been consistently reassuring.

When humans wield such awesome power as was being developed in the 1950s, ignorance is not bliss. In the early days of the nuclear era, government scientists believed that ingested radiation was safe. By 1956, however, they understood that milk from cows exposed to radioactive fallout could contain strontium 90, which was then deposited in human bones, where it wreaked havoc. Nonetheless, the tailings that piled up outside the uranium mines producing the raw material for nuclear weapons were used as filler dirt for homes, schoolyards, and roads. As a people, we were naive about the dangers of radiation. As a child, I remember going into a shoe store that featured an X-ray machine. Customers were encouraged to stick their feet into it so they could wiggle their toes and watch their toe bones dance—no nurses with lead aprons required.

In 1963 the chairman of the Atomic Energy Commission, Glenn Seaborg, asked a noted medical physicist named John Gofman to take a second look at the effects of low-level radiation. Seaborg and the AEC's taxpayer-funded club of atomic boosters expected a reassuring report, but Gofman and his colleagues at what was then called the Lawrence Radiation Laboratory in Livermore, California, reached startling conclusions. They reported that the government standard for "safe" exposure to radiation was way too high. They recommended that it be reduced tenfold, from 170 millirads a year to just 17 millirads. Otherwise, they said, people with weakened immune systems, especially the elderly and developing fetuses, would be at risk. They concluded that as many as 32,000 additional deaths could occur each year.[4] In response to their findings, Gofman and his colleagues were vehemently attacked by Seaborg and his AEC staff for their "irresponsible" heresy. Their work continued to be maligned until 1972, when further studies by the National Academy of Sciences reached very similar conclusions.

While the debate over the danger of low-level radiation raged on, our military was experimenting on the people it had publicly pledged to protect. Their Cold War exemption from democratic norms was not a prescription for ethical behavior. More than a thousand people—prisoners, the retarded, terminally ill patients, pregnant women, and the impoverished—were exposed to radiation in experiments between 1944 and the early 1970s, often without their consent or knowledge, and certainly without a complete understanding of the risks and consequences. African Americans were especially well represented among the targeted groups. The information given to gain consent was often misleading and the research was identified as "medical," inducing near-automatic trust.

The agencies doing the military's bidding included highly respected institutions like the University of Chicago, MIT, Harvard, Columbia,

Vanderbilt, and Massachusetts General Hospital. The experiments were varied. In one, plutonium was injected into unknowing patients. In another, radioactive pills were given to eight hundred pregnant women. In Washington and Oregon, the testicles of prisoners were irradiated so heavily that the experiments ended with vasectomies. (Catholic prisoners were excluded from these experiments, in deference to the papal edicts about birth control.)[5]

In the 1950s and 1960s the Atomic Energy Commission was to public health and safety what a drive-by shooting is to justice. By 1974 its reputation had become so stained that it was given a new name, the Nuclear Regulatory Commission. But it was still staffed by the same rubber-stamping bureaucrats who had validated the earlier atomic era. And it had the same quasi-judicial and quasi-legislative powers that the AEC had had, so its decisions were just as skewed, exclusive, and unaccountable. Risks and costs were still downplayed, especially if those risks and costs could be passed on without liability to powerless others. The fairness of how those risks and rewards were distributed was still not on the agenda. Known dangers were still officially ignored. The agency's reputation for arrogance and exclusion survived the letterhead changes intact, as anyone who has attended a recent NRC hearing can attest.

The advent of nuclear weaponry and the Cold War race to develop ever bigger weapons, and ever more of them, resulted in the contamination of vast tracts of land in the United States and the Soviet Union, as well as hundreds of smaller sites around the world. Unlike the disasters we were accustomed to, radioactive contamination did not shake us, drown us, or burn us down. Exposure was not obvious, contamination was not recognized, and danger was not acknowledged. The full, unintended consequences of radiation were a mystery to be unraveled the hard way—with flesh and blood, over time. Nuclear fallout compelled questions that we answered in our bones.

You didn't have to live or soldier downwind from above-ground testing to be included in the great Cold War game of nuclear roulette. You didn't have to drink and eat downwind from a leaking reactor to get cancer. The facilities associated with nuclear weapons production were a minefield of chemicals, heavy metals, and radioactive substances that were poorly monitored and incompletely understood. Safety was inadequate

239

for the thousands of workers who toiled there daily. They were told they were safe and realized they had been misled only after noticing how many fellow workers were suffering and dying.

The danger began at the very front end of the production process, in the uranium mines, because the ore itself is dangerously radioactive. The first victims of the nuclear era were the most powerless and sub-jugated populations in America. Uranium, the raw material for both nuclear weapons and nuclear energy, is often found on the ground of indigenous peoples and ethnic minorities, both here and abroad. In the 1950s there was a uranium boom, and uranium was prospected and mined across the American Southwest. Places like Moab, Utah, became sprawling trailer towns. A culture of speculation spread. Prospectors got rich overnight, built castles and bought boats, then went bust.

Mines were poorly ventilated and miners poorly trained in the art of radiation safety. Rules were ignored in the rush to get the yellow ore out of the ground. Soon cancer stalked the first generations of uranium miners, many of them poorly paid Navajos. Miners and their kin, who lived near the mines and the piles of tailings that blew around in the wind, began to die—slowly at first, then with accelerating frequency. All were assured by government scientists that their mines and mills were safe. The scientists either didn't appreciate the risks or covered them up—it is hard to say which, since those who knowingly deny danger and are subsequently caught lying routinely plead ignorance.

Like the downwinders, the uranium miners who have struggled for compensation have become lost in a bureaucratic maze that they claim is designed to keep them filling out papers until they either die off or give up. Here again, the anecdotal evidence of high cancer rates in Indian uranium-mining communities is overwhelming, but official epidemiological studies dismiss the statistics as coming from population samples that are too small to be conclusive—a common problem in rural villages.[6]

At the beginning of the nuclear age, we were as naive as John Wayne's cowboy hat was white. It would have been hard for us to fathom the dangers of the power that we were toying with, in an era before intercontinental missiles, the global balance of terror, and melting reactors. We had full faith in our human powers to unlock and master the power of nature. Progress was in full industrialized swing. And who could have imagined the lethal, long-lived power of the soft yellow stone encrusted in the earth? Even Marie Curie, credited with unlocking the first secrets of radioactivity, didn't understand. She downplayed the danger and ultimately died of cancer from inhaling her own experiments.

The uranium for Marie Curie's pioneering research was dug in the 1920s in Utah. The small tunnels the miners dug can still be seen in the Chinle Formation, beneath gray and lavender mounds of ancient volcanic ash, at the mouth of Grand Wash in Capitol Reef National Park. There is something eerily metaphoric about those dark sockets, now barred and chained, in the midst of such timeless natural splendor—the way our prideful desire for mastery of the elements drilled holes in the heart of desert beauty that, now abandoned, have become dangerous traps.

Those inside the mines and weapons facilities were not alone. Outside the gates, untracked emissions and secret dumping contaminated air, water, and soil. Radioactive contamination can remain dangerously potent for hundreds of years and can be carried wherever wind and water will take it. Cleanup is now under way at 114 of the nation's nuclear facilities, civilian and military alike.[7] The South has Pantex in Texas, Oak Ridge National Laboratory in Tennessee, Savannah River in South Carolina, and the Shearon Harris nuclear power plant in North Carolina, site of the largest radioactive waste storage pools in the country. The West has Rocky Flats in Colorado and Hanford Nuclear Reservation in Washington state. In the heartland, there's the Fernald Feed Material Production Center in Ohio and the Paducah Gaseous Diffusion Plant in Kentucky.

The Hanford Nuclear Reservation is a typical example of the nightmare we have created. It covers 1,460 square kilometers in south-central Washington along the banks of the Columbia River. Plutonium produced at Hanford went into the first nuclear explosion ever—the test at Alamogordo, New Mexico, in July 1945—and into the bomb dropped on Hiroshima. Big corporations like Westinghouse, Rockwell, and Battelle grew fat on Hanford contracts during the Cold War, and the site enjoyed full support from surrounding communities, mindful of the jobs it brought and proud of its contributions to meeting Cold War imperatives. A local high school football team's helmets bore the image of a mushroom cloud. Now, so many years later, workers and residents from surrounding communities are struggling to understand the impact of plutonium processing on local health.

The statistics are staggering. Hanford buried 18,000,000 cubic feet of "low-level" radioactive waste and 3,900,000 cubic feet of plutonium-contaminated, or transuranic, waste. It discharged 210,000,000,000 gallons of radioactive waste into groundwater. More than 500,000 gallons of *high-level* nuclear waste has leaked from Hanford's storage tanks. Radioactive wastes have gone into the Columbia River.[8]

It is hard to calculate the costs of our nation's nuclear mismanagement, not least because they will be accruing for many generations to come. The cleanup at Rocky Flats alone costs us $2 million a day.[9] Current estimates are that over the next seventy-five years, American taxpayers will spend from $100 billion to half a trillion dollars to clean up, secure, store, and bury our accumulated waste and contaminated ground. And the estimates have steadily climbed over the years, as new damage is continually discovered. The cost to ecosystem integrity, of course, cannot be measured. The National Research Council points out that even after "cleanup," many lands will be too contaminated to turn over to public use.[10]

At about the time John Gofman was warning of the dangers of low-level radiation in the United States, Dr. Andrei Sakharov was issuing similar warnings to the Soviet nuclear regime. Sakharov was a world-renowned physicist and the father of the Soviet nuclear bomb. He was twice awarded the Order of Lenin, his empire's highest honor, for his weapons-related work.

But in 1958 he concluded that nuclear weapons could more accurately be described as biological weapons, characterized by disease and chronic illness that would kill millions long after the blinding flash that burnt flesh. His research showed him that even very low levels of ingested radiation could cause mutations in DNA that would damage immune systems in humans and accelerate the mutation of microorganisms. When he considered the convergence of mutated viruses with humans who had weakened immune systems, nuclear weapons took on a new dimension. Unlike conventional weapons, which accomplished their destruction immediately and locally, nuclear weapons would have an impact that would spread over time and migrate far from any targeted area.

The radiation dispersed by a 50-megaton nuclear test in the Soviet Union, Sakharov calculated, would induce genetic mutations that would eventually accelerate or cause a half-million to a million deaths.[11] And as the megatonnage of tests increased dramatically over time, so would the radiation released into the atmosphere. Add the deaths that could be attributed to U.S. testing, and the death toll would be in the millions.

Sakharov's most prophetic insight was linking the synergistic effects of widespread radiation in very low doses with reduced genetic integrity, the growth of new viruses, and lowered immune system functioning. It was a dark vision of how the profound connections we share with the physical world, our embodiment in nature that poets and philosophers celebrate, can also become pathways to destruction.

Tragically, in an era that had not experienced AIDS, chronic fatigue syndrome, toxic shock, or the wide range of other immune system dysfunctions that we live with today, the prophetic nature of Sakharov's conclusions went mostly unheeded. In fact, he was pulled from his pedestal by enraged Soviet generals and eventually sent into internal exile. Even from exile, however, he bravely and eloquently continued to rail against the nuclear madness he had helped create.

After the Berlin Wall fell and the Soviet empire collapsed, Sakharov was returned to a place of honor and respect. By then an AIDS epidemic was sweeping through the fetid forests of central Africa. Although the emergence of AIDS and so many other chronic, deadly autoimmune illnesses cannot be conclusively tied to radiation from nuclear testing and is, no doubt, the consequence of many converging factors, these illnesses' resonance with Sakharov's model is striking. AIDS originated in the high-rainfall areas of Africa whose people had, twenty years before, registered the highest levels in the world of strontium 90 in their bones after heavy fallout from nuclear tests in the atmosphere.

In another decade, the AIDS epidemic that is still decimating central Africa would reach Russia and central Asia. Sakharov would be long gone, his warnings about the essentially biological nature of nuclear weapons largely forgotten by governments and their corporate sponsors. A new generation, however, is acting on his belief that low levels of nuclear radiation that do not have immediate, obvious, or easily measured consequences may contribute to illness in significant, unintended, and insidious ways.

Today the Soviet Union is gone, and the Cold War arms race that Sakharov railed at is over. Yet the nuclear nightmare continues, now reconfigured to include the possibility of regional conflicts in the Middle East, the Indian subcontinent, or the Korean peninsula. So-called dirty bombs wielded by terrorists and nuclear blackmail by desperate despots are now part of the equation.

In the new world of nuclear one-upmanship, weapons are fashioned using enriched uranium from power plants, making the symbiotic relationship of the two sides of the nuclear coin—nuclear energy and weapons production—clearer than ever. If the world should agree tomorrow to ban nuclear weapons altogether, the challenge of cleaning up the testing, production, and storage facilities and securing the arsenals will still be with us—as will the detritus of the "peaceful atom."

The Perpetual Peril of the Peaceful Atom

Our self-destructive affair with the atom was born of fear. Hitler's troops were storming across Europe and his Luftwaffe was bombing Britain when refugee scientists from Germany warned the Roosevelt administration that a Nazi A-bomb was in the works. America launched its race to beat the new Nazi weapon when we joined the war, but in an odd twist, we used the weapon against Japan, not Germany, and ended up racing the Soviet Union, not Germany, into the nuclear abyss. Again, fear drove us on.

By contrast, the launch of the peaceful atom was driven by hope. Harnessing the atom to produce energy for industry promised utopia, not annihilation. While we regarded nuclear weapons with trepidation and dismay, nuclear power seemed like a godsend. In his role as the principal booster for atomic power in the early 1950s, Atomic Energy Commission chairman Glenn Seaborg promised that "planetary engineering" would spawn legions of nuclear reactors, each with "its own little Eden."[1] The new world of nuclear technology would include homes built from uranium that would generate their own power and cities that would radiate heat to melt snow. In September 1954, a close advisor to then President Dwight Eisenhower and another AEC chairman, Lewis Strauss, offered this oft-quoted promise: "It is not too much to expect that our children will enjoy in their homes electrical energy too cheap to meter."[2] There was talk about using atomic bombs for construction, perhaps to carve out harbors or to dig a "panatomic canal." When Disneyland opened in 1955, it featured "Our Friend the Atom" in its perky take on the future, Tomorrowland.

In a nuclear reactor the atom is used, essentially, to boil water. That boiling water is used to turn turbines that make electricity. Although the average American had trouble comprehending the nature of atomic power, peaceful or otherwise, electricity was commonly regarded as a good thing. As recently as the 1930s, lots of Americans did not have it. The Roosevelt administration had promoted rural electrification, touting the benefits of light and heat for homes and reliable energy for businesses and industry. Building up the nation's electric infrastructure with dams, coal-fired plants, and power lines was a way of putting people in a depressed economy to work. Electricity meant jobs during the Depression, and in the postwar era it meant "all-electric homes" complete with a television, which in turn carried advertisements for electrical appliances to wash our dishes, dry our clothes, vacuum our rugs, and save our labor. If atomic power meant cheap electricity—well, who could question that? By the mid-1960s big dams were out and big reactors were in.

It was not just Americans who could benefit from nuclear power. In a special address to the United Nations in 1953, President Eisenhower promised infinite benefits for people all around the globe from our "Atoms for Peace" program. It was important to show the world that we were not just the people who had incinerated Hiroshima and then, in a second act that many regarded as unnecessary, obliterated Nagasaki. Yes, we now dominated half of the world by virtue of our nuclear weapons of mass destruction, but we were also good guys who were willing to share the benefits of our mastery over the atomic genie that our superior engineering had enslaved. For our Soviet adversaries, too, the ability to build nuclear energy infrastructure abroad was a source of pride and a means of enlisting foreign allies. Big technology, of course, came with big bucks, and big bucks could fill many pockets, especially those of the local political elite, whether in our allies' countries or our own.

The peaceful atom had a similar mollifying effect at home, helping to head off any popular discontent with the new and enormous public expenditures on the nuclear arms race, which of course were also justified by the fear that the Commies had the bomb and would use it if we didn't deter them. Nuclear power was the spoonful of sugar that helped the nuclear weapons medicine go down, an antidote to the fear and sacrifice associated with the arms race.

The development of civilian nuclear power accomplished other goals that complemented the aims of the military. The nuclear weapons infrastructure required thousands of engineers and skilled workers. It required facilities to mine, process, and enrich uranium. It required lots of technological components. The expertise, workers, and facilities required for civilian nuclear power were complementary and convergent. According to early concepts of how nuclear energy would work, nuclear power plants would use enriched uranium as fuel. Spent fuel could then be reprocessed, essentially recycled, into weapons-grade plutonium or new reactor fuel. This plan was short-circuited by President Jimmy Carter in 1977, however, because it was too expensive, workers at the first reprocessing facilities to be developed were getting sick, and the product itself, enriched uranium, was too hard to track and too dangerous if it got into the wrong hands. In the beginning, however, nuclear power was imagined as a self-sustaining industrial cycle.

Back then, nuclear power was an alternative energy—alternative to solar. In 1952, the last year of his administration, President Harry Truman's Paley Commission outlined an energy future for the nation built around the power of the sun. The commission envisioned 15,000 solar-powered homes by 1975.[3] A solar-powered future, however, was seen as threatening by the nation's powerful utilities. Solar power would be a decentralized means of generating energy that could grow outside the electricity infrastructure already in place. That could threaten the profits of private utilities, which were already competing with the big new public utilities created by the Roosevelt administration, such as the Tennessee Valley Authority and the Bonneville Power Administration. Utilities, large and small, public and private, lobbied hard to defeat solar power. When the Republicans and Eisenhower took over from Truman and the Democrats in 1953, solar power was taken off the table and nuclear power was put on it.

During the 1950s, the rush toward domestic nuclear power acquired a self-interested momentum. The Atomic Energy Commission was a burgeoning and unchecked bureaucracy that was building a political and financial empire, much like the Bureau of Reclamation during the dam-building era. The AEC was supported in its plans to make domestic energy generation go nuclear by the large private utilities, which recognized the opportunity such a move represented for them.

Ironically, although they feared a decentralized solar infrastructure, the private utilities could not muster the dollars or tolerate the risks required to develop a domestic nuclear power infrastructure. The government would pick up the tab for research and development, but then there was waste disposal, insurance, and the construction of highly complex plants. Only the private utilities' government-subsidized rivals, like the TVA and Bonneville, could muster the courage, cash, and credit to gamble on nuclear power plants. Bonneville had experience in engineering and operating big dams, which gave it the confidence to take on nuclear power. TVA had a powerful network of political allies that could help it cope with management and regulatory issues and win the subsidies it needed to succeed.

Eventually, a tide of subsidies to design, build, and operate nuclear power plants and then dispose of troublesome wastes would lift all ships, large and small. After private investors balked at the costs of nuclear development, the government established a pattern of heavy taxpayer subsidies that continues today.

When the enormous risks associated with radiation exposure and nuclear accidents became apparent—at least to insurance analysts, who were paid to know—the feds also stepped in to deal with them. In 1957 Congress passed the Price-Anderson Act to cap civilian claims against nuclear power providers, to exempt the utilities from lawsuits, and to create a half-billion-dollar federal pool to be used for claims. Price-Anderson remains a key prop for the nuclear industry and was renewed as recently as 2002. To further sweeten the deal, state regulators often based rates on how much money the nuclear utilities sank into their physical plants, so that the cost overruns they incurred would eventually be soaked up by ratepayers and taxpayers. This, of course, encouraged cost overruns by unscrupulous contractors.

With utopian promises made, subsidies in place, and public utility investors lined up, the nuclear-plant bandwagon began to roll. Soon everyone wanted one. Regulators did their best to get out of the way, with the constant traffic of personnel between regulatory agencies and the industry they regulated also diminishing regulatory pressure. Over the industry's first two decades, more than two hundred nuclear reactors were built or planned in the United States. President Richard Nixon promised a thousand U.S. reactors by the year 2000.[4] Then the bandwagon suffered a series of flat tires.

There had been hints of what was to come. A controversial breeder reactor near Detroit, designed to produce plutonium, had a partial fuel meltdown in 1966, coming close to being an American Chernobyl. In Idaho in 1961, three men died after getting too close to nuclear fuel rods as they carried out "routine" preparations for the startup of a reactor in Idaho Falls. Their heads and hands had to be removed from their bodies and buried with other radioactive waste.[5] Then, in 1969, physicist John Gofman released his disturbing research on the unanticipated dangers and consequences of even very low levels of radiation.

In addition, early in the 1960s, *Silent Spring* author Rachel Carson and others had raised the public's consciousness about the dangers of environmental toxins to wildlife and health. Next, the anti–Vietnam War movement led people to question all sorts of governing assumptions and priorities, including the necessity of huge nuclear weapons arsenals and the myth of efficient and safe nuclear power. New federal laws passed in the early 1970s, like the National Environmental Policy Act, required planners to take a closer look at the environmental impacts of proposed new projects.

Against the background of all of these influences, the modern environmental movement emerged, and in communities across the land, local groups formed to oppose nuclear reactors. In California the focus was Diablo Canyon and a proposed reactor at Bodega Head. In New York it was the Shoreham power plant. In 1978, some 20,000 protesters gathered to stop a reactor at Seabrook, New Hampshire. And then, the next year, came Three Mile Island.

Ironically, it was the "peaceful," domesticated nuclear twin that blew up first, undermining faith in our ability to tame the conjoined nuclear Frankensteins we had created. In March 1979, a nuclear reactor at Three Mile Island in Pennsylvania basically melted down. Human error was blamed, although design flaws helped to set up and then compound the errors. When the reactor went out of control, virtually all of the fuel in the containment area turned into radioactive molten metal that threatened to explode. The entire eastern seaboard hung on the brink.

Fortunately, an explosion was avoided, but large amounts of radiation leaked into the atmosphere. We will never know just how much, or how many people were exposed and at what levels, because monitoring systems downwind were quickly pushed beyond their scales of measurement and shut down. We do know that hundreds of area residents were poisoned and became ill, and millions changed their minds about nuclear energy. Six weeks after Three Mile Island, 125,000 demonstrators marched on the Capitol in Washington, D.C., to demand an end to nuclear power. Later that fall 200,000 packed Manhattan's Battery Park.[6]

In 1986, the most devastating industrial accident in human history happened in the country least prepared to deal with it. The Chernobyl nuclear reactor, in what is now the independent nation of Ukraine, suffered a catastrophic meltdown. The exact causes of the accident are still debated, but it is safe to say that it occurred within the interface between a poorly designed, poorly built reactor and the human miscalculation that is, sooner or later, inevitable when operating highly complex technology. Soviet authorities were slow to respond and covered up by habit.

Although more than 5 million people were immediately exposed to fallout, only 135,000 were evacuated. No effort was made to keep people from eating food and drinking water that had been contaminated by fallout. Soviet officials kept vital information from their European neighbors that would have warned them to take precautions in time.[7]

Cancer, chronic illness, and immune system disorders became epidemic in Ukraine and neighboring Belarus within a decade of the meltdown,[8] but the full dimensions of the tragedy are still unknown. In 1992 Vladimir Chernousenko, a Soviet scientist charged with accounting for the consequences of the disaster, stated that the radiation released by Chernobyl was the equivalent of a thousand Hiroshima-sized bombs, a much higher figure than previous estimates. Dying of cancer himself, he claimed to be one of the 7,000 to 10,000 soldiers, volunteers, workers, and scientists who had rushed in to battle the reactor fire and cover the radioactive remains and who were dying within a few years of their exposure. Chernousenko and other scientists have linked Chernobyl to rising morbidity rates in the former Soviet republics, suggesting that the ill effects of a catastrophic meltdown can ripple through a population's health for decades afterward.

At the time Chernobyl blew, millions of Europeans had been taking to the streets since the early 1980s to protest plans to install new missiles on their territory, which they feared would invite a Soviet first strike. Commercial nuclear power, though, was still commonly regarded as safe and necessary. Chernobyl changed all that. It entered the popular vocabulary as a code word for disaster, but it could as readily be used to describe what may have been a tipping point in history.

Over the breakfast table in my kitchen, I asked a visiting Russian scientist and a dissident citizen leader why they thought the Soviet Union had collapsed. They conferred briefly and laughed when their answers turned out to be the same. "Two things: networked computers and Chernobyl," their translator said. "Once we could communicate via computer, they couldn't suppress information anymore, and we could communicate and coordinate quickly. Chernobyl was proof, once and for all, that the Soviet system was a dangerous failure. People were literally sick and tired."

As we look back today, we can see that the atomic era revealed the consequences of astonishing technological prowess wedded to a profound ignorance of the impact of environmental degradation on public health and land. A powerful new technology in the hands of an engineering elite who are almost impossible to hold accountable is, apparently, a recipe for misinformation, cover-ups, downplayed risks, outright lies, and criminal neglect. At least, that is what has been revealed by the evidence accrued during the AEC era. We would be wise to acknowledge our mistakes and learn from them, because the history of nuclear power—both nuclear weaponry and nuclear energy—not only forms the backdrop for current struggles to keep the waste stream of the nuclear industry from landing on native desert lands, but also draws attention to the sort of technological hubris that raises the stakes in our development of new technologies. All our efforts to reconnect and re-store may be in vain if we do not learn to curb and contain masterful new developments like genetic engineering and nanotechnologies.

The American landscape has been transformed over centuries in ways that reflect our changing regard for it and our relationship with it. Before World War II, we had ample evidence that our impact was large. We had seen, after all, how we had turned the Great Plains, once abundant with bison and long grass, into a dust bowl. But nothing prepared us for the postwar era of subtle, sudden, and widespread contamination. We are now capable of poisoning whole landscapes haphazardly, with little understanding of how the damage we do comes home to our blood and bones.

The story of the atomic era informs the current debates about what to do with that period's detritus. When today's anti-nuclear activists argue that plans to ship nuclear waste across the heartland and bury it on Western deserts are ill-considered, dangerous, unfair, and deceptive, they point to the folly and tragedy of that formative era. They ask how anyone can trust a nuclear establishment that has been wrong, dead wrong, for so long. Just as the abolitionist movement of the nineteenth century was propelled forward by a growing awareness of the evils of slavery and its terrible human cost, today's movement to end nuclear weapons and nuclear power has developed against the backdrop of the environmental and human degradation wrought by the nuclear regime.

Nuclear history began fifty years ago in my backyard near the set of John Wayne's movie in St. George, but the massive struggle to contain the radioactive waste produced by that age is just beginning. My desert backyard is once again the front line.

THREE

How the Evil Yellow Ore Returns

"The evil yellow ore is trying to return." It's October 2001, and Corbin Harney is standing in the center of a circle of ragged activists in the middle of Skull Valley. The activists come from across the nation, but mostly from Utah and Nevada. They have come to network, share, and coordinate their struggle to keep the Great Basin Desert from becoming the nation's nuclear dumping ground. Corbin is a Western Shoshone elder who is a leader in his tribe's struggle to hang on to a once great desert landscape that has been fragmented and strafed by the U.S. military.

Today he is here to defend Yucca Mountain, Nevada. Yucca Mountain is in the middle of the Great Basin Desert, which covers almost all of Nevada, parts of Oregon and Idaho, and much of Utah. It is high, dry, and sparsely populated, all factors that make it a likely candidate to be the nation's repository for the most irradiated substance on earth, spent fuel rods from nuclear reactors. Skull Valley, where Corbin is standing, is on the easternmost rim of the Great Basin Desert. It is the proposed site for "temporarily" storing the fuel rods while awaiting construction of the Yucca Mountain facility.

Margene Bullcreek has invited the grassroots activists to gather at her Skull Valley home on the Goshute Indian reservation because she is under siege. When her Goshute neighbors agreed to trade their ancestral ground and tribal sovereignty to a consortium of powerful utility corporations in return for undetermined riches, Margene said no. Not here, not on top of my grandmother's bones. Not here where I cut willows for the cradles of my babies. "This place is peaceful," she tells me, as we gaze out at the gracefully undulating horizon, now muted into pastel shades of blue, gray, and pink by the fading sunlight.

Dinner is about to be served to Margene's two hundred guests by the Nevada-based Shundahai Network, which has much experience in the art of feeding crowds from a big tent, having nourished the annual flock of demonstrators who gather to protest weapons testing at the Nevada Nuclear Test Site near Las Vegas. The food is basic, vegetarian, and wholesome—tasty, if not delicious. Corbin is saying grace, Shoshone style. He talks softly in a mix of English and his native tongue, turning slowly, facing his circled audience, speaking words of wisdom about the connectedness of being alive, the reciprocal nature of life, and the nurturing presence of "our Mother Earth." The word shundahai, a Shoshone expression of the relationship he is describing, is repeated throughout. Corbin's voice is a plain but hypnotic monotone.

His message is not eloquent and, if divorced from his presence, it might be read as corny and trite. But Corbin Harney pulls it off because he is weathered, sincere, and wise. Although he speaks the part well, he doesn't look like the visionary spiritual leader he is. His large head bristles with close-cropped gray hair, and he is dressed in a plain, faded shirt and jeans. His skin is burnt-gold leather, his fingers thick and rough. He might be the guy who sells melons out of a truck on the side of the road. It is his encountered presence that transcends his common appearance. He is self-possessed.

Later he tells me he attended formal school for only one week in his eighty years. "I avoided school successfully until I was fifteen. Then they caught me and made me go. I was there for a few days because it took me that long to figure out how to escape." He smiles. I see pride and mischief in his eyes. It has become clear to me, while listening to him speak, that Corbin thinks white people are caught up in a strange kind of madness. It is sad, even tragic, to him, and he has no regrets about having avoided our collective delusions and the self-destructive pursuits they generate. He has been trying to pierce white people's self-centered arrogance all his life, mostly in struggles against an array of agencies that have power over Indians, from the Bureau of Indian Affairs to the Department of Energy. By systematically kidnapping Indian children from their homes and isolating them in boarding schools where they were forbidden to speak in their native tongues, the BIA did its best to eradicate Indian languages, a sure way of killing off a culture. This went on from the late nineteenth century through most of the twentieth.

Corbin's adherence to a way of experiencing the world as a whole and expressing reverence for what he perceives is remarkable in the face of what the Western Shoshone have endured. Over the past fifty years, most of the Shoshone's traditional lands have been seized and occupied by the U.S. military. The Nevada Test Site, Nellis Air Force Bombing Range, China Lake Naval Weapons Center, Edwards Air Force Base, Fort Irwin Military Reservation, Twentynine Palms Marine Corps Base, and various other military operations have turned much of their culture's habitat into an environmental sacrifice zone on a scale previously seen only in places like Kazakhstan, where the former Soviet Union did most of its nuclear weapons testing. The last hundred years of history have been a kind of Shoshone apocalypse. Corbin has had a long, hard life, full of much loss and betrayal. I would expect some bitterness and anger, but I sense none. This day I hear only sadness and pity. And tiredness, too. The fools are busy yet again, and Corbin must be up and after them.

Corbin, in his wisdom, can point to our failure and folly, but he is not about narrowly focused solutions. He wants to block nuclear waste not only from his backyard, but from all backyards. How, I ask? He says he wants to abolish nuclear weapons and nuclear power too, because the world is a living web that is animated and holy and nuclear weapons and power are not compatible with that world. But like the other activists camped out in Skull Valley, today he is focused on the formally sanctioned "solution" that our government wants to impose on him and his people, a solution that he believes is racist, shortsighted, and bound to fail.

Corbin and the others realize that even if the nation agreed to abolish nuclear weapons and power tomorrow, we would still have to deal with a waste stream that would be lethal and dangerous for thousands

255

of years. There are no good solutions, the anti-nuclear activists tell me, but shipping the waste to deserts for burial solves nothing—it just enables the nuclear industry to make more waste, thereby compounding the problem and making it even more intractable. The activists are out to stop the enablers. Corbin, for one, thinks that asking him for a solution is just plain silly. "You whites been doing this nuclear power for fifty years and you still don't know how to fix it. You gonna wait until this old man tells you how?"

Visiting with Corbin reminds me that while on the trail of these visionaries, I have discovered a kind of continuum of humble vision. On one end are the practical activists and advocates who translate bold ideas into first steps and then second steps. They are no less visionary for translating a vision into the realm of proposal, plan, and policy, or for working their alchemy in courts and councils. Then, in the middle perhaps, are those like the conservation biologists, who empower the activists with knowledge and create compelling new contexts for regarding the world and acting upon it.

Finally, at the far end of that continuum, are folks like Corbin. His vision and contribution are more visceral. He is a storyteller at heart, and he listens to the world directly. He insists that animals talk and finds it amusing that we take our refusal to listen to them as proof that they don't—but he is sad for us, sad that we miss what they could teach us. He doesn't need a pet psychic to help him talk to his horse or a Jungian analyst to discern the archetypes in his dreams. He reminds his listeners that there are other ways of being, in a world that is more present and available than we admit. We can change the way we live.

After the meal is cleaned up, some of the women head for Margene's sweat lodge. My wife wants to go but cannot join them. She forgot her bathing suit, and the Goshute women had qualified their invitation to join them in the sweat lodge with a polite request for modest attire only. "This ain't no Rastafarian Rainbow Festival," I hear between the lines. "Good for them," I think, then wonder if my response is one more sign that I am getting older, like when I look into the mirror in the morning and catch myself shaving my father.

I drift over to Sammy Blackbear, a leader of the dissident Goshute faction. We have just learned that Salt Lake City's mayor, Rocky Anderson, will join us the next day for the concluding press conference, and we talk about how impressed we are that he would drive sixty miles and back to show support. "He gets it," I tell Sammy, "and he's not afraid to stand with us." Elsewhere in Utah, such bold political behavior is unknown. Away from the culturally diverse streets of Salt Lake City, Anderson is loathed with a virulence that is a strange measure of how threatened some Utahns feel when confronted with provocative ideas that challenge comforting assumptions.

Sammy shares with me his latest take on the legal struggle to have Leon Bear's tribal regime declared illegitimate and to install his own anti-Bear faction. Leon Bear is the disputed leader of the small but sovereign band of 125 Skull Valley Goshutes, the majority of whom now live far from the reservation, in the gambling town of Wendover to the west or Tooele and Salt Lake City to the east. Bear cut a deal with a consortium of utilities called Private Fuel Storage to park 40,000 tons of spent nuclear fuel rods in Skull Valley until a permanent repository is built at Yucca Mountain. He has been accused by his opponents of misusing funds, cutting secret deals, and engaging in sneaky politics. Sammy is trying to make the charges stick. His take on things is always optimistic. "Any day now," he tells me, "Leon is going to jail."[1]

As Sammy briefs me on the latest developments, we are close enough to Leon Bear's home that I swear I can see the setting sun glinting off the roof of his shiny new pickup truck in the driveway, next to his shiny new motor home. Bear has been well rewarded for signing a deal to allow the construction of a $3.1 billion nuclear waste storage facility on the Skull Valley reservation.

Margene Bullcreek, in contrast, would benefit if the encampment left one of its portable toilets behind, since the electricity and plumbing in her home are less than iffy. The Bullcreek septic tank is full, and her tribal payments have been cut off and applied to an absurd $91,245.66 bill assessed her by Bear's government for fines, interest, and administrative costs.[2] The fines are for such transgressions as grazing her horses on tribal lands without Bear's permission, and that particular fine is ten times what a lease to graze a horse would cost anywhere else in Tooele County. I wonder if Margene's shoulders are broad enough to withstand Bear's heavy hand.

"It's easy to tell who supports Leon's deal and who doesn't," said a friend who investigated the situation for *Time* magazine. "The supporters have new double-cab pickups and trailers to pull their toys, and the traditionals drive around in old wrecks that are wired together and duct-taped." The people of Skull Valley have always lived in or on the edge of poverty, but theirs was a poverty shared by all. Now the struggle over the radioactive waste disposal scheme has divided the Goshutes into haves and have-nots.

Have-not has been the rule. The Goshutes, or Kusiutta, are America's aborigines; they have been dream-walking our spare desert interior for thousands of years. They migrated between distant springs and hunted rabbits, snakes, reptiles, and deer. They gathered, winnowed, and ground wild grass seeds into a mush that was a tribal staple. They harvested pine nuts. They knew drought and starvation but, Margene told me, "Life out here was never easy, but the land sustained us and we knew how to live on it."

Then, 150 years ago, Brigham Young and his Mormon refugees arrived, explored, and settled down. They came by the tens of thousands to land that had sustained only thin and scattered populations. They took over the springs, cut timber, killed the game, and set their cattle loose on sensitive grasslands. Before long, the Goshutes were starving and resorted to killing the animals that were gnawing on their portion of the food web.

The cowboys got angry when the "naked heathens" ate the cows that were eating their habitat. In May 1850, Brigham Young, the governor of the new territory, complained to the federal government, "We cannot live with bad Indians." Utah's natives were "doing no good here to themselves or anybody else." Their ancestral ground was nothing but "naked rock and soil, naked Indians and wolves" who were "annoying and destructive to property and peace." The area's wolves, of course, were developing a taste for lamb and beef because their own food web and habitat had been torn apart by the settlers. The Mormons, Young wrote, were "trying to shoot, trap, and poison the wolves," but they needed help removing the Indians.[3]

The feds balked, but a year later, after starving Goshutes helped themselves to fifteen head of cows and horses, a "Tooele Expedition" was organized by the territorial government. The quasi-cavalry chased the Goshutes all over hell and back. They would see some Indians in the distance and charge over, only to find that they "had principally re-located," as their report put it, by the time the cowboy-soldiers got there. After a few days the expedition was "melted down," in the words of its commander. At last they found the camp and the slaughtered cattle hanging in the branches to dry.[4]

The expedition's leader, Captain William McBride, sent for reinforcements. "We wish without a moment's hesitation to send us about a pound of arsenic. We want to give the Indians well a flavour," he wrote. "A little strychnine would be of fine service and serve instead of salt to their too-fresh meat." His report concluded with a three-line appeal:[5]

Don't forget the arsenic!
Don't forget the spade and the arsenic!
Don't forget the spade, strychnine, and arsenic!

In a few decades, the Mormon settlers' occupation of the Goshutes' former habitat was complete. The tribe had been thoroughly demoralized by such genocidal war crimes. Reduced to living in brush huts in dry valleys where they ate grasshoppers to avoid further starvation, they were famously described by Mark Twain on one of his journeys west in the late nineteenth century as the lowest form of human being on the planet, a label that today's Goshutes have thoroughly absorbed.

I once sat in a meeting in Ibapah, the Skull Valley band's neighboring Goshute community at the foot of the Deep Creek Mountains, and listened to a young Goshute woman make a tearful confession. When she goes to powwows, she told the group, she tries to pass herself off as a Shoshone, Piute, or Ute because even among Indians, Goshutes have low status and are stigmatized. Others, their eyes welling with tears, acknowledged they had done the same. On the drive back to Salt Lake City, Forrest Cuch, the Ute director of the Utah Bureau of Indian Affairs, shook his head and told me, "Self-hatred is a most destructive force. It is killing us long after the last bullet was fired."

In 1918, the 18,000-acre Skull Valley reservation was created, and the government tried to teach the Goshutes to be farmers. Farming didn't take, but the white government did succeed in all but eliminating the Goshute language. That's an old story. What is unique in the Goshute version is how the U.S. government then surrounded the Indians with the most poisonous activities and contaminated habitat imaginable. The Goshutes, having survived frontier racism and then an era of paternalistic neglect, are now on the front lines of environmental racism.

Teryl Hunsaker took no guff. He was proud to be a man who gets things done. During his career as a high school shop teacher, he expected his students to do their work and behave themselves in the process. It was about improvement. And God help you if you crossed him. In a town where people substituted "heck" for "hell" and "dang" for "damn," Hunsaker was known for the cussing that peppered his volatile outbursts. His anger was sudden and unpredictable, even legendary. Stories circulated that he once threw a piece of metal at a student who was goofing off and stapled another in the shoulder when he angered him.

In a Mormon culture, where being nice is an unspoken rule, Hunsaker's hot temper and erratic behavior did not exactly fit the preferred model. That he was not only forgiven for his trespasses but frequently endorsed despite them is a measure of his other personality—the no-nonsense guy who makes things happen, the practical man who taught a generation of boys to fix and build things and raise animals for cash or food. He was elected mayor of Grantsville, Utah, while still a young man, then Tooele County commissioner twice after he retired from teaching. He could be an abrasive SOB sometimes, but people liked him and trusted him.

Commissioner Hunsaker was not exactly the philosophical type, but he had a clear philosophy: Land generated wealth. Period, end of story. Wealth that was real, reliable, useful, and right was based on land. You tore metals or minerals out of the ground, cut lumber, grew crops, grazed, or bought, sold, and leased acreage. You harnessed what little water was available for drinking or irrigation. Even the Great Salt Lake could be profitably mined. Call that a plain, old-fashioned way of thinking, but it worked, was proven, was tried and true, dammit.

"How about tourism?" I once asked. "Bullshit!" he replied. Who wants to make beds and clear the slop from tables when yuppies from California are through eating? Sure, tourism was fine and he had done a lot to promote it, but it was off to the side, unreliable, uncontrollable. Land—that was where it was at, and if you didn't grasp that, you didn't have your feet on the ground.

Here's another thing you need to get straight, he'd say: the most good for the most people. What was "good," of course, were jobs that enabled men to care for their families. It was also good to develop a source of revenue other than the voters' own wallets to support services to them, like recreation facilities for families to enjoy. That should be obvious, too.

Hunsaker bristles today when his critics question whether the revenue he has developed from importing hazardous waste into the county has compromised people's health. After all, tax dollars from hazardous waste imported into his county helped build a big new hospital in Tooele without overloading property tax bills—so don't tell him he doesn't have public health in mind. And don't go talking about ecosystems and health to Hunsaker—he's not a believer. Nothing's been proven, he'll tell you. It's just speculation. One last thing: Patriotism. Hey, none of that "killing John Wayne" crap for the commissioner. The Duke is still the duke to him. Keep your hands off him, Pilgrim.

Commissioner Hunsaker's political fiefdom, Tooele County, had a lot of land and most of it was, according to the prevailing philosophy so unabashedly expressed by the commissioner, useless. Vast stretches of dry high desert could not support man or beast, held no precious metals or minerals, and were unsuitable for crops of any kind. They were, however, remote and sparsely populated.

During World War II, when the feds were looking to construct an inland depot that Japan's fighter planes would not be able to reach, the Tooele Army Depot was built to the east of the Goshute reservation. Eventually that depot would be expanded to accommodate half the nation's stockpile of chemical weapons. Then two controversial incinerators for burning that aging stockpile would be tacked on. To the west of the Goshutes, Wendover Air Base was built to train the crew of the *Enola Gay,* the bomber that dropped the big one on Hiroshima. Then a vast bombing range was carved out of the desert so that jets from Hill Air Force Base in Ogden, Utah, could practice the art of aerial warfare.

Meanwhile, to the immediate west of the Goshutes, the Dugway Proving Grounds was developed to test biological, chemical, and radiological weapons. More than a thousand open-air tests involving nerve gas and anthrax were conducted directly upwind from the Goshute communities. The tests were halted after one went awry in 1968 and more than 6,400 sheep in Skull Valley dropped, rolled, convulsed, stuck their sheepy feet in the air, and croaked. No health survey of the Goshutes living in the valley at that time has ever been conducted.

If Tooele County's leaders, who had suffered though the grinding scarcity of the Depression, realized the advantages of welcoming secure government jobs into the area, the military also saw opportunities. The West Desert was so geographically removed that activities which would never be tolerated anywhere else could be conducted there without much scrutiny or complaint. In the post–World War II years, the locals were hungry and already had a high tolerance for risk, since underground mining had been a predominant occupation for much of the county's history, until it was succeeded by open-pit mining at the nearby Kennecott copper mine. So the locals were willing to live with munitions stacked all around them. And they could be gullibly patriotic, such as in one Dugway experiment where civilian volunteers got extra pay, fifty cents a day, to let mosquitoes infected with encephalitis bite them.

The military opened the West Desert gate to private industry. A magnesium refinery was built, with Tooele County's encouragement, in the early 1960s. It spewed about 80 percent of the nation's "point source" chlorine gas emissions, and today it regularly tops the Toxics Release Inventory's list of worst polluters in the nation. Its ownership has changed often; the latest owner is a billionaire who is constructing what is reputed to be the largest private mansion in the country in the Hamptons on Long Island. After a while, some Goshutes began to get the picture: the desert is where white men go to do what they don't dare do in their own backyards. They got a small piece of the poisonous pie themselves when they landed a contract for a Hercules rocket-motor testing site.

An era of corporate dumping and burning began in earnest in the late 1980s, when peace broke out briefly and the government decommissioned some military bases, including the Tooele Army Depot. The resulting job loss was scary for the region. The time had come to diversify the local economy, officials decided, so a large swath of desert west of town, called the West Desert Hazardous Industries Area, was zoned for business by Hunsaker's predecessors on the county commission. Two commercial toxic waste incinerators, a dump for hazardous waste, and a dump for "low-level" radioactive waste went into the zone.

Teryl Hunsaker was elected cowboy-in-chief of a county commonly called the most toxic place in America, and he was proud of it. "My hell," he'd say, "we're solving a problem!" I once wrote that one of his fellow county commissioners had turned the West Desert from a military toilet into a pay toilet. The commissioner reportedly laughed when he read that and then used my line enthusiastically to describe himself to others.

The word was out: Tooele County was where you could do business, so make an offer. Leon Bear certainly got the word. Bear had succeeded his father as chairman of the Skull Valley band of the Goshutes. The previous Chairman Bear had once told a crowded hearing in Grantsville that spent fuel rods were safe because, after all, they were "spent"—this from a man who had just toured nuclear plants throughout Europe as a guest of utility companies so he could learn all about nuclear power.

The younger Bear was smarter and more sophisticated than his dad. The prince of paupers was tired of poverty and insecurity, tired of the indignities suffered by his people. Like many of the small band of a hundred or so, he wanted out. Out and up. But how? The band tried operating a recycling plant, but it went belly up. Then they realized that they could get a lot of money to participate in a study of whether their reservation would be a suitable site for an MRS facility. MRS was an acronym for monitored retrievable storage, a key component of the nation's plan for nuclear waste disposal.

During the formative stages of the nuclear energy industry, the federal government gave it massive subsidies to keep it growing. As originally conceived, nuclear power was supposed to reprocess "spent" reactor fuel into new fuel. The reactor rods that push fission in the reactor's core are packed with enriched uranium pellets. They become "spent" in an economic sense when they are no longer useful as a fuel and become, instead, a costly liability. At that time, they are anything but "spent" in a radioactive sense. In fact, they are among the most irradiated substances on the planet and, unshielded, could kill an unwary bystander in less than a minute. They remain dangerously radioactive for tens of thousands of years.

Reprocessing these spent fuel rods proved to be too dangerous and expensive, as well as risky to the nation's security. Enriched uranium could find its way into weapons of mass destruction, like those held today by India, Pakistan, and North Korea. And too many workers in the processing facilities were getting sick. When reprocessing was abandoned, the spent fuel rods had nowhere to go. They had lost their place in the loop. Now what? America had the nuclear orphan from hell in its hands.

The short-term answers were made up as the country went along. Spent fuel rods went into cooling pools after they were pulled, to lower their temperatures and reduce their volatility. When the pools got too crowded, the rods went into dry storage, usually very near the reactor that produced them. Dry storage meant the rods were wrapped in specially designed shields within casks.

As the spent fuel rods in casks accumulated on site, the utilities that owned the reactors lobbied the government hard to come up with a plan for disposal. If the accumulated fuel rods in their casks could not be moved away, they argued, power plants might have to shut down because of the lack of storage room. People who lived near the power plants and used the energy they generated were wary of the risks of living near the consequences of their power source. Storage was costly, so if costs could not be passed on, nuclear power wouldn't be able to compete with other energy sources.

The feds agreed with the nuclear utilities. Local citizens would not tolerate the accumulation of fuel near dense populations, on river plains, or perched along the coast. The costs of moving the fuel rods, burying them, monitoring them endlessly, and conducting the inevitable remediation would be too much for the corporations and their rate-paying customers to handle. The nuclear industry would collapse from the load. To keep the nuclear utilities propped up, the taxpayers would have to take over, the very citizens whose legitimate concerns compelled the removal of the spent fuel rods. As the nuclear utilities backed away from the bills falling due, they smilingly reiterated to the public that they were "competitive" and "clean."

The process was supposed to go like this: First, the feds would identify scientifically appropriate locations for both a "permanent" repository, where waste could be buried for at least 10,000 years, and a "temporary" location, where waste shipped away from the utilities could await burial. It was assumed that the so-called permanent repository would be very expensive and would take a long time to complete, thus the need for a temporary site in the meantime.

Once the sites meeting the scientific criteria had been identified, the feds would select two to develop. The plan was formalized in the National Waste Policy Act, passed by Congress in 1982. The act included a provision that the temporary site and the permanent site could not be in the same state.

Sounds straightforward enough, but like so much else in nuclear history, it didn't work out as promised. First, scientific studies identified deep hardrock or old dry caverns as the best repository option. But those sorts of sites were in the Midwest and East, where political opposition would be too tough, so they kept on looking, ignoring their original criteria and lowering their standards as they searched. Once the scientific criteria had been compromised, political criteria took over, and politics has driven the process ever since.

It was clear that any community near a proposed nuclear waste repository was going to resist. A small, impoverished community would be the easiest to roll over. And Indian reservations needed development, right? They could get hundreds of thousands of dollars to simply consider the proposal. Unemployed tribal members would be hired to "study" the ways that nuclear waste would be shipped and stored. The sociological and political criteria were met, and economics provided a validating cover.

Thus the U.S. government polled Indian reservations regarding their interest in taking spent nuclear fuel, an instance of environmental racism matched only by the distribution of blankets infected with smallpox in frontier days or, perhaps, meat salted with arsenic and strychnine in the days of the Mormon settlers. There were few takers among the tribes, but Leon Bear's dad, under the guidance of the band's attorney, raised the band's collective hand, and soon the checks were rolling in. Or at least they were rolling toward those who supported the deal. A significant number of Skull Valley Goshutes opposed the plan, and the band became bitterly divided.

Meanwhile, back at the radioactive ranch, otherwise known as the Nuclear Regulatory Commission, a decision regarding the permanent repository was closing in on Nevada. The federal nuclear facilitators had an eye on Yucca Mountain, a hundred miles northwest of Las

Vegas. It didn't meet the scientific criteria; it was made of porous volcanic rock and was in an area that was very seismically active. It had even experienced volcanic activity within the past 10,000 years, a period of time equal to the time for which the site was supposed to be safe in the future.

For that matter, the desert surrounding Yucca Mountain had been underwater within the same rough time period. Until very recent geologic time, Lakes Lahontan and Bonneville had been twin inland seas that gathered in the Great Basin. According to that time scale, the nuclear repository inside Yucca Mountain was to be built during a dry spell. In an era of global warming, who could tell what the shape of the land would be thousands of years in the future?

Yucca Mountain had one thing going for it—it was in Nevada, and Nevada had a total congressional delegation of three at the time. And these three were easy to overcome. The legislation targeting Yucca Mountain was popularly known as the "screw Nevada" bill. Besides, Nevada already had the test site for nuclear weapons. They had skilled atomic workers—or, at least, willing workers who had a high tolerance for risk if the paycheck and benefits were sufficient. Yucca Mountain, in fact, was surrounded by the Nevada Test Site.

Having spent all their political capital on the unexpectedly protracted process of choosing a permanent repository, the feds abandoned their search for a temporary storage site. Three tribes had been in the running for that project. One was the Mescalero Apaches in New Mexico, who engaged in such divisive political infighting that the feds gave up on them. Another tribe was in Nevada, and the rules prohibited the two sites from being in the same state. The remaining tribe was the Goshutes. The federal game was over, but if Leon Bear, now chairman of the Skull Valley band, was worried that the gravy train of study money would stop, he didn't have to fret long.

A consortium of private utilities that owned nuclear power plants decided that if the feds could not designate and develop a temporary storage site to relieve them of their waste stream while a permanent repository was prepared, they needed a kind of nuclear-waste Plan B. The members of the consortium changed over time and so did their corporate names, but the consortium included Southern California Edison, Consolidated Edison, Florida Power & Light, Genoa Fuel Tech, GPU

Nuclear Corporation, Indiana/Michigan Power, Southern Nuclear Operating Company, and Xcel Energy. They had reactors in Minnesota, Michigan, New York, Florida, Wisconsin, Pennsylvania, California, Alabama, and Georgia. The consortium was known by its initials, PFS, short for Private Fuel Storage.

PFS realized that the Skull Valley band could be a cheap and easy solution to their problem. And by cutting a deal to "temporarily" dump their waste on an Indian reservation, they could avoid the usual legal and political constraints, since the tribe's sovereignty exempted them from state and federal regulations. Although Leon Bear refuses to reveal the terms of the contract he signed with PFS in 1997, it was generally assumed that the Goshutes were paid around $200 million.

However, Judy Fahys, a reporter for the *Salt Lake Tribune,* uncovered documents showing that the sum was much less, perhaps as low as $40 million, a fraction of what the deal was worth to PFS. The combined income of the entire Skull Valley band, Fahys points out, is less than a million dollars a year, so $40 million is a lot of money to them. But the eight utilities that make up the Private Fuel Storage consortium have a combined income of $119 billion. They could have afforded to pay much more for a facility that would enable them to keep on doing business. One tribe, for instance, had asked for $1 billion up front and $1 million per year after that; the Department of Energy and the industry representatives who heard the offer never blinked an eye, according to Representative Richard Stallings of Idaho. When the Goshutes negotiated, on the other hand, their attorney was barred from the bargaining table because he caused too much "friction."[6]

PFS spokespeople, of course, present the deal as a good deed and certainly not their idea. "They came to us!" exclaimed the smiling CEO of Private Fuel Storage when I debated him before a convention of Utah real estate agents in Tucson (yes, the Utah Realtors' convention was held out of state). "What if the tribal government changes hands and the people decide they don't want to be a repository after all?" a woman in the audience asked. The CEO evaded the question, but the audience insisted that he answer, whereupon he deferred to his corporate attorney. "Well," said the attorney, "a deal is a deal." Even a smiley face has a bottom line.

The locals in Tooele County were easy marks, too. PFS found a price that the county could live with, between $90 million and $300 million over time for providing services and support. The governor, however, refused to go along. A member of a large downwinder family from southern Utah, Mike Leavitt asserted his power. He seized the only road into the valley and declared it off-limits to nuclear waste, saying it would come into Utah "over my dead body." County commissioner Hunsaker fussed and fumed in response and threatened to build a parallel road next to the one Leavitt had seized. Eventually the state legislature joined the governor in opposition to PFS and passed legislation designed to thwart the Skull Valley project. PFS, in turn, took the state to court. Salt Lake City mayor Rocky Anderson, aware that PFS could bring spent fuel rods on trains through the city, added his arguments to what was becoming a consensus of opinion across the state, Hunsaker et al. excepted.

The Utah congressional delegation eventually added their voices of opposition, when it was clear that it was politically safe to oppose the PFS project at home and, indeed, couldn't be avoided. Congressman Jim Hansen took the lead. His rage was genuine: If PFS parked 4,000 casks of spent nuclear fuel in Skull Valley, fighter jets flying from Hill Air Force Base in northern Utah would have to avoid Skull Valley, which was otherwise the logical and common way to approach the Utah Test and Training Range, where the fighters practiced warfare. Hill was the economic engine of Hansen's district, and he could be counted on to fight like a bulldog to keep it open because thousands of jobs were at stake. His district was hooked on military spending. He slapped the table emphatically at an NRC hearing in Grantsville and vowed to block the deal.

As it turned out, having Jim Hansen on your team was not necessarily an advantage, despite the seniority and power he had accumulated over two decades on the Hill. Hansen's opposition was convoluted. When Utah realized it could block a PFS rail line into the proposed Skull Valley site by getting the Cedar Mountains, on the western side of the valley, designated as wilderness, Hansen decided his vehicle to accomplish the task was a Defense Department authorization bill—despite the fact that he was then chair of the House Natural Resources Committee, the usual place for generating wilderness designations. The language of the legislation that Hansen tucked into the defense bill would have turned all of Utah's West Desert into a military colony, governed by the military and subject to its priorities. His colleagues, unwilling to blatantly compromise the Wilderness Act, uninterested in giving Hansen's favorite Air Force base a competitive advantage over their own, and unwilling to help Utah block nuclear waste that could be shipped from their districts to Utah, killed his legislation.

Once the Hansen attempt at blockage, offered in the closing weeks of his last term, was defeated, Governor Leavitt could have accomplished the same thing by simply asking the Bureau of Land Management to manage Wilderness Study Areas in the Cedar Mountains by the book. But that would have looked bad when the governor and his Republican Party went on to fight wilderness designations in southern Utah. It would seem contradictory when they tried to push out new roads through other Wilderness Study Areas.

Hansen's legislative fumble at the end of his long run in Congress might be excused as a simple case of overreaching, but Leavitt's acquiescence revealed that although he had pledged that the nuclear waste would come in only over his dead body, his opposition to wilderness designation was just as strong. His political base, after all, was in rural Utah, where limitations on grazing, drilling, and road building in wilderness are regarded as more threatening than living next to a nuclear waste pit.

Meanwhile, Utah's own environmental regulatory agencies built a case against the PFS plan. They didn't have a lot of experience arguing in favor of the land and against development, but they collected powerful evidence of seismic activity in Skull Valley and conjured a vision of thousands of huge upright casks tipping over on their cement pads, their stability disrupted in a geologic game of pick-up sticks. The Nuclear Regulatory Commission, always the powerful enabler of the industry, denied their claims and ruled against reality.

People who live on the desert understand that the Skull Valley site is risky because we live with earthquakes, wildfires, flash floods, and avalanches. We live embedded in a landscape where chaos, catastrophe, and disturbance reign and cannot be constrained. The unthinkable happens here all the time. Here as everywhere, we have seen trains derail and tankers explode on highways. But unlike everywhere else, F-16s crash regularly here. Missiles go astray. Nerve gas gets loose and sheep herds drop dead. Well after 9/11, the NRC refused to study the likelihood of a terrorist attack on waste shipments or on 4,000 giant casks sitting in a wide open-valley under the desert sun.

Eventually, however, in early 2003, a licensing board that advises the NRC on safety issues ruled that the risk of fighter jets crashing into the PFS facility was too great. PFS amended its plan and appealed the ruling to the NRC. In the summer of 2003, the NRC's decision was still pending. Opponents of the plan were not optimistic that the NRC would take its own advice.

There are powerful reasons why the Western Shoshone find common ground with the Goshutes to their east and offer them support and counsel. They are also living inside the sacrifice zone. The Western Shoshone's ancestral ground comprises Yucca Mountain and the Nevada Test Site, so they are deadly familiar with the kind of radioactive racism the Goshutes are only now learning about.

Traditionally, Western Shoshone habitat covered the whole Great Basin Desert. For thousands of years the Shoshone lived well within the limits of their habitat, until white people upset the balance. First, trappers decimated beaver populations along the Humboldt River. Then a constant stream of wagon trains on their way to the California gold rush competed for game and water. In 1862, a fort was built in Ruby Valley, Nevada, to protect the settlers' passage. Colonel Patrick Connor of the California Volunteers, who manned the fort, ordered his men to "destroy every male Indian you encounter."[7]

By 1863, hundreds of Western Shoshone had been massacred, and the tribe, desperate for safety, signed the Treaty of Ruby Valley. One hundred and fifty years later, the Shoshone were still arguing with the state of Nevada and the federal government over the terms of the treaty: whether the Western Shoshone were entitled to the vast landscapes of the Great Basin Desert or only to the small, barren reservations to which they had retreated.

The Nevada Test Site, according to Western Shoshone leaders like Corbin Harney, added insult to injury. If you make the case, as Corbin does, that the white government in Washington is morally bankrupt, mentally unbalanced, dangerous, and utterly lacking in the consciousness and knowledge required to manage a landscape with integrity, the Nevada Test Site is Exhibit A.

Since the advent of the current nuclear era, the Nevada Test Site has been where we rehearsed Armageddon. The site is big—1,350 square miles splayed out in the middle of Nellis Air Force Base, which is the size of Connecticut or Belgium. The Nevada Test Site is bigger than Yosemite or Rhode Island. It had to be vast to hold our nuclear testing program in its arms—928 above- and below-ground nuclear weapons tests were conducted there.

Among the brown mountains is one gray one. To understand how a geophysical feature would affect the nuclear blast pattern, a 44-kiloton device nicknamed Smoky was detonated on a seven-hundred-foot tower next to the once brown mountain. The resulting explosion blew the soil off the mountain, right down to the gray bedrock below.[8]

Above-ground testing moved underground in the early 1960s, so in addition to the craters from bombs like the one that covered John Wayne in radioactive fallout, the test site is also covered by playas that are moonscapes of subsistence craters made when the earth below collapsed from the force of underground tests. A 104-kiloton test in 1962 moved 12 million tons of earth in a millisecond. Sometimes cracks opened on the surface of the craters and radioactive smoke and dust billowed skyward. The test site is a radioactive landscape that must be monitored and quarantined for a thousand years.

Now add Yucca Mountain. Yucca was sacred to the Shoshone as a high point that intersected earth and sky, a place where the power of the wind and sun was manifested. Mountains are, according to the Shoshone belief system, places of emergence and creation that are packed with life force and energy.[9]

Yucca Mountain was also slated to be packed with more than forty years' worth of spent nuclear fuel rods—thousands of them, shipped from nuclear power plants in every corner of the nation—and sealed for at least 10,000 years. Construction is under way. A gigantic special machine had been constructed to bore a titanic tunnel into the mountainside. It had almost breached an aquifer and the critical Ghost Dance Fault, named after a millennial Indian movement that swept across the West from the Great Basin during the sad era when the utter defeat of the Indians became apparent.

At the turn of the nineteenth and twentieth centuries, Indians tried to dance the buffalo back into life and dance the destructive white demons away. At the turn of the twenty-first century, whites are trying to spend away the nuclear demons that haunt them. So far, our money has been little more effective than the Ghost Dancers' prayers in banishing our respective demons. We have already spent close to $4 billion developing the repository, a drop in the bucket compared to the final cost, which could top $60 billion, making it the most expensive construction project ever. If completed, Yucca will cost more than the Hoover, Grand Coulee, and Glen Canyon Dams together. Throw in the Alaska pipeline, the Panama Canal, and the World Trade Center, and you start to get an idea of how much the infrastructure for nuclear waste disposal will cost. Desperate to get a handle on the burgeoning expenses, the Department of Energy is already unilaterally redefining the rules, standards, and procedures developed to guide the repository design and construction, in order to move the project along.

If the Nevada Test Site exhibits the dark side of human endeavor, the Shoshones offer light. Shoshone consciousness has been inspiring to a generation of anti-nuclear demonstrators who have held annual protests at the test site from the 1970s through the present. Hence the Shoshone word shundahai was chosen for the name of the network of grassroots activists trying to link the struggle to curb nuclear weapons development with the struggle to keep nuclear waste from getting dumped next to the military sacrifice zone. The Shundahai Network's mission statement reads, "We seek to abolish all nuclear weapons and put an end to weapons testing. We advocate phasing out nuclear energy and ending transportation and dumping of nuclear waste."

Reinard Knutsen of the Shundahai Network has organized the 2001 gathering in Skull Valley. Reinard is a veteran of the Nevada Test Site Peace Camp, which grew out of an earlier era of protest against the development and maintenance of nuclear weaponry. A Franciscan nun named Sister Rosemary initiated a Lenten vigil at the test site in 1977. The protest/pilgrimage was repeated each spring and attracted a growing number of citizens who were convinced that the madness of the arms race had to be confronted. Quakers joined early, then peace advocates from other religious denominations, then pagans and nonreligious activists too. The staging area next to the test site became known as the Peace Camp. In 1985, in the wake of massive demonstrations in Europe against increasingly provocative missile deployment, the activists expanded their equinox vigil to a thirty-five-day protest.

A year later and across the globe, in 1986, Chernobyl blew up and melted down. Then, in early 1989, an underground blast in Kazakhstan, the central Asian republic where the Soviets tested most of their nuclear devices, vented radiation into the atmosphere. Soon after, the Kazakh poet Olzhas Suleimenov appeared live on Soviet television to read his poetry, but instead surprised his viewers and would-be censors with a statement condemning nuclear testing and calling for public meetings. A robust anti-nuclear movement in Kazakhstan resulted, and its leaders expressed solidarity with the protesters in Nevada.[10]

We cannot know for sure how much the synergy between protesters in the Soviet Union and the United States contributed to the demise of the Soviet empire in that fateful year of 1989, but the convergent perspectives of people living in landscapes that had been captured by their competing militaries were inspiring. Each side's desert populations found that they shared unifying concerns and threats regardless of which side of the Cold War ramparts they hunkered behind. Maybe the enemy wasn't a foreign power after all, but a local elite and their prevailing mind-set.

The Nevada protests thinned as the Cold War ebbed. The protesters who continued to show up at the Peace Camp each spring redefined the context for their struggle. They realized how suicidal weapons were wedded to ecocide. Each year thousands of them would walk onto the test site and as far into restricted areas as they could before being arrested by guards. As described by Rebecca Solnit in her illuminating account of that era, *Savage Dreams: A Journey into the Landscape Wars of the American West,* protesters symbolically reclaimed land that they understood had been taken from the Western Shoshone people. They walked over the line and into the sacrifice zone to ritualistically weave the land back into its ecological web.

In an amusing twist of fate, when the American children of Cold War affluence, earnest young people like Reinard Knutsen, turned away from the underlying assumptions of their culture, they fell into the arms of the most defeated and discredited culture on the continent, the Western Shoshone. Reinard Knutsen decided to make the hard work of beating nuclear swords into plowshares his calling, and he became Corbin's right-hand man at Shundahai. "A lot of what I do is build alliances," says Reinard. "I travel a lot. It's satisfying to see people who did not realize they have so much in common find one another. Ultimately, nobody benefits from what we're doing with nuclear technology. Even those who profit from it are going to suffer in the long run. People are waking up to that, and when they do, we put them together."

Shundahai's bridge stretches all the way to Washington, D.C. Kevin Kamps has come to Skull Valley from the Nuclear Information and Resource Service in D.C., and Lisa Gue has traveled from Public Citizen's Washington office. Lisa traveled here by conventional means, but Kevin drove, pulling a trailer with a giant inflatable dumbbell strapped to it, a mock-up of the shipping casks for spent nuclear fuel rods.

The inflatable cask is a prop he uses to tell communities along the route from D.C. to Nevada about Mobile Chernobyl, the name given to the tens of thousands of shipments it will take to send 77,000 tons of waste to Yucca Mountain. Estimates of the number of accidents that can be expected range from 90 to 950, depending on how you crunch the numbers. No realistic assessment denies there will be accidents. If your community sits on the route of spent nuclear fuel, Kevin tells them, and at least 50 million Americans have that dubious honor, then you'd better understand that accidents are inevitable. It's just a matter of where, when, and how bad.

Spilling nuclear waste is not like spilling hogs or even caustic chemicals on the highway or a rail line. The resulting disruption and required remediation could cost an urban area like Salt Lake County well over $100 billion, according to Dr. Marvin Resnikoff, a consultant on nuclear waste hired by the state of Utah. What price do you put on a watershed if a shipment goes over a bridge or derails by a riverbank? What price do you put on the lives of those who, exposed by wind or rain after an accident or a terrorist attack, suffer and die? Over the long run, and it will be a long run, transporting nuclear waste is like a game of Russian roulette. Sooner or later a radioactive bullet will kill a river, a wetland, a forest, or a coast somewhere. There will be a spill from a nuclear waste shipment that is equivalent to the wreck of the *Exxon Valdez.*

Along the route he takes with the inflatable cask in tow, Kevin often recruits others based on their self-interest. "I don't want that stuff shipped through my backyard!" is the frequent response, one that parallels the understandable sentiment of those who live in the shadow of the stored waste that is now crowding power plant pools and dry-cask storage yards—"Get that stuff outta here!" The nuclear waste policy war has turned into a nationwide game of hot potato as the fuel rods are spent, stored, shipped, and stored some more. At each turn, nobody wants them nearby.

Again, the activists who oppose the shipping and burial of nuclear waste do not offer ready alternatives. The first step in finding a solution that is acceptable, they say, is acknowledging that the solution being imposed today is unfair and is no solution at all. Rather than solve the problem of what to do with the waste, we are transferring the problem, its costs, and its consequences to others so that the root problem—the production of more dangerous waste—can continue indefinitely.

As Kevin pulls his trailer along the route that nuclear waste will take, he tries to expand the context for stopping Mobile Chernobyl so that it becomes more inclusive. The leap from "not in my backyard" to "not in anyone's backyard" is far easier to make if you are simply on the nuclear route than if the fuel rods are already in your backyard.

The leap of moral commitment Debbie Katz took, then, is amazing. She helped build a grassroots organization, the Citizens Awareness Network, that makes common cause with the people far away who would be poisoned tomorrow by the waste that sickens the families and neighbors of CAN members today. CAN members are mostly in Massachusetts and Vermont. When Debbie speaks to a full tent on the first day of the Skull Valley rally, there is not a dry eye in the house. Her conviction is inspiring. Later she tells me her story.

I became involved in 1991 against my will. I was living in rural Massachusetts with my husband and two children. I had worked in New York City for many years as a social worker at an alcohol treatment facility in the Bowery, organizing a senior citizen food co-op in the Bronx, at the women's shelter, working with the mentally retarded, working as a consultant at a nursing home for transfer trauma, etc. My husband and I had put in many years of service, and we were burned out. We continued counseling in New York, but we moved to western Massachusetts and tried to live a much simpler life there. I guess you could say we were in retreat.

Three things happened to change all that. The EPA held a meeting about what they were going to "permit" Yankee Rowe, our local nuclear power plant, to "release" into our local river. Lightning struck the Yankee Rowe and Vermont Yankee reactors at the same time on Father's Day. I live four and a half miles from Rowe and about sixteen miles from Vermont Yankee. The lightning knocked out communications to the Rowe reactor control room. That was interesting. Finally, the Union of Concerned Scientists released a report saying that the Rowe reactor vessel could shatter like glass in the event of an accidental loss of coolant.

People in the community began to meet regularly, about ninety people a week. I did not want to get involved. I was adverse to granola-eating New Agers, and that's who I thought the "environmentalists" were. Also, I had joked for about twenty years that we lived in the "meltdown zone" for Rowe. I had felt that my inability to carry a child to term had to do with radiation exposure, but I figured if I knocked ten years off my life, that was my business. Then the Three Mile Island accident affected me greatly, and I worried about our traveling down to New York City as the accident continued.

My husband and a friend of ours began to attend the meetings and get involved. I continued to resist, but eventually gave in to their pressure. It was summer; the room was hot and sticky. I thought I'd only stay for a little while. All our kids were playing outside. It seemed so bucolic, and yet what we talked about terrified me and made me sick. It was as if I woke up from a dream to a nightmare. I was terribly worried about my children; we had adopted them when they were babies; they were born in Texas. I realized I had brought them to a place that could hurt them, and that I had to be so stupid and thoughtless to do that. I put their lives in danger. We were up many, many nights examining our folly.

I realized that I felt intimidated in Rowe to express my concerns—that I had silenced myself from questioning what was going on. Rowe had become rich through the nuclear business. Franklin County is a poor rural county. We live on dirt roads without sewer systems or streetlights. We were afraid of ostracism and, more than that, retaliation. Coming home from meetings at first, we would worry about being followed. That happened. Being involved with other people engaging in this struggle to shut Rowe down, gaining knowledge about our local nuke, and finding my voice actually took my fear away. I felt connected to a community of people committed to fighting corporate control of our community. We have been threatened many times and followed, but we are less afraid now then we were all those years in our alienated retreat.

"Why did you stay with it?" I ask her. "Why are you here now, so far from home?"

There were many reasons. We closed Rowe. There is nothing like success to validate your work. But there were other issues that have driven my choices. All those nights we stayed up learning about nuclear power and recognizing our ignorance and our fear of technology and science—our believing that we could not have a voice in decisions that vitally affected our community because we were too "stupid"—led us to look at certain painful truths.

At a public relations meeting in Shelburne Falls with local selectmen, townspeople, and nuclear executives, a local asked, "Since the reactor has no containment, if there was an accident, wouldn't it topple over into our local river and contaminate it?" A chemist from the reactor got up and said, "We've been dumping in that river for thirty years, so what's the difference?" We were shocked. We realized that we didn't even know how our local nuke worked. All that time they were dumping waste in our river, and we were oblivious.

We set up a team of mostly women to investigate the records for Rowe at the local public document room in Greenfield. I began reading old records on what Rowe had dumped into the river—the river our kids swam in! Farmland is adjacent to that river! Schools are adjacent to it! I was shaking. I was sure that my calculations were wrong. I actually called an expert I knew to verify that I was correct. Rowe had been dumping thousands of curies a year into the river for years due to faulty fuel rods.

We assembled the documentation. Our focus changed from the consequences of an accident to the standard operation of the nuke and the community becoming a nuclear waste dump for the reactor. We eventually did the same for Vermont Yankee, which releases its waste into the air. I was furious. They knew that they were using the community as a garbage can for their toxic waste, and they didn't care! Not only didn't they care, they relied on people being too intimidated to find out the truth. This was what we called the "meltdown in democracy."

As we recognized our inability to protect our children, we realized that we knew that there were many sick people in our town and the surrounding towns along the Deerfield River, where Yankee Rowe dumped its waste. We realized that we had acted opportunistically—not just from ignorance—that we were willing to ignore their suffering and the suffering in our community because we were not directly affected by it. This was unconscionable. We could not accept our own well-being at the expense of others. We couldn't just save our own children; we had to protect everyone's.

Yankee Rowe began a rapid decommissioning of the reactor—shipping its toxic waste to Barnwell, South Carolina. We found out that Barnwell was a sister city to us—46 percent African American, poor and rural. If we didn't want our children hurt, we couldn't accept other children being hurt. This is the ethics of waste. We organized "caravan of conscience" tours to go ahead of the waste—alerting transport and dump communities and forming an alliance to end the sacrifice of any community.

This is really hard for us. This waste has made us sick and devastated our community. We have a tenfold increase in Down syndrome, statistical significance in cancers, high rates of learning-disabled children (both my kids are) and disabled children. What has made us sick, we are stuck with until there is a scientifically sound and environmentally just solution. I live between two high-level waste dumps, both targets for terrorism. Yet the waste cannot be moved.

"Did you have role models?" I ask. "Who inspired you?"

"There are few women that are acknowledged in this society for doing anything," Debbie says. "I took the mothers and grandmothers of the disappeared in Argentina, who protested and fought for the lives of their dead and dying children. It has also become clear to me that much of the fight involving toxics—nuclear and other contaminants—is done by women for their children and others. In their lives, women are always dealing with protection, organizing, and cleaning up. So maybe it's natural that women find themselves fighting for their children, fighting to stop contamination, and forcing corporations to clean up their messes.

"I was intimidated at first," Debbie says, "and I believed my voice was insignificant. But I decided we can't leave it up to a handful of corporations to determine what kind of world we live in. That's a melt-down of democracy. And when we do find the courage to stop them, they pit sacrifice communities against one another—mine against yours. Unity is hard to accomplish under these circumstances. No one wants this monstrous waste in their community, but we are stuck at the end of the fuel chain with each other. So we must work together to end the cycle of contamination and sacrifice.

"I am a Taoist," Debbie tells me as we say good-bye. "Life may be suffering in itself, but it is the suffering that the people bring on themselves and others that can end. We can prevail."

FOUR

Activists vs. Enablers

Jason Groenewold came to ski. He grew up in Wisconsin and gradu-
ated as a business major from a college in Minnesota, so Utah's winter
temperatures seemed relatively mild and a welcome change. And Utah
gets snow—great snow, lots of it. When cold winds from the north
sweep across our unfreezing saltwater Serengeti, the Great Salt Lake, a
phenomenon known as the "lake effect" happens. As the frosty winter
winds move over the warmer water beneath them, the resulting con-
densation loads them with fine snow that banks up against Utah's
Wasatch Range, burying its ski resorts in deep powder.

Jason's focus on the slopes, however, didn't last. Shortly after he arrived in the summer of 1997, he learned about the federal government's
plans to incinerate munitions filled with nerve agents like VX, mustard,
and sarin, which were stockpiled at eight depots across the nation. Half
of the nation's arsenal was parked in an Army depot in Tooele, and a
prototype incinerator was already burning nerve agent there. The national program's first full-scale incinerator was being built next to the
prototype. It was huge and incredibly complicated, and had grown a

billion-dollar price tag. And it was happening southwest of Salt Lake City, just upwind from the ski slopes Jason had come to enjoy.

Incineration, generally, was a controversial technology stigmatized by its highly toxic emissions and its frequent failures to operate as intended. The inherent problems and risks associated with incinerating garbage and toxic waste had been thoroughly exposed during struggles to halt the construction of incinerators in other communities across the globe where people were on the losing side of the economic and racial divide—places like Pine Bluff, Arkansas, and Anniston, Alabama, where the Army planned to incinerate chemical weapons.

The problem with the notion of burning chemical warfare agents seemed obvious to Jason. If you take an exceedingly poisonous substance and treat it with very high heat in a system that concludes with an open stack, what happens when something goes wrong and "upset conditions" are experienced? Mistakes are bound to happen, and when the inevitable oops happens the bad stuff will go out the open stack, propelled by intense heat. Even if we say we don't know for certain what happens once dioxins, heavy metals, and other toxic emissions spread through food webs and watersheds, we are still allowing downwinders to become guinea pigs.

And who, Jason asked, is running this experiment? The Army's incineration program did not enjoy a confidence-building history. The program was already ten years behind schedule and 700 percent over budget in 1997. A parade of whistle-blowers, including the incinerator's safety manager and its general manager, had walked out.

"What are we going to do?" he asked when we first met. An earnest young man, I thought, obviously smart and appropriately alarmed. I had been tilting at the Army's chemical weapons establishment for a few years by then, and I fear I may have come across as jaded. I knew it was a protracted struggle, and Jason was looking for results right away. "Whatever we can," I replied.

An organization I helped found and build, Families Against Incinerator Risk, was the voice of opposition to the incineration program in Utah, and it was in shambles. Lisa Puchner, FAIR's principal cofounder and backbone during its formative years, had also hoped for quick results. She had thrown herself hard at the Army incineration machine, then gotten burned out and moved on. While Lisa was minding

FAIR, I had been consumed for more than a year with a parallel struggle to force an infamous magnesium refinery to clean up, a story I have told elsewhere,[1] and I did not relish the prospect of rescuing FAIR. So I gave the reins of the faltering organization to Jason—a dubious present and a total gamble.

Fresh out of college, barely twentysomething, possessing little political savvy and no organizing experience, Jason Groenewold was given $4,000 from the Chemical Weapons Working Group, a national alliance of grassroots groups opposing incineration. It was enough to pay the rent on a small office for a few months and get a phone and some office supplies. He got an old donated computer that we joked was on the verge of a Y1K crisis.

To raise enough money to pay his wages, Jason would have to pound the sidewalks each night, canvassing door to door with a petition against incineration, making his case and collecting checks and cash by porch light. It was tough, but he learned the arts of political persuasion very quickly. It didn't hurt that he was tall and blessed with classic good looks, or that he was gracious and mature beyond his years. He could even charm his opponents who, ironically, often questioned Jason's credibility since he was paid to attend and speak at public hearings, even though his pay was a slim fraction of the wages paid to the corporate hired guns he was there to counter.

Four years after his inauspicious launch, Jason was voted Activist of the Year by *Salt Lake City Weekly*. He had led FAIR through numerous court battles over chemical weapons incineration and had been instrumental in forcing a garbage incinerator to clean up, triggering the overthrow of its arrogant managers in the process. He had become a master of the FAIR line: that the decisions we make about what we allow into our air, water, and soil get translated into flesh and blood, so it is important that those decisions get made in a way that is open, inclusive, informed, and accountable. It's about democracy and how citizens can make a difference. Risk is not a technical matter of calculating potential harm but an ethical question more properly answered in a civic dialogue about what is fair. Who is put at risk, and who benefits?

Jason became a regular on Utah television and radio. Print reporters conferred with him daily. Five years after his stint raising money for his meals by pounding the pavement and knocking on doors, FAIR had an annual budget of $200,000 and a paid staff of three. When FAIR moved from challenging incineration to addressing radioactive waste issues, no one put those issues on the public's map more effectively than Jason Groenewold.

Our campaign to stop the West Desert from becoming the nation's nuclear dumping ground started in Ed Firmage's meeting room at the University of Utah's College of Law in the fall of 2000. Five or six of us would meet there every Wednesday night and wring our hands. Private Fuel Storage had just cut its deal with Leon Bear and company. Governor Leavitt had noticed, but it was questionable whether he would have the spine and stamina to oppose the powerful PFS utilities in a protracted struggle. Yucca Mountain wasn't on the nation's radar screen yet. Envirocare, a private company that had developed a radioactive waste dump on the West Desert, wanted to take much hotter classifications of waste at their landfill. The Great Basin Desert, so often abused, was under attack again. An entire landscape that stretched through four states was being turned into a vast, contaminated environmental sacrifice zone. And here we were, all six of us, wondering what to do about it.

Ed Firmage was a renowned professor of law who had led a David vs. Goliath struggle once before in the late 1970s and early 1980s. At that time, the U.S. military wanted to cover the Great Basin Desert with MX missiles hidden in railroad cars, a basing mode that would have made Utah and Nevada primary targets for Soviet missiles. The idea was simple: hundreds of thermonuclear warheads would be shuttled between thousands of pod-encased silos spread across an area of the Great Basin Desert the size of New England. The Soviets, unable to know in which pods the missiles were installed, would have to hit them all, and the number of pods would be the same as the number of Soviet missiles. So to get them all, they would have to shoot their whole wad right at the beginning of a nuclear war. Either that, or build a lot more missiles to aim at us.

During the Cold War, that is what the United States called defense. The MX system would be so daunting that some feared the Soviets would be tempted to launch a preemptive strike if we decided to deploy it. Ed led a successful grassroots movement to stop the madness. He did what most of us in Utah considered impossible—he got the Church of Jesus Christ of Latter-day Saints, popularly known as the Mormon Church, to abandon its characteristic restraint and defend Utah's environment.

Ed's reputation as a brilliant young attorney and a leading intellectual in Mormon culture was established during the 1960s and 1970s. He was a White House fellow to Vice President Hubert Humphrey. He loved the Constitution and was a genius at interpreting it. The University of Utah prized his contribution and wanted to keep him. The Mormon Church was proud to call him their own, too. Everyone said there would be a place at the top of the patriarchal pyramid for young Ed Firmage someday. His success in organizing the defeat of the nuclear bull's-eye drawn on Mormondom's Great Basin kingdom should have consolidated his stellar reputation; it would become, instead, a departure point.

After the MX scheme was defeated, many of those Ed had mobilized settled back into their habitual ways of seeing the world. Not Ed. He kept going because his eyes had been opened anew. He translated the MX struggle into a global context. Just as the American military-nuclear axis would have turned Utah and Nevada into expendable military colonies, he realized, other people across the globe were also being sacrificed by their governments' military-nuclear programs.

Ed sought out relationships with people from around the world who were, each in his or her own community and habitat, bearing the costs and risks of nuclear power and armaments. In the process he became an advocate for peace, reconciliation, and dialogue. Today Ed counts the Dalai Lama and other spiritual leaders around the world as close personal friends. There were hard trade-offs along the way, however. He lost a wife and his beloved church. He was cast out of the eternal Mormon hierarchy that was once his assumed destiny.

Physically, Ed Firmage fits his name. He is short, stocky, and handsome in his own way, as so many fit, self-confident, and intelligent people are. Wire-rimmed glasses and ready humor soften a strong demeanor. Ed is often described as charismatic and brilliant. Once in a while, he would get carried away in the telling of a fascinating war story, taking a little too long to return to the table so we could discuss what to do right now. But, all in all, Ed was the old wizard in our band of political adventurers, the inspiring and beloved Gandalf in our hobbit-like quest to return the nuclear ring. He called us together, shared his vision of a better world, and gave us our quest.

Ed's intellectual energy, honesty, and passionate commitment were infectious, but the challenge ahead seemed overwhelming. How to shape consciousness and change habits, raise questions, challenge assumptions, convey alternatives, and make new and revealing information available? And how to counter the inevitable response from those with very deep pockets and powerful networks?

This is what our small group discovered about how it is done: six people go out, and each one convinces three more people to join in. Each of those three must find three more. As they recruit, they become educated so they can make their case. People gather information individually and then share it. A knowledge base grows and a context emerges. A division of labor also emerges as people find niches. Workshops are taught, letters are written, legislators phoned, hearings attended, editorial boards visited, packets made and mailed, and debates held. Media are courted, from talk radio to the nightly news, from alternative weeklies to the most established morning paper. Grants are written, donations solicited, endless meetings attended. A growing movement is by nature inclusive because allies are sought, and practicing inclusion requires retranslating the context into an expanding tent. Web sites are built and e-mail lists are made. These days the Internet is an indispensable organizing tool and information source.

Since the organizational hierarchy that is usually preestablished in most formal campaigns is missing, consensus has to be reached continually. It takes relentless energy and orchestration. Ed was our muse, but Jason Groenewold was our maestro. An effective vision is a picture not just of where you are going, but also of how you are going to get there.

Eventually the campaign became magnetic, drawing others who saw common cause but had different motives. We started with activists inclined to see moral principles at stake and ended up with real estate agents worried about declining property values along transportation routes and Rotarians worried about taxpayer liabilities. It would not be unfair to characterize many who joined the campaign as NIMBYs, people who did not want nuclear waste in their own backyards. They didn't want it in anyone's backyard but insisted that if it had to go somewhere its placement should be fair. NIMBYs are often characterized as selfish, but they are also motivated by democratic concerns for fairness and accountability. They could make a compelling case that since Utah had no nuclear reactors and was a net energy exporter, it was unfair to saddle Utahns with the risks, costs, and liabilities of waste from a process that did not benefit them. Governor Leavitt was fond of asking, "If it's safe to store, then why not keep it where it is, and let those who benefited from it in the first place figure out what to do with it?" Far from solving a national problem, he argued, we are letting utility customers and taxpayers from other states shift their burden to us.

As people studied the dilemma of what to do with the waste, it was easy to see that the problem was intractable. Nobody anywhere in the world had come up with a good answer for what to do with a waste stream that could be dangerous and problematic for thousands of years and was exceedingly difficult to contain. Europeans were giving up on the "solution" we had selected—landfilling nuclear waste—and were beginning to understand that nuclear power would have to be phased out so that its waste problems were not compounded over time.

If you looked at the problem long enough, you were bound to bump up against one drawback after another. Recycle it? Workers in reprocessing plants got sick, and the recycled fuel rods could be turned into weapons and instruments of terror that could be used against us. Bury it? A temporary solution at best, given the long life of the waste and the dynamic nature of the earth's geology and climate over time.

It seemed like the national effort to find a solution to our nuclear waste problem was no closer to a realistic, acceptable solution despite decades of study and billions of dollars invested. We would have to go back to the drawing board at some point and look again. Meanwhile, making even more nuclear waste made no sense. Turning the desert into a nuclear dump so that the inevitable day of reckoning could be postponed a little longer didn't solve the problem; it allowed it to continue.

Our Wednesday evening meetings soon overfilled Ed's meeting room in the law library as new participants swelled our ranks. We moved to roomier venues here and there around the city. In my mind, among the interested stakeholders and potential allies who visited us in the early days, Seldom Seen Smith was the most colorful and compelling. Seldom Seen was a fictional character of Ed Abbey, a member of the Monkey Wrench Gang in Abbey's novel of the same name. Abbey's character was a "jack Mormon," that is, a born-and-bred Mormon who had strayed far from the fold as an adult. He was a back-country and river guide who knew the land by heart and had more in common with the old Anasazi of the canyons than the pious bishops in town. Smith mourned the loss of his beloved Glen Canyon when the Colorado River was stopped by pale cement and the cheery blue death of Lake Powell spread over its golden flow. With his fellow monkey-wrenchers, he conspired to bring the big dam down.

Everyone knew that Abbey had based Seldom Seen Smith on his hiking and river-running companion Ken Sleight. Ken was a legend, not only because of his friendship with Saint Abbey but because, like his fictional persona, he did know the back-of-beyond like the back of his hand. In a case of life imitating art, Ken was there when Dave Foreman and his original Earth First!ers threw a plastic crack over the side of the Glen Canyon Dam, ritualistically destroying the structure and kicking off their bodacious drive to defend the last wildlands of America. Though he still preferred to be seldom seen and was pushing beyond seventy years of age, Ken Sleight was now engaged in a new struggle, one that resonated with the one to keep spent fuel from coming to the West Desert. He had to talk to us face to face.

The lanky desert rat bounced into the room, smiled shyly, looked everyone straight in the eye one at a time, shook hands vigorously, and got down to business. He wanted us to be aware of a problem way down south in San Juan County, down in Indian country. In the late 1970s, a corporation called Energy Fuels planned to construct and operate a uranium mill on White Mesa, three miles south of Blanding, Utah, on U.S. Highway 191, just three miles north of a Southern Ute Indian reservation. The Utes claimed the mill would violate sacred burial grounds.

Ken Sleight and concerned archaeologists argued that this would indeed be a desecration since the mill area was covered by Anasazi sites and artifacts. The state, in fact, had identified about two hundred archaeological sites, many untouched, that covered the ground in question. The piles of tailings from the mill would destroy most of the sites. The Nuclear Regulatory Commission, predictably enough, ignored the evidence and green-lighted the project. We could all go looking for arrowheads somewhere else, they seemed to say, but uranium is important. Energy Fuels then made plans to mine the White Mesa uranium near the Havasupai reservation in the Grand Canyon. The Indians protested, but the feds approved.

Energy Fuels declared bankruptcy in 1995, and the White Mesa mill they had built and operated was bought by International Uranium Corporation. Ken claimed that International Uranium was really developing a nuclear waste dump disguised as a uranium mill that would reprocess tailings and other contaminated soils shipped in from out of state, including places as far away as New York, Tennessee, Missouri, and Massachusetts. The "recycled" uranium would supposedly be used to make new fuel for the nuclear power industry.

A mill operates according to a different set of standards than a landfill. When toxic uranium tailings are shipped to a new mill for further processing, they become "alternate feed" instead of contaminated waste. Only a fraction of the billions of pounds of nasty stuff shipped to the White Mesa site has actually been processed, however. As long as the ruse of a mill could be maintained, White Mesa would not be subject to the laws and safeguards governing dumps, as insufficient as they are.

But when Ken showed county commissioners the photos he had taken of dust from the accumulated piles blowing far and wide, they were unconcerned. One commissioner asked him why, if he thought it was dangerous, did he go up there to take the pictures? International Uranium was hiring local truck drivers to appease the area's residents, always desperate for jobs, but not training them in how to handle hazardous waste. Truck after truck rolled across scant watersheds and through town, where drivers sometimes parked in the wind while they got a bite to eat.

Now the mill was seeking to further amend its license so it could take hotter loads from nuclear complexes across the country. Ken was challenging International Uranium, and he was angry with local county commissioners for siding with the company instead of area residents and their health. He was especially mad at Governor Leavitt for ranting against nuclear waste in the north of the state but ignoring the plight of those who lived near the White Mesa mill/dump. "Whose side is he on? We're not even getting the information we need to be smart. The track record of this company needs to be known. Public disclosure would certainly increase the company's accountability, and there'd be fewer mistakes." The guv's behavior, Ken offered, was "treacherous and hypocritical."

It was all of a piece, he told me. Atomic testing was deceitful because it was harmful and the government didn't want the people to know that. Health and safety were ignored to get uranium out of the ground. People in southern Utah had suffered enough, and now this company was going to reopen the wounds and pour uranium in them. The desert and its scattered denizens didn't count. "We learned the hard way what science is confirming—there is no safe radiation dose. I read that book about Alice Stewart, *The Woman Who Knew Too Much*, and I think she got it right. She showed that fallout increased infant mortality worldwide. Everybody suffered, but not like us down there in the Four Corners country. We got a dose here from fallout and a dose there from uranium tailings and, heck, it all adds up. I read the obituaries and I think we've got a cancer epidemic, but the feds won't do a thorough epidemiological study because they're afraid they'll be held accountable."

Kevin Kamps appreciates the irony of Utah and Nevada occupying the front line in the struggle over nuclear waste policies. On the one hand, it is unfortunate that the ill-prepared citizens of Utah and Nevada find themselves in the forefront of a struggle to halt the nuclear waste juggernaut, since they are the least likely to succeed. The state's thin history of grassroots and labor organizing means its citizens have not yet acquired the skills, experiences, and native leadership to defend themselves. The cultural reticence of the Mormon majority about confronting authority, wedded to a self-conscious patriotism, also inhibits civic engagement. A one-party system, in Utah anyway, does not generate public discourse. The traditional hostility of the state's governors and legislators to environmental regulation leads to weak interpretation and enforcement of the rules that might shield citizens. Corporations like Private Fuel Storage and International Uranium Corporation know all this, of course—they look for it and count on it.

On the other hand, we were fortunate to be first, to read the map early and smell the giant's breath as he appeared on our horizon. Communities across the country were still asleep and oblivious. Oh sure, they would be wary of the usual accidents that could happen on the interstate highways and railroads that intersected every urban sprawl, every watershed, and most habitats. They had seen trains fly off bridges, crumple into tunnels and explode in flame, or spill their tanks of chemicals into neighborhoods. Those of us who have never been evacuated at some time or known someone who has had to run from danger have at least seen the helicopter shots on television—misty toxic clouds hugging the earth, black and orange smoke roiling up into the sky, dead fish floating, and men in hazmat hoods and disposable coveralls, their gloves taped to their sleeves. But did they know Mobile Chernobyl was coming?

Kevin Kamps is trying to warn them. Several months a year he is on the road, following the routes nuclear waste shipments will take on their way to Yucca Mountain and Skull Valley, towing his trailer with the giant dumbbell simulating a shipping container for spent nuclear fuel. Kevin rides from town to town like a nuclear Paul Revere shouting, "Mobile Chernobyl is coming!" That evocative phrase embodying "the transportation issue," as more sedate observers refer to it, is one the nuclear industry abhors and scorns. "Exaggeration and fearmongering," they charge.

Kevin will let you decide. He can go almost anywhere and find an audience, because a map of the United States showing the routes for shipping spent nuclear fuel and other high-level wastes to Yucca Mountain and Skull Valley is so varicose that the whole country is covered. The movement of at least 2,000 shipments a year for decades, he warns, could result in hundreds of accidents over time.

Kevin makes his case in a road show that could be called "Truth or Consequences." Picture a dog-and-pony show where the dog is Frankenstein and the pony is Godzilla. He points to the mock shipping cask and explains that the real ones are much larger, so heavy that only specially designed trucks and railroad cars can carry them. Imagine that my little trailer is a 165-foot trailer, he says, so big it takes an engine at each end to push it on a triple-axle car. Each train could carry the cesium equivalent of more than two hundred Hiroshima-sized bombs. What if one is hit by terrorists or there is an accident? Even if the material is not released and spread by an explosion, a jumble of cracked casks in a train or a truck wreck could be exceedingly dangerous to handle.

They tell you these casks are safe, he says, but they are relying mostly on computer modeling. There are films that the nuclear utilities play for the public that show shipping containers being dropped and crashed and burned. He refutes every assurance that corporate container makers and government facilitators have given. Dropped from thirty feet onto an unyielding surface? A mere thirty-mile-per-hour fender-bender. Capable of withstanding a 1,500-degree fire for thirty minutes? A mere house fire; both propane and jet fuel burn hotter and longer.

"Your message is intended to alarm. What kind of objections do you get?" I ask.

"There's the one about it being a solution—that shipping the fuel across the country to Yucca Mountain is a way to solve the nuclear waste problem," he says. "Of course, it isn't."

"I get that too, all the time," I reply. "If you don't like the solution, they say, then what's your solution—how would you solve the problem? Because we have to do something. I tell them we're not solving a problem but allowing it to be re-created over and over. Allowing others to avoid the consequences of their behavior is not solving, it's enabling. The Great Basin Desert is being turned into a nuclear enabler for some very toxic collective behavior."

"Exactly!" he chimes in. "We have a forty-year accumulation of spent nuclear fuel sitting around outside power plants. If we take twenty years to ship it out west while we continue to produce more of it, we don't end up with zero spent fuel sitting near reactors in the East and Midwest. We'll have enough to fill both Yucca Mountain and Skull Valley and still have fuel rods in dry-cask storage near the reactors. Then, of course, it goes up from there until you expand Yucca Mountain or find another repository." His logic seems obvious to me, but I look for holes.

"What if they figure out a way to safely reprocess it?" I ask.

"Well, they've been working on that for fifty years, pouring a lot of money into research because they're desperate for an alternative, but the science still isn't there. It's too dangerous and it's too costly." You trade one problem for another—the spent fuel rods are gone, but the world is awash in materials that can be turned into weapons of mass destruction or used as "dirty bombs" by terrorists. Storage risks, costs, and liabilities turn into security risks, costs, and liabilities. Time to cut bait, Kevin says.

The movement to alert people along transportation routes in the United States, Kevin tells me, is in its infancy. It is in Germany, where the radioactive waste issue has been most controversial, that one finds the most sophisticated movement of people against nuclear waste shipments. German activists traveled regularly to America in the 1970s to learn nonviolent action strategies from anti-nuclear protesters in places like Seabrook, New Hampshire. They put what they learned into practice during Europe's massive anti-missile deployment demonstrations in the early 1980s. When the German government tried to develop an interim repository site for nuclear waste, activists were ready.

Germany, like the United States, chose geological storage for its high-level nuclear waste. It selected a salt dome near the small farming community of Gorleben in the Wendland region. As the government prepared the site for shipments by rail, a hundred grassroots groups collectively known as the Burger Initiative organized to block them. Their slogan was *"Wir stellen uns quer,"* "We stand in the way."

On April 25, 1995, the first shipment was made, unannounced. On short notice, 3,000 people blocked the tracks. Getting through them cost the government $15 million. In 1996, another shipment was attempted. This time 9,000 determined protesters blocked the route. About 19,000 police were thrown into a pitched battle to clear the route. The bill was $40 million. In 1997, a third shipment went to Gorleben, accompanied by 30,000 police. They fought pitched battles all along the way. Rail lines were sabotaged. Farmers blocked roads with tractors and even dug them up. Young people lay down on the tracks or danced and played music on them. When the phalanx of police and the giant cask of nuclear fuel rods reached Dannenberg/Gorleben, 20,000 protesters met them. In the ensuing nuclear rugby match, 500 were arrested and 175 injured. Cost: $100 million.

Although Germany is more dependent on nuclear energy than the United States, getting 30 percent of its energy from nukes compared to our 20 percent, it has decided to walk away from its national nuclear experiment. There will be no more new plants, and Germans are deliberately planning how to transition to cleaner and renewable power sources. Germany has no rich oil fields to turn to and no fossil fuel colonies out there either. Its investment in alternatives to replace a major portion of its energy infrastructure will put the country at an expensive disadvantage in the short run, but as Germany moves ahead of us in developing solar, wind, and hydrogen alternatives that they can market to the world, they may well end up laughing last.

The Beltway is a long way from Berlin. On Pennsylvania Avenue, across from the Library of Congress and one flight up from the tantalizing aromas of the Hunan Restaurant, is a warren of offices inhabited by the staff of Public Citizen. The entrance is marked by a plain bronze-like plaque and, most afternoons, a begging man who is politely tolerated. The sidewalk in front is full of a diverse mix of people. The working poor sit in a window at the neighboring burrito shop, watching the fashionable women leaving the adjacent hair salon to join the flow of young Capitol Hill staffers and middle-aged bureaucrats. At this hour, many of them are leaving work and heading for the Hawk 'n' Dove bar just down the street. A disheveled old drunk stumbles among the crowd, raising capital for his addiction. There is no elevator in the building and security in the lobby is tight, an ironic contrast to the loose ambience found upstairs, in Public Citizen's offices.

I had not anticipated wrestling with a large inflatable mock-up of a nuclear storage cask during my visit, but the deflated cask had to get to Federal Express right away to make it to a demonstration in the Midwest. Lisa Gue, whom I'm here to meet, is busy with loose ends in the Public Citizen offices, so I volunteer to help. A Public Citizen staffer and I stuff the unwieldy model into a box that almost bursts, duct-tape the damn thing on every lip and seam we can find, and lug it in a sling to the FedEx outlet on the corner, where we cajole the shipping agent into overlooking its bulgy noncompliance and taking it anyway. When I get back to the office, Lisa is still making phone calls. The Yucca Mountain vote is coming up soon, and she is working sixteen-hour days.

I look around. For the umpteenth time I observe that activists tend to be information rich and clerically poor. Too bad, because they are also overcommitted and need help. Everywhere files have degenerated into piles that have become dislocated and scattered. There is abundant evidence of poor collation follow-through: copious stacks of paper left over when they'd had just the right number of some documents they were putting into packets but too many of others.

In one office, loose papers form a soft talus slope against a wall. Every available surface is covered with haphazard heaps of reports, memos, position papers, clippings, and flyers—a white kaleidoscope of communication. A cartoon on the wall shows an angry man with a gun warning, "Go ahead, make one more change. . . . " In the central meeting room, speakerphones compete for space with the scattered debris of an interrupted envelope-stuffing project. Coffee stains mark cheap office furniture.

The walls of individual offices are covered with posters reflecting the diverse concerns of the activists who occupy them, from "Free Tibet" to "No NAFTA." Campaign finance reform, electrical utility issues, anti-globalization, and clean energy are well represented, but the favorite decor seems to be the propaganda of current and past Public Citizen campaigns. A massive papier-mâché puppet of Joe Camel occupies the corner of one office, and related bumper stickers abound. Because democracy is eroding on so many fronts, Public Citizen has diverse targets. Lisa shares offices with other researchers, activists, and advocates. Later I visit a Public Citizen office in another building—the health and litigation wing—and find fresh paint, no piles, and matching furniture. Doctors and lawyers, apparently, get clerical assistance.

Lisa works on nuclear waste issues, and Public Citizen has just released a report on the individual member utilities that formed Private Fuel Storage.[2] The paper exposes the reputations of the utilities, aiming to give citizens an idea of the integrity and credibility they can expect from the companies during their collective effort to stow their waste in Skull Valley. Lisa is doing her best to share the findings with the public.

According to Public Citizen's research, Southern California Edison and its parent company, Edison International, have a reputation for hiding profits, avoiding accountability, breaking promises, and exploiting Native Americans. Southern California Edison exerted enormous lobbying power to get deregulation passed in California and profited heavily, at consumer expense, when deregulation began. Edison International transferred hundreds of millions of dollars in SoCal Edison profits and bought a profitable Swiss telecommunications company with the extracted funds. Then, once Edison International had bled SoCal dry, SoCal claimed it was on the verge of bankruptcy and needed the help of taxpayers and ratepayers. This so-called near bankruptcy was then used as a rationale to argue for the renewal of nuclear power. Now there's nerve.[3]

One can only imagine how much responsibility such a company will take for an unprofitable spent nuclear fuel site once the radioactive hot potato has been passed to the backyard of Utah taxpayers: "Tag, you're it." Or, to glimpse the future, examine SoCal Edison's broken promise to create wetlands and marine reefs to compensate for the damage done when its California nuclear plant was built. Those projects were promised as part of its licensing agreement; it even collected a rate increase worth $106 million to pay for them. But it spent only $2.7 million of the money on its intended use and refused to follow through.[4]

SoCal Edison also owns a huge coal-fired power plant on the Navajo Indian reservation that, in 1998, spewed 46,000 tons of nitrous oxide, 17 million tons of carbon dioxide, and 564 pounds of deadly mercury into the Arizona reservation's environment. The coal that fires that plant comes from a controversial mine at Black Mesa on the Hopi Indian reservation, where black lung and silicosis are becoming epidemic. The coal is slurried across Hopi and Navajo land through a poorly constructed and maintained pipeline that wastes precious tribal water and pollutes streams and wildlife.

Florida Power & Light, another PFS member, has been fined hundreds of thousands of dollars for its poor nuclear safety record, including leaking radioactive water, lack of emergency planning, and failure to make needed repairs. Employees who discovered such serious violations were fired; Clinton administration Labor Secretary Robert Reich said of the company's actions, "The evidence of retaliatory intent is overwhelming." When FPL and a company called Entergy agreed to a mega-merger in 2000, FPL's top executives quickly pocketed $62 million in incentive pay for making the deal. A short time later, when the deal fell through, those executives refused to return the money to the shareholders.[5]

The safety record of PFS member GPU Nuclear Corporation is among the worst in the nation. GPU, after all, owned the infamous Three Mile Island nuclear reactor, site of the worst nuclear accident in U.S. history. For six years prior to the Three Mile Island disaster, GPU falsified the data on the reactor's coolant leak-rate so it could avoid a shutdown order that would have averted the crisis. Safety problems at

Three Mile Island continue, and in 1997 GPU was fined $210,000 for numerous safety violations. During energy deregulation in New Jersey and Pennsylvania, GPU managed to dump most of its debt from past power plant boondoggles on consumers and taxpayers.[6]

When Xcel Energy, the leading PFS partner, planned to build its Prairie Island nuclear power plant in Minnesota, it told the Prairie Island Indian community next door that it would be a "steam generator." For years Xcel denied that its plant was polluting the Mississippi River, but eventually it conceded that it was releasing tritium, a known carcinogen, into the water. Like its PFS partner companies, Xcel has been fined hundreds of thousands of dollars for violations. Xcel is the largest customer of Manitoba Hydro, which currently faces a hundred lawsuits for its mistreatment of native peoples and destruction of indigenous communities through dam building and displacement.[7]

Given these utilities' controversial records in their own service communities, can we expect their behaviors to improve when they move their act to faraway Utah? Is it reasonable to think that they will become more accountable, more truthful, more cooperative, and more solicitous of the opinions of others? Or will their behavior just get worse? These are the kinds of questions Public Citizen and activists like Lisa Gue are good at asking. If you want to practice democracy well and wisely, they say, follow the money and focus some light on the players. The collective decisions we make about what we allow into our air, water, and soil are more likely to protect the environment and public health if those decisions are open, inclusive, informed, and accountable. The health of our natural environments is dependent on the health of our civic environments.

Eventually, Lisa escapes the office. We take a cab to the Afghani restaurant where we're meeting Kevin Kamps, and she tells me her story. Although she strikes me as near thirty, she seems to have a political savvy far beyond her years. No wonder—she started early, inspired by her parents while growing up in Alberta. "My mom was a nutritionist. I remember her disapproval when the church took Burger King up on its offer to supply a cheap orange 'beverage' to us kids at Sunday morning coffee hour. When her complaints to the church's board didn't yield results, Mom decided to take our nutrition into her own hands. My parents stopped contributing financially to the church and instead dropped off a case of 100 percent orange juice with no sugar added each month. Eventually the board came around, and my parents went back to tithing in cash instead of orange juice."

The church's coffee was next on the list. The coffee was served in Styrofoam cups. It was the mid-1980s, and Lisa was learning about environmental issues. She made a dozen signs showing a Styrofoam cup covered by the international "no" symbol above the slogan "Save the Ozone Layer." At coffee hour she set out stacks of nondisposable coffee mugs next to the Styrofoam cups and stood by with an offer to wash the mugs. When she had gained enough converts, she recruited help and organized them into a washing rotation. "Within a few months," she says proudly, "the Styrofoam cups had been phased out and the congregation was fund-raising for a dishwasher." She was twelve. A couple of years later she organized fellow students to lobby for remodeling the girls' locker room in the school gym, then started an environmental club that contracted with a recycler to take the scrap paper they collected. "Maybe early success gave me the expectation of winning," she guesses.

In college she was influenced by Canadian scientist and environmental leader David Suzuki, whose critique uses classic economic models to expose how limitless growth externalizes costs to the environment. She studied international development and focused on structural changes in networks of global trade, joined "radical" student groups, and helped organize a festival for youth in Cuba. She eventually ended up working for the World Council of Churches in Europe, where she participated in the first big anti-globalization demonstrations in Geneva. When she reached the front line of one protest, a Swiss policeman picked her up, politely muttered, *"Excusez-moi, Mademoiselle,"* and threw her back over the barricade she had crossed.

"These struggles are part of who I am," Lisa says now. "It's about conscious and intentional living and nurturing supportive and sustainable communities. I've learned that change is hard to make and that relationships are more important than outcomes. I've learned to walk the tightrope between the need for radical change and the need to work within the current system. I've learned it takes a lot of energy to win credibility as a young woman, to have a voice and to be effective."

At the restaurant, Kevin Kamps joins us. He started early, too. "It was seventh or eighth grade in Michigan, where I grew up. Physicians for Social Responsibility put out information on what would happen to Kalamazoo if there was a nuclear war, and it made me think about how insane the arms race was. I was in Earlham College in Indiana when I got hooked. I dropped out to walk across America—part of the 500th anniversary of Columbus's landing in 1992." He spent nine months walking with anti-nuclear activists and Indians, learning about nuclear power and how Indians in places like Prairie Island were being targeted. "I was impressed with how rigged the whole process is," he concludes. "We need to rewrite the process."

It's my turn. The political process we must use to collectively define our problems, set goals, and make plans to reach them is dysfunctional and corrupted. The citizens I am trying to activate are reluctant to get involved because they feel they are competing in an arena where the rules are rigged. Also, many who think ecologically are turned off by a political system that rubs against the grain of their sensibilities. The model of the political system that I was taught was politics as a football game, I tell them. Two sides devise strategies that are implemented on a field bound by rules and referees. Points are accumulated and a score is kept. At some point a winner is declared, and we all go on to the next contest. We use this football model throughout our public culture. Businesspeople are especially attracted to it—it fits an environment driven by markets, hard measures, and bottom lines. Mental models are important because they orient and guide attitude and behavior, for better or worse.

The football model, however, appeals less and less to ordinary citizens, who are tired of politicians who remind them of game-show hosts and are reluctant to go up against the best teams money can buy. Well, here's some good news. The cultural bifurcation we are experiencing now is not so linear and controlled. And change happens across a much broader time scale than we generally allow ourselves. Real social change is complex, and the football model does not explain it.

A better analogy of how cultures change, emerge, and unfold can be found in a musical jam session. Each player comes to the session with his or her own instrument, favorite musical themes, and an open ear. Each instrument has its own unique qualities. When the players begin, a theme emerges, and variations on the theme are explored until the session shifts to a new theme that is in turn developed, explored, exhausted, and abandoned. Evolution itself is like that. Our civic culture is also always in process, feeding on itself and unfolding like a great complex jam session where the music never stops.

I like this analogy because I can leave my helmet at home, and I don't have to worry about the score or whether I win or lose. The fat lady never sings. I just have to know how to play my instrument—my civic voice. If I keep an open ear and bring my themes to the session, those themes eventually get mixed in, come around, and grow in unexpected ways. That's why a handful of people with a compelling and timely message can make a difference. I have seen it happen over and over despite the odds against us.

As Lisa would tell you, the way you live here now is your instrument. So learn your instrument well, and come to the jam session. Blow your horn. Hit the highest note you can reach. Sing with all your heart. Throughout our lives, we are constantly given the choice to avoid or embrace our roles as citizens. When we avoid the challenges of creating viable and healthy communities together, we get nuclear sacrifice zones, enabled and sanctioned by our indifference.

I left Washington, D.C., the next day. A few days later, on July 9, 2002, Congress voted overwhelmingly to send nuclear waste to Yucca Mountain. Lisa and Kevin accepted the outcome and moved on to work on the next phase of opposition to Mobile Chernobyl—alerting citizens along transportation routes, making maps, informing people about risks and alternatives, empowering new local groups, building alliances, lobbying to block more money for Yucca Mountain construction, doing the research, and looking for opportunities to make their case known. I went back to Utah to face Khosrow Semnani.

A Glowing Account of Horatio Alger's ABCs

Imagining a world that is better than the one you are in is easy enough. Translating that vision into the real world is tough. If the history of our struggle to deal with nuclear waste is a story of failed policies and broken promises, the next phase may be one of cutthroat competition, corruption, and deceit. The intractable problem of keeping nuclear waste from contaminating ecosystems and destroying health is now being turned over to the private sector. And the individuals and corporations that have risen to the challenge are more interested in making fortunes than in saving the environment or protecting human health. Idealistic anti-nuclear activists, no matter how insightful and determined, enter an arena that is hard to play in because the players change constantly, the rules are broken or ignored, and a kind of ruthless venality seldom seen since the robber-baron era of American capitalism drives the game. The pro-nuclear side has visionaries of its own, of course. Like Khosrow Semnani.

Semnani had forty-seven bucks in his pocket when he arrived in America via London and Montreal. He was chasing the American dream but was low on cash. He had learned to be an enterprising man from his father, who had had five wives and seven children to support. Semnani senior went from cotton farmer to car dealer to ice maker in their native Iran. In the late 1960s Semnani left Iran for England, where he went to school in between waiting on tables and selling shoes. Determined to get into an American university, he got as far as Montreal before running out of money. He came to Utah in 1969 to seek a loan from an Iranian professor at Brigham Young University, a friend of his brother. But the professor was on sabbatical and Semnani was broke. So he got busy mowing lawns and painting houses. Eventually, he talked his way into Westminster College in Salt Lake City, cutting a deal for the tuition he could not afford, and studied chemistry and physics. Then he got a master's degree in engineering administration, mopping floors as a custodian for $1.35 an hour in his spare time. He has been cleaning up ever since.[1]

After graduation he worked as a research chemist at Kennecott's massive open-pit copper mine in Utah and learned about the refining of metals. For most of this continent's industrial history, mining and industrial waste that contained heavy metals and toxic chemicals was simply dumped into rivers, piled in the wind, or landfilled. When the EPA set guidelines for the disposal of hazardous waste in the 1970s, Semnani saw an opportunity to apply his experience to a burgeoning new market. The Resource Conservation Recovery Act went into effect in 1976 and stopped the practice of dumping contaminated waste in county landfills for a fraction of what it would cost to dispose of it responsibly. Semnani realized that a facility that could take in hazardous mining and radioactive wastes could also make lots of money. His experience in metal refining made him uniquely qualified to understand the sophisticated engineering as well as the complicated regulation that would be involved, and he knew it.[2]

At the time, Khos, as his friends called him, was making a modest $27,000 a year. He talked bankers into lending him enough money to buy an isolated tract of land called Grassy Mountain, about sixty miles west of Salt Lake City in Utah's West Desert. Lacking capital for improvements, he hand-dug trenches on the site with a shovel. He also got sweetheart treatment from the Tooele County commissioners, who were looking for a way to make their desert backyard profitable and saw in Semnani the kind of toxics entrepreneur they had been waiting for. Tooele County had a long history of underground and open pit mining. As that industry was playing out, an era of mining waste streams was beginning, and Semnani seemed to have a bead on it.

In the early 1980s, the government developed a site on Utah's West Desert to dispose of uranium tailings. The radioactive tailings came from a uranium mill that had become surrounded by homes as sprawl from Salt Lake County began to spread across its broad valley. The tailings were in the way, and everyone wanted them out of there. The government put in a rail line and a power line, sank monitoring wells, and otherwise developed the so-called Clive facility in Utah's West Desert. The troublesome tailings were then shoveled into railroad cars and shipped to Clive for burial.

The disposal of radioactive waste in the West Desert generated interest in how other toxic wastes could be handled at remote desert locations in Utah. Semnani bought the Clive facility in 1987, after the tailings from the uranium mill had all been buried.[3] A legislative audit suggested he paid a fraction of what the property was worth. The following year, the Tooele County commissioners created what they called the West Desert Hazardous Industries Area, which included the Clive facility, and encouraged further development—Tooele County was open for business. Two toxic waste incinerators and a huge hazardous waste dump quickly followed.

In the meantime, Khosrow Semnani was attempting to obtain official approval to open up Clive again as a dump for so-called dirty dirt, radioactive soil mixed with other contaminants. There were no radioactive waste dumps on private property anywhere in the nation, so the permitting process was complicated and unprecedented. When approval was granted, Semnani incorporated and went into the radioactive waste business.[4] He gave his company the tree-hugging moniker of Envirocare.

Semnani's timing was excellent. The U.S. government's plan for handling our growing pile of nuclear waste was collapsing in the late 1980s, and the questions we needed to ask each other as citizens about the real costs, risks, and liabilities of the nuclear industry, and about whether nuclear technology is sustainable, were not being asked. That dialogue was supplanted by competition among corporations to define waste-disposal plans by themselves and for themselves. Civic discourse was ceded by the government to the private sector, to the waste-disposal businesses that were organizing to pick up the ball the feds were eager to drop.

The West's newest land rush is for access to desert dumps. Where we once put pioneer settlers into arid landscapes that could not sustain their farming practices, as if farming without water were possible, we are now facilitating a waste industry as if landfilling without consequences is possible. In an earlier era, dam building became an end in itself when the private corporations that built big dams and their government agency allies drove public policy and sucked up big budgets. Later, nuclear reactors were built across the country, also without an inclusive and open public dialogue about their merits and dangers.

In the case of the developing nuclear waste industry, however, policy and planning were turned over to the private sector almost from the beginning. The first lobbyists to hit the ground had considerable de facto power over policy right away. Rather than learn how important an open, inclusive civic dialogue can be in shaping technology so that it is sustainable and wise, the federal government simply skipped over paying the usual lip service to public involvement, instead delivering a set of blueprints with lots of blank space for the private sector to fill in. Publicly funded state agencies stood by to facilitate their plans.

The competition to fill in the blanks was intense. Players switched sides, spied on and undermined each other, and conspired. The Nuclear Regulatory Commission refereed on the federal level, and state regulatory agencies directed traffic locally. Khosrow Semnani could compete with the best. "I welcome regulation," he told me, "because I can meet the standards and the requirements, and my competitors cannot." In the emerging political environment, where the boundaries between abdicating government regulators and aspiring entrepreneurs were bleeding into one another, winning the competition also required gaining political access and advantage.

The perils of this mix became apparent in the relationship between Semnani and Larry Anderson, the director of Utah's Division of Radiation Control. To put Envirocare into operation, Semnani had to acquire permits to develop and run a "low-level" radioactive waste site. Low-level radioactive waste is anything less hot than spent reactor fuel rods (which alone are categorized as high-level) and comes in three bitter flavors—A, B, and C. The A-level waste is generally the least dangerous—mostly soils contaminated by mine tailings, refinery wastes, or the various processes that occur as raw uranium moves up the chain of refinement on its way to becoming concentrated, hot, and usable. Semnani requested permits for A-level waste only.

As the nation's first and only privately owned commercial radioactive waste disposal site, Envirocare would be a kind of bridge between the traditional and expected responsibility of the government to ensure the public's interest and safety, and the new policy direction of privatizing radioactive waste disposal. This was to be accomplished without the benefit of civic dialogue or even much public scrutiny. To make it more interesting yet, competition to get permits was cutthroat. The stakes were certainly high for Khosrow Semnani—should he fail to turn his West Desert land into a sanctioned waste disposal site, he'd be stuck with a piece of economically useless contaminated ground and the liabilities that would carry.

Think *Survivor* in Utah's West Desert. Alliances are made and broken as the players conspire their way to the grand prize by eliminating competitors from the island. And in the end, those whose torches have been extinguished get their chance to "dis" the winner by dragging up old grudges and misunderstandings. In the case of our West Desert episodes, Larry Anderson brought along a bullhorn and a box of documents to the last tiki-hut show. Instead of voting for the final survivor, he relit his torch and set fire to the set. In 1996, the by-then former director of Utah's Division of Radiation Control sued Khosrow Semnani, claiming that he was owed millions of dollars for helping Semnani start Envirocare. Anderson claimed that Semnani had hired him to do "consulting" while Semnani was obtaining permits for Envirocare from the agency that Anderson himself ran! Semnani had already paid Anderson $600,000 in cash, gold coins, and real estate. Where, asked Anderson, is the rest of my money?[5]

That Anderson filed suit at all is a powerful indication that the rules guiding behavior among regulators and the regulated were confusing to at least one important participant; otherwise Anderson's suit would have to be seen as a kind of legal suicide. Either that, or Anderson was blind to what the state of Utah later described as an obvious conflict of interest. Given the nuclear industry's history of shameless bureaucratic enabling followed by the further blurring of the boundaries between government agencies and privately owned corporations, Anderson might be forgiven for asking, "What conflict of interest?"

Semnani responded to Anderson's suit and its obvious implications of corruption by striking hard and early. Anderson, he claimed, had extorted the money and a condominium from him. He, Semnani, was the mere victim of a corrupt bureaucrat, cornered, with no place to go but down. A heated public squabble ensued. Anderson was eventually charged with tax evasion; meanwhile, Semnani bargained his way down to a misdemeanor tax charge for failing to report his gifts to Anderson. He agreed to pay a $100,000 fine and to surrender his CEO position to another man while retaining sole ownership of the corporation. In return for his guilty plea, he helped put Anderson in prison for two and a half years for tax evasion after a trial that featured accounts of cash hidden in magazines and exchanged in elevators.

Interestingly, Anderson was acquitted of charges that he used his government position to extort money from Semnani, and Semnani was never charged with bribery. The difference between extortion and bribery can be a matter of who brings it up first—the government official who wants to be rewarded for his cooperation, or the client who is willing to pay for that cooperation. When the desperate entrepreneur and the clueless good ol' boy were in each other's embrace, it was hard to tell if they were wrestling or dancing and, if dancing, who was leading. The jury's mixed verdict indicates that they too saw, in the peculiar personal dynamics between Khosrow Semnani and Larry Anderson, a two-sided coin that was hard to read while it was spinning.

Semnani's coins, it was revealed during the Anderson trial, have been well and widely sown. A former Utah governor accepted a $65,000 "personal loan," a state senator accepted a loan of $108,000, and a member of the Radiation Control Board got a loan guarantee for $15,000. By the end of 2001, Utah governor Mike Leavitt's various campaign funds had received $85,000 in contributions generated from Envirocare, and the campaigns of many Utah legislators have also benefited from Semnani's largesse.

Leading charities have also received big donations, and Semnani's generosity is rewarded with goodwill. Friends describe him as a devout father and husband and an American patriot who also wants to see democracy develop in his native Iran, where he has donated money to build schools and clinics. A leading Salt Lake City newspaper has described him as possessing the kind of good looks and "smooth Ricardo Montalban charm" that opens doors and gets a seat at the best tables.[6]

People like Cindy King, however, who have been approached by Semnani's lawyers rather than his legion of lobbyists, may be forgiven if the charm wears thin. For fifteen years, King led the Utah Sierra Club chapter's effort to monitor the state's various hazardous waste activities. In January 2001, Semnani's lawyers hit her with a defamation suit that accused her of conspiring with Envirocare's competitors and sowing false information. According to the suit, King and ten others, including a Utah state representative, spread lies that Semnani was financing Middle East extremists, diverting radioactive materials to weapons brokers for delivery to Arab countries, having sex with female regulators, and getting CIA protection to boot.[7]

Cindy King sees it differently. "I've been SLAPPed," she told me. "It's that simple." SLAPPs—strategic lawsuits against public participation—are what some corporations use to keep their public critics quiet. A SLAPP is designed to intimidate critics, to tie up their time and resources, to drain them financially, to harass them and undermine their credibility, to fish for information, and to warn those around them to back off. When one critic is attacked in front of others, an enhanced civic dialogue does not follow. SLAPPS are usually characterized by an imbalance of power—Cindy King was a graduate student with a loan to pay, Khosrow Semnani a multimillionaire with a planeload of prominent attorneys at his beck and call. By the summer of 2003, the suit against King was asking for more than $140 million.

If the charges Semnani makes against King are true, of course, he has every right to be offended, to claim damage, and to insist that his business issues be discussed responsibly; but Semnani and Envirocare have sued when they disagree with the facts their critics cite. After Envirocare CEO Charles Judd threatened litigation against an out-of-state consultant hired by the state of Utah to outline ways of taxing the company, the man fled the state and didn't look back. An intern for a citizens' group advocating higher taxes on radioactive waste was sued for allegedly getting some statistics wrong.[8] When opponents crunch the numbers or interpret them differently than Envirocare does, they get threatened by the company.

Jason Groenewold, the young director of Families Against Inciner-ator Risk, got a threatening letter after an article critical of Semnani appeared in FAIR's newsletter. "You are on notice that you have defamed Mr. Semnani, Envirocare, and other honorable people," the letter warned. A FAIR employee quit when she realized how readily Envirocare sues over the kinds of factual errors, differences in interpretation, and ambiguities that are a normal aspect of civil discourse in a democracy.

Personally, I have seen both the broad smile and the razor-sharp bite behind it. Though a critic of much of what goes on in the West Desert, I left Envirocare alone as long as it was handling only A-level waste. I know folks in Colorado who are glad to see playground fill that includes uranium mine tailings dug up and shipped away for remote disposal. I can agree that such detritus of past mistakes should go to someplace like Envirocare's Clive facility. B- and C-level waste, however, is another ballgame. In 1999 Envirocare sought state permission to take these hotter wastes, and I spoke up. Immediately, the Semnani charm machine was cranked up and aimed at me. "Why not meet at Cuppa Joe's for a little talk?" his aide suggested, and I agreed. Jason Groenewold made the arrangements, and we went together.

Semnani's aide was young, clean-cut, and well dressed, I remember, and seemed to fall somewhere between an administrative assistant and a manservant. Semnani himself was impeccably dressed, carefully coiffed, and deliberately calm. He comes across as reasonable, smart, and sincere. He is earnest, listens intently, and analyzes carefully. He is a gracious and solicitous chemical engineer—a bit like a cross between a pharmacist and a funeral director.

This is what Jason and I told him: the utilities that own nuclear reactors built during the reactor boom of the 1960s and 1970s were starting to tear out, redesign, and rebuild their aging infrastructure. The legal and political costs of developing new sites and getting new permits for nuclear plants, however, were prohibitive—add them to the equation, and nuclear power can't compete with lower-cost alternatives. So the existing hundred-plus sites in the United States already occupied by the first generation of reactors would have to serve as the sites for the next generation of reactors. Old ones out, new ones in.

All that debris from the old ones would have to go somewhere, and the corporation that could capture the market for that waste could make billions. Although B- and C-level waste includes a wide range of materials with widely varying degrees of radioactivity, it also includes curtains, pipes, and equipment from corroded reactors that are arguably as hot as the spent fuel rods Private Fuel Storage hopes to unload on Skull Valley. We do not want that waste moving through Utah, we told him, and we do not want it buried in the West Desert for our children's grandchildren to monitor and maintain.

We did not tell him this: B- and C-level waste, along with spent fuel, is the nuclear industry's Achilles' heel. If the people who use nuclear power are able to benefit from it and then export the costs, consequences, risks, and liabilities to Western deserts, then the costs, consequences, risks, and liabilities will be reproduced again and again. But if people have to face the consequences of their choices and live with them, they are far more likely to abandon nuclear power as a clearly unsustainable energy source and develop energy sources that we can all live with. Again, as with spent fuel, we are unwilling to abide what others cannot while turning the West Desert into a nuclear enabler.

To his credit, Semnani did not claim, as Envirocare often did in its later public presentations on the meaning of low-level waste, that B- and C-level wastes were materials such as medical waste, parts found in smoke alarms, and the illuminating paint on highway reflector signs. He acknowledged that B and C were going to be mostly reactor debris. He hadn't gotten rich by misunderstanding the market. Someone had to take that waste, he argued, and he could do it safely and without harm to the environment. The people of Utah would get jobs and revenue in return. "Trust me," he told us. "I can do this." Also, he warned us, be wary. His competitors were sneaky and would try to use us against him. We parted amicably, and he encouraged us to keep in touch and to call whenever we needed to understand the facts.

Our next encounter was strange. One busy afternoon, I ducked into a fast-food outlet (I am ashamed to admit) to grab a quick chicken sandwich between meetings, one of those mass-murdered and processed contrivances that is closer to an agenda item than a food item. I got in line behind a dark-haired man in a dark blue suit, his back to me. The suit was expensive, sleek, and crisp. I notice these things because my own demeanor is hopelessly rumpled. My ties invariably become visual menus of what I eat on my lunch hour, and my wrinkled pants and shirts are scarred by pen marks. Suddenly, the spiffy dude I was admiring turned around. "Chip!" Semnani proclaimed. "Khosrow!" I replied.

An awkward moment followed. I cracked a joke. "Gosh, I hope your being in Carl's Jr. isn't a measure of your company's financial outlook." The thought that a multimillionaire whose annual income was commonly estimated in the eight-digit range would be eating at Carl's Jr. was in itself amusing. He laughed politely, and we both made a point of fixing our gazes on the menu board over the counter. More awkward silence. He broke it. "Well, I suppose that since we are here together, we should sit down and eat and talk," he offered. I agreed. I can't remember what he ordered.

We talked for an hour. I wanted to talk about his application for permission to take B- and C-level wastes, but he was obsessed with recent legislative moves to add significantly to the taxes he would have to collect from his customers for taking their A-level waste.

I told him I felt ambivalent about taxing his company because in my experience, regulators become hostage to revenue. If a state regulator knows that a local government or the state is dependent on revenue generated by a polluter, that polluter can expect to get any variance, exception, expansion, or change in the rules he wants. Some state agencies and whole federal departments, like the Department of Energy or the Nuclear Regulatory Commission, have such a symbiotic relationship with the corporations they regulate that they are more like facilitators than regulators—more pimp than chaperone. To a bureaucrat or politician, revenue is like profit is to a CEO or stockholder—it is not just desirable, it is imperative.

On the other hand, taxing is a way for government to create incentives and disincentives. If a bad habit becomes too expensive, businesses develop other options to replace the habit they can't afford. But in the meantime, an industry with rising costs will struggle to cut them wherever it is expedient. "Transportation costs are what will get cut, right?" I asked.

"What else can be done?" he replied. His reply may have been rhetorical, a way of expressing agreement with my anti-tax tone. A closer look at transportation issues does not favor Envirocare. If transportation of spent nuclear fuel rods across the nation to Skull Valley by Private Fuel Storage is a legitimate concern, then the transportation of B- and C-level waste on its way to Envirocare is also worthy of close scrutiny. Spent fuel will at least go out under a spotlight. The industry knows that one bad accident could be a show-stopper.

Disposing of B and C, however, will require many thousands more shipments of cargoes that are varied, mixed, and uncertain. They will go mostly by truck in all sorts of weather and with relatively little monitoring and tracking. The routes they choose will cover the nation. Government at all levels is unprepared to assess the risks, enforce the rules, or handle the consequences. And accidents are as inevitable as rain. Those trucks packed with nuclear debris, like shipments of spent fuel, cross watersheds and go over aquifers. They can spill into rivers and streams or tip over into the wind. On their way to the designated environmental sacrifice zone, they could create unintended sacrifice zones along the way. Debris could be, like used fuel rods, a terrible and haunting rogue waste stream.

Semnani became a bit agitated as we talked. He expressed sincere exasperation. He had submitted every document, cooperated with every test, filled out every form, and participated in dozens of public hearings but nothing, he complained, would satisfy the citizen activists from the Sierra Club and FAIR. In turn, I told him that going to hearings is frustrating for citizens, too, because we can only offer comments that are almost always ignored or overridden. Real power and real involvement would put citizens at the table early, when criteria are being decided that will shape all the decisions that follow. I cited the example of a process that citizens, state regulators, and the Army had used to identify alternatives to chemical weapons incineration. It was a model for getting stakeholders to set the agenda and rules together. He nodded his head but concluded that he had to operate under a set of rules and according to a process that was already in place. What else could he do?

Whatever goodwill we generated in our brief and unexpected encounter has long since evaporated. FAIR went after the B- and C-level waste issue, and Jason got a threatening letter. And whatever insights Khosrow Semnani may have gleaned from our burger-joint conversation about the wisdom of honoring a democratic civic dialogue, they had obviously faded a year later. In 2001, Envirocare decided to side-step what little public participation was called for in the official rules by going after legislative approval of a B- and C-level waste permit before public hearings were completed. Envirocare had put the legislative cart in front of the public-participation horse. As ineffectual as public hearings can be for citizens seeking to make their concerns known, they at least offer the chance to influence a decision.

Jason went to work. He worked the media, worked the phone, recruited help, wrote press releases, made packets, held meetings, gave interviews, conferred, cajoled, persuaded, and confronted. Awareness grew within the public and among the local media, generating a kind of positive feedback loop. The journalists did their job well and the public responded positively, thus encouraging reporters to dig deeper. At a hearing held in Salt Lake City at the Department of Environmental Quality on January 4, 2001, before the legislature had taken any action on Envirocare's permit, more than one hundred people swelled through the doors to speak up. A few weeks later, on February 1, another hundred-plus crowded a public hearing.

Such hearings are, unfortunately, normally attended by a literal handful of activist monitors, people like Jason Groenewold who show up, keep track, and speak out so the rest of us can be spared the dreadful tedium of such affairs—a tedium that can either put you to sleep or send your blood pressure through the roof. On these nights, however, speaker after speaker passionately opposed Envirocare's permit and condemned its arrogance in seeking to have the legislature approve its permit prematurely. Envirocare workers were there, too, shuttled over from Tooele County on a company bus. They were equally passionate in defense of the "necessary and important work" they were doing. But the hearing was dominated by the opponents.

That day, a poll in the *Deseret News* showed that 84 percent of Utahns opposed B- and C-level waste coming into the state. Envirocare's spokesmen complained that the average citizen couldn't distinguish between its proposed permit for B and C and the controversy over the Private Fuel Storage plan to put spent fuel in Skull Valley. Nevertheless, the writing was on the wall. The morning after the second crowded hearing, Donna and Jerry Spangler of the *Deseret News* had the scoop—Envirocare's strategists would soon announce that they had withdrawn their application for a permit from the current legislative session. Later, in July, they announced that they had suspended their effort to win legislative approval altogether, although nobody doubted they would resume their efforts once public opinion changed or citizen watchdogs looked away.

The battle was won, but the waste wars were far from over. Envirocare got the Utah Division of Radiation Control to grant them the permission they needed to expand their operation into the B- and C-level waste market, giving them five years to come back to the legislature to complete the next step. They could bide their time and wait until the moment was right to approach the legislature. Of course, in the meantime, competitors were trying to move in line ahead of them. The Radiation Control Board was not inclined to let that happen.

In Utah, our watchdog agencies have long been more like lapdogs, lapdogs that know only one trick: roll over. Even so, the attitude of the Radiation Control Board toward Envirocare's application for permission to take B and C waste was remarkable, somewhere between a red carpet and a greased slide. Commissioner Teryl Hunsaker, Tooele County's chief nuke-booster, sat on the board. He attended one meeting with an Envirocare sticker pasted across his heart. No wonder—Tooele County is hooked on the revenue Envirocare contributes, about 20 percent of the county's total tax income. Revenue from Envirocare built the Deseret Peak Complex, which includes a demolition-derby arena, rodeo grounds, a motorcycle track, a swimming pool, baseball fields, and a mining museum.

In 2002, FAIR was preparing for a campaign to keep Envirocare from getting legislative approval for B- and C-level radioactive waste. Out of the blue, we got a clear signal that our opposition to Envirocare's plans had successfully raised awareness. A group of powerful movers and shakers took it over as their own, including a Democratic leader, a member of a wealthy publishing family, a businessman who sat on the state Board of Regents, and the state's teachers union.

This unlikely coalition announced that it would be backing a campaign to put an initiative on the November 2002 ballot to impose much higher taxes on the A-level waste Envirocare was already importing and to ban B and C wastes altogether. The initiative would also require reform of the Division of Radiation Control, the agency that regulated Envirocare, to inhibit traffic in personnel between the agency and Envirocare's payroll. The increased taxes would go to support an over-loaded educational system and programs for the homeless. To pull it off, the coalition was prepared to spend hundreds of thousands of dollars to collect signatures across the state and then counter an expected frontal assault from Envirocare.

Semnani outspent the initiative backers—$4 million to less than $1 million—aiming to spread the notion that the initiative was too complex, too confusing, and unfair to Envirocare. Jason Groenewold devoted exhausting days and nights to countering Envirocare's arguments, but as they say, money talks. Envirocare's public relations team cast the initiative as nothing more than a plot hatched by competitors to put it out of business.

In reality, the initiative was an attempt to open up the decision-making process, but it was a flawed effort, and Envirocare succeeded in sowing doubts among Utahns. After the blitz of competing television ads was over, voters were confused. Most were not happy with their choices and were wary of both sides. Holding their noses, they poked their ballots, and the initiative went down by a two-to-one margin.

At least some in the Utah legislature thought that inviting in B- and C-level waste was a great idea, although they weren't sure Envirocare was the right receptacle. The B and C market was potentially huge, they reasoned, so it could provide a fat revenue stream for years to come. Thus a bill that would have banned B and C waste from being imported into Utah was gutted, then killed on the floor of the legislature in 2003. Legislators created a task force to "study" the issue and turned it over to a legislator who had wondered aloud if the state ought to be developing its very own high-level nuclear repository. That way, he argued, the state could make all the money instead of the Goshutes, and it could be located on the southern edge of the state, to keep shipments of spent fuel from coming through the populated Salt Lake valley and Wasatch Front. San Juan County, in the heart of the redrock wildlands of the Colorado Plateau, volunteered itself as a potential site. The International Uranium Corporation facility there at White Mesa, the one that Ken "Seldom Seen" Sleight had railed against, was a likely location.

By the time Yucca Mountain is made operational and filled, if that day ever comes, there will be enough spent fuel rods in America to fill Yucca

Mountain and Skull Valley and still leave some in dry-cask storage near the reactors that produced them. If by that time the state of Utah has developed a site for high-level nuclear waste storage, there may be a market for its services—call it Yucca II. A Yucca II, of course, will require a Mobile Chernobyl II. At what point will we see the pattern? And when will we realize that this is a national problem that cannot be banished to desert colonies?

Jason Groenewold finished the legislative session of 2003 exhausted. Utah's legislature is hard to take on a daily basis. A day of lobbying on the Hill is a lot like being trapped in a phone booth with Elmer Fudd's evil twin. The legislature is predominantly composed of old white men, a term that also describes most of the younger men, who are hopelessly nearsighted and cranky when challenged. They busy themselves with bills forcing the University of Utah to accept the presence of concealed weapons, making the teaching of sex education punishable, assigning a "porn czar" to watch us closely, and ranting about same-sex marriages, partial-birth abortions, the Pledge of Allegiance, prayer, and the Ten Commandments. But Utah's natural virtue, the integrity of our health and environment, is always for sale if you can show them the money—the pious turn to pimps on a dime whenever Mother Nature is up for bid.

Meanwhile, new allegations of corruption have surfaced in court documents filed by Charles Judd, who took over as CEO of Envirocare when the courts ordered Khosrow Semnani to step back in the wake of the Larry Anderson debacle. After years of building deals and strategizing together, Semnani and Judd had a falling-out over money. Judd sued his former partner and then, in the spring of 2003, asked Tooele County to let him open his own radioactive waste facility, right next door to Envirocare.[9]

Envirocare's neighboring hazardous waste dumps are bought and sold often. They are like chess pieces in the developing competition to capture ground and contracts as the nation dumps its most obnoxious and dangerous waste on the desert West. It is hard for the locals to keep track of the facility names. "Was it the USPCI dump that became Laidlaw before it became Safety-Kleen?" I once joked to a friend. "And what became of Aptus?" "Well," he replied, "it's not Safety-Kleen anymore, because they went bankrupt; now it's Clean Harbors." Given the nature of the waste and its potential to damage the land, our health, and our wallets, trying to solve our waste-stream crisis in such a speculative, cut-throat, and potentially corrupt arena is a lot like learning how to clean a loaded gun in the middle of a barroom brawl.

There is much to admire about Khosrow Semnani—his hard work, his bold gambles, his success in the face of cunning competition, his generosity and personal charm. He's a smart fellow who started with dirty dirt and learned to glow with the flow. But he is also a man who instinctively assumes conspiracy and the need for secrecy, who sues at the drop of a hat to intimidate critics, who can afford to buy the kind of access to political leaders that ordinary citizens don't enjoy, and who has a troubled history of paying public officials to get what he wants. Should we let such a man have the power to shape our national policy for disposing of radioactive wastes? Even if we accept his argument that he is a victim—a self-made Horatio Alger mugged by a venal bureaucrat on the road to the American dream—he still paid and kept silent because it was what he "had to do." For me, the doubts add up. I want to vote on a guy like Semnani before I hand him the levers of power and let him shape my grandchildren's future.

Because the consequences of handling nuclear waste—be it high-level wastes from spent reactor fuel or "low-level" wastes from processing uranium into fuel and weapons or rebuilding infrastructure—are so high, it is wise to be careful. A careful process is one that is open and accountable, honest and fair. The privatization of the radioactive waste stream, as seen in the case of Khosrow Semnani's Envirocare, is clearly not open, accountable, honest, or fair. It is vicious and secret. The competition to capture the radioactive marketplace is driven by criteria that guarantee the sacrifice of safety, environmental integrity, and public health for profit and power. Some things are best handled in the public arena. The Nuclear Regulatory Commission may be the lapdog of nuclear industry and in need of a thorough overhaul. Perhaps it should be abandoned outright for a democratic alternative we have yet to craft. But privatization is not the alternative.

The nuclear landscape of the West that the rest of the nation is creating is also a land of hard and confusing choices. The story of how we are dealing with the poisons we have made—poisons that can take down whole watersheds, habitats, and populations—does not inspire confidence. Our best efforts fall short. Perhaps the time has come to consider a bolder choice that has always been before us, although we have long refused to acknowledge its presence—abolition.

SIX

Abolition and Precaution

Abolition. It is not a word we use lightly. It has an absolute ring to it. We save it for things like slavery. We abolished slavery. We did so because slavery was monstrous and wrong—no exceptions. Can we apply the term to the nuclear monster we have created? Shouldn't we be more compromising and practical? After all, we don't want to give up X-rays when our bones are broken, and how about treatments for cancer? Sometimes the nuclear genie wears a white hat.

Although anti-nuclear protesters have an aura of abolition about them, they do not often use the word. You can read a lot of literature generated by Families Against Incinerator Risk, Public Citizen, and the Nuclear Information and Resource Service and never see the term captured in print. The Shundahai Network, on the other hand, is explicit about its abolitionist aim. Shundahai's perspective is earth-based and views nuclear technology as completely incompatible with a living planet. Public Citizen is more intent on creating the means to exercise popular control over our ecological commons and on altering the means by which we wrestle value from the land. If the collective decisions we make about what we allow into the air, water, and soil eventually get translated into public health and well-being; then we are wise to be open, inclusive, informed, and accountable. That would be the Public Citizen perspective.

Even if they don't say "abolition," most of the activists I have met think about it. But they are much more likely to speak of "ending" nuclear weapons and power or "walking away" from nuclear energy. They talk about transitions and a "phaseout." They encourage the development of alternative sources of energy like wind, solar, and hydrogen because they understand that abandoning nuclear power will require alternatives. They may look like they are doing the business-as-usual of environmental activism and only playing defense, but they are really trying to accomplish something greater. They understand that beyond the latest battle and the next one around the corner, they are facing a nuclear regime that cannot be abided and sustained. If they block it at each turn and contain it long enough, they believe, the public will eventually understand what they are doing and agree that enough is enough. Then we will be ready to create a new energy paradigm.

The problem of spent fuel rods may grab our attention, but there is more, much more. The production of spent fuel rods and the production of plutonium for 32,000 nuclear warheads left 265 million tons of uranium mine tailings littering the landscape. Plutonium processing also left us with 91 million gallons of high-level waste that must be secured. Add that and the tailings to a half-million tons of depleted uranium and millions of cubic feet of contaminated tools, metal scraps, oils, solvents, and other waste from both weapons and energy production, and you could fill a train that would stretch around the equator and then some. Isn't that enough? At what point are we ready to pull the plug?

If the policy debates over what to do with the nuclear wastes that have been generated took place within the context of an agreement to phase out nuclear power altogether, the debate would, I suspect, look much different. The development of repositories at Skull Valley and Yucca Mountain would, at least, not be seen by opponents as the first steps in the eventual sacrifice of the Great Basin Desert to enable a corrupt and unsustainable industry that has a waste stream that keeps on coming. For better or worse, it would be seen as part of a plan to put nuclear power down for good.

The countries that, like Germany, have concluded that there is no good solution to the problem of nuclear waste, so it is wiser to leave nuclear power behind and find alternative sources of energy, have realized that the process will be long and tricky. In the United States, where just over a hundred nuclear power plants produce about a fifth of the nation's energy, phasing out nuclear power would take at least a decade, probably two or three, and the waste problem we now face would remain and even grow during that closing phase. But if everyone agreed that phaseout was the ultimate goal, many of the activists I know would be more amenable than they now appear to be to some of the plans for shipping, consolidating, and temporarily storing nuclear waste until better solutions are developed and a consensus about those solutions is formed.

In the current context, temporary fixes are unacceptable because they keep the nuclear industry going despite the compounding of its waste-stream problems and the inherent unfairness of how those problems are being "solved." As the lines are currently drawn, nuclear power has a waste stream that requires the industry to identify sacrifice zones, bully its way through the door to those zones, and then pretend that the waste buried there can be forever contained. It aggravates anti-nuclear activists that we are still not ready to admit that nuclear technology is not sustainable. An army of industry and government technicians insists that we can get by if we just invest more money in the same old engineering approach that has never yet come close to solving the problems of what to do with the waste.

There is good reason to think that neither Skull Valley nor Yucca Mountain would be chosen for nuclear waste disposal if a rational process prevailed and the decision was made on scientific merits alone, given the commonsense notion that putting highly volatile waste in a landscape characterized by geologic catastrophe is not wise. Both science and common sense would tell us to go back to the drawing board and find a better way. Instead of storing spent fuel in steel casks alone, we might cover them with a layer of copper, as Sweden is doing, and bury them deeper in granite, surrounded by a layer of impervious clay to inhibit moisture transport. That is not "the answer," but it is better than what we are doing. We might also vitrify the waste in glass. We might figure out better ways to store it on site or regionally until we can devise some way of recycling it with "fast reactors" that are now in the earliest stages of development, assuming the new technology is any better—a big and dubious assumption.

All these added layers and steps of precaution would be costly and would make obvious what activists like Kevin Kamps, Jason Groenewold, and Lisa Gue already recognize—if we "did it right," nuclear energy would clearly be unaffordable and could not compete with alternative energy sources. By insisting that we handle nuclear waste in a thorough, precautionary way without cutting corners, anti-nuclear activists are in effect advocating a de facto abolition of nuclear power because it is not affordable or competitive when done right—as opposed to our current system, in which the government and its industry clients decide what to do with nuclear waste while ignoring public concerns, then announce the decisions and defend them against all comers. The task of forging a socially acceptable plan would be complicated and difficult, but no less so than the current intractable conflicts we are experiencing. It is doubtful that the Department of Energy or the Nuclear Regulatory Commission could pull off this feat, since their credibility is long gone.

Perhaps we do not hear the word "abolition" used in dialogues about nuclear energy because it is reserved for discussions of weapons. Lately it has been easy to feel nostalgic for the Cold War era of mutually assured destruction, which now seems considerably more manageable than our era of unpredictable threats: nuclear-armed rogue states, unilateral and preemptive strikes, and dirty-bomb terrorists. As more states add nuclear weapons to their arsenals and engage in regional conflicts fueled by powerful religious and cultural differences, Armageddon may have many cousins. And given the abundance of potent processed uranium and plutonium left over from decades of Cold War weapons production—and the plentiful opportunities to steal weapons outright, especially in the former Soviet Union—the prospect of terrorists using dirty bombs to further their causes and seek revenge seems almost inevitable.

Although I have chosen to address the problems of nuclear waste mainly in the energy sector, the crises of proliferation, security, and waste in the weapons sector are worse. The post-9/11 doctrines of the Bush regime are fueling rather than discouraging proliferation as nations like North Korea and Iran realize that they can avoid Saddam

Hussein's fate if they arm quickly. And now we are hearing mad proposals from the Bush administration for the development of "bunker-buster" nuclear weapons.

A nuclear conflict, of course, cannot be contained. If Pakistan and India lob nuclear missiles across their borders at each other, the resulting radiation will circle the globe. What disease vectors will spread from the corpses of the 20 million innocents caught in the cross fire? Like slavery, nuclear weapons technology is morally repugnant. What else can you say about weapons that can kill millions indiscriminately and destroy whole habitats or spread disease across the globe? What do you call an industry that has consistently misrepresented its costs, dangers, and consequences and then transferred them to the weakest and most vulnerable communities it can find? How do you redeem a technology that may have shortened the life spans of millions of people already, according to Andrei Sakharov, father of the Soviet nuclear arsenal turned nuclear dissident? How do we regard a technology that will threaten life for millennia to come?

Democracy empowers choice. The requirements of nuclear technology—its scale, its scope, its capital costs, the enormity of its consequences, and the need to control its spread—invite authoritarian decision-making. If no state wants the waste but some state has to take it, then, by golly, force will have to be applied. Nevada may have been targeted to bear the costs and consequences of our weapons programs because of its vast geography and sparse demographics and because deserts are ecosystems that we have only recently learned to appreciate and respect. But Nevada was also politically weak because of its small congressional delegation. Likewise, Utah is now targeted as a dump for both spent fuel and reactor debris because it is a desert land and relatively powerless. Abolition is a bold word that says citizens can assert control over this most undemocratic technology and stop it, start over, and make different choices.

Finding ways to put an undemocratic and self-destructive technology back in its cage is half the challenge. Finding new ways of looking at our world that acknowledge its complexity and emphasize precaution is the other half. We will have to admit we don't know everything. We can catch a glimpse of how that might work in the Precautionary Principle.

First enunciated and then written into German environmental law in the 1970s, the Precautionary Principle appeared on the world stage at the Earth Summit in Rio de Janeiro, Brazil, in 1992. It was identified there as a key principle for guiding policies ranging from the regulation of chemicals in the environment to global warming. In contrast to our current approach, which demands incontrovertible proof of harm before a corporation's product or waste can be banned or even, in many cases, limited, the Precautionary Principle shifts the burden of proof and recognizes that, given the natural world's inherent complexity, absolute proof is not reasonable. Instead, where there are potential threats of serious or irreversible damage, the absence of scientific certainty is not a green light to proceed or an excuse not to take restorative action. If you have scientific uncertainty and the likelihood of harm, you take preventive action and look for alternatives.

The Precautionary Principle was further delineated at the Wingspread Conference in Wisconsin, a gathering of scientists concerned about the impact of chemical pollutants on public health, in 1998. Since then, it has spread like a prairie fire into laws and policies across the globe, especially in Europe, and is now emerging in the United States. The city of San Francisco, for example, formally adopted it as a guideline in 2003.

Carolyn Raffensperger, an enthusiastic advocate of the Precautionary Principle, prefers the subtle adverb "microbially" to describe how the principle has spread into our political culture and its regulatory regimes. Raffensperger co-edited the book *Protecting Public Health and the Environment: Implementing the Precautionary Principle,* which provides a thorough explanation of how the principle might be realized throughout our society. The principle is not just another policy trend, she emphasizes, but a profoundly different way of looking at the world and then asking different questions of it. Instead of asking, "Is this level of risk acceptable?" you ask, "Are there alternatives that are less risky?" You scan the horizon for problems using concepts from ecology and evolutionary biology instead of using toxicology alone as a guide. So instead of asking, "Is this level of exposure safe for a 150-pound male?" you ask, "How does nature work, and what are the unintended consequences that could follow?" Rudimentary cost-benefit analysis, which often leads to schemes to pass costs on to the environment or to the powerless, is replaced with an inquiry that emphasizes ethics, inclusiveness, and wholeness: Who benefits? Who, including birds and animals and future generations, is left at risk?[1]

At heart, the Precautionary Principle recognizes that the health of the individual cannot be separated from the well-being of his or her community, which is likewise embedded in the wholeness of the ecosystem that sustains that community. Although the translation of this root insight is new and potentially revolutionary, the Precautionary Principle just makes sense, and in one guise or another, we've all heard it: What goes around, comes around. Safety first. An ounce of prevention is worth a pound of cure. Or, as my grandmother was fond of reminding me, look before you leap.

The wisdom of precaution and the sorry history of nuclear technology should inform our consideration of new technologies being developed the old-fashioned way: driven by profit and expediency, without regard for or knowledge about long-term or holistic consequences. Biotechnology and nanotechnology are inherently far more complex than nuclear technology. How will we cope when genetically altered organisms, clones, and self-replicating nanocreatures wreak unanticipated havoc? Will they be any easier to call back than radiation? Stepping back, admitting failure, stopping, and then dealing with the consequences of nuclear technology could be a profoundly instructive experience. In an age when we can clone and splice, transplant and annihilate, it might be useful to practice capturing a dangerous technology that has escaped our intentions, attentions, and assumptions and putting it back in a box.

As a library development consultant for the state of Utah, I encouraged many local governments to make long-range plans for public library service. Five-year plans were a stretch for most mayors and commissioners, and ten-year plans were out of the question. A 10,000-year plan would be laughable. Nevertheless, that is what the builders at Yucca Mountain are supposed to create. The radioactive rods entombed there must not leak for that long, even though they will be hot and dangerous for thousands of years longer. To foresee whether they will leak, many variables must be considered. Geologic structure and the movement of moisture within strata, climate and weather, the durability of the canisters and their rate of corrosion, earthquakes, floods, and even the possibility of renewed volcanic activity must be factored in. To coordinate so many variables into a projection of risks, a computer model has been built. It is called total system performance assessment, a name that expresses the kind of technocratic arrogance that Corbin Harney, a Western Shoshone with no formal education, would find fundamentally ignorant.

Although he is not familiar with the word "nonlinear" (I asked him), Corbin knows intuitively that the earth changes and responds like a living being in ways that are not predictable, logical, or measurable. In fact, Corbin says the earth is a living being, a being far more powerful than the animals she created and nurtures, including us "two-leggeds." You can take his words literally and dismiss them as animistic nonsense, or you can see that he is really talking about our place in the world and what we can know. We can measure the losses we have already sustained during our struggle to contain nuclear technology in dollars and lives, but there is more at stake. How the land we live on generates health is a process that is more complex than we will ever fathom, but we have clear evidence that generating radioactive waste harms the integrity and vitality of ecosystems and health alike.

When the time bombs we have buried in our grandchildren's grandchildren's future go off, they will curse us for our failure to see or acknowledge the consequences of our behaviors, for our failure to practice precaution, and for our failure to love them enough. By then they will understand that there is no safe parking lot. Radiation is a patient killer with a global reach. Now or later, here or there, reactors or bombs, a little or a lot—it's all the same to the King of Death by Degree. You can choose your poison, he says with a confident grin, but it is poison no matter what you choose or how you swallow it. Given the thousands of years that it will retain its health-vanquishing powers, radiation from nuclear waste will surely migrate throughout the land.

"Migration," that natural-sounding term for radioactive materials attaching themselves to the air we breathe, the water we drink, and the food we eat, is not supposed to happen, of course, unless someone screws up and there is an accident or unless a terrorist uses our radioactive waste as a weapon. But living downstream or downwind from the supposedly safe production of nuclear power may lead to exposures we have not identified, tracked, or acknowledged.

A recent peer-reviewed study by researchers from the nonprofit Radiation and Public Health Project looked at the cancer rates of "host communities" in an area where eight nuclear power plants had been closed for at least two years, leaving a seventy-mile or better nuclear-free radius. The study concluded that infant mortality rates and childhood cancer rates dropped a significant average of 17 percent in those communities after reactors ceased operating. In one case, infant deaths and childhood cancers dropped 42 percent. The average decline for the rest of the nation during the same period was 8 percent. The study's data hint at the hidden toll of sickness and death caused by the nation's nuclear power plants. About 22 million people live within fifty miles of New York's Indian Point reactor alone.[2]

Sometimes migration is facilitated in surprising ways. Last year, 110 billion pounds of commercial fertilizer and 4.2 million pounds of sewage sludge were spread on cropland, home gardens, public parks, golf courses, and school lawns. Full disclosure of fertilizer ingredients is not required in most states, so it is hard to know what those fertilizers and sludge contained. We ought to know, though, because "recycling" hazardous waste into fertilizer and sludge is a popular business practice. Billions of pounds of hazardous waste, including radioactive waste, are "recycled" into fertilizer each year. Elements in mining and industrial waste that are beneficial to plant growth and that are also found in hazardous waste—such as nitrogen, phosphorus, zinc, manganese, copper, calcium, boron, and sulfur—can be added to fertilizer with little regard for what is attached to them. Thus arsenic, mercury, cadmium, lead, PCBs, dioxin, and plutonium may go along for the ride. Corporations that would rather make a buck off their waste than pay to dispose of it safely are eager to mine sumps, tailings, holding ponds, furnaces, and even pollution control devices for metals to sell as fertilizer additives.

Southeast of Denver, the Lowry Landfill Superfund site sends nerve gas residues, dioxin, industrial solvents, and radioactive plutonium, americium, radium, and strontium 90 down a seventeen-mile pipeline into the Denver Metro sewage treatment plant, where it is processed into "biosolids," otherwise known as sludge, that are used to grow wheat.[3]

At some point, of course, the parking lot of waste that is so hot it cannot be flushed or farmed out will become overloaded. Just as we ran out of rivers for big dams to kill, we will eventually run out of deserts for big dumps to kill. At that point we will have to stop making nuclear waste, but it will always be with us—ticking away like a time bomb that will inevitably explode slowly and invisibly. Fear of the nuclear menace, like fear of global warming and rampant extinction, is now our fate.

Health itself is an ecological process. Ecosystems are soil, air, and water. When we eat, drink, and breathe, we incorporate soil, air, and water. Because we trade food in a global economy, we eat from a wide range of ecosystems, and the local characteristics of ecosystems are consumed globally. This is the karmic law of ecology: all are interdependent and all are interconnected. What goes around, comes around. Bad stuff blows back.

"Why don't you move away?" I am frequently asked by those who worry about my proximity to danger and see my continual engagement with the West Desert as a futile obsession. The question reveals our crisis of perception. The notion that you can preserve or restore health by running away to a safe haven mirrors the notion that you can exile nuclear waste in the desert and then keep it there forever. My answer is simple: you can move, but you can't stop eating.

We can reconnect broken landscapes by expanding the fragments and creating linkages between them. We can breach dams and restore drowned habitat. But if we do not summon the wit and courage to reverse the path of technology that cannot be sustained and abided, our efforts will be in vain. Or perhaps Sakharov's nightmare—that radioactive fallout will weaken immune systems while increasing viral mutation—will come true, and humans will be felled by epidemics triggered by fallout. Nuclear technology has put us all at death's door, and time and circumstance are waiting to kick us through it. If that happens, then maybe the land, absent our troubling hands, will have the opportunity to reconnect and restore on its own. No one in his or her right mind would wish for that scenario. No one who knows the history of nuclear technology, however, would deny the possibility. If we can choose our future, and I believe we can, then we should do so mindfully, attentively, deliberately, and hopefully. Now.

Epilogue

Three years after I walked in the Vermont woods with Sue Morse, volunteers trained by Keeping Track are still out there, learning about the land and sharing what they learn with others. The vocabulary, concepts, and principles developed by conservation biologists and then advocated by the Wildlands Project are becoming common. You can hear them in civic dialogues about land use and in the planning documents of government agencies and land trusts. College professors give voice to them in their classrooms, and newspaper reporters write them down for popular consumption. Despite the efforts of the Bush regime to gut decades of environmental law and policy, and despite the financial hard times that environmental nonprofits are facing in the post-9/11 economy, a sea change in our consciousness continues to build.

Will that sea change break over us in time to wash us clean? I don't know. There are dark clouds on the horizon. I am especially concerned about the introduction into the wild of evolutionary pollution from genetically engineered plants. But I remain optimistic. H. G. Wells said, "The future is a race between catastrophe and education." I am betting we can learn.

In the summer of 2003, the Glen Canyon Institute moved its offices from Flagstaff, Arizona, near the ghost of Glen Canyon, to Salt Lake City, near media and courts, signaling a shift in its campaign from doing the science to doing politics and litigation. Heat has been an unexpected ally. Years of drought have lowered the Lake Powell reservoir to a little more than half its highest volume, exposing for the first time in decades canyons that are legendary for their beauty. A photo in the *Salt Lake Tribune* in August 2003 showed Rich Ingebretsen standing under a recently uncovered arch with his arms raised in the air. He remains confident that he can push the reservoir down and keep it there. The international movement to stop new dams and take down old ones continues to build momentum. The wisdom of conserving and restoring watersheds is becoming a given. The question that remains is how to do so.

It is harder to be optimistic about the abolition of nuclear weapons and reactors. It is hard to imagine the country embracing abolition and the Precautionary Principle while our government is caught up in the mad doctrine of preemptive war, proposing resumed nuclear testing and new kinds of nuclear weapons and encouraging nuclear utilities to build new reactors. When it comes to the nuclear juggernaut, there seems to be more wit in a wren than in humankind. Our confusion is equal to our fear, and our fear is a match for our arrogance. Nothing humble here. Lessons are still to be learned.

At the end of my journey, I see reconnection, restoration, and abolition on a continuum of consciousness and will. It is easier to save something you haven't yet destroyed than to bring it back after you have trashed it. It is harder yet to stop powerful habits, even habits that are ultimately self-destructive, once you have become invested in them and your dependence reinforces them.

The stories I have told may seem unconnected because the issues they concern are so varied. But the visionary activists I encountered would connect easily if introduced to one another. Sue Morse would find Corbin Harney fascinating and might even teach the wise old Shoshone a thing or two about tracking. Kevin Kamps would find much in common with Rich Ingebretsen. One wants to take down nuclear reactors, and the other wants to take down a big dam. They are two Davids with different Goliaths, but beyond the details that delineate their struggles, both understand technocratic arrogance and the concealed price of progress that are common to each of their challenges. Rich Ingebretsen would admire Lisa Gue and Leanne Klyza Linck. Michael Soulé would have something cogent to say to each of them, and each of them would be eager to hear what that would be.

Despite their differences, these activists share a sense of wonder, even awe, at the way an interlaced and ever morphing natural world continues to emerge and evolve all around us. They respect those processes. They are inspired by nature's diversity and resilience. They have learned that our health and well-being are inseparable from the integrity of whole ecosystems that hold us in their webs. They attempt to communicate bold visions, based on modest assumptions about how nature works, that are compelling to many and provocative to all. They are committed to acting on what they have learned and making a difference.

The people I have profiled here may not have all the answers we need to set the world right. Most of them would admit that they are still searching for those answers and that their work is far from finished. But we would be wise to listen to them, learn from them, and encourage them. They have taught me that our biological communion with the world is real and that honoring the living communities that sustain us is right. And that my journey is not over, but has just begun. Hope is our horizon.

NOTES

RECONNECTION

1. Keeping Track, Watching Hawks

1. Joshua Brown, "Keeping Track: In Step with Bears, Bobcats, and Other Beasts," *Wild Earth,* Fall–Winter 2001–2002, p. 32.

2. Mark Gerard Hengeshaugh, *Creatures of Habitat: The Changing Nature of Wildlife and Wild Places in Utah and the Intermountain West* (Logan: Utah State University Press, 2001), p. 145.

3. Gretchen C. Daily, ed., *Nature's Services: Societal Dependence on Natural Ecosystems* (Washington, D.C.: Island Press, 1997).

4. Gretchen C. Daily and Katherine Ellison, *The New Economy of Nature: The Quest to Make Conservation Profitable* (Washington, D.C.: Island Press, 2003).

5. Sandra Steingraber, *Having Faith: An Ecologist's Journey to Motherhood* (Cambridge, MA: Perseus Publishing, 2001), pp. 65–67.

2. It's a Trickster World—Just Ask Coyote

1. Michael E. Soulé and Bruce A. Wilcox, eds., *Conservation Biology: An Evolutionary-Ecological Perspective* (Sunderland, MA: Sinauer Associates, 1980), p. 8.

2. Michael E. Soulé, "What Is Conservation Biology?" *Bioscience,* December 1985, pp. 727–734.

3. George Wuerthner, "The Coming of the Wolf," *California Wild,* Winter 2000, p. 28.

4. Mollie Matteson, "The Land of Absence," in David Clarke Burks, ed., *Place of the Wild* (Washington, D.C.: Island Press, 1994), p. 98.

5. Rick McIntyre, ed., *War Against the Wolf: America's Campaign to Exterminate the Wolf* (Stillwater, MN: Voyageur Press, 1995), p. 72.

6. Davis Sheremata, "The Predators Run the Show," *Alberta Report,* November 2, 1998, p. 19.

3. Putting the Wolf at the Door

1. Dave Foreman, "The River Wild," *Wild Earth,* Winter 1998/99, pp. 1–4.

2. Ibid., p. 4.

4. How to Fill Sky Islands with Parrots and Jaguars

1. Dave Foreman et al., "The Sky Islands Wildlands Network: Diverse, Beautiful, Wild—and Globally Important," *Wild Earth,* Spring 2000, p. 13.

2. Julia Wondolleck and Steven Yaffee, *Making Collaboration Work* (Washington, D.C.: Island Press, 2000).

5. Making the Map Meaningful

1. David Havlick, *No Place Distant* (Washington, D.C.: Island Press, 2002), pp. 4–5.

7. I Used to Stomp on Grasshoppers, but Oysters Made Me Stop

1. Jeffrey Lockwood, "The Death of the Super Hopper: How Early Settlers Unwittingly Drove Their Nemesis Extinct, and What It Means Today," *High Country News,* February 3, 2003, p. 1.

2. Barbara Kingsolver, *High Tide in Tucson: Essays from Now or Never* (New York: HarperCollins, 1995), pp. 1–16.

RESTORATION

1. Flash Flood: Driven by Unquenchable Thirst into the Path of Danger

1. Dominy quote—"the . . . Colorado . . . is a son of a bitch." Ken Verdoia, "Glen Canyon: A Dam, Water, and the West," KUED-TV, 1999.

2. Flashback: From Suicidal Fool to Prophetic-Hydro Hero, John Wesley Powell's Strange Trip Downriver

1. "Worthless" quote from member of Powell's party. George Bradley quoted by Edward Dolnick in *Down the Great Unknown: John Wesley Powell's 1869 Journey of Discovery and Tragedy Through the Grand Canyon* (New York: HarperCollins, 2001), p. 36.

2. Ken Verdoia, "Glen Canyon: A Dam, Water, and the West," KUED-TV, 1999.

3. Dammed If You Do, Damned If You Don't: Dominy vs. Brower

1. Verdoia, "Glen Canyon: A Dam, Water, and the West."

2. Marc Reisner, *Cadillac Desert: The American West and Its Disappearing Water* (New York, Penguin, 1986), p. 218.

3. Ibid.

4. Aldo Leopold, *A Sand County Almanac,* quoted in Sandra Postel, *Last Oasis: Facing Water Scarcity* (New York: W. W. Norton, 1992), p. xx (prologue).

5. Richard Ingebretsen, "The History of Glen Canyon Dam," *Zephyr,* February/March 2002.

6. David Brower, "walk around our gardens" quote.

7. David Brower, letter to *San Francisco Chronicle,* June 9, 1966, p. 13.

8. Verdoia, "Glen Canyon: A Dam, Water, and the West."

9. Russell Martin, *A Story That Stands Like a Dam: Glen Canyon and the Struggle for the Soul of the West* (Salt Lake City: University of Utah Press, 1999), p. 205.

10. Ibid., p. 211.

11. Verdoia, "Glen Canyon: A Dam, Water, and the West."

12. Katie Lee, *Glen Canyon River Journeys* (CD), Katydid Music, Jerome A2, 1998.

4. Faux Flood: Diverting Disaster by Inviting Chaos

1. Char Miller, ed., *Water in the West: A High Country News Reader* (Corvallis, Oregon State University Press, 2000), p. 92.

5. Flash Forward: The Draining Debate over Powell's Dead Body

1. Statistics from Glen Canyon Institute. "Citizen's Environmental Assessment on the Decommissioning of Glen Canyon Dam" (Flagstaff, AZ: Glen Canyon Institute, 2000).

2. Jim Wolf, "How Low Should Lake Powell Go?" *Salt Lake Tribune,* October 11, 1995.

3. "Cadillac Desert: Water and the Transformation of Nature," KTEH, San Jose and Trans-Pacific Television, 1997 documentary.

6. A Ridiculous Idea Whose Time Has Come

1. Ed Abbey, *The Monkey Wrench Gang* (New York: HarperCollins, 1975).

2. Martin, *A Story That Stands Like a Dam,* p. 291.

3. Ibid., p. 292.

4. Ed Abbey, "The Damnation of a Canyon," in *Beyond the Wall* (New York: Henry Holt, 1984).

5. Ed Abbey, *Down the River* (New York: Penguin, 1991), p. 13.

6. All quotations in this section from U.S. House Committee on Resources, Subcommittee on National Parks and Public Lands and Subcommittee on Water and Power, "Hearing on Sierra Club Proposal to Decommission Glen Canyon Dam," 105th Congress, Xth Session, September 24, 1997.

7. All quotations in this section from Glen Canyon Institute, "Citizens' Environmental Assessment," 2000.

7. Fire in the Water: Salmon as Gift or Commodity

1. Jim Lichatowich, *Salmon Without Rivers: A History of the Pacific Salmon Crisis* (Washington, D.C.: Island Press, 1999) pp. 10–20.

2. David Duncan, "Salmon's Second Coming," *Sierra Magazine,* March/April 2000, p. 32.

3. William Dietrich, *Northwest Passage: The Great Columbia River* (New York: Simon and Schuster, 1995), cited in Charles Little, "Books for the Wilderness," *Wilderness,* Summer 1995, p. 34.

4. Duncan, "Salmon's Second Coming," p. 37.

5. Jerry Adler, "The Great Salmon Debate," *Newsweek,* October 28, 2002, p. 55.

6. Duncan, "Salmon's Second Coming," p. 34.

7. Lichatowich, *Salmon Without Rivers,* pp. 33–36.

8. Following the Money Through Fear and Loathing

1. Utah Rivers Council, "Mirage in the Desert: Property Tax Subsidies for Water," 2002.

2. Quoted in Dan McCool, ed., *Waters of Zion: The Politics of Water in Utah* (Salt Lake City: University of Utah Press, 1995), p. 163.

3. Jon R. Luoma, "Water for Profit," *Mother Jones,* November/December 2002, p. 37.

9. White Elephants in the Boneyard of Pride

1. Patrick McCully, *Silenced Rivers: The Ecology and Politics of Large Dams* (London: Zed Books, 2001), p. 24.

2. Ibid., p. 14.

3. Michael Parfit, "Water," *National Geographic* special issue, 1993, p. 58.

4. McCully, *Silenced Rivers,* p. 5.

5. Ibid., p. 3.

6. Ibid., pp. 6–7.

7. Ibid., p. 7.

8. Ibid., p. 175.

9. Ibid., p. 337.

10. Patrick McCully, "After the Deluge: The Urgent Need for Reparations for Dam Victims," *Cultural Survival Quarterly,* Fall 1999.

11. Arundhati Roy, description of plight of displaced peoples in India, *The Cost of Living* (New York: Modern Library, 1999), pp. 1–90.

12. McCully, *Silenced Rivers,* p. 70.

13. Ibid., pp. 74–75.

14. Ibid., pp. 39–40.

15. Ibid., p. 94.

16. Ibid., p. 55.

17. Elizabeth Grossman, *Watershed: The Undamming of America* (New York: Counterpoint Press, 2002), p. 3.

ABOLITION

1. First, They Killed John Wayne

1. Norm Clarke, "Author: Hughes' Memos Show He Knew Risks of Radioactive Movie Site," *Las Vegas Review-Journal,* October 10, 2001.

2. Ibid.

3. Carole Gallagher, *American Ground Zero: The Secret Nuclear War* (Cambridge, MA: MIT Press, 1993), p. xxiii.

4. John Gofman and Arthur Tamplin, *Poisoned Power: The Case Against Nuclear Power Plants* (Emmaus, PA: Rodale Press, 1971), pp. 24–25.

5. Arjun Makhijani, Howard Hu, and Katherine Yih (eds.), *Nuclear Wastelands: A Global Guide to Nuclear Weapons Production and Its Health and Environmental Effects* (Cambridge: MIT Press, 1995), pp. 178–184.

6. Valerie L. Kuletz, *The Tainted Desert: Environmental and Social Ruin in the American West* (New York: Routledge, 1998), pp. 25–29.

7. Ibid., p. 84.

8. Michael E. Long, "Half Life: The Lethal Legacy of America's Nuclear Waste," *National Geographic,* July 2002, p. 8.

9. Ibid., p. 14.

10. National Research Council, *Long-term Institutional Management of U.S. Department of Energy Legacy Waste Sites* (Washington, D.C.: National Academies Press, 2002).

11. Jay M. Gould and Benjamin A. Goldman, *Deadly Deceit: Low Level Radiation, High Level Cover-up* (New York: Four Walls Eight Windows, 1990), p. 127.

2. The Perpetual Peril of the Peaceful Atom

1. Harvey Wasserman, *The Last Energy War: The Battle over Utility Deregulation* (New York: Seven Stories Press, 1999), p. 31.

2. Ibid.

3. Ibid., p. 30.

4. Ibid., p. 35.

5. Anna Gyorgi, *No Nukes: Everyone's Guide to Nuclear Power* (Boston: South End Press, 1979), p. 15.

6. Wasserman, *The Last Energy War,* pp. 47–48.

7. "What Chernobyl Did: Not Just a Nuclear Explosion," *The Economist,* April 27, 1991, pp. 19–21.

8. Jay M. Gould, "Chernobyl: The Hidden Tragedy," *The Nation,* March 15, 1993, p. 331.

3. How the Evil Yellow Ore Returns

1. Sammy's attitude represents the triumph of hope over experience. Two years later, in the summer of 2003, Bear will still be in power and Sammy, Margene, and other dissidents will be charged by Bear's government with "treason" in an attempt to strip them of all their tribal rights and rewards.

2. Judy Fahys, "Goshutes Who Have Opposed Nuclear Waste Are Out in Cold," *Salt Lake Tribune,* January 6, 2003.

3. Will Bagley, "Goshutes Feared Two Savage Enemies: Starvation and the White Man," *Salt Lake Tribune,* October 13, 2002.

4. Ibid.

5. Ibid.

6. Judy Fahys, "Draft Shows Seamy Side of N-Waste Deal," *Salt Lake Tribune,* September 29, 2002.

7. Michelle Nijhuis, "Land or Money," *High Country News,* August 5, 2002, p. 8.

8. William L. Fox, "Radioactive Road Trip," *Orion,* January/February 2003, p. 35.

9. Kuletz, *The Tainted Desert,* p. 132.

10. Rebecca Solnit, *Savage Dreams: A Journey into the Landscape Wars of the American West* (Berkeley: University of California Press, 1999), pp. 25–26.

4. Activists vs. Enablers

1. Chip Ward, *Canaries on the Rim: Living Downwind in the West* (New York: Verso, 1999), pp. 189–214.

2. Public Citizen's Critical Mass Energy and Environment Program, "Another Nuclear Rip-off: Unmasking Private Fuel Storage," July 2001.

3. Ibid., pp. 24–28.

4. Ibid., p. 26.

5. Ibid., pp. 28–31.

6. Ibid., pp. 31–34.

7. Ibid, pp. 38–42.

5. A Glowing Account of Horatio Alger's ABCs

1. Doug Robinson, "Semnani Living American Dream," *Deseret News,* November 7, 2002.

2. Ibid.

3. Katharine Biele, "A Matter of Waste: Getting to the Bottom of Utah's Most Controversial Ballot Initiative," *Salt Lake City Weekly,* October 31, 2002.

4. Ibid.

5. Robinson, "Semnani Living American Dream."

6. Ibid.

7. Jerry D. Spangler and Donna Kemp Spangler, "Envirocare Foes Fear Legal Lash," *Deseret News,* November 7, 2002.

8. Ibid.

9. Brent Israelsen and Linda Fantin, "Leucadia Tried to Buy Envirocare Last Year, Sources Say," *Salt Lake Tribune,* October 5, 2002.

6. Abolition and Precaution

1. Derek Jensen, "Carolyn Raffensperger on the Revolutionary Idea of Putting Safety First," *The Sun,* November 2002, pp. 5–13.

2. Carolyn McConnell, "When Nuclear Plants Close, Infant Death and Childhood Cancer Drop," *Yes! A Journal of Positive Futures,* Spring 2002, p. 25.

3. Diane Olson Rutter, "A Growing Concern: Hazardous Waste in Fertilizer," *Catalyst,* 2003, pp. 16–20.

ACKNOWLEDGMENTS

I wrote this book in whatever "spare time" I could make in my full life, juggling my career as a library administrator, my second career as a citizen activist/advocate, and my third but most important career as a husband and father. My family empowered me, especially my wife, Linda. I owe this book to her encouragement, patience, and generosity. The interest of my children—Brian, Carly, and Tyler—never flagged. As always, their love sustains me.

I am thankful to Nancy Tessman and my colleagues at the Salt Lake City Public Library for tolerating my "writing days," my frequent distractions, and my obsessions. Together we are redefining the place of the public library in our urban culture—a place where democracy is practiced, ideas and information are shared openly, and diversity is honored and celebrated. My career as a librarian does not run beside my life as a writer and activist, it informs and complements it.

Writing this book has been like taking a demanding but rewarding journey. At the trailhead was my friend and mentor Mike Davis, who introduced me to the surprising notion that I could and should write another book. Friend and fellow activist Rebecca Solnit helped me organize my gear for the expedition, and fellow board member/advocate Bert Fingerhut steered me to Island Press. Jonathan Cobb, my editor at Island/Shearwater, was a skilled, insightful, wise, and gentle guide for the remainder of the trek. I am also thankful for Jonathan's stamina and experience. Along the way I received welcome advice from Tom Butler, Allison Jones, Zach Frankel, and Jason Groenewold. The folks at Island Press, where this hike concluded, were extraordinary without exception.

A primary goal of this book is to serve as a bridge for readers to the rich and growing literature available on the topics covered. Also, because I am a librarian by profession, I must acknowledge great books that were maps along the way. I hope my introductory account of island biogeography and conservation biology inspires readers to seek out David Quammen's masterpiece, *The Song of the Dodo: Island Biogeography in an Age of Extinctions.* Likewise, readers who want a comprehensive assessment of the folly of dam building worldwide and the people's movement to resist should read Patrick McCully's powerful and instructive critique, *Silenced Rivers: The Ecology and Politics of Large Dams.*

I am fortunate to have so many family members, friends, and colleagues who encourage, teach, and inspire me—too many to name, but worthy of this heartfelt gesture of gratitude. You know who you are.

INDEX

Index